LONDON'S TURNING

London's Turning
Thames Gateway: Prospects and Legacy

Edited by
PHILIP COHEN
University of East London

and

MICHAEL J. RUSTIN
University of East London

ASHGATE

Published by
Ashgate Publishing Limited
Gower House
Croft Road
Aldershot
Hampshire GU11 3HR
England

Ashgate Publishing Company
Suite 420
101 Cherry Street
Burlington, VT 05401-4405
USA

Ashgate website: http://www.ashgate.com

British Library Cataloguing in Publication Data
London's turning : the making of Thames Gateway. - (Design
  and the built environment series)
  1. Thames Gateway 2. City planning - England - London
  3. Docks - Remodeling for other use - England - London
  4. Urban renewal - England - London
  I. Cohen, Philip II. Rustin, Michael J.
  307.1'216'09421

  ISBN-13: 9780754670636

Library of Congress Cataloging-in-Publication Data
London's turning : the making of Thames Gateway / edited by Philip Cohen and
Michael J. Rustin.
    p. cm. -- (Design and the built environment)
  Includes index.
  ISBN 978-0-7546-7063-6 (alk. paper)
  1. Urban renewal--England--Thames River Estuary. 2. Urban renewal--England--
London. 3. City planning--England--Thames River Estuary. 4. City planning--
England--London. 5. Thames Gateway. I. Cohen, Phil. II. Rustin, Michael J.

  HT178.G72T435 2008
  307.3'41609422--dc22

                                                                    2007042387

Printed and bound in Great Britain by MPG Books Ltd, Bodmin, Cornwall.

Contents

PART 2: CASE STUDIES IN URBAN CHANGE

List of Figures, Plates and Tables

Figures

Plates

Tables

List of Contributors

The Editors

Philip Cohen is the founder director of the London East Research Institute and Professor of Urban Studies at the University of East London. He has researched the impact of structural change on East London communities for the past 20 years. Among his publications are *Knuckle Sandwich: Growing Up in the Working Class City* (with David Robins) (1978), *Rethinking the Youth Question: Education, Labour and Cultural Studies* (1998), *New Ethnicities, Old Racisms* (1999), *Finding the Way Home* (2007) and *Questioning Ethnographies* (2008). He is also a published poet, with a first collection *Like as If* due out next year.

Michael J. Rustin is a Professor of Sociology at the University of East London, and a Visiting Professor at the Tavistock Clinic. He is author of *The Good Society and the Inner World: Psychoanalysis, Culture, Politics* (1991) and *Reason and Unreason: Psychoanalysis, Science and Politics* (2001) and, with Margaret Rustin, of *Narratives of Love Psychoanalysis and Loss: Studies in Modern Children's Fiction* (1987/2001) and *Mirror to Nature: Drama and Society* (2002). He was co-editor (with Tim Butler) and contributor to *Rising in the East: The Regeneration of East London* (1996) and contributed to Tim Butler (ed.), *Eastern Promise: Education and Social Renewal in London's Docklands* (2000).

Other Contributors

Andrew Blake is Associate Head of the School of Social Sciences, Media and Cultural Studies at the University of East London and a consultant on cultural policy with a performing background as a saxophonist and composer. He has written widely on music and the creative industries, sport, and consumer culture and his short book *The Irresistible Rise of Harry Potter* (2002) has been translated into five languages.

Penny Bernstock is Senior Lecturer in Social Policy at the University of East London. She has worked as researcher in a monitoring group exploring the impact of the regeneration of London Docklands on local communities. She recently completed her PhD at the London School of Economics and has since been working on a study that has explored housing development in the Thames Gateway and the use of S106 planning gain agreements.

Karina Berzins is a freelance consultant and a Visiting Research Fellow with the London East Research Institute. She has carried out extensive research on cultural tourism and the night-time urban economy.

Tim Butler is Professor of Geography at Kings College London. He worked at the University of East London for many years where he edited *Rising East* and the collections *Rising in the East* (1996) and *Eastern Promise* (2000). His most recent book is *London Calling* (2003).

Andrew Calcutt is convenor of MA Journalism and Society at the University of East London, and editor of *Rising East*, a journal published by London East Research Institute which explores the re-making of East London and the reconfiguration of its relations with the wider world. His previous publications include *Arrested Development: Pop Culture and the Erosion of Adulthood* (2001) and *BritCult: an A-Z of British Popular Culture* (2004). His research is concerned with attempts to re-connect society in a period after politics.

Massimo De Angeles is Principal Lecturer in Development Studies at the University of East London. He is an economist with a special interest in the impact of globalisation of local and regional economic development. His most recent book is *The Beginning of History* (Pluto 2007).

Michael Edwards is Professor of Planning at the Bartlett School of Architecture. He has researched and written widely on issues of land use, strategic planning, economic development and urban regeneration.

Michael Keith is Professor of Sociology at Goldsmiths College and Director of the Centre for Urban and Community Research. He was leader of Tower Hamlets Council and also Chair of the London Thames Gateway Partnership. He has published many books on aspects of contemporary urban theory and policy, the most recent being *After the Cosmopolitan* (2005).

Iain MacRury is Principal Lecturer in Cultural Studies and Creative Industries at the University of East London and Director of London East Consultancies. He conducted research for London City Airport on the community impact of its master plan. He has also published a number of books on advertising and promotional communications. He is the co-editor (with Gavin Poynter) of the forthcoming Ashgate book *Olympic Cities*.

William Mann is a partner in Witherford Watson Mann Architects. His architectural practice is concerned with developing a framework of environmental sustainability as sensitive to the social ecology of neighbourhoods as it is the fabric of the public urban realm. He has carried out extensive research into the historical and geographical coordinates of urban change in East London and Thames Gateway.

John Marriott is Reader in History at the University of East London, where he directs the Raphael Samuel Centre for Metropolitan History. His books include *Labourism in East London* (1994) and *The Other Empire* (2005). He is currently developing a project on Lost Industries in Thames Gateway with Eastside Heritage.

Han Meyer is Professor of Urban Design and Planning at the Technological University of Delft. He is chief planning advisor to the City of Rotterdam and the architect of 'hydraulic urbanism'. His ideas are developed in *Port and City* (1998) and *Water Cities* (2005)

Gareth Millington is a lecturer in sociology at Roehampton College. His current research is concerned with community relations between 'established' and 'outsider' groups in Southend-on-Sea, Essex with particular attention given to the role that place plays as a context for these relations. An article based on this work has recently been published in *Social and Cultural Geography.*

Alice Sampson is Senior Research Fellow at the Centre for Institutional Studies at the University of East London. She has carried out numerous studies evaluating regeneration projects in East London and contributed regularly to *Rising East.*

Paul Watt is a Lecturer in Sociology at Birkbeck, University of London and a Visiting Fellow at the London East Research Institute, University of East London. His interests include urban social polarisation in relation to housing and employment, and more generally the inter-relationships between the social and spatial parameters of inequality and exclusion. Recent publications include a paper on London working-class council tenants in the *International Journal of Urban and Regional Research* (2006), and a co-authored book with Tim Butler, *Understanding Social Inequality* published by Sage (2007).

Preface and Acknowledgements

Our first and greatest debt is to our fellow contributors who not only turned in their chapters on time, but responded positively to our editorial comments and suggestions.

There are a number of colleagues and associates whose work does not appear here but who have nevertheless made a significant contribution to this project. Syd Jeffers, Tom Wengraf and others who attended the LERI reading group on Thames Gateway made many useful comments and suggestions which we have drawn upon. John Lock and Carole Snee, who have a hands on role in developing the University's regeneration strategy, especially in relation to Thames Gateway, have been an unfailing source of local intelligence.

We would also like to thank Geoff Mulgan of the Young Foundation for hosting a series of seminars on the theme, and indeed with the title, of this book and to all those who took part and gave papers.

Finally, thanks to Jason Ditton and Alex Werner of the Museum of London for permission to use some of the illustrative material. We hope these photographs and maps as well as the text itself will help readers who have yet to explore the Thames Gateway to set out on their own account. While it is always better to travel hopefully, especially when you are not sure quite where you will arrive, it may sometimes be as useful to navigate one's pessimism with the aid of maps drawn by those who do not necessarily depend on such encouragement to embark on the journey. As we think this book shows, even these more negative lines of thought can be productive in ultimately leading us in a more fruitful direction.

Philip Cohen and Michael J. Rustin
London East Research Institute
Royal Docks Newham, London
July 2007

Editorial Introduction

Philip Cohen and Michael J. Rustin

The title of this book, *London's Turning*, refers to the ambition to shift the unequal balance of London's development from the generally affluent west to the relatively deprived east of the city and its region. The history of this imbalance is in part a consequence of London's physical geography which has become overlain with socio-economic and cultural distinctions. To the east of the City of London, the River Thames soon becomes wide and hard to cross – there is only one overland crossing east of Tower Bridge to this day, though one has long been projected and may before long be built. The river flows through flat land which used to be marshy and susceptible to flood; this flood plain offers few vistas and panoramas of the kind which have always attracted the settlements of the better-off, except long views of the river itself. The prevailing wind, and of course the river's flow, is from the west, thus the east got the worst of the city's dirt, in its various forms – noxious industries, waste products, smells, polluted water – while those who could avoid these hazards stayed upstream. Of course modern technology, and indeed deindustrialisation, has made many of these original geographical disadvantages irrelevant today. But their effects live on, east and west, in the quality and texture of the built environment, in the types and locations of enterprises, and in the more intangible but nevertheless influential factors of social and cultural capital, in the capacities of the population to compete with those of other zones of the city for well-paid and satisfying work.

The Thames Gateway plan for sustainable communities to give it its full title, is a comprehensive attempt to tackle these issues. As such it is the largest and most complex project of urban regeneration ever undertaken in the UK. It has been compared, in proportionate scale, to the rebuilding that took place after the Great Fire of London, or to all the New Towns that were built after World War II. It involves the building of affordable homes for upwards of half a million people; the construction of a new transport network to attract people, goods and inward investment from across Europe; the creation of a whole new apparatus of governance to regulate London's historic turn to the east; the attempt to create a sustainable green environment out of some of the most polluted brown field sites in the country. And now, superimposed on this, the London 2012 Olympics ....

All this is being proposed against the background of widespread public scepticism about master plans and grand projects, coupled with concerns about the impact of global warming on London's flood protection systems, and the fear that market led construction of mass housing will lead to Los Angeles type urban sprawl. Will Thames Gateway be a bigger and better (and hence in some views worse) version of Docklands? Will the polarisations of race and class that have occurred on the Isle of Dogs be displaced downriver and reproduced in Thurrock? Will the new deregulated regionalism generate a 'space of flows' in which the global knowledge economy and the local hidden economy combine to absorb the communities of labour made redundant by the decline of Fordism? Or will the outcome be new kinds of inequality, new forms of social immobility and peri-urban deprivation?

The Thames Gateway plan has produced a voluminous documentation, much of it frankly promotional, some of simply a collation of existing statistical data, little of it theoretically informed. There is also considerable media coverage, most of it negative, which has contributed to fixing a public image of the plan as an unwieldy, ill-conceived adventure in governmental megalomania. Yet for a project of this magnitude and social importance, it is very research-light. Notwithstanding the current emphasis on evidence-based policymaking there has been little attempt to grasp the impact of the project as a whole or to generate locally grounded case studies.[1] *London's Turning* sets out to remedy this by providing a critical assessment of the 'the Thames Gateway effect'. We trace the genealogy of the plan and explore its limits and conditions of realisation in and through a detailed examination of the problems of urban change it seeks to address. We use the plan as a lens through which to look at a series of important questions of social theory, urban policy and governmental practice, but we are also concerned to look at some of the possible answers.

The book is produced by members and associates of the London East Research Institute. The Institute was set up in 2002 to bring together the work on regeneration being done at the University of East London. The Institute built on earlier work but extended its scope and scale to focus on the Olympics and Thames Gateway.[2] From the outset we have emphasised the importance of building a collaborative and interdisciplinary research culture which critically engages with the changes that are going on in our midst. This book has not been written from the academic sidelines. The university is a key player in Thames Gateway and the work we do at LERI is produced from a position of direct engagement in the regeneration process.

However in putting this book together and in presenting its rationale we have resisted the temptation to impose any more editorial cohesion on our project than

---

1   A recent survey of the policy-oriented research literature undertaken by Oxford Brookes University identified a number of sectoral lacuna, but interestingly did not comment on the paucity of generic studies. See Oxford Brookes University (2006), 'Thames Gateway Evidence Review', London: Department for Communities and Local Government.

2   This earlier work appeared in *Rising in the East: the Regeneration of East London*, edited by Tim Butler and Michael Rustin (1996) and *Eastern Promise*, edited by Tim Butler, (2000) and the journal *Rising East*. A companion volume to the present book on Olympic cities. Our current journal, *Rising East On Line* (www.risingeast.org), combines academic studies with topical debates and photojournalism and focuses on regeneration in East London and Thames Gateway.

its subject matter could reasonably sustain. The Thames Gateway plan has elicited much public controversy and the job of the book is to reflect the full spectrum of academic opinion and policy debate. As a result there are many different kinds of arguments assembled here and our contributors certainly do not speak with one voice, let alone provide a common preferred reading of the same set planning texts. The book allows readers to sample different opinions, perspectives, and priorities and invites you to form your own judgement. Some of our contributors are deeply committed to the Thames Gateway project and still optimistic about what it may deliver. The alternatives, they argue, will almost certainly be worse. Others take a more sanguine or sceptical view and suggest that an alternative approach to regeneration is both necessary and possible.

This multiplicity of standpoints has also in part dictated how the book is organised. We are not hubristic enough to think that everyone will want to read the whole book from cover to cover, although our ideal reader – that implausible editorial construct- would of course do so!

We have deliberately designed the contents page to make it possible to pick and choose. But we also want to encourage the reader to take risks – to jump into topics and universes of discourse with which they may not initially be familiar. Thus architects and urban designers will find much to stimulate them in a chapter by a sociologist about the lived demographics of the big move east; equally social geographers will recognise much of their current concerns about city/country relations in a chapter by an architect on the changing forms of East London's urban fabric.

This is not a book just for those professionally engaged in regeneration, although we hope it will have much to say to them. It is designed to make sense of Thames Gateway to a much wider audience who have heard about it more as a rumour, or a news story, than as something which directly concerns them. And that includes a large number of people who live and work in the designated zones of change! Finally those who are interested in more general debates about the direction of change in contemporary forms of culture, economy and polity will find here a rich source book.

At this point it is worth entering a further caveat. Although the book takes a comprehensive view of both the official mapping and lived territories comprised by Thames Gateway, it does not aim or claim to be an all inclusive inventory of the issues raised by the plan sector by policy sector. For example there are no chapters on health, or social welfare, transport, civil engineering or education as such. This is not because we think these areas are unimportant or that joined up policy thinking should not address them. On the contrary you will find many of these issues discussed here as part of larger arguments and analyses about the changing nature of regeneration. We decided however not to organise the book into discrete policy areas but as far as possible to identify and explore cross cutting themes. One of the great challenges posed by the Thames Gateway is to break down the professional and institutional silos that currently exist, as much within the academy as within the world of local and central government and we have tried to encourage that process in the way we have put the book together.

There is also a method in the madness. We have divided the book into two parts, broadly corresponding to the scope and scale of the contributions. In Part 1 we have asked our contributors to situate the Thames Gateway project within a wider set of debates about different cultures of modernity and postmodernity in contemporary urbanism. Contributors examine the origins and development of the plan in relation to the history of London, Docklands and port cities; we focus on the post-war development of British town planning and the more recent narrative turn in planning theory and practice; contributors also engage with the great debate on sustainability, focussing here on local issues of population density, neighbourhood ecology and the urban fabric, as well as the rhetoric and reality of globalisation. The impact of New Labour's commitment to the cultural turn in urban regeneration, and the role of the heritage industry in the branding of Thames Gateway is another important refrain.

Part 2 presents a series of detailed case studies into the impact of urban planning and demographic change on the material, social and cultural environment of London's growth downriver. New forms of ethnic gentrification, and the development of the eastern hinterlands, the lived demographics of population movement – and immobility – between city and country and, the role which 106 planning agreements play in regulating housing provision, these form a distinctive cluster of studies; the attempt to create new cultural hubs, for example in Stratford and Southend, linked into holiday and night time economies are another focus as is the effect of 'splintering urbanism' associated with the creation of premium sites around new transport hubs such as London City Airport and the proposed Thames Gateway Bridge.

The implications of these changes for redistributive strategies of urban development, and in particular for implementing anything like sustainable community, are drawn out in two concluding chapters; one focuses on issues of land use and sets out a possible policy for regulating the region's economic growth in the interest of all its citizens. In a tailpiece the editors build on some of the arguments advanced elsewhere in the book about the unequal impact of de-industrialisation and the failure of the cultural turn in regeneration to consider ways of tackling the democratic deficit in regional planning. Drawing on some of the ideas which Bruno Latour has recently advanced about how to widen and deepen the practice of political assembly, we make a modest proposal for regenerating the process of civic engagement with the Thames Gateway plan.

As we move into what is proclaimed to be a new political era, where change is the order of the day, and where the issues of affordable housing and the devolution of 'power to the people' has moved to the top of the rhetorical agenda, it seems important to take a longer term view of London's historic turn to the east. We hope this book will help inform the public deliberations that now have to take place if the heroic ambition of Thames Gateway to transform the prospects of the region, and not least of those communities who have been left behind by the advent of the new economy, is to be translated into social fact on the ground. With so much at stake we cannot afford to fail.

PART 1
Big Pictures, Small Details

Plate 1.1   Photograph of Royal Docks 1952. Author's photograph

Plate 1.2   Photograph of Royal Docks 2008. Author's photograph

Chapter 1

Ex-ports: The Laboratory Role of the London Docklands[1]

Han Meyer

In port-cities all over the world docklands are the subject of radical changes and transformations, but the London Docklands area is by far the biggest, with the most extensive and radical transformations, with effects on the spatial, economic and social structure of the whole metropolitan and regional area, which even have national and international importance. Because of the enormous scale, the radical character of the transformations and wider meaning of these transformations, studying and discussing the London Docklands has a worldwide relevance. The area is a laboratory from which every port-city can learn lessons.

London as well as the Dutch port-cities can be considered as trend-setting types of port-cities over many centuries, alternating with each other in playing a leading role in the international port economy, but also in playing a leading role in the planning and design of paradigmatic relationships between port and city.

During the twentieth century, the London region and Holland became two showcases of modern urban planning: Sir Patrick Abercrombie's Greater London Plan (1946), Cornelis van Eesteren's Amsterdam Extension Plan of (1934) and Cor van Traa's reconstruction plan for Rotterdam (1946) were considered as the most important examples of modern city-planning in that period. Lewis Mumford, acknowledged worldwide as an important international expert on city planning at that time, celebrated the London and Dutch experiences as setting examples for every city.[2] All these typical modernistic plans demonstrated the ambition to plan and to control urban society by planning and controlling the spatial framework of the city. However, in all these plans the *port* was considered to be a world which it was not possible to plan and control and which should be excluded from the daily urban world.

The question of regeneration of port areas, especially in these countries most strongly influenced by modernism over many decades, puts something essential on the table concerning urban planning in general: these areas seem to have a great potential to function as the start of a another type of urban planning – not only

---

1   This chapter is based on my book *City and Port – Transformation of Port-cities, London Barcelona New York Rotterdam*, Utrecht, International Books, 1999.

2   Lewis Mumford, *The City in History: Its Origins, Its Transformations, and Its Prospects*, Harcourt, Brace and World, New York, 1961.

because of the possibility of spectacular waterfronts, but especially because these areas escaped from the control of the modernistic planning machine.

The development of port-cities can be regarded as the most manifest examples of the general process of *modernisation*. In general, the process of modernisation concerns the development of a balance between the process of globalisation and the ambitions of local communities to improve the conditions of daily life. A second aspect of this modernisation process concerns the relation between urbanisation and the natural conditions of the territory, which should be revised in order to avoid an overly aggressive exploitation of nature, soil, water and air. These two themes are as old as the city itself, and especially as old as the port-city.

Establishing new relations between the local and global and between urbanisation and nature is important nowadays because of the scale of these developments worldwide. During the next 35 years, a 100 per cent increase of the population living in cities all over the world of is expected,[3] especially in developing countries, and most of this unprecedented urbanisation will take place in coast and delta areas. The developments in China are illustrative: more than 90 per cent of the Chinese industrial economy is concentrated in the coastal zones, where 330 port-cities are taking care of the worldwide distribution of the new products of the Chinese economy; all of these 330 port-cities seem to be trying to become the largest port in the world.[4] It means that all the delta-areas of this enormous country are colonised by industrial and urban developments, with tremendous effects on the quality of urban life and on the quality of the natural environment.

China is currently an extreme example of this, but similar processes are happening in other parts of Asia, in Africa and Latin-America, while port-cities and port-regions in the 'western world' find themselves in the process of structural reorganisation, de-industrialisation and urbanisation. More than ever, coastal zones – and especially port-cities – are the backbone of economic traffic and urban development all over the world.

These processes of exploding economic growth and intensification in port-areas are developing parallel to two other important processes:

- the increasing need for an approach to urban development which pays attention to the specific cultural and historic identity of cities and regions, related to the general desire for local communities which have a clear identity, as a counterweight to the processes of globalisation;
- the increasing need for a careful approach to the natural environment, especially the water-systems of rivers, deltas and coastal areas.

Port-cities have already played a role as laboratories of modernisation for many centuries. Port-cities represent in the most explicit and critical ways new approaches to the two above-mentioned 'great themes' – the relation between the global and the local, and the relation between urbanisation and the natural territory.

---

3   According to UNESCO calculations.
4   James Wang, *New Trends in Port-City Interactions in China*, IACP-conference, Rotterdam, 2005.

From the early phase of modern urban development, from the thirteenth and fourteenth centuries, until the end of the twentieth century, there have been two contrasting ways of responding to these two 'great themes'. In earlier times too, the case of the London Docklands had an important role as a 'trendsetter'.

The First Arrangement: The Port-City as Intermediate Zone

The first arrangement, developed in most western port-cities from the late Middle Ages until the middle of the nineteenth century, was characterised by a strong interweaving of both port and urban infrastructure and of the natural conditions of the landscape and the port infrastructure. The construction of the port infrastructure was made possible by the presence of natural artefacts such as bays, creeks, etc. The development, construction and maintenance of the port and urban infrastructure were combined in one policy. City and port were interwoven with each other; the port was located near or on the immediate border of the city. In this enclosed system of the port-city, the harbour was a marketplace – the final destination on the transportation route – and the port's infrastructure was organised within the enclosed boundary of the city.

However, this integration of urban system and port system was effected in different ways. The difference of Dutch and British port-cities is illustrative; very similar but dealing with different local configurations of the relations between water and territory and with different relationships between public and private initiatives.

In the Dutch port-cities – the most important centres of world trade during the seventeenth century – the urban port infrastructure was a transformed and manipulated part of the landscape drainage system. The systems of harbours and canals in cities like Amsterdam and Rotterdam were developed and constructed as public works; they functioned as port infrastructure as well as drainage systems and as the primary elements of the urban fabric. This enabled merchants and port entrepreneurs to build relatively small warehouses and depots beside the canals. The elements of hydraulic engineering – canals, quays, dykes, dams and sluices – were at the same time the main framework of the urban fabric. The quays and dykes were the most important urban streets; the dam was the main square and the core of the Dutch water-city. City, port and water-management infrastructure were completely interwoven.

In London, on the contrary, a large-scale port infrastructure, initiated and constructed by public authorities, did not exist. Here special companies, such as the West India Company and the East India Company, played a main role in the development of port equipment. During the 1700s, these companies gave emphasis to the development of a new type of buildings. During this period the port of London was concentrated on the River Thames, where ships could lie in the roads and could be loaded and unloaded at the riverbanks. The integration of port and city in London was demonstrated by the scale of building, with the famous Adelphi building by Robert Adams as the most prestigious and famous exemplification of the modern port-city of mid-eighteenth-century. London had taken over the leading role as the most important trade centre of the world from Holland, and the Adelphi was the demonstration *par excellence* of the city that 'ruled the waves'.

The Second Arrangement: Creating Sharp Borders

While the Adelphi represented the peak of the special relationship between city and port, at the same time it marked its end. From the end of the eighteenth century London developed a quite different type of port infrastructure, by creating a brand new landscape of docklands. The *dock* was an innovative invention, which enabled mass ship-handling, protected against the tidal movement of the water, (which is rather extreme in London) and protected against robbery and raids, which was an established tradition on the open and unprotected water of the River Thames. The initiative, lay-out and construction of the docks was the result of initiatives by the companies, who originally owned and ruled these docks.

The moving of the port activities from the riverbanks to the new docks resulted in a sharp separation between city and port, which would deeply influence the spatial development of other western port-cities.

In many port-cities, it took a long time – from the middle of the nineteenth century to the beginning of the twentieth century – for the development of a totally different relationship between port and city to take place. During the nineteenth century there was a great deal of construction of new large-scale public works of basins, quays and warehouses – designed and constructed by professional departments of public works, which also were responsible for the extension of the city and the water-management of the city – in many continental port-cities, for instance, in Holland. On the other hand, the first signs of specialisation and autonomous development of the port as an independent entity also became visible in the continental port-cities. From the 1920s and 1930s a new, modernistic arrangement of port-city relations was developed that finally departed radically from the original arrangement. Planning institutions became convinced that it was no longer fruitful to combine the scale of the port with the development of the city. An inspiring example for this new separation was the case of the London Docklands.

The London Docklands also became a showcase of something which other cities tried to avoid: the destiny of the leftover land between the docks as residential areas for the poorest people of the city. This London East End was made famous by Charles Dickens' novels, which described the poor and miserable conditions of the people in this zone, most of them dependent on employment in the port. The separation of city and port became part of a social policy, intended to insulate the urban community from the raw and strange world of the ships and the port.

During the post-World War II decades, the separation of port and city was concluded. Rotterdam, the world's largest port from 1961, built its new port and industrial complexes even further away from the city. In many cases, clear distinctions – in terms of both policy and space – were made between the industrialised port landscape, the city and the green landscape.

Port and urban planning came off worse in processes which were dominated by a conceptual separation between urban social values and large-scale infrastructures. The large *technical* framework of the large-scale infrastructure, including the port infrastructure, was regarded as being in conflict with the social, public domain of the city.

The Twenty-first Century: Towards a Third Arrangement of Port-City Landscape

As a result of the policy of concentrating all port activities outside the urban territory, many old dockland areas constructed in the eighteenth and nineteenth centuries lost their original function and instead became key targets of policies of urban regeneration in most European and North-American port-cities. Such famous examples as Baltimore's Inner Harbour, New York's Battery Park City, Barcelona's Moll de la Fusta and Rotterdam's Kop van Zuid established a new orientation of the city on the water, and created an urban waterfront which could play a major role in the economic and social regeneration of the whole city.

At first sight, the redevelopment of the London Docklands seemed to be part of this international series of urban regeneration projects. The big differences seem to be the scale and the more or less autonomous position of the London Docklands Development Corporation, which was allowed to follow a development policy which did not have to take much account of the interests of the surrounding communities. However, not only is the regeneration of Docklands a larger development than other examples of its kind, but its scale also creates the possibility that Docklands might become the forerunner of a comprehensive planning policy in large-scale delta areas.

At the time of writing, the situation of the urban water edges is changing. The port and transport economy and technology are undergoing fundamental changes. Some port activities need more large-scale concentration, deep water, etc.; other port and transport activities need greater decentralisation combined with an effective logistic organisation. Modern ports no longer have the linear character of the transit port, but consist of various specialised distribution hubs, which together make up a network.

Moreover, a new approach to water management is necessary. In previous times, 'modern' water management seemed to produce greater safety, but it also reduced the potential economic and recreational use of the land. Now, however, the management of water is itself being confronted with objective limits. A series of floods and near-floods all over Europe in the 1990s demonstrated that belief in total control of the water system an illusion. Existing water management policy, with its repeated strengthening and raising of the level of dykes, narrowing the rivers and increasing pumping-power in the polders (in Holland) showed that it had no answer to the fundamental effects of climate change. Radical changes in approach are giving a stronger emphasis on 'dynamic' and 'elastic' types of water management, which allow more space to the water in the rivers, more space for temporary water storage in the lowlands, and the replacement of the narrow forms of coastal defence by a wider zone of artificial as well as natural defences of dunes, beaches, inlets, islands and breakwaters. The change from a static towards a dynamic water management – from 'hard' towards 'soft' forms of coastal defence – also offers new opportunities for economic development, especially for port development and recreation.

Finally, the character of urbanisation has changed fundamentally. Because of increasing mobility and new communication and information technologies, the 'daily urban systems' in the western world exist on an increasingly regional scale. However, in the large metropolitan areas there is a growing separation between the regional systems occupied on a daily basis by the urban middle class, and the world of the poor and the disadvantaged, who lack any linkage to the infrastructure of the modern information and communication technology. Urban planning and urban design should take into consideration not only the regional as the relevant scale of the modern city, but also the problem of how to enable every citizen to experience and participate in the urban world in its new regional form.

The new circumstances concerning water management, port development and city development challenge us to find a new approach to the transformation of the urbanised delta landscape, with more coherent relationships between landscape, urbanisation and port development, and between landscape design, urban design and hydraulic engineering.

Port-cities have a major responsibility for creating a new balance within the natural territory, which includes the water itself, the infrastructure of the port system and the public domain of the urban system. The design of the new urban waterfronts, the re-conversion of obsolete docklands and the lay-out of new port terminals have, in their combination, the potential to function as a coherent framework for the urbanising landscape and as the core of a public domain at a new, regional scale.

This new approach to planning and designing port regions creates the need to reconsider the existing assignment of duties of planning institutions and authorities. Existing separations between port authorities, city planning departments and institutions responsible for the landscale should be turned into their collaboration or even their converging. Related to these considerations, the redevelopment of the London Docklands could play an important role in the development of the larger Thames Gateway area.

Such a redevelopment strategy implies some principles which need to be elaborated during the planning and design process:

1) *Time and the long term*
   An area such as the Thames Gateway needs a long-term perspective, which sets out clear *conditions* for urbanisation, environmental qualities and economic (port related) activities for the next 30 to 50 years without, however, seeking to impose a detailed blueprint.
2) *A regional scale and local projects*
   A vision for development with a long-term perspective is needed on a regional scale. But at the same time it is important to define *projects* that can play a role as 'generators' of this regional perspective at the local scale and with

implementation in the short term. These projects should pay particular attention to the ways in which economic, social and environmental aspects are linked together. They play a role as the 'workbench' of the laboratory: each project can learn from the other projects and linkages between economy, social aspects and environment can be improved during the process.

3) *Considering river and docklands as a new type of public domain*
   The river and the Docklands have the possibility to become the core of a public space on the regional scale. This partly natural, partly manufactured landscape is a neutral spatial structure which is owned by nobody and at the same time can be accepted and used by everyone. It is a carrier of the specific urban history of London and expresses the specific natural conditions of the landscape. Developing the river and the Docklands as a public domain of regional significance means that the Docklands should be transformed into a public feature, not only for the immediate surrounding districts, but for all people of the Thames Gateway region. The creation of public access entrance to this new public domain, and of possibilities for its public use, will be of fundamental importance in the development of the London region as a recognisable spatial and social coherent entity.

4) *Interweaving port and city*
   This interweaving becomes more and more important for the city as well for the port. Examples of this are to be found in Seattle, Hong Kong and Barcelona: these cities exploit their ports as important public and urban features, combined with facilities for panoramic views, recreation, fishing, parks, etc. The port activity itself can be 'rediscovered' as a feature with a spectacular dimension which contributes to the identity of the city. In return, the city has become more important to the port, because the latter becomes more dependent on logistic and financial infrastructures, which prefer to locate themselves in 'interesting' urban areas. This new interchange between city and port should be elaborated as part of the regional and long-term strategy.

5) *Creating conditions for complexity and sustainability*
   The changing climate and rising sea level make it necessary to create the conditions in which changing water levels can be managed. It means that new, innovative solutions must be developed to combine a sustainable system of water management with specific types of urbanisation and/or recreational facilities. New types of environments can be developed, which can play an exciting and generative role in the development of the river and Docklands areas as a public domain.

The challenge is not to *plan* what exactly should happen and what not, but to *create conditions* for a new urban, regional and environmental complexity. The London Docklands and the Thames Gateway together are one of the few examples in the world where it might be possible to create these conditions.

It will be extremely difficult both to manage this process and invent good innovative solutions. But if it can do so, London could become a showcase of international importance for such a development.

Chapter 2

Smokestack: The Industrial History of Thames Gateway

John Marriott

Several years ago, when these matters were more fashionable, London's problematic and contradictory location within the industrial history of the nation received considerable attention. London, it was argued, was unlike so many of the great urban centres of the midlands and the north in that it was not begat of the Industrial Revolution. Despite the fact that London remained the greatest centre of production and consumption, it was seen to possess few of the features that defined the experience of industrialisation. Large factory production and heavy engineering, for example, were conspicuous by their absence. London manufacturing continued to be dominated by small-scale workshops employing fewer than 25 persons because the capital was simply too remote from the sources of coal and iron ore and land was too expensive to allow it to compete successfully with the burgeoning industrial heartlands.[1] Thus, although the most important metropolitan industries – clothing, furniture and printing – were mechanised in the course of the nineteenth century by widespread adoption of the sewing machine and the band-saw, the organisation of labour and production remained largely unaffected. J.L. Hammond captured prevailing sentiment when he declared that the Industrial Revolution was a storm cloud that passed over London but broke elsewhere.[2]

Such fine epigrams, however, reveal only part of a complicated story. To suggest that London was completely inured to the influence of the Industrial Revolution is patently false. The threat of the impending storm forced metropolitan producers to seek refuge in industries such as clothing, furniture and luxury items which

---

1   Peter Hall, *The Industries of London Since 1861*, London, Hutchinson, 1962; Gareth Stedman Jones, *Outcast London. A Study of the Relationship between Classes in Victorian Society*, Oxford, Clarendon Press, 1971; Raphael Samuel, 'The Workshop of the World: Steam Power and Hand Technology in Mid-Victorian Britain', *History Workshop Journal*, No. 3, Spring 1977, pp. 6–72; Leonard Schwarz, *London in the Age of Industrialisation: Entrepreneurs, Labour Force and Living Conditions, 1700–1850*, Cambridge, Cambridge University Press, 1992.

2   J.L. Hammond, 'The Industrial Revolution and Discontent', *New Statesman*, 21 March 1925. This piece was a review of Dorothy George's wonderful *London Life in the Eighteenth Century* (London, K. Paul, Trench, Trubner and Co., 1925) which had argued along similar lines. I am indebted to Simon McKeon for tracking down the reference.

had long been established to meet the seemingly insatiable demands of the metropolitan bourgeoisie. Other industries such as engineering and shipbuilding, for which London had an enviable reputation, fared badly. The emergence of iron-clad vessels driven by steam fatally weakened London's tradition of shipbuilding by dramatically cutting the demand for wooden ships; any attempt to switch production had to surmount the seemingly insuperable barrier posed by its disadvantageous location. Then the crash of the Overend-Gurney discount house in 1866 rendered irreversible the long-term decline of this metropolitan industry in particular and heavy manufacturing more generally.

To privilege heavy industry in this way, however, is somewhat myopic for it understates other vital dimensions of London's modernisation. Before industrialisation took hold in the first decades of the nineteenth century, London had established itself as the world centre of commerce and finance. Such authority was built on and sustained by a communications infrastructure, at the heart of which stood the Thames and an extensive docklands complex. Toward the close of the eighteenth century, powerful merchant traders combined with developers to construct the West India Docks on the Isle of Dogs. This was soon followed by Wapping, East India, Surrey and St Katharine's docks: with the completion of the Victoria Dock in 1855 London possessed the largest and most modern docks in the world, capable of accommodating the new breed of ocean-going ships. More than any other feature on the metropolitan landscape, docklands represented the capital's modernity, celebrated time and again in paintings, etchings and feature articles. And for good reason. The docks brought together finance, commercial and entrepreneurial capital. The Victoria Dock, for example, was financed by the City and built by entrepreneurs previously responsible for some of the most ambitious railway development schemes in Britain and abroad. More than this, the docks nurtured and sustained a large range of associated industries including ship repair yards, foundries, coopers and rope makers.[3] Advanced hydraulic lifting gear in the Victoria Docks accelerated the unloading of seaborne coal from the north-east, thereby reducing its cost and compensating for London's remoteness from the country's mines. This ready supply of cheap coal in turn gave rise to massive gas and related chemical industries.[4]

Metropolitan industries varied considerably in terms of what they produced and how production was organised. London attracted such variety because it remained the largest centre of consumption, and although locational disadvantages proved decisive in the long term for the fortunes of heavier industries, London's supremacy as a manufacturing centre remained unchallenged. This renders any

---

3   Roy Porter, *London. A Social History*, London, Hamish Hamilton, 1994, p. 190.

4   John Marriott, 'West Ham: London's Industrial Centre and Gateway to the world', I: 'Rapid Growth, 1870–1923' and II: 'Stagnation and Decline, 1923–1939', *The London Journal*, Vols 13 (1988), pp. 121–42 and 14 (1989), pp. 43–58.

definitive statement on the impact of the Industrial Revolution on London difficult, if not impossible.[5]

As a way of out this impasse, I believe, with David Green, that we have to alter the terms of the debate.[6] In foregrounding mechanised factory production, historians have defined the Industrial Revolution too narrowly. Well into the nineteenth century, small-scale production retained a significant presence on Britain's industrial landscape because it was sufficiently versatile and adaptable to compete successfully against mechanised production.[7] Furthermore, an emphasis on production tends to understate the importance of the service sector, which overall contributed more to economic growth than manufacturing. These qualifications force a radical reassessment of the impact of the Industrial Revolution on the metropolitan economy.

London's Manufacturing Heartland

I wish to approach the matter rather differently and intend to begin by rethinking the spatial boundaries of the metropolis, for it is not only the Industrial Revolution that has been defined too narrowly but the metropolis itself. Scholarly research on London's industrialisation has taken the outer boundary to be that defined by the administrative limit of the London County Council. To the east, therefore, London stopped at the River Lea which marked the eastern edge of Poplar; south of the Thames its limit was the eastern edge of Woolwich. The narrowness of this spatial definition has resulted in a highly partial and distorted view of the industrial history of the metropolis; by including these 'suburbs' in the account (that is, what we now recognise to be the bulk of the metropolitan Thames Gateway), we gain a rather different picture overall.

Take as just one example data on workforces attached to particular industries conventionally thought to be outside London. At their height in the decades around 1900, the Great Eastern Locomotive works at Stratford in West Ham employed 7,000, the Thames Ironworks in Canning Town 6,000, Siemens in Woolwich 7,000, Woolwich Arsenal 70,000, Beckton Gasworks 10,000 and Ford's at Dagenham 15,000. At a time when London was putatively dominated by small-scale production units, these figures point to a rather different experience. It is true that historians have noted the existence of such industrial concentrations, particularly in the remarkable case of West Ham, but they are invariably viewed as part of the distinct experience of outer London or the outskirts, and are therefore considered beyond legitimate interest. To the contrary, I wish to argue that because the movement of capital did not recognise administrative boundaries

---

5   This is the implication of the recent argument in Francis Sheppard, *London. A History*, Oxford, Oxford University Press, 1998, ch. 14.

6   David R. Green, 'The Metropolitan Economy: Continuity and Change, 1800–1939', in Keith Hoggart and David R. Green (eds), *London. A New Metropolitan Geography*, London, Edward Arnold, 1991, pp. 8 – 9.

7   Samuel, 'The Workshop of the World'.

this industrial experience was almost entirely metropolitan, albeit one mediated by the privileged access to the Thames and hence to overseas markets that the region as a whole possessed.[8]

Features of this distinct experience can be traced back to what would conventionally be described as the pre-industrial period. Thames shipbuilding, for example, dates from the sixteenth century when royal dockyards were constructed at Woolwich, Deptford and Erith. Benefiting from proximity to the metropolis and ready access to the sea, this tradition and its associated trades were to survive until the twentieth century.[9] The Woolwich dockyard began with the building of the flagship *Henri Grace à Dieu* in 1513, the fitting of which was completed at Erith where the river had an adequate draught. By Elizabethan times Woolwich and Deptford yards were major sites; here were built all the navy's big ships, supplemented by orders from private trading companies such as the Muscovy and Levant Companies. Private yards, although smaller, were rather more numerous. Among the first established was the Blackwall Shipyard in 1588 at the north-eastern edge of the Isle of Dogs, later to be taken over by the East India Company and greatly extended. By the eighteenth century London and its environs to the east had at least 16 significant yards.[10] Shipbuilding and ship repair gave rise to a host of associated trades. The majority were traditional such as coopering, sail and rope making, but included also were proto-industrial firms. Crowley's iron manufacturers, for example, moved to Greenwich in 1704 to supply the naval shipyard with anchors, nails, tools and locks, and cast iron cannon and other ironware to EastIndiamen built in private yards nearby.[11]

Another nascent industry characteristic of the region which was to play a considerable role in long-term development was that of armaments. As early as the late sixteenth century the Royal Palace at Greenwich was established as a site of arms manufacture, but following increased demand during the Civil War and the continued need to fit ships with guns and ammunition a new location was sought at Woolwich; this eventually became the great Royal Arsenal. Much of the gunpowder was supplied by the Board of Ordnance's Powderhouse, moved out of London to a remote site on Greenwich marsh in 1694, wherein were stored up to 8,000 barrels of gunpowder, much to the consternation of local inhabitants who eventually petitioned parliament for its removal to Purfleet.[12]

Underscoring much of the industrial development that was to transform the region in the nineteenth century was coal, but here again the region displayed evidence of significant early activity. Some of the first experiments in converting

---

8   The boundaries I choose here are those encompassing the existing London boroughs of Barking and Dagenham, Bexley, Greenwich and Newham.

9   Philip Banbury, *Shipbuilders of the Thames and Medway*, Newton Abbot, David and Charles, 1971.

10   Ibid., p. 20.

11   M.W. Flinn, *Men of Iron. The Crowleys in the Early Iron Industry*, Edinburgh, Edinburgh University Press, 1962.

12   Mary Mills, *Greenwich Marsh. The 300 Years before the Dome*, London, M. Wright, 1999, pp. 24 – 9.

coal to coke took place in the mid-seventeenth century when John Winter and Thomas Peyton established works at Greenwich and Deptford, most probably in connection with the established copperas industry. Over the ensuing 150 years this industry grew steadily as the value of coke in iron smelting, and of coal tar in shipbuilding came to be realised. Then in the early nineteenth century the gas industry took off.[13]

London's Industrial Revolution

In the course of the nineteenth century this embryonic industrialisation matured and greatly expanded, transforming the region into a manufacturing centre which in terms of mechanisation, production and organisation rivalled any in the country. At the heart of this transformation were the docks and shipbuilding, sustained by the arterial Thames. The first phase in the modernisation of the London docks complex took place over 1790–1810. During this period the old London Docks were extended and the Commercial Docks, East and West India Docks constructed. This development transformed a metropolitan riverscape that had remained largely unchanged since the late fifteenth century and consolidated London's position as the great centre of world trade and commerce.[14] The direct impact on industry, however, was slight. Apart from expansion in traditional riverside trades and warehousing there was little industrial growth; Poplar and its vicinity remained undeveloped until mid-century.

More important was the completion of the Victoria Docks in 1855. Like so many proximate riverside areas, the southern reaches of West Ham were below the high water mark of the Thames; subject to constant flooding, the marshland was unsuitable for industrial settlement, but then a series of developments took place which presaged an extraordinary industrial development. During the 1830s the Eastern Counties Railway line linking London to Norwich was built. The line passed through Stratford which subsequently emerged as a major locomotive works, but arguably its influence in promoting a branch line to the south was of greater long-term significance. In 1846 a small group of important railway developers including Kennard, Brassey, Peto and Bidder completed a line from Stratford to the junction of the River Lea, ostensibly to distribute seaborne coal from a wharf recently constructed by the Northumberland and Durham Coal Company. The line was immediately extended to North Woolwich in order to capture busy commuter traffic from south of the Thames. Having opened up the riverside area, the contractors then embarked on a scheme to build the Victoria Dock, which when complete in 1855 was the largest and most advanced dock in the world, capable of accommodating the new breed of large steamships.[15] As in

13   Mary Mills, *The Early East London Gas Industry and its Waste Products*, London, M. Wright, 1999.

14   Royal Commission on Historical Monuments of England, *Survey of London*, Vol. XLIII, London, 1994.

15   Marriott, 'West Ham', I.

Poplar, the immediate impact of the docks was limited. Despite the developing communications infrastructure, the area was unknown and too remote from London. The decision of W.T. Henley to build a submarine cable and telegraph works at North Woolwich in 1856 astonished his friends, and in 1874 when Henry Tate established a sugar refinery in what became known as Silvertown a member of his family questioned his sanity, claiming that the workforce would either drown or go down with swamp fever.

However, the docks did offer facilities for the cheapest coal in London, and this was to prove critical to the development of the region as a whole. Coal from the north east was already imported into the area, and had been instrumental in the establishment in 1837 and subsequent expansion of the shipbuilders Ditchburn and Mare situated either side of the Lea adjacent to the coal wharves, and the firm of Coles Child, coke manufacturer and lime burner, on the Greenwich peninsula, which in 1840 could announce it was the largest manufacturer of coke, and because of advances in loading could offer coke and coal at 'a considerable reduction in price'.[16]

The real transformation, however, was brought about by the successful introduction of steam colliers and the enterprise of William Cory. In 1852 the first steam collier journeyed from north-eastern coalfields to Poplar. The round trip took 120 hours, including 24 for unloading; two sailing colliers would have been required to transport the same tonnage of coal, and the trip would have taken at least a month.[17] From then the coal shipped by steam colliers increased dramatically, from 85,000 tons in 1855 to 600,000 tons in 1858. Soon after completion of the Victoria Dock, Cory & Son built batteries of hydraulic cranes on the foreshore and on a converted floating derrick in the dock itself. Another was built in 1865. Within ten years the firm was unloading 1.5m tons of the 2.75m tons of coal shipped to London, giving seaborne coal a decisive advantage over inland coal for industrial use which, despite setbacks, it was able to sustain until World War I.[18] Over this period, the reliability of steam colliers combined with increased size and more efficient unloading guaranteed bulk supplies to riverside industries which steadily expanded; in turn the proportion of seaborne coal for industrial rather than domestic consumption increased. Cory also played a critical role in the industrial development of Erith. By this time sizeable coal wharves had been established by the Beadle brothers to supply the needs of the fledgling engineering industry.[19] In 1898 they, along with the seven other large metropolitan coal distributors, amalgamated into a single company controlled by Cory. The new firm controlled 70 per cent of the import of seaborne coal.[20]

---

16   *Kentish Mercury*, cited in Mary Mills, *Greenwich Marsh*, p. 74. She also notes that many of the streets in the vicinity were named after Durham coalfields.

17   R. Smith, *Sea Coal for London: History of the Coal Factors in the London Market*, London, Longman, 1961, p. 285.

18   Ibid., pp. 338–40.

19   For some interesting insights into this episode see Charles Beadle, *Reminiscences of a Victorian*, privately published, 1924.

20   Ibid., p. 343.

In the second half of the nineteenth century a number of nascent metropolitan industries which relied heavily on abundant and reliable supplies of cheap coal, expanded and reached maturity. Shipbuilding, chemicals, gas, armaments, cables and heavy engineering benefited greatly, and as a result were to feature prominently in the industrial landscape of the region as a whole.

Shipbuilding and Engineering

The shipbuilding firm of Mare & Co. had established a yard on the Poplar side of the Lea in 1837, extending the premises to Canning Town in 1846. The firm attracted admiralty contracts, but following huge losses over the ironwork for Westminster Bridge and gunboats for the Crimea, Mare was declared bankrupt in 1856. The yard was taken over by Peter Rolt and reformed as the Thames Ironworks and Shipbuilding Co. Before its eventual closure in 1912 it became the greatest of the London shipbuilders, responsible for the construction in 1860 of the first iron-clad warship HMS *Warrior* and a succession of prestigious vessels before finally completing HMS *Thunderer* in 1911. This success was in part dependent upon a large on-site foundry which reconstituted iron from scrap. The works thus made its own angle irons and plates and undertook projects that posed difficult engineering challenges, such as in 1855, when it was contracted by the Royal Arsenal to construct a 42-ton mortar, the largest ever made, and later the ironworks for important constructions including Hammersmith Bridge and Alexandra Palace.[21] During the 1860s, however, the manufacture of armour plate became an increasingly complex process controlled almost entirely by northern manufacturers; despite the works' diversification into civil and electrical engineering projects, this undercut its viability so contributing to its eventual demise.[22]

Continuing a tradition dating back centuries, Greenwich also emerged at the heart of Thames shipbuilding in an age of iron and steam. The marine engineers and shipbuilders Maudslay, Sons and Field, originally established at Lambeth in 1814, moved to East Greenwich in 1864. The firm specialised in the construction of marine engines; indeed, the first steamships on the Thames, the first to cross the Atlantic to America and the first to make a steam passage to India were all provided with Maudslay's engines. So complete was its dominance in the early years of steam that Maudslay's was the only Thames firm to receive Admiralty contracts. For a brief period it built ships at East Greenwich, but faced increasing competition from rival engineers and shipbuilders before closure in 1900.[23] The most important of these was John Penn & Son which began operating out of Greenwich in 1800. Penn supplied many of the engines for the fast steamships

21   O.F.G. Hogg, *The Royal Arsenal. Its Background, Origins and Subsequent History*, Oxford, Oxford University Press, 1963, p. 787.

22   Banbury, *Shipbuilders of the Thames and Medway*, pp. 268–74.

23   Ibid., pp. 198–203.

built by Ditchburn and Mare, and later the Thames Ironworks including the *Warrior* and the *Thunderer* with which it amalgamated in 1899.[24]

By the time the Chicago engineering firm Fraser & Chalmers Ltd opened up a new plant at Erith in 1891 the tradition of Thames shipbuilding was in terminal decline. The firm had emerged as the major supplier of mining equipment to the gold mining fields of South Africa, and it was under the influence of the Rothschild and De Beers families that closer geographical links were sought. In the belief that the Maxim Nordenfelt Gun Company (see later) were willing to sell part of their property in Erith, and conscious of the locational advantages of the site, the company purchased the necessary land and within a year manufacture commenced.[25] Initially, orders were hit badly by the American depression, and the company considered closing Erith, but it was decided that the plant was critical to the development of the business in Africa and Britain. Throughout the 1890s production of boilers, engines and machine parts steadily increased, no less than 99 per cent of which were for export. Employment levels fluctuated between 600 and 1000, and then increased; by 1910 the plant had a workforce of 1630. Production fell during World War I, at the end of which the company was taken over by the General Electric Co. Production diversified into machinery for the iron and steel industry, but the plant continued to decline.

Gas and Chemicals

Simultaneously, other industries began to move to the area to take advantage of seaborne coal, the most important of which was gas. So-called gas light and coke companies were originally established in the first half of the nineteenth century to manufacture gas for lights and coke for the workplace.[26] The majority of the companies were small, but with advances in technology, increased industrial use of gas and coke, and cheaper supplies of coal to the metropolis, more sizable plants were built. By the 1860s it was apparent that the numerous small plants of one of the major producers, the Gas Light & Coke Company, were proving expensive and inefficient, so the company sought an alternative site with good facilities. In 1868 Gallions Reach to the east of West Ham was chosen; when the works was completed two years later Beckton was the largest gas plant in the world. Its supply of coal was unloaded by a series of hydraulic cranes mounted on a T-shaped pier which extended over 100 metres into the Thames. And across the Thames at the edge of the Greenwich peninsula the company's great rival – the South Metropolitan Gas Company – built in the early 1880s what was the latest and proved to be the last of the massive metropolitan gasworks. It alone consumed over one sixth of London's seaborne coal at the turn of the century.[27]

---

24 Ibid., pp. 224–7.

25 D.M. Smith, *Fraser & Chalmers. The First Hundred Years*, unpublished manuscript, 1967.

26 Mary Mills, *The Early East London Gas Industry and its Waste Products*, pp. 20–21.

27 Smith, *Sea Coal for London*, p. 340.

Cheap, abundant coal not only encouraged the establishment of sizable industrial concerns but also stimulated the growth of subsidiary industries utilising coal by-products. In 1856 Burt, Boulton and Haywood moved to Silvertown; by 1876 it was the largest tar distillers in the world, consuming 12m gallons of gas tar annually. Numerous other chemical and allied firms followed as result of which West Ham acquired a reputation as a refuge for noxious industries expelled from London by restrictive bye-laws; but more powerful economic motives operated and better explain their migration. As in West Ham across the river, the ready supply of coal to Greenwich gave rise to numerous chemical firms processing by-products, most notably that of Frank Hills which moved to the area in 1845 and developed new techniques for perfecting chemical processes.[28] Hills bestrode the Thames since he also owned a large chemical factory at Stratford, and was later to take control of the Thames Ironworks. After his death in 1895, the Greenwich works was sold to, and incorporated into the South Metropolitan Gas Works.

Cable and Telegraphy

The extent to which the region controlled the development of cable communication in the nineteenth century was remarkable. The early years of cable construction were dominated by British entrepreneurs and investors who, despite the heavy risks, were attracted by the prospects and excitement of this truly revolutionary technology. All the major firms – the Telegraph Construction and Maintenance Co., Siemens Brothers, the India Rubber, Gutta Percha and Telegraph Works, W.T. Henley Telegraph Works and Callender's Cables – which together made the majority of the world's cables, occupied extensive riverside sites in Silvertown, Woolwich and Erith where they could exploit fully the locational advantages offered and draw on up-to-date knowledge of cable making, insulation and electrical distribution necessary to the success of such capital-intensive ventures.

The telegraph and submarine cable industry of Greenwich had its origins in rope making. In 1837 the local firm Enderby's, which had pioneered the use of coal tar in making insulated rope, was approached by William Cooke, inventor of the telegraph, to help develop an electric telegraph cable across the Thames.[29] Submarine cables presented different sets of problems, the resolution to which depended upon active cooperation of diverse industries including wire rope making and gutta percha manufacture. By 1850 William Kuper and Co. was already established as a major manufacturer of wire rope when it moved from Camberwell to Greenwich in 1852. Under the leadership of Richard Glass and George Elliott the company (now Glass Elliott) began to manufacture wire cable in 1854, and soon secured major contracts for submarine cables, culminating in the Atlantic cable, begun in 1856 and completed, after numerous setbacks, in 1858. An alliance with W.T. Henley was formed, and together they sought new premises before Henley decided to move over the river to North Woolwich where the firm could take advantage of Silver's rubber and waterproof works which had

28   Mills, *Greenwich Marsh*, pp. 167–9.
29   Ibid., p. 51.

settled in the area a few years earlier. Silver's was soon to float a public company called the India Rubber, Gutta Percha and Telegraph Works and expanded overseas, particularly in the Americas; by the turn of the century it employed 4,000. In 1864 Glass Elliott, underwritten with capital provided by John Pender, the dominant figure in telegraph company finance, sought similar cooperation when it merged with the Gutta Percha Co. to form the Telegraph Construction and Maintenance Co.[30] The new firm manufactured new Atlantic cables in 1864 and again in 1866 – both of which were laid by Brunel's *Great Eastern* – and was the driving force behind cables in South America, as a result of which it emerged as the major cable manufacturer.[31]

It was at this time that the German engineering firm of Siemens and Halske decided to establish a permanent staff in London better to take advantage of the opportunities opening up to British firms in cable manufacture. The original factory was at Millbank, but in 1863 the firm moved to Woolwich as independent manufacturers of submarine cables. A number of small overseas contracts were secured, but then in 1868 the brothers, who 'had accustomed themselves to think upon an imperial scale',[32] won a contract from a British government recovering in the aftermath of the Indian revolt to construct and lay the Indo-European line. The line ran from Lowestoft to Teheran via France, Prussia and Russia, where it connected with the existing line to India. Completed in 1871 with an in-built automatic relay system, it dramatically increased the speed and frequency of signalling. Over the next decade Siemens laid over 12,000 miles of cable in Europe and the Americas, including in 1873 the first direct submarine cable to the United States.[33]

Long-distance and submarine cable manufacture peaked in the 1880s and then steadily declined. This affected the fortunes of most of the major firms, but Siemens was able to diversify and expand, largely because of determined entrepreneurship in electrical engineering pioneered at their Stafford plant opened in 1900.[34] At Godalming in 1881, the company built the world's first commercial generating station which was used to provide electricity for incandescent lamps in homes and in street lighting, and as the industrial use of electric power gradually increased became a major supplier to the mining, textiles, transport, and iron and steel industries. While the Woolwich site concentrated on cable manufacture employment fluctuated wildly from a weekly average of 239 in 1876 to 1,735 in

---

30   J.D. Scott, *Siemens Brothers, 1858–1958. An Essay in the History of Industry*, London, Wiedenfeld and Nicolson, 1958, p. 54.

31   Jorma Ahvenainen, *The European Cable Companies in South America before the First World War*, Helsinki, Academia Scientiarum Fennica, 2004.

32   Ibid., p. 36.

33   William Pole, *The Life of Sir William Siemens*, London, John Murray, 1888, pp. 206–10.

34   In the 1870s a catalogue described the firm as 'Telegraph Engineers, Manufacturers of Submarine and Subterranean Cables, Materials for Overground Lines, Iron Telegraph Poles, Insulators, Instruments, Batteries, Electric Mine Exploders, and Telegraph Apparatus of all kinds' (cited in Scott, *Siemens Brothers*, p. 45).

1884.[35] As cables declined and Woolwich took on more responsibility for electrical equipment, so employment increased reaching a peak of just under 10,000 during World War II.

The other important cable manufacturer, Callender's, moved to Erith in 1880 where it found a riverside site suitable for loading heavy cables. Originally supplying bitumen from Trinidad to the construction industry, the firm undertook successful experiments to produce a cheaper form of insulation for electric cables which enabled it quickly to exploit the opportunities offered by developments in telegraphy and power supply. Until 1896 most contracts were for electric lighting, but then, reformed as Callender's Cable & Construction Co. and with the services of Samuel Canning who had been chief engineer of the rival Telegraph Construction Co., the firm expanded rapidly. It attracted a steady flow of contracts to provide and lay cables domestically and overseas – mostly within the empire – for power distribution including lighting, railway and tramway electrification schemes, and telegraphy.[36] Further expansion followed in the twentieth century as the company benefited from the general increase in use of electricity, boosted by construction of the national grid after 1926.

Armaments

The armaments and explosive industry had a presence in the region dating back to the late sixteenth century when an ordnance store was sited in Woolwich to provide the dockyards at Greenwich, Deptford and Woolwich with guns and cannon balls, but it was with the development of the Woolwich Arsenal that the full impact of the industry was felt. Until 1716 the state contracted private firms to undertake the manufacture of iron and brass guns but following an explosion at the main foundry in Moorfields production was transferred to Woolwich. Named by George III as the Royal Arsenal after a visit to the site in 1805, and boosted by demands occasioned by the Napoleonic and Crimean wars and the Indian revolt, the works fast developed into a modern armaments factory with access to the most advanced scientific and engineering knowledge. At the height of its production during World War I the site of 1,300 acres was occupied by gun and carriage factories, a laboratory, and mechanical engineering and building works departments.[37] Employment levels fluctuated with the extent of British military involvement, reaching peaks of 5,000 in 1814, over 10,000 in 1861, 20,000 in 1901, a remarkable 73,000 in 1917, and then, following dispersal of arms production, 32,000 in 1940.[38]

Massive though the presence of the Arsenal was, it did not have monopoly over arms production in the region. The Maxim Gun Co., which had been set up in 1884 to manufacture the revolutionary machine gun occupied a small site at Crayford. Three years later Nordenfelt Guns and Ammunition Co., which also

35 Scott, *Siemens Brothers*, p. 193.
36 R.M. Morgan, *Callender's, 1882–1945*, Prescot, BICC plc, 1982, pp. 43–8.
37 Hogg, *The Royal Arsenal*, p. 950.
38 Ibid., pp. 1289–90.

manufactured machine guns, bought a ten acre site for an ordnance factory in nearby Erith. In 1888 the two firms merged to form Maxim Nordenfelt, largely thanks to the acumen of the financier Lord Rothschild and steel company director Albert Vickers, both of whom became major shareholders in the new company.[39] Its most important product was the famous Maxim gun which was used with such devastating effect by the British in Africa, but the company did not attract sufficient government contracts in the 1890s, and was taken over by Vickers in 1897. Vickers, Sons and Maxim continued to operate on both sites, and in the period leading to 1914 as the government came to recognise that it could not rely as it had previously upon Royal Ordnance factories to meet the nation's military needs, the company emerged as a major armaments manufacturer. The plant at Erith was reorganised and expanded to manufacture the Maxim gun, develop the Vickers gun – which would soon supersede the Maxim – and produce breech mechanisms for the larger guns made at Vickers' plant in Sheffield; within a decade the Erith site occupied 18 acres and employed over 4,000 workers. The outbreak of war saw the company overwhelmed with orders, as a result of which production increased dramatically, particularly at Crayford where the workforce at the height of the war reached 14,500. At the time the two factories turned out over 1,000 guns per week.[40] After the war production was diverted to machine tools, sporting guns and domestic appliances with little success. In 1927 Vickers merged with its great rival Armstrong. Four years later the Erith factory closed.

Brunner Mond established a chemical works at a riverside site in West Silvertown in 1893, initially to manufacture caustic soda. Production ceased in 1912, but with the urgent demand for high explosive shells after the outbreak of the war, the factory was one of those sought out by the Explosives Supply Department to purify TNT. Despite heightened fears of the risks to local residents, production began in 1915 and continued even though a safer and more efficient plant was built at Northwich early in 1916.[41] Early in 1917 an explosion took place which devastated the surrounding housing, killed 73 people, and entered into local mythology.[42]

The complex interrelationships established among riverside sites during industrialisation is nicely illustrated by the exploits of Samuel Williams. Williams started a lighterage business on the Thames in 1855, specialising in timber and ice. In 1861 he purchased a steam tug made in Greenwich (the first on the Thames), and then a steam dredger with which he delivered millions of tons of Thames ballast to the new site of the Beckton gasworks.[43] With a decade Williams & Son had built a fleet of eight tugs, largely as a result of a lucrative contract on

---

39   Scott, *Vickers. A History*, p. 39.

40   Ibid., p. 105.

41   *The First Fifty Years of Brunner Mond & Co. 1873–1923*, Northwich, Brunner Mond, 1923.

42   Graham Hill and Howard Bloch (eds), *The Silvertown Explosion*, Stroud, Tempus, 2003.

43   L.T.C. Rolt, 'Samuel Williams & Sons, 1855–1955', in *A Company's Story and its Setting. Samuel Williams & Sons Ltd, 1855–1955*, Samuel Williams, 1955, p. 45.

construction of the Thames Embankment, opened a coal bunkering depot in the Victoria Docks and operated special barges to transport tar, creosote and ammoniacal liquor to Beckton's chemical works, on the basis of which it secured a 60-year contract in 1875.

In a move the long-term importance of which could not have been foreseen, the company purchased riverside land in 1887 that had originally been acquired by the Dagenham Dock Co. for the nascent dock scheme. Instead of developing the docks, however, Williams & Son decided to create an industrial estate. By using London's rubbish and spoilage from construction of the underground to build up the marshland, 600 acres of land were systematically reclaimed by the company in the period leading to 1914; coal wharves and jetties for the handling of sea-borne coal were installed by pioneering use of reinforced concrete, and in 1909 a railway terminus was completed. In 1911 the dock had its moment of fame when it was provided with a deep water jetty to accommodate HMS *Thunderer*, the last ship built by the Thames Ironworks, which was towed down river to be fitted out.

Soon after the war the Ford Motor Co., which had established a factory at Manchester in 1911, decided to relocate production to Dagenham. The site not only offered abundant cheap land and good river communication but – because of the building of the nearby Becontree estate by the London County Council in the 1920s for approximately 100,000 residents displaced from East London – a ready supply also of cheap labour. Ford's purchased all the land owned by Williams to the east of the dock area and in 1929 began work. Roads, railway tracks and bridges were constructed, and to stabilise the ground on which the factory was to stand 22,000 concrete piles cast by Williams were driven to a depth of 25 metres. When complete the works was virtually self-contained with its own power station, foundry and gas plants and a massive jetty and cranes capable of unloading the largest cargo ships.[44] The presence of Ford's, however, gave rise to other factories connected to the motor industry as a result of which Barking and Dagenham attracted significant numbers of medium and heavy engineering firms.

Epilogue

By exploring the experience of a region to the east of London generally thought to be outside its general purview, this chapter has attempted to revisit the industrial history of the metropolis. Industrialisation of the region may have differed in scale and intensity, periodisation and trajectory, but it is the commonalities and complex interdependencies that persuade us of the importance of thinking about the region as a totality and of its neglected contribution to London's industrial history. This shared experience derived from locational advantages offered by riverside sites. These had long been recognised and were critical to the region's proto-industrialisation, but in the nineteenth century the active confluence of access to the river and hence overseas markets, completion of an extensive docks

---

44   David Burgess-Wise, *Ford at Dagenham*, Derby, Breedon Books, 2001, p. 31.

and transport infrastructure, availability of cheap land, proximity to the London market and City finance, abundant coal supplies, and networks of associated industries promoted a dramatic new phase in the region's industrial history as numerous sizable factories settled and expanded. Here too came among the age's great engineers – Maudslay, Telford, Rennie, Brunel, Stephenson, Mare, Trevithick, Hancock, Hudson, Siemens, Bessemer and Congreve – to secure their reputation in the shipbuilding, chemical, locomotive, armaments and cable works of the region.[45]

The twentieth century witnessed the demise of this industry; today it survives only in collective and official memories, in its archaeological heritage, and in a few isolated outposts such at Tate and Lyle. This part of the story is framed by the history of Britain's industrial and imperial decline, but it is complicated by specific local factors. Given the history of the decline of Thames shipbuilding, the Thames Ironworks survived beyond its time, but its closure in 1912 was forced by the government's refusal to award further contracts. The decline of the Royal Arsenal followed the decision to disperse armaments manufacture in the period leading to the outbreak of World War II. The interwar years witnessed general stagnation as many established industries failed to adapt to changing economic circumstances, and the locational advantages that had originally attracted them to the region proved more elusive. Few genuinely new industries settled. Even the one obvious exception – Ford's at Dagenham – never had the level of success that was anticipated. The war provided opportunities for many firms to boost production, but this was only a temporary respite. In the postwar period the relentless decline continued until the region ceased as a major manufacturer. Mergers and takeovers took place which served to stay execution for while, but the closure of the docks in the 1970s finally sealed the fate of the region.

45   Banbury, *Shipbuilders of the Thames*, p. 20; Mills, *Greenwich Marsh*.

Chapter 3

One Hundred and Twenty Years of Regeneration, from East London to the Thames Gateway: Fluctuations of Housing Type and City Form

William Mann

Since the establishment of metropolitan government in 1888, 120 years ago, it has been a guiding principle for those governing London that the East End is in need of regeneration. The symptoms have varied between social, environmental and economic ills, and the physical cures implemented have ranged from dispersal to concentration and from low to high density – until, in time, ills and cures have blurred. With the promise to repair degraded environments and lift disadvantaged communities, the Thames Gateway follows this lineage, but with public sector attentions spread over an area of unprecedented size.

This chapter is an episodic historical account of the attempts to renew East London, from the 1880s to the present; this account is broadly paralleled by a topographic journey eastwards from Shoreditch and Whitechapel to Poplar and on to Silvertown and Barking in the London Thames Gateway. My focus is on the types of residential buildings used in regeneration projects in successive periods and locations – houses, tenements and towers – and on the forms of collective space in which these sit – courts and closes, streets and parks. My aim in examining these types and forms in some contextual detail is to explore the continuities and changes in social intent behind these projects of physical regeneration, as well as to study the relation between the form of the city as a whole and its constitutent dwellings. By setting ten years and six miles in the London Thames Gateway against 120 years and three miles of historical and topographical background, I aim to highlight the nature of current practice in relation to issues of density, public space and the form of the metropolis.[1]

---

1   Inevitably, given the wide historical and geographical scope, my narrative is drawn from a piecemeal examination of the extensive literature on regeneration in the area. Equally, given my profession (I am an architect and urban designer, not an academic) it is drawn from personal observation over a decade exploring and designing projects for corners of this vast area. I hope that the detailed insights that professional work has afforded me are complementary to the micro- and macro-narratives of the area.

East London in the Late Nineteenth Century

By the 1880s East London extended uninterrupted to the River Lea, three miles from the City. The predominant residential urban forms at this time in the east were court or alley developments, with houses clustered around a common space, and fine-grained street structures lined with terraces of two storey terrace houses, commonly referred to as 'cottages'. Little trace survives of the former, except in the slightly contorted structure or unusual dimensions of the urban grain along parts of Shoreditch High Street and Whitechapel High Street; however, it is worth recording these, if only to note the existence of more intimate forms and scales of collective space.

The terraced 'cottages', built in the eighteenth and nineteenth centuries, were tightly packed, one room wide and two or three rooms deep, with a small yard at the back. In parts of East London the rear wall of the kitchen was as little as 5 metres from the back of the property behind. The cottages defined hard-edged, intimate streets, generally referred to as 'turnings' (the street to the rear was called the 'back-double'). As Young and Willmott observed in their 1957 study of Bethnal Green:

> The residents of the turning, who usually make up a sort of 'village' of 100 to 200 people, have their own places to meet, where few outsiders come – practically every turning has its one or two pubs, its two or three shops, and its 'bookie's runner'. [2]

Charles Booth's *Map Descriptive of London Poverty* of 1888–89 (Figure 3.1) helpfully set out for the new London County Council the state of East London. Dividing the population into seven income classes, from 'Upper-middle and Upper classes: Wealthy' to 'Lowest class. Vicious, semi-criminal', it shows with great clarity the disparities in income between the city's West and East Ends. Where the wealthy are spread across the West End, the East End is mapped in the colours of the honest working classes, crossed by ribbons of shopkeeper red, and interspersed with patches of black – alleys, courts and street networks damned under the name of 'rookeries'[3], with the meanest of them sketching an arc at the eastern edge of the city, from Shoreditch to Whitechapel. This map was to serve as a plan of action for a series of interventions over the following years.

'Improvement'

In his essay 'Rookeries and Model Dwellings',[4] Robin Evans challenges the conflation of income, housing and morality implicit in Booth's classification. He

---

2   Michael Young and Peter Willmott, *Family and Kinship in East London*, London, Penguin, 1957, p. 109.
3   Literally, 'the collective nests of rooks': the name was intended to emphasise the meanness of the dwellings, and the absence of demarcation between families.
4   Robin Evans, 'Rookeries and Model Dwellings: English Housing Reform and the Moralities of Private Space', in *Translations from Drawing to Building and Other Essays*,

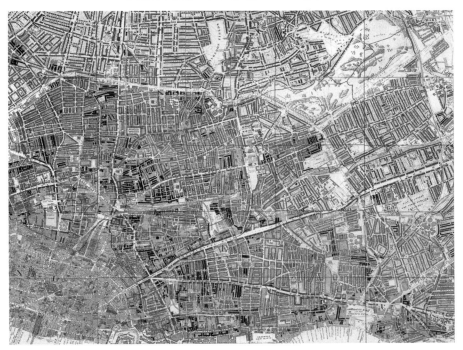

Figure 3.1   **Charles Booth – map descriptive of London Poverty 1898–89, sheets 1, 2 and 5 combined © The Library of the London School of Economics and Political Science**

interprets the rendering in black of the lowest-class dwellings as an expression of the Victorian fear of the 'contagion of immorality'. Just as earlier maps had plotted everything from disease to the 'modern plague' of alcoholism, the colouring of Booth's map suggests that the immorality and criminality of the rookeries would be liable to spread if not destroyed. According to Evans, what shocked the Victorian social reformers as much as poor sanitation or overcrowding was the blurring of public and private and the mixing of sexes and generations in the lodging-houses and subdivided cottages of the 'rookeries'.

The tenement block quickly became the building type applied in the redevelopment of the rookeries, with a number of distinctive features aimed at taming the disorderly sociability of the narrow streets and courts. Communal areas were kept minimal and open to public surveillance, dwellings were designed for nuclear families (parents and children only), with clear differentiation between room functions. Generous living rooms combined with the closure of public houses were intended to enforce middle-class habits of private living. Indeed, because of its clearly normative character, 'model housing' remained unpopular for a long time,

London, AA Publications, 1997, pp. 93–117.

and even sometimes unlet, leaving social reformers puzzled that 'the habits and tastes and desires of the people are to a large extent hostile to improvement'.[5]

So, the courts and alleys between Fashion Street and Whitechapel High Street were slated for demolition in 1876 (by the Metropolitan Board of Works) after a campaign led by Canon Samuel Barnet of nearby St Jude's church, and were finally replaced by the six-storey Rothschild Buildings in 1887, stern and utilitarian in appearance, the only concession to ornament being the brick gateway that still stands in Wentworth Street. The low terraces of the 'Old Nichol' slum, beside St Leonard's, Shoreditch, though built barely 50 years previously, were replaced with the tall tenements of the Boundary Road estate (1893–96) by the London County Council, which took up and developed the architecture of the apartment or 'mansion' blocks of the wealthier West End, with elaborately banded stone and brickwork, and large gables to the main elevation (Figures 3.2 and 3.3).

Both developments replaced the intimate collective spaces (modest streets and small courts) and diffuse networks of urban spaces (fine-grained street grids) with clear central spaces. In the case of Rothschild Buildings, the hard internal court served as collective space, a focus for this enclave of Jewish émigrés from Eastern Europe, and play area for the children who initially made up 665 of the population of 1,162 (in 198 flats) in 1899. While critics at the time argued that these 'barracks' (as tenements became generally known) would destroy the individualism of the residents, Jerry White's oral history[6] provides a useful corrective, showing that in certain circumstances – shared religion, diverse origins and incomes and a well-defined common space – an intense communality could and did exist in the 'model dwellings'.

By contrast, the Boundary Road scheme is built around a circular central public space, Arnold Circus, in which the demolition spoil was landscaped into a mound, topped with a small park and a bandstand. Now ringed with mature trees, it is a place of considerable character, but appears to be a further development of the anaesthetic or buffer character of many London squares, more for looking at that being in: it is the narrow communal yards between the blocks that appear now to be the locus of communal life.

For all their differences, these developments established the basic template for the redevelopment of East London until World War II, gradually replacing houses and streets from the bottom and progressively the middle of Booth's classification with robustly built new tenements. 'Improvement' proved hard to resist and, over the next century or so, this would entail a wholesale transfer of the population from houses to apartments between the City and the River Lea. As Lionel Esher has commented, slum clearance targets followed a pattern of 'perpetual recession. By 1939 half the so-called slums of 1931 had been cleared, but many more were to be added to the other half'[7] before the programme would be brought to a halt.

---

5   Lewis Dibdin, 'Dwellings of the Poor', in Evans, ibid., p. 110.
6   Jerry White, *Rothschild Buildings: Life in an East End Tenement Block 1887–1920*, London, Pimlico, 2003.
7   Lionel Esher, *A Broken Wave: The Rebuilding of England 1940–1980*, London, Allen Lane, 1981, p. 26.

Figure 3.2   **Old Nichol Street, known as 'the Jago', 1880s. Photo: London Metropolitan Archive**

Figure 3.3   **Boundary Road Estate, Shoreditch. Photo: Witherford Watson Mann Architects**

Apartments or Houses

Residents' perceptions of the old and new forms of accommodation were starkly expressed in the polarisation of 'cottages' and 'barracks'. These perceptions are just one facet of a debate over the respective merits of apartment buildings and houses that has raged since the mid-nineteenth century. The following impassioned pleas date originally from 1878 and 1937, but sound remarkably familiar and topical:

> London's architects, developers and residents should stop building the interminable lines of thoroughfares … bordered with equally interminable lines of houses … each inhabited by one and the same family, and should instead start to construct apartment houses in the Parisian style.[8]

> One look at the advertisements of the building speculators in the English newspapers is sufficient to show that Englishmen want to live in a cottage. And yet …. Nowadays many people believe it is an improvement to build tall houses like those which are to be found in other large cities. London has apparently been panic-stricken and has abandoned the English traditions …. London, the capital of English civilisation, has caught the infection of Continental experiments which are at variance with the whole character and tendency of the city![9]

---

8   William H. White (1878), 'On Middle Class Houses in Paris and Central London', lecture to the Royal Institute of British Architects Marcus, Sharon, *Apartment Stories. City and Home in Nineteenth Century Paris and London*, Berkeley, CA, University of California Press, 1999, p. 83.

9   Steen Eiler Rasmussen, *London: The Unique City*, Oxford, Jonathan Cape, 1948, pp. 392–6 and 404.

The Garden Suburbs

As fast as houses were demolished, more houses would spring up further to the east; the extension of London's rail network provided the impetus and support for extensive development beyond the city's edge.

In Stratford and Barking, these followed the compact, fine-grained but repetitive lines of the workers' cottages of East London. After World War I, housing would increasingly take the forms advocated by the Garden City movement – though predominantly as garden suburbs rather than self-sufficient settlements. Curiously, London's first garden suburb at Hampstead was the culmination of Samuel and Henrietta Barnett's campaigns for the working classes of Whitechapel, which ran from the redevelopment of the Flower and Dean Rookery, the establishment of the University Settlement, Toynbee Hall, to the Whitechapel Library and Art Gallery. While the Hampstead location may be considered a strange choice to benefit the 'labouring classes' of London, the template established by architects Barry Parker and Raymond Unwin in 1909 proved remarkably persuasive: the characteristic U-, S- and W-plan blocks of compact low-rise houses enfolding small closes, beside an area of wilder landscape providing recreational space and separation from the city.

These architectural and urban tactics formed the basis for the development of the Becontree estate, east of Barking, built between 1919 and 1935, comprising no fewer than 24,000 houses on what until then had been agricultural land. The tension between Garden City and garden suburb is expressed in the LCC's description of the estate as 'a township *more or less* complete in itself' (my italics): and while the overall plan suggests self-sufficiency, the built reality proved more mundane. The plan looks like a half remembered diagram from Ebenezer Howard's foundational text 'Garden Cities of Tomorrow', with an open belt of heathland separating the estate from neighbouring areas, and five roads radiating from a central point, designated originally as the location of a Civic Centre and a park. With the estate split across three boroughs, the planned Civic Centre ended up at the north-eastern edge, and any semblance of urbanity for the inhabitants was focused on small local parades of shops close to the railway stations, and seven cavernous pubs scattered across the estate.

Yet while deployment and redeployment of the forms of the garden suburb across a vast area only increase the sense of monotony and disorientation, at the small scale, the closes which punctuate the urban blocks served as the focal points for local sociability which for some was experienced as every bit as intense as the East End they had left behind. Peter Willmott's *The Evolution of a Community: A Study of Dagenham After Forty Years*, traces both the endurance of old habits of sociability and the emergence of more detached attitudes, noting that 'the familiar patterns have flourished in certain kinds of streets – ones which have something of the physical form of the old East End "turnings"'.[10]

---

10   Peter Willmott, *The Evolution of a Community: A Study of Dagenham After Forty Years*, London, Routledge and Kegan Paul, 1963, p. 83.

In the late 1920s attention switched, as Roy Porter recounts, 'from great peripheral estates to blocks of flats in inner London. Whereas cottages comprised over 85 per cent of the output between 1919 and 1927, by 1939 something like 90 per cent were flats'.[11] This paralleled changes of policy outside of Britain, in particular in Vienna, where the Social Democratic administration performed a similar switch from developing garden suburbs outside the city (their immediate postwar policy) to building dense apartment complexes around the city's inner edge,[12] a change that has been interpreted as an attempt to maintain their political constituency. The forms of the garden city started to inflect the LCC's inner city projects (Figure 3.4).

**Figure 3.4   LCC estate, Coate Street, Bethnal Green, East London, 2005.
Photo: Witherford Watson Mann Architects**

While earlier tenements had followed existing street patterns, from the 1920s onwards increasingly ingenious, sometimes tortuous, layouts were deployed. A typical example from the 1930s can be found at Tenter Street in Spitalfields, where an outer and an inner U-plan block define a service courtyard between, all

11   Roy Porter, *London: A Social History*, London, Harvard University Press, 1996, p. 310.

12   Manfredo Tafuri, *Vienne La Rouge: La Politique Immobiliere de la Vienne socialiste, 1919–1933*, Brussels, Mardaga, 1981.

stairs, decks and bins, while the smaller block defines a pleasant courtyard with fruit trees on a carpet of grass, devoid of any signs of life. Without any avant-garde aspirations, these blocks quietly anaesthetised the street and intensified the sociability and conflicts of the common courtyard.

From Howard to 'the Vertical Garden City'

Ebenezer Howard, the anarchist who initiated the Garden City movement, was not without ideas for the urbanised areas of the city. His thesis about the community benefits of the uplift in land values caused by the creation of garden cities had a corollary in the anticipated depressive effects on property and land values in central London:

> de-magnetise that people, convince large numbers of them that they can better their condition in every way by migrating elsewhere, and what becomes of monopoly value? Its spell is broken, and the great bubble bursts ... [I]magine the population of London falling, and falling rapidly; the migrating population establishing themselves where rents are extremely low, and where their work is within easy walking distance of their homes! Obviously, house-property in London will fall in rental value, and fall enormously. Slum property will sink to zero, and the whole working population will move into houses of a class quite above those which they can now afford to occupy. ... These wretched slums will be pulled down, and their sites occupied by parks, recreation grounds and allotment gardens. And this change, as well as many others, will be effected not at the expense of the ratepayers, but almost entirely at the expense of the landlord class. ... Nor will, I think, the compulsion of any Act of Parliament be necessary to effect this result: it will probably be achieved by the voluntary action of the landowners, compelled, by a Nemesis from whom there is no escape, to make some restitution for the great injustice which they have so long committed.[13]

Howard's prediction proved uncannily accurate: yet everything happened somewhat differently, since change in London was enacted by forceful wartime and post-war governments, and the depression in inner-city property values, though palpable, would eventually reverse. A different nemesis, in the form of aerial bombardment provided an impetus for the reduction and dispersal of population. In the 1943 County of London Plan and 1944 Greater London Plan, Patrick Abercrombie set out Howard's principles of population reduction in the inner city, a green belt and Garden Cities (the New Towns) around London with great diagrammatic clarity and surprisingly precise detail. The form of the city was presented as a series of concentric rings – with a ring motorway skirting its outer edge, a detail you will not find in Howard.

Part of the logic of the creation of the New Towns was to allow 'the bombed and blighted areas of east and south-east London ... to be rebuilt at adequate

---

13   Ebenezer Howard, *Garden Cities of Tomorrow*, London, Faber 1965 (1st edn, 1898), pp. 154–6.

standards, with small gardens for families with children'.[14] Yet the LCC's bomb damage maps – a new set of 'plague' maps of chilling beauty to equal Booth's – show between 70 and 90 per cent of the housing stock of East London escaped serious damage (the proportion decreases in proximity to docks and industrial areas) (Figure 3.5). The 'cottages' were torn down and replaced with new, slightly larger ones with more generous gardens and greener surroundings, mixed with a relatively low proportion of apartments. The template was set out in the Lansbury estate, Poplar, which was developed by the LCC as a showcase for the redevelopment of the city for the 1951 Festival of Britain. The houses, which formed the majority of the accommodation, were modest; the market square, with its arcades, curved brickwork fronts and bay windows and demonstrative clock-tower has the feel of a piazza, humane in scale, its details mundane with touches of elegance; heights rose to the six storey apartment blocks at the west end, with relatively generous swathes of green space between. In John Summerson's assessment: 'It is not exciting, but it is important and worth close attention, because here is the first realisation of a formula for urban redevelopment which appears to have great merit. Here, conceivably, may be the first step towards redemption of our disgusting cities.'[15]

At Lansbury, Abercrombie's skilful synthesis of Garden City and modernist city planning appears in retrospect to have been fragile. Space for industry and employment which had been woven through the fabric of the East End, and was also an important consideration for Howard, appears to have been of marginal concern. The expansive new areas of green space were never allocated the necessary capital funds to be established as parks or gardens of any quality, while the maintenance budget would increasingly be challenged. But such issues, which give an indication of the long term sustainability of a redevelopment model, take a long time to come to the surface or to be understood. In the meantime, redevelopment of the East End, and demolition of existing neighbourhoods, accelerated, and increasingly followed a medium- and high-rise template.

The architect Ernö Goldfinger, who had written a popular book championing the County of London Plan,[16] extrapolated from this interpretation of Abercrombie's proposals for London to realise something of the spirit that Le Corbusier would refer to as 'the Vertical Garden City'. His Balfron Tower, 1968, just to the north-east of the Lansbury Estate, replaced the tightly packed streets of workers' cottages with maisonettes stacked in a 26 storey tower, accessed by nine bridges from the distinctive lift and services tower, flanking a small park with a lower apartment block. Many tenants were drawn from the surrounding area, with former neighbours sharing the same access 'streets'. Yet as one of Goldfinger's

14   Peter Hall and Colin Ward, *Sociable Cities, The Legacy of Ebeneezer Howard*, Chichester, Wiley, 1998, pp. 49–50.

15   John Summerson, review in *the New Statesman*, 16 June 1951, quoted in Nick Tiratsoo, 'The London County Council and the Case of Lansbury', in *Rassegna 75*, 'Architecture and Public Administration', Milan 1998, p. 114.

16   E.J. Carter and Ernö Goldfinger, *The County of London Plan Explained*, London, Penguin Book, 1945.

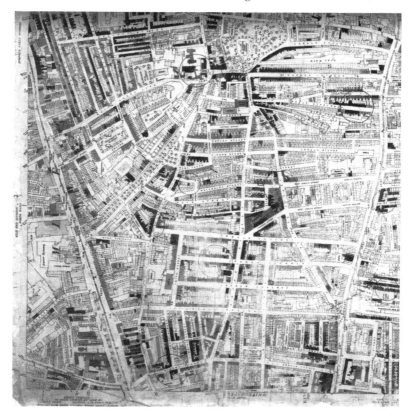

Figure 3.5   Bomb damage maps excerpts from nos. 51, 52, 63, 64.
© London Topographical Society

biographers has written 'the poor lift provision may have done as much to facilitate interaction as the corridor/street idea, with tenants talking to each other as they waited for a lift to arrive'.[17] Balfron Tower shows the replacement of the intimate streets of Poplar with a new, sublime scale, to parallel that of the A102 urban motorway carved through the area (Figure 3.6).

Yet we should be careful about over-emphasising the anxiety associated with previous tower experiments, recognising that these were but a small proportion of development.[18] What was most destructive was the scale of redevelopment, the wholesale nature of the change, and the introverted planning of the new

---

17   Nigel Warburton, *Ernö Goldfinger – the Life of an Architect*, Oxford, Routledge, 2004, p. 161.

18   With self-selection of tenants (as at the Balfron's twin, the Trellick Tower in Ladbroke Grove) and careful management, it is clear that towers can form part of successful urban communities. Indeed, when the Holly Street Estate in Hackney was redeveloped, one tower was retained and refurbished, and many of the older residents, who no longer

Figure 3.6   Balfron Tower, Poplar, under construction, late 1960s. © Tower Hamlets Local History Library

developments; for example, community centres and shops were located at the centre of an estate rather than the edge, where they might serve as a point of contact with a wider area. Already in 1956, Young and Willmott had argued for different priorities and different tactics to avoid the wholesale dislocation of fine-grained family and community networks, arguing for 'sacrificing some of the many projected open spaces ... putting some factories rather than residences in high flatted buildings ... and saving as many as possible of the existing houses'.[19] Yet large-scale redevelopment continued for a further 20 years: city neighbourhoods were transformed into 'estates', the static, centrally-planned composition of uses supporting the architects' narrow functionalism, making uses or lifestyles other than those originally planned hard to accommodate. The scale of the undertaking defeated consistency (not a bad thing perhaps, but the basis of the project) and exhausted resources before the task was completed. The 500 hectares of the East End 'comprehensively redeveloped' after the war form a landscape of considerable visual variety but little urban or social coherence. Occasional intact blocks of

---

had young children but had positive memories of high-rise living from the early days of the estate, chose to live there.

19   Young and Willmott, *Family and Kinship in East London*, pp. 197–8.

terrace housing sit amongst the sometimes grand courtyard blocks, and the slabs and towers set in scrubby parkland. Mile End Park is finally maturing as a park with diverse uses, characters and publics, more than 50 years after its appearance in Abercrombie's County of London Plan. Destruction is relatively quick work, but cities are slow to construct or remake, both financially and socially.

The combination of comprehensive redevelopment and population dispersal transformed the East End beyond recognition. The population diminished and changed composition. Indeed, comparison of census figures in 1901 and 2001 suggests that in one area the evolution from house to apartment dwelling has been accompanied by a 75 per cent reduction of population – there are half as many residential units as before and half as many residents per household.[20] A different, but equally dramatic, official statistic notes a 25 per cent reduction in London's population as a whole between 1961 and 1994. The physical fabric and the ethnic mix of the East End have both changed fundamentally since Booth's study: yet the area is still deeply marked by social deprivation, relative both to national and London-wide standards. The overlap between Booth's 1889 map and the Greater London Authority's 'London Index of Deprivation' is uncannily close.

Already during the slow tilt towards greater district and site densities – from Abercrombie to high-rise – a few architects had explored 'low-rise, high-density' solutions, such as those at Fleet Road and Branch Hill,[21] by innovative architects at the London Borough of Camden. Recalling the compact layouts of the workers' cottages, the rhythmically repetitive low blocks of houses and maisonettes were interspersed with small gardens and narrow pedestrian streets.

Throughout the 1970s and early 1980s, with London's population and industry declining and thus relatively low pressure on land use, and with political support for community involvement in planning, a high proportion of family accommodation was built. Compact layouts of houses and maisonettes – generally medium rather than high density – became increasingly common. With its original Jewish constituency steadily leaving the area, slowly being replaced by a new wave of migrants from Bangladesh, Rothschild Buildings was demolished in the 1970s, its austere, penitential bulk replaced by two- and three-storey pitched roof houses around a series of courts. In Spitalfields, as at Coin Street, near Waterloo, high-density office development was faced down by sustained community campaigning, achieving a temporary reversal of values, and realising pockets of the low, green, permeable city that Howard and Abercrombie had envisaged.

Docklands 1980s and 1990s: From Clearance to Infill, from Openness to Enclaves

A radically different approach to the regeneration of the East End was put in place in the early 1980s, when the Thatcher government set up a Development

---

20   Unpublished research by John Baker of the Leabank Project Group in relation to the Aberfeldy Estate, Poplar.

21   Christoph Grafe, 'Les Terrasses de Camden: The Hanging Gardens of North London Revisited', *OASE*, 61, 2003.

Corporation – the favoured instrument of the Garden City movement – to redevelop declining areas within the city, the extensive dock areas. Rejection of the public sector-led regeneration of the post-war period was axiomatic: the vast majority of development was carried out by private sector developers, with the new office cluster at Canary Wharf catering for the newly deregulated financial services industry and high-value apartments for sale lining the riverfront and docksides.

Where the social housing programme of the late nineteenth century was motivated by fear of the 'contagion' of poverty, the development of Docklands appears to testify to an opposite belief: the 'trickle down effect', whereby, in urban terms, the injection of business activity and high-value housing should help spread entrepreneurialism and wealth to the wider area. In practice, the residents of adjacent areas have not had the skills to access employment in the financial services sector that makes up much of the office market and the disparity of income limits the extent of shared use of retail or local services.

The almost inevitable outcome of this was that new developments were realised as closed enclaves: Docklands re-established urban apartments as the preferred development form and showed that a strong market existed for a (selective) urban lifestyle, albeit behind the protective physical barriers of dock walls and transport infrastructure. While the stereotype of Docklands is of laissez-faire city-building, defensive site layouts and enclosures seem both consistent and deliberate. Thus Poplar is separated by the Docklands Light Railway and by the six lanes of highway from Canary Wharf, immediately to the south, and linked by a single footbridge. Equally, the majority of dock basins are introverted enclaves, disconnected from the wider area; in Woolwich, the first step in the redevelopment of the Arsenal as a residential site was the reconstruction of the boundary wall which had been demolished with the construction of the A206. Paul Barker has written that 'In the urban landscape, the docks were like prisons, carving out huge, secretive chunks of territory. No one apart from those who worked there ever went inside'.[22] This disconnection is still in place.

With the dockside sites to the west of the River Lea built out and demand still buoyant, private developers have turned their attention in recent years to the Regent's Canal and the canalised River Lea (navigation). While much smaller in scale to Docklands developments, the common logic of these sites quickly becomes apparent. Several developments, such as Victoria Wharf (Figure 3.7) and 'Urban Island' at Three Mills, use the waterways in the manner of a moat to establish a distance to neighbouring areas, guaranteeing privacy and light. The waterside is the front, open and glazed, while the street side is closed and defensive; the ground floor is given over to an undercroft of car parking, elevating residences from any direct contact with the environs.

For all the enthusiasm expressed in sales literature for the 'vibrant' life of the local streets/market/pubs, the relationship with the rest of the city that these developments offer their residents is primarily visual – the tensions of urban life are reduced to a skyline, recalling Patrick Keillor's provocative statement: "in the

22   Paul Barker, 'London Witness', *Prospect*, April 2005, p. 45.

**Figure 3.7   Victoria Wharf, Mile End, East London, 2005. Photo: Witherford
                Watson Mann Architects**

UK, the subjective transformation of landscape seems to offer the individual a way to oppose the poverty of everyday surroundings. As individuals, we can't rebuild the public transport system, or re-empower local democracy, but we can poeticise our relationship with their dilapidation'.[23]

The Thames Gateway

Even while the regeneration of the dock areas was stuttering in the recession of the early 1990s, further growth and regeneration was being planned by the interventionists of the Conservative government. At the opening of Canary Wharf in 1991, Environment Secretary Michael Heseltine signalled his intent to bring the 'barren areas' of the 'East Thames Corridor' 'back into more valuable use'.[24] Stretching 62 kilometres out from the Lea Valley to Southend and the Isle of Sheppey on either side of the Thames estuary, traced by satellite in the cold blue of retreating industry, this vast area has become the receptacle for many confused hopes and fears.

The Thames Gateway's scale, form and current condition all challenge our perceptions of London. The distance from Stratford to Southend is ten miles more than that from Heathrow to the Lea – a whole city. The linear form appears to break through the concentric rings so clearly established by Abercrombie, internalised in the intervening years in our perceptions of the city. The area is made up of declining industrial uses, abandoned workings including the extensive chalk pits left behind by the cement industry, and cut through by major road and railway infrastructure.

The linear form is the greatest distraction, raising spectres – or hopes – of a 'linear city' stretching out into the marshes: it is, in fact, no more than an administrative boundary, and a weak one at that. The area is one of a number of development corridors which radiate out of London, the strongest of which runs westward from Heathrow along the M4 towards Bristol, with others north to Stansted and Cambridge, and south to Gatwick and Brighton. With the wide tidal Thames in the middle, the Thames Gateway is in fact two bundles of transport infrastructure and supported development (the A13 and London – Southend railway north of the river, and the A2, M20 and North Kent railway to the south), bound together more closely in the city's inner edge, and with intermittent links further east (the planned Beckton–Crossness bridge, the DLR to Woolwich, the existing Dartford bridge and tunnel). New infrastructure will support the development of the area, most particularly the Channel Tunnel Rail Link's stations at Stratford in the Lea Valley and Ebbsfleet south of the river near Dartford. In Peter Hall's characterisation, the Thames Gateway is 'a discontinuous development corridor'.[25]

23   P. Keillor, 'Popular Science', in The British Council, *Landscape* (2000) p. 61–7.

24   Quoted by David Milliband, speech to the Thames Gateway Forum, 23 November 2005.

25   Hall and Ward, *Sociable Cities*, p. 155.

Hall and Ward give one of the clearest characterisations of the Thames Gateway I have read:

> it is not and will not be a Linear City, much as that phrase makes good journalistic copy. It will be linear: the Thames ensures that. It will be urban, though it will also be rural; there will be a complex intercalation of urban areas and intervening green belts, green strips, green wedges. It will not at all be a single monolithic city; it will be something altogether more complex than that, a corridor with multiple centres large and small, with residential areas strung out between them. It will also have a great deal of intervening open space: the urban elements are separated by vast spaces of marsh or quarried chalk, always backed by the equally vast expanse of the tidal Thames.[26]

Perhaps the Thames Gateway is best seen as a reassertion of the 'tentacular city', with development stretching out along major arteries, that Abercrombie sought to suppress and remodel. As Lionel Escher comments, Abercrombie's annular representations were always somewhat misrepresentative:

> In fact, any diagram of the built-up area in 1945 reveals it to be not annular at all but tentacular – an ink-blot spreading out along its main road and rail radials. Only by chopping off the tentacles could the rings be given credibility. Perhaps unconsciously influenced by Clough Williams-Ellis's successful 'England and the Octopus' Abercrombie could not see any octopus as benign, and gave no consideration (as the Danes were doing for Copenhagen) to fairly high density tentacular growth as a concept that could be as valid as the planet-and-moons concept he adopted.[27]

Two conclusions follow from this characterisation of the Thames Gateway. Firstly, while the planning model may be both innovative and site-specific in terms of regional planning, it does not appear to be the case that we are talking about a completely new kind of city, rather an evolution of aspects of the city we already know. Neither the greatest expectations nor worst fears for this area appear to be justified. Secondly, it is dangerous to generalise about the Thames Gateway. Discontinuous development of widely varying conditions (in particular in terms of public transport accessibility) requires much specific attention before generic conclusions can be drawn. Here my account strays from the tangible realities of displaced communities, demolished streets and new buildings and residents to paper schemes, because of the long gestation of projects in the Thames Gateway. While things are unlikely to turn out exactly as currently planned, there is enough evidence to make observations and raise questions about the direction that the development of East London appears to be taking.

26 Ibid., pp. 157–8.
27 Esher, *A Broken Wave*, pp. 98–9.

City Form and Building Type

Abercrombie's plans were underpinned by clearly defined principles on the relations between buildings, neighbourhoods and the city as a whole. While the rationality was, in parts, speculative, and was progressively bypassed, as on the issues of density and building height, the plans extrapolated from 50 years of regeneration practice. Importantly, they were helped in their initial years by the purposefulness of a war government and the opportunities of an aftermath economy. The London Thames Gateway can rely on no such rationalised or habitual relation between city form and building type; equally, whatever favourable economic conditions may once have been in place have given way to the housing boom which in part reflects a structural imbalance between high demand and slowly growing supply. Furthermore, the profound shift in development paradigms that occurred in the 1980s leaves current practice strongly connected to the economics of the Docklands paradigm and only weakly to more collective, social goals – however flawed – of post-war regeneration.

Without a strong connection to the wider city-form, density and building type are increasingly determined by interpretations of what is viable, mostly slewed to high density assumptions, but, equally, susceptible to any revision of assumptions (as, for example, would be likely in any strong economic cycle). While there are thoughtful, long-term policies and public sector proposals on the release of industrial land, on the use of the river and waterways for transportation of bulky goods (including waste), and on forming existing public open spaces and undeveloped landscapes in to a network – the 'East London Green Grid' – issues of development density and building height are subject to relatively light-touch control. Perhaps this should not be surprising – it is the financial return on development that must bear the brunt of affordable housing requirements, land remediation costs and transport and social infrastructure. However, a recent study, undertaken by URS and Patel Taylor Architects for the Greater London Authority[28] showed that in 2004/05 67 per cent of schemes were granted permission at densities above those recommended in the London Plan, a figure that rises to 77 per cent in East London.

In several current schemes in the Lea Valley, densities are high, approaching and surpassing those of the city centre, opening up strange but interesting faultlines. One tower currently being developed by the Poplar HARCA housing association has separate access cores for private and social tenants, while at Leamouth by Canning Town, Ballymore have submitted a cluster of towers for planning permission, with a school on the bottom six floors of a 23-storey block.

Further east, in Silvertown and Barking, two recent schemes offer more familiar perspectives. At Thames Barrier Park in Silvertown, Sergison Bates Architects are designing a scheme of 1,000 homes for Barratts, at a density of 160 units/hectare (Figure 3.8). Composed of six blocks, five of these are apartment blocks with a U-plan (open to the south), and one is a 12-storey tower. While

---

28   URS and Patel Taylor, *London Plan Density Matrix Review*, London, Greater London Authority, 2006, p. 26.

the architectural form and articulation of these blocks has a familiar tenement character, a diverse set of street, court and garden spaces is formed by the blocks; sitting between the Docklands Light Railway viaduct, under which sports facilities are proposed (in the manner of the Westway) and the Thames Barrier Park itself, the scheme has the potential to offer public spaces that are spatially defined and clearly 'owned' in the manner of the old East End, being generous in quantity and differentiated in use. We have to speak of 'potential' here, since the scheme is not yet built (though of course the park is), and the burden of the preceding illustrations of housing development in East London suggests a degree of caution in terms of the provision and maintenance of public space.

In Barking, architect Peter Barber (with Jestico and Whiles, for East Thames Housing Group and Acorn Homes) has resurrected the cause of low-rise medium-density housing development. The scheme consists mainly of two- and three-storey houses, flats and maisonettes facing defined, narrow streets to the front and small gardens to the rear (Figure 3.9). Roof terraces to the upper maisonettes and flats give a crenellated form to the streets, which step down the gentle slope, emphasising the composition of individual houses. A five-storey apartment building and a ten-storey tower frame a more generous public space, a planted square close to the pedestrian route to the town centre. The scheme has only recently been completed; it will be interesting to see how a population of greater class and ethnic diversity will negotiate these proximities and whether this development form will support a degree of the communality that existed in the equally dense but socially homogeneous Bethnal Green that Young and Willmott described.

Further east, Peter Hall has argued:

> What is in question here is garden suburbs. By definition, they will be suburbs, for three main reasons. First, however many jobs we can and should provide in the corridor itself, many of the people who come to live here will find employment in central London, while relatively few are likely to find suitable employment right on their own front doorsteps. Second, the linear form means that the predominant direction of movement will be east to west, or vice versa, along the spines. And third, they will be built by private builders working to sell their houses in the market and the market shows that the majority of people are going to be looking for fairly conventional single-family housing with private garden space.[29]

At Barking Riverside, just to the south of the heroic but flawed Becontree estate, this contention is being challenged. Led by a joint venture of Bellway Homes and English Partnerships and designed by Dutch master planners Maxwan, the proposals raise densities far above the garden suburb norm that Hall appears to envisage. Relatively compact layouts will keep building heights mostly between two and six storeys: the first phase will start at approximately 60 units/hectare, with houses and gardens, rising to 100–150 units/hectare for the majority of the development, with apartment blocks around garden courts, and 320 units/hectare along a part of the river front, in the form of apartment blocks with towers of up

---

29   Hall and Ward, *Sociable Cities*, pp. 159–60.

Figure 3.8 **Thames Barrier Park** **Figure 3.9** **New housing, Barking, by**
housing, Silvertown, by **Peter Barber Architects/**
Sergison Bates Architects. **Jestico and Whiles**
© Sergison Bates **Architects. Photo:**
Architects **Witherford Watson Mann**
Architects

to 20 storeys. The development is ringed by generous parks (in part imposed by the presence of power lines), and will be served by a bus connection to Barking and Romford (the East London Transit) and an extension of the Docklands Light Railway (the subject of protracted negotiations on public sector funding).

The masterplan is sophisticated and is supported by a complex and cultured set of guidelines which, if implemented, will lead to a visually diverse and socially varied development with generous public realm. Yet its form as a 'vertical garden suburb', made up predominantly of apartments, poses many questions. Will it have (or develop) the amenities to support a relatively autonomous urban community? The presumption is the opposite to Becontree, where a centre was presumed but not delivered, while at Barking Riverside two local centres and one district centre are proposed with what appear to be relatively modest retail and public service provision. Can you make an urban quarter without significant presence of workspace? Will the predominantly higher densities in this location prove viable in the long term and will policy and local opinion support these densities in 15 years time when the final phase is due to be built – will this 'vertical garden suburb' become more city or more suburb than the proposals seem to suggest? At least the masterplan appears sufficiently versatile to permit both these eventualities.

A further important question is whether the improved public transport links will compensate the relative lack of road and pedestrian links to the wider area. As at Becontree, where the bridges over the railway lines were not supplemented, and therefore the layout followed on from the alignment of the existing rural lanes, no new road connections or foot and cycle connections are currently proposed to the north (to Barking and the A13) or to the west (across the River Roding, to the Royal Docks). The acceptance of profound severance by the area's linear infrastructures contrasts fundamentally with Maxwan's masterplan for Leidsche Rijn, the extension of Utrecht, where the increasing densities of development are culminating in a continuous platform over the A12 motorway, which will be developed at high densities, and graded into the surrounding land levels, a solution which recently received approval and funding.

Conclusion

Two relatively simple patterns of behaviour can be observed in this trawl of nearly 120 years of regeneration practice in East London.

My account shows the significant fluctuations in terms of development densities and preferred building types that have occurred over this period. The extremes are the redevelopment of the Rothschild Buildings site at 50 units/hectare in the 1970s, within half a mile of the City, and the present acceptance of 300 units/hectare three and six miles to the east in Canning Town and Barking. The regular cycle of change – from tenements to houses and back to tenements again across the 1880s to the 1930s; from houses and apartments to apartments and towers from the 1940s to the 1960s; and from houses in the 1970s to apartments in the 1990s, to the higher densities and high-rises currently projected – has inevitably meant that the fit between the overall structure of the city and its neighbourhoods and buildings has fluctuated between close fit, loose fit and mismatch. This danger seems once again to be present in the London Thames Gateway.

**Figure 3.10   View of a street as envisaged in one of the medium density
                 neighbourhoods at Barking Riverside. Courtesy of Maxwan
                 Architects and Urbanists**

I have sketched the underlying moral arguments deployed in support of renewal. Victorian efforts to regenerate East London were infused with the spirit of social engineering; the injunction for residents to live more privately and less publicly weakened from a controlling ambition to a liberating impulse coloured by strong anti-urban prejudice; the injection of a spirit of enterprise into the area refocused the moral intent, but was rendered (inevitably?) ineffective by the tools of delivery. With lifestyle choice a defining principle for politics and development alike, there is little trace in current initiatives of social engineering. Yet the London Plan expresses an implicit alignment of the virtues of sustainability and social cohesion with the harsh realities of development viability, as illustrated by the following statement by the Mayor: 'London has been developed as a relatively low density city and we must build in future at higher density – not just to increase housing supply and make best use of urban land – but to secure the benefits from higher density, high quality vibrant urban development'.[30] This proposition will require significant and ongoing examination and further underpinning. Otherwise, it is more than likely to be tested to, and beyond, its limits.

---

30   Ken Livingstone, quoted in Greater London Authority press release 'Mayor urges higher density housing in London', 5 July 2002.

Chapter 4

Daring to Plan? Concepts and Models of Urban Regeneration in Thames Gateway

Michael Keith

How should we make sense of the Thames Gateway? With its uncertain genealogy, its shifting geography and a sense of its limited appeal in the imaginaries of people that live east of Tower Bridge is it no more than a politician's fiction or a bureaucratic chimera?

The most comprehensive attempt to provide a vision for what has been described as the largest regeneration project in Europe has been provided by Department of Communities and Local Government's Interim Thames Gateway Plan, published in November 2006. The projected numbers of homes and jobs associated with this major transformation have changed regularly in recent years between the agencies responsible for making official estimates but the numbers of jobs and homes predicted have generally risen, based on bullish underlying assumptions about the forward trajectories of London's growth and an aspiration to direct this transformation towards the part of the city most beset by postindustrial decline. The 2006 Thames Gateway Plan targets the creation of 180,000 jobs in the region and 160,000 homes between 2001 and 2016 (Thames Gateway Delivery Unit, 2006a, 2006b).

In 2005 in a piece of work conducted for the Secretary of State, the polling company MORI suggested that a significant problem with this story of grand scale city transformation was that it lacked 'a narrative' to make sense of the change. Similarly, with a fairly limited evidence base, the lobbying think tank the IPPR suggested that the Thames Gateway story was neither understood nor believed by people that lived or might live in the future in this new subregion of London (Bennett and Morris, 2006). At one level this might appear no more than a public relations concern with how to promote the Thames Gateway project. But in this chapter I want to suggest that there is in reality much at stake in the attempt to generate a plausible narrative of city transformation. A closer examination of the competing frames through which the Gateway is made visible undermines some commonly held oppositions between 'top down' and 'bottom up' change, politically left and right wing understandings of city regeneration, and community versus market led models of social change.

Flesh and Stone: Between Lego Builders and Community Heroes

A New Compass for Contemporary Urbanism

Within different traditions of urban theory there has been a tendency to conceptualise city change two-dimensionally. At one extreme various paradigmatic approaches and even whole sub-disciplines have tended to regard the city as a functioning unit and have sought to maximise social good through optimising spatial configuration. The discipline of planning rests on a claim to know the good city; the architectural challenge of the modern (after Heidegger) requiring a coming to terms with the pastoral and counter pastoral readings of 'dwelling in the fourfold' (Heynen, 1999: pp. 14–19). Within the spatial disciplines of geography and social policy technocratic knowledges are produced which appeal to and depend on this functionalism; modelling or elaborating transport networks, built form and social organisation for the cities of tomorrow.

In contrast, various strands of 'radical', Marxian and post-structuralist urbanisms have appealed to an exposure of the city's artifice as their principal intellectual function. An analysis of the hidden power structures of regimes of governance, the logic of capital seen in patterns of uneven development and the coded norms of class, race, gender and sexuality located in the social order are the outcome of intellectual labours of great integrity which have an unremittingly deconstructionist purpose at their heart. The purpose of intellectual labour in such analysis is to expose the normative basis of processes that remain beyond the control of the academic gaze, rather than to improve their practical functioning. The register of voice is properly critical but scholars and academics in the critical tradition sometimes fail to engage with the policymakers and the politicians because their deconstructions are not always matched by the pragmatics required to devise alternative visions of the future city.

But when we begin to analyse the future of the metropolis this two-dimensional dialogue of the deaf between the critics of city transformation and the handmaidens of regeneration becomes more complex. We immediately run into some deeper entanglements of the moral and the empirical which do not necessarily fit our conventional binary divide of critics and technocrats. Decisions about the role of existing markets and the construction of new markets require analysis both of what is empirically plausible and what is ethically desirable in structuring city growth. Categories of identity politics do not always sit easily with each other, let alone with competing alternative moral imperatives that, rather than focusing on the existing city, might dwell on the city that is yet to come (Simone, 2004). A sense of urbanism that stresses the community obligations of 'the known' and the familiar sits in tension with a tradition of city thinking that privileges abstract senses of obligation, an ethics of hospitality or a privileging of 'the unknown' and the treatment of the stranger. These are contrasting ways of thinking about the moral order of the metropolitan.

I have argued elsewhere (Keith, 2005) that the constitutive tensions between the liberal and the communitarian strands of thinking in moral philosophy create a tension in 'city thinking' that is as important in structuring a moral compass for the city as the alternative axis which contrasts deconstruction and functionality.

These tensions can bring together odd bedfellows. Those preferring a more egalitarian social settlement may rarely disagree about ends but nevertheless differ massively about means. Suspicion of the power of the state shares with suspicion of the market a scepticism that calls into question the essential commitments and genealogy of western liberalism. 'Anti-statism' appeals both to the conventional right and the left of the political spectrum and can be articulated as both a critique of the social engineering of the New East End (Dench et al., 2006; Keith, 2006) and as a new leftist nostalgia for the anti-statism of the Thatcher era (Pearmain, 2006). The tensions between *notions of liberalism* that privilege the rational ordering of the social, and *notions of the communitarian* that privilege the anthropological construction of the moral order might need to be taken seriously. Both perspectives are relevant if we are to reconcile the logic of the 'Lego builders' that foreground the bricks and mortar of city regeneration and the appeal of the 'community heroes' that appeal to the known social world to be placed within an understanding of the particular histories and geographies of this part of old London (Keith, 2005).

Further, urban studies needs to take more seriously both the ethical lessons of the governmentality debates that draw on Foucault's late work to refigure an understanding of the problem of liberal government in political theory (Rose, 1999; Rabinow, 2003) and the materialistic lessons of the new economic sociology that considers the entanglements of state and society which define the social construction of new markets (Callon, 1998; Mackenzie, 2006; White, 2002).

If we complicate the stale debates between old right and old left with a more nuanced compass that recognises the tensions between rational organisation and sentimental appeal, justice and loyalty, community and liberal government, we may begin to understand the different narratives that are used to make sense of the Thames Gateway. What is not said can be as important as what is said. For example, a foregrounding of community that fails to recognise the new travel to work areas emerging from the old economic base will not capture the dynamism of city change. Alongside continued deindustrialisation in sites like Fords in Dagenham there is an economic engine at Canary Wharf that has created what is arguably the second largest financial district in Europe in the heart of the Gateway itself; with over 80,000 jobs on site and a potential to grow over the next decade to 200,000 jobs (compared with an annual daily commute to the Square Mile of the City of approximately 300,000). In deciding who will get these jobs, what configuration of homes and transport will service this new economy and how London's travel to work patterns can be reconfigured by the capacity of public transport and the construction of new labour markets and their subjectivities, there are many dimensions to take into account. These include the logics of house-building and of economic development, the cacophany of Olympian rhetoric, and the risk of reproducing new forms of racial inequality.

The Thames Gateway, in other words is a confluence of socio-economic realities and regeneration stories. It is simply not possible to detach the future of this part of London from the emergent housing markets and the cartographies of travel to work areas that are in fact both artefacts of the state. Narratives of the Gateway are much more than a matter of PR, since they help to shape policy-options. The Gateway envisaged as downmarket solution to the supply problems of low cost home ownership implies a suburban lack of aspiration. The Barker report, which is economically numerate but institutionally ignorant of the way the housing market is structured by legal, planning and political processes, amplifies this disappointing vision. However, a state-sponsored model that privileges development by fiat and by land site is hardly likely to win support from either the market or the community. And, in contrast again, a Sim City aspiration that stresses high-quality city life based on architecturally informed rhetorics of successful urbanism risks economic illiteracy if it fails to consider both the massive legacy costs of brownfield cleaning or the neo-Ricardian facts of life of large rental differences between Canada Square and the Royal Docks.

These new multiple realities, the complications of their spatial logics and their present pasts, contrast starkly with the simple ways in which in the immediate post war era faith in social engineering prompted the mapping of a 'London of bubbles' – a new London where community development was to sit organically alongside economic development in neatly constrained new neighbourhoods.

Would these new pluralities make Patrick Abercrombie turn in his grave? In the 1940s the reformer, planner and author of both the *County of London Plan* and the *Greater London Plan* had the temerity to attempt to rationalise London through mapping its future, choreographing its city spaces and land uses down to the smallest plot sizes. In contrast, in recent years the bullish literatures around the future of the city have suggested that the capital will be the site of sustained employment and population growth over the next two decades but are much more vague than Abercrombie about its configuration. Ken Livingstone's London Plan, the Deputy Prime Minister's Sustainable Communities Plan and the No. 10 Strategy Unit's London Analytical Report have all have echoed the mantra of growth. Looking eastwards from Tower Bridge, the Thames Gateway subregion has been earmarked to be the heart of this growth. Identifying the opportunities provided by carious tracts of brownfield deindustrialisation, the area is cast as the location for new forms of policy intervention (such as the return of Urban Development Corporations) and as a test bed for market responses to the housing boom of the early twenty-first century.

The notion of growth foregrounds a debate on what sort of a city London might become. In regional government Lord Rogers' Architecture and Urbanism Unit at the Greater London Authority attempted to deploy best practice urban design standards in the creation of new city spaces. In contrast, the *Guardian*'s architectural critic Jonathan Glancey (2001a) has characterised the plans for the Gateway as a colonisation of the cockney Siberia. Multiple realities confound a rerun of Abercrombie today. These include the plural geographies that follow from the demographics of the city region; the growth profiles of different sectors of the economy, and the demands placed on the welfare state, in fulfilling its role of social reproduction, to generate a labour force 'fit for purpose' for the new twenty-first-century market places. There are also the tensions between idealist conceptions of how people might dwell in the city, and the more prosaic realities of the building of homes on which the rest of this chapter concentrates.

The lens through which London is made visible structures our thinking about the dynamics of its present and the potential of its future. In particular, in thinking about housing development we might consider how the languages of city transformation inflect the relationship between state governance and institutionalised property markets. It is not the first time that the forces of city change have focused on housing but for the Gateway to realise its potential for twenty-first-century London a clearer set of analytical dynamics is needed than is usually obtained from the nebulous lexicon of urban regeneration.

It is possible to figure London through the lens of housing demand and it is essential to take the measure of such demand against feasible housing supply. (Hence the supply side concerns with mass production, planning inhibitions and regionalisation of Housing Corporation funding in London.) It is also possible to figure London in terms of its job growth in key economic sectors. The commensurability of these two future visions is moot. Both sit uneasily with an interdisciplinary invocation of city building that might be loosely captured under the rubric of 'urbanism', except that the notion of urbanism is itself susceptible to annexation by the discipline of architecture.

Urban Renaissance

At its most optimistic the lessons of urbanism point to the possibilities of urban renaissance. At their crudest this might be identified with Lord Rogers' ideas, as set out in his Reith lectures of 1999, his subsequent publications and his work with John Prescott's Urban Task Force and as an advisor to the Mayor of London in the early 2000s. But their genealogy stretches further back. Most obviously, the coincidence of city growth and modernity in the late nineteenth/early twentieth century prompted many debates about the ability to plan and build the civilised metropolis with adequate residences for the citizens of the city. In Germany the Bauhaus was driven by such concerns and much of the Werkbund's brave efforts in cities such as Weimar Frankfurt epitomised a social democratic aim to mass build equity (Heynen, 1999: Lash, 1999). Significantly, the Werkbund triggered a major debate around the interplay of high numbers, rational interest and quality outcomes in housing provision.

Though they can seem like caricatures, there are really four principles which inform most contemporary urban renaissance rhetoric:

- by building densely it should be possible to maximise the value of a single acre of land;
- by maximising the value of a single acre of land it should be possible to *levy* significant amounts of social value against enhanced profit, translated into social housing at affordable levels of rent (and moot levels of subsidy and purchase price);

- by creating a new and *rational* planning framework the self-interest of the former principle and the equity of the latter principle should be harnessed to produce mixed development;
- finally, this should produce a high quality public realm and – with the immediate gains of Section 106[1] and the longer term gains of a sustainable revenue base from rents and a tax base from residents and businesses – it should be possible to engineer the future city. Or at least that is the script.

The Dynamics of Change: The Background to Growth Numbers

Three reasons point towards the need for increased housing numbers in the Gateway area.

Economic Production and London

In 2003 we saw a collapse in the commercial office market with Foster's landmark Swiss Re building struggling to let space, and with considerable turbulence around the future of Canary Wharf Group, which was once an FT100 listed company on the basis of a single property portfolio on the Isle of Dogs. London's bullish projections around employment growth have looked less plausible in the 2004–2007 period than in the early years of the decade.[2] But this potential for continued employment growth in the east of London appears likely from forecasts of the financial services and business services sectors and the investment decisions of major corporates such as Citigroup, Clifford Chance, Barclays, and HSBC that have located on the CWG estate in recent years. The numbers of jobs on the estate itself will exceed 100,000 in the near future arising from buildings already coming through the ground. The cyclical trend of oversupply and depression of commercial office markets should not detract from the scale of this change. In 2007 one sign of a return to growth both in London generally and on the Wharf has appeared in the newly incorporated form of Songbird; the venture that emerged from the commercial property downturn when a struggle for control over the old Canary Wharf Group between Brascan, Paul Reichman (formerly of Olympia and York) and Morgan Stanley concluded largely to the advantage of the latter, with a return to expansion of the estate. The old ODPM (now DCLG) recognised the new financial and business services sectors on the Isle of Dogs as having the potential to drive the employment base up to 200,000 on the estate and in the related commercial developments in the adjacent Wood Wharf and Millennium Quarters. The impact of such change on housing demand is considerable, and will be mediated through the uneven impacts of poor transport infrastructure

---

1   On Section 106 agreements, see Penny Bernstock's chapter in this volume.
2   See, for example, the claim that 'Taking our long-term projected output growth of 2.5 per cent this gives rise to a total employment increase of 970,000 between 2003 and 2026, equal to 22 per cent of total employment in 2003' (Cooper, 2005).

both eastwards and westwards, and continued uncertainty (mitigated slightly in mid-2007) about the future of Crossrail.

Social Reproduction

Following the 1990s boom and related population growth, the south-east in general, and London in particular, faced labour shortages in key markets which facilitate the social reproduction of economic growth, though in some economic sectors demand has been matched by 'A8' migration from the accession countries of Eastern Europe. However, welfare state workers essential to the affluent city cannot afford to live in London or survive on national public sector pay settlements that incentivise moving away from the city to low-cost areas of residence outside the south-east. In essence, the city faces a problem of reproduction of itself alongside the production of affluence. As is most clearly seen in the debates around the chimeric search for a definition of the key worker, the city struggles to provide the supply of labour needed to support the civil institutions and the public sector itself. So in the first years of the new century, town halls across London sought to identify those public sector workers who would be granted privileged access to social housing by being defined as 'key workers'. This definition normally started with nurses and teachers and rapidly expanded to include other occupations where labour shortages hindered recruitment, for example, in the 'caring professions' of social services. The need to provide affordable housing for such a labour force is in this sense a condition of production. This echoes the institutional logic of Manuel Castells' definition of the city as a site of social reproduction and collective consumption. More prosaically in an era where 'liveability' is a key measure of metropolitan competition, the presence of a labour force that services not only economic growth but also consumption patterns and social infrastructure gives rise to a new form of housing crisis whose definition is not entirely philanthropic.

Household Demographics

A third reason for the growth in households is culturally produced rather than being the outcome of cyclical commercial demand. Long-term reductions in household size and increasing numbers of households generate demand for additional residential units. Many of the estates in the inner part of the Gateway reveal of pattern of mass overcrowding and suppressed residential demand. In many areas of gentrification there is demand for dwellings for smaller families at rental and purchase prices which are beyond the range of many who need them.

Though linked, these sources of demand may generate different dynamics of spatial preference and fluctuations over time. The recent Treasury-commissioned Barker housing review has highlighted supply side constraints in bringing land forward, has cited the rational tendency for private developers to protect profits by deliberately limiting supply in some contexts and has put a spotlight on the relationship between housing subsidy and the roles of both developers and registered social landlords. This analysis has three consequences. It makes it essential to reconsider the appropriate mediation of public interest and private profit. It demands a reconsideration of the complicated institutional architecture which includes regeneration agencies, social housing provision, housing subsidy, English Partnerships, local authorities and the newly-developed London Housing Board. The merger of English Partnerships and the Housing Corporation into a single new body, Communities England, which was announced in 2007, is perhaps the most significant statement of commitment to a 'new social engineering' that emerges from this way of thinking. But perhaps most significantly, Barker raises a question about the trade-offs between quality development in specific places and the rapid achievement of housing numbers in large tracts of land deemed suitable for development.

It is clearly the case that the vast majority of the housing numbers in the Gateway will need to be developed by the private sector, even by models which maximise the elements of social housing in the transformation. But the exact balance of private, low-cost (subsidised) and rental property is subject to political deliberation and social mediation, which returns us to the desirable balance between the rational ordering of liberal government, state direction and the ethnographic realities of 'real places'. The legacy of the property-buying fascination of the British in comparison with their continental peers will determine whether new models of housing tenure that involve flexible fractionalisation of ownership and renting can really be developed. This in turn implies a set of normative assumptions about the individuals, families, ethnicities and faiths that might occupy these new developments. The interface between an implicit white communitarian norm and the diversities of cosmopolitan London raises massive questions about integration and cohesion in these development sites.

But certain institutional changes might restructure the relationship between public interest and the market and the way such a relationship translates into housing outcomes. Post-Barker, housing subsidies may be paid to property developers and the Registered Social Landlords (housing associations) are to become developers in their own right, or hybrid characters, working in the space between the provision of public goods and of private residences. Planning law might attempt value capture through hypothecating future tax revenues in areas of physical infrastructure change. The principle of *polluter pays* could be mitigated by subsidies for the development of brownfield sites. Such changes suggest thinking carefully about the spaces of the Thames Gateway that will be developed in new models of residential change, and about the timing of such change. They logically demand a politics which both accepts the role of the market and brings back into play the potential to plan the city.

Thinking Spatially and the London of the Prime Ministers Strategy Unit

In an important piece of research, led by Geoff Mulgan (then) at the Prime Minister's Strategy Unit (PMSU), a diagnosis of London's present and prognosis of its future was published in the London Analytical Report of 2003. In relation to the growth agenda it makes two significant points.

Its analysis conceptualises London's economy with relatively little reference to its geographical variations. It offers no explanation of where London's economic growth will be realised. It extrapolates exponentially from trends, but neither analyses the dynamics behind these trends (i.e. the problem of a hypothetical future cast as an extrapolation of yesterday's events) nor (more significantly) develops an understanding of where the jobs growth (putatively an additional 300,000 skilled jobs by 2010) will take place. In terms of the latter claim – given that the daily commute to the geographical area of the City Corporation equals approximately 300,000 – we could be talking about a 'new square mile' of jobs added to the London economy in the next six years. Where will they be located?

The London of this relatively recent report does not recognise the Thames Gateway at all as a possible spatial answer to either housing growth or job growth. The housing sections of the report (PMSU, 2003: pp. 48–71 and particularly 70) highlights the limited potential for London housing growth eastwards and suggests instead that the resolution of the housing supply problems are to be found in the inner suburban and central rings of London. This is undoubtedly true if analysis were to be based on extrapolated trends only, but it disregards other possible dynamics. The current number of 10,000–15,000 new builds a year in London which the Report describes reinforces Barker but potentially underplays the possibility that the intervention of regeneration agencies might restructure residential preference. For example by 'making places' such as Docklands it was possible to create a new market for housing expansion in a part of London where previously there had been *low* demand over a long period. This demands an understanding of the *space-economy* of London and the capacity of institutional change to maximise the potential of the city and create new places within it. In short, this planning vision of London's future challenges (if only implicitly) the city's ability to build new communities, avoiding any definite view of the relative roles of social engineering and the market place in determining outcomes.

Temporality and the Gateway Paradox

Part of the argument of this chapter is that the tensions in city building need to be seen as outcomes of the root problems of liberal government; not least the tension between the state's attempt to facilitate metropolitan development and the housing market's inclination, competence or facility to provide new housing units in the areas most essential to the public good. When we consider the time-scales of city change in the Gateway we can see that the differential demands made by players, organisations and institutions can lead to some suboptimal outcomes.

One example of this was seen in the summer 2003 update of the Sustainable Communities Plan, which had population growth numbers for Thames Gateway that may well be too high over the short term but too low over the long term. This arises because of:

a) *the understandable need* to deliver a vision that is financially realistic and not over-ambitious on the longer-term supply side. With contemporary trends of new house build at 10,000–20,000 units per annum a very large proportion of London's annual build would need to take place in the Gateway to meet even the modest targets for housing new build in the Sustainable Communities summer 2003 update. (These are well below the revised figures put forward in 2007.) This points to a broader debate about the plausibility of a step change in the supply side of housing units;

b) *the understandable* desire to be seen deliver over the electoral cycle;

c) *the understandable manner* in which the model in the sustainable communities update is driven by the dynamics of the housing new build crisis (the historically low numbers of new build) rather than by the regional employment potential of the Gateway (300,000 new skilled jobs in London 2004–2010 (PMSU), and by the global city growth pressures in the London and south-east economy)

A paradox arises because the resulting model of growth in the Gateway aims at financial modesty and limited demands on the Treasury, but as a result of this it is fiscally wasteful and economically sub-optimal.

Over the long term, lower aspirations could translate into suburbanised low quality development at below 'urban renaissance' densities. Physical infrastructure becomes *more expensive* because the costing/population growth ratio leads to *higher per capita costs* for each fixed cost public sector infrastructure decision. For example in investment decisions about public transport, the numerator (population growth) diminishes and the denominator (investment costs for any specific public transport project – e.g. Crossrail or Docklands Light Railway (DLR) extensions) remains fixed. Already at least one consultant has attempted to claim that if population targets are set at the levels of the summer 2003 targets, then there is no need for some of the major physical infrastructure projects that are in reality central to the future of the Gateway. There is effectively a chicken and egg argument that links together population density, growth targets and infrastructure investment. Higher growth targets are consequently economically performative in persuading the Treasury to invest upfront in transport infrastructure and socially normative in constructing implicitly the sorts of community that will arise from this development. They are also subject to the usual unintended consequences of policy decisions, for example, in the larger demands that would be placed on the development control process (potentially to the detriment of democratic scrutiny or buy-in to the planning system).

Over the short term, the overambitious targets for delivery costs exaggerate the public sector investment bill needed to realise the Sustainable Communities vision. Physical infrastructure becomes *more expensive* because the costing/time growth ratio leads to *higher per annum costs* for each fixed cost public sector infrastructure decision. For example, in public transport investment decisions the numerator (population growth) diminishes and the denominator (investment costs for any specific public transport project per annum) increases.

Consequently the worries will be:

a) as a *housing driven* model the planning framework of the Sustainable Communities Plan and the Thames Gateway more generally will be dislocated from the *economic drivers* which would demand greater transport infrastructure investment. Put simply it is possible to realise modest housing targets in East London without infrastructure spend but it is not possible to realise a jobs-driven economic model without this. As a result south-eastern economic growth is potentially jeopardised if places such as the new business district of the Isle of Dogs cannot be *made to work*;

b) the buy-in to the significance of the Gateway for London at regional governmental level potentially dissipates as the 'Global City' thrust of the London Plan is jeopardised;

c) the buy-in at local government level is jeopardised because boroughs to the east of London that are the subject of medium-term patterns of deindustrialisation see the future they are offered in terms of low-quality suburbanisation which will bring few new jobs, limited social infrastructure and the 'export' of the overcrowded inner East End to the less densely populated outer London boroughs. A caricature of these tendencies was at the heart of the electoral successes of the (fascist) British National Party in the 2006 local government elections when they became the second largest party in the town hall in Barking and Dagenham, winning all but one of the seats that they contested.

The Institutional Architecture for Delivery

In the post-war decades of the twentieth century we have witnessed a crisis of faith in the project of social engineering. The broadly consensual settlement of the Keynesian Welfare State was subjected to trenchant critique from liberalisms of both left and right. The command systems of state power were seen as oppressive (from the left), the structures of welfarism were seen as bloated and inefficient (from the right). The city articulations of this Keynesian era are frequently paraded as evidence for the prosecution from all points on this left/right spectrum: the tower blocks of the inner city and the wastelands of some of the new towns become iconic. But the iconography is performative, proclaiming the failure of hope as much as factually describing a failure of delivery.

In the final two decades of the twentieth century, a critical liberalism (again of both the left and the right) displaced such grandiose ambitions across the world. But the 1980s and 1990s highlighted the failures of this liberalism. The market – *sans* state – cannot be trusted to protect the public interest in the reshaping of the dual cities of polarisation and social exclusion. So in the last decade of that century the pendulum swung back tentatively to a belief in land-use planning, not least in order to supply the housing needs of London. And so – equally tentatively – we might look to cities across the globe for whom this penny has already dropped. For example, to Shanghai, where Pudong expands exponentially and even to New York, where the changing demands of the city underscore much of the debate around the shape of the city post-9/11.

At the heart of the debate is the degree to which we believe in a bureaucratic rationality that might consciously erase or mediate particular interests in delivering the principles of urban regeneration. Perversely, Jonathan Glancey's own book on London (2001b) was dedicated to the work of Frank Pick, the exemplary bureaucrat whose dedicated service to a London Underground he celebrates as having been constructed to meet socially defined needs of the city more than the imperatives of the market. The sort of vision needed for a civilised expansion of the Gateway demands exactly the sort of bureaucratic commitment to the expansion of the city which was exemplified in the Underground lines that precipitated 20th century London expansion. This is precisely the regulation of interest that the Gateway demands for reasons that depend equally on the need to optimise public expenditure and to generate social value. For Max Weber, bureaucracy represented 'a discharge of business according to calculable rule and *"without regard for persons"*' (Weber, 2007, p. 215; emphasis original) and 'the abstract regularity of the execution of authority'. We are searching for a bureaucratically efficient method of delivering the future city. But do we dare to whisper that bureaucracy might be a positive force for good as much as a pejorative metaphor for conventional governance? This would point to a need to consider the abilities of the institutions in the Gateway to develop optimal renaissance change.

Conclusion

In considering the future of the eastern pie slice of London that includes the Thames Gateway, higher housing numbers and densities are not only possible but imperative if we are to deliver both high-quality urban change and social inclusion. High numbers can be achieved. They depend on achieving a harmonious institutional architecture from a governmental maze that might have confused Theseus. Among the entities that need to be linked together are the London Housing Board, the two new urban district councils in the Gateway, the role of the Housing Corporation/English Partnerships/Communities England, the hybrid forms of Registered Social Landlord and developers, the London Development Agency, the Olympic legacy, the big spending departments and regional and local government.

There is a default model. The concentrations of brownfield land within the perimeter of the M25 have the potential to provide plentiful housing land and serious residential growth if the lessons of the Barker review were to be read principally in terms of planning-induced supply constraints. Although density can become a fetish it is a fact that, while high density costs more in the short term, it yields higher financial and social returns in the long term. Relatively low-cost intervention could produce low-density housing in East London that would create the required residential numbers in some post-industrial areas. But it would be a future of low-cost mixed estates of low quality. It is not quite the post-1945 nightmare of utopian social engineering gone wrong. The default is rather a model of low-quality, economically suboptimal suburbanisation. But this would be a waste of the opportunity of a generation.

East London deserves better than this. Analytical clarity is needed to ensure that the timescales of public investment and the geographical planning of residential numbers are mediated through a new architecture of governance. The Thames Gateway has the capacity to save much of the Green Belt (through the densification of polluted industrial land). It has the potential to provide extraordinary new places for residence and employment at the highest quality. The vision for the Gateway was bravely set out in the original Sustainable Communities Plan, but it is is potentially diminished by a numbers-driven logic which seeks greater returns from Milton Keynes and more rural parts of the country better served by transport infrastructure. The challenge is to harness both market and state to deliver this vision. The Thames Gateway will provide the litmus test for the plausibility of urban renaissance.

In his recent book on the extraordinary growth phenomenon that is modern China, Will Hutton defends the enlightenment tradition of the west and suggests that people should have more faith in the ideas which made possible western affluence. His diagnosis rests on the assertion that beneficial globalisation requires both China and America to remember the Enlightenment principles that first sustained economic and political pluralism and the institutional forms that followed from this. (These included a free press, an independent judiciary, independent knowledge production and an effective state.) He suggests that this might be captured by 'an approach to living, whose spirit the great Enlightenment philosopher Immanuel Kant summed up simply to "dare to know"' (Hutton, 2007; p. 51). A reflexive synthesis of traditions of urbanism that recognises the tensions and the incommensurabilities of city building in the twenty-first century (in China or in the UK) might prompt us to consider – in the face of the cheap and easy critiques of left and right, communitarian and liberal – if perhaps the time has come to ask if we 'dare to plan' the Thames Gateway.

References

Bennett, J. and Morris, J., *Thames Gateway People: The Aspirations and Attitudes of Prospective and Existing Residents of Thames Gateway*, London, IPPR, 2006.

Callon, M., *The Laws of Markets*, Oxford, Blackwell, 1998.

Cooper, E., 'Working Future: Employment Projections for London by Sector', Working Paper 1, GLA Economics/Volterra, December 2005: http://www.london.gov.uk/mayor/economic_unit/docs/wp14_working_future.rtf.

Dench, G., Gavron, K. and Young, M., *The New East End; Kinship, Race and Conflict*, London, Profile Books, 2006.

Glancey, J., 'Cowboy Builder', *Guardian*, 19 February 2001a.

Glancey, J., *London: Bread and Circuses*, London, Verso, 2001b).

Greater London Assembly, 'The London Plan (draft). Draft Spatial Development Strategy for London'.

Heynen, H., *Architecture and Modernity: A Critique*, Cambridge, MA, MIT Press, 1999.

Hutton, W., *The Writing on the Wall: Why We Must Embrace China as a Partner or Face it as an Enemy*, London, Little Brown, 2007.

Keith, M. *After the Cosmopolitan: Multicultural Cities and the Future of Racism*, London and New York, Routledge, 2005.

Keith, M., 'We Should not Confuse Nostalgia with History: Cosy Notions of the White Working Class Hinder our Understanding of Migration', *Guardian*, 7 March 2006.

Lash, S., *Another Modernity: A Different Rationality*, Oxford, Blackwell, 1999.

Office of the Deputy Prime Minister, *Sustainable Communities: Building for the Future*, London, HMSO, 2003.

Mackenzie, D., *An Engine, Not a Camera: How Financial Models Shape Markets*, Cambridge, MA and London, MIT Press, 2006.

Pearmain, A., 'Labour Must Die', *London: Soundings*, 2006: http://www.lwbooks.co.uk/journals/articles/pearmain06.html.

Prime Minister's Strategy Unit, *London Analytical Report*, London, PMSU, 2003.

Rabinow, P., *Anthropos Today: Reflections on Modern Equipment*, Princeton, NJ, Princeton University Press, 2003.

Rose, N., *Powers of Freedom: Reframing Political Thought*, Cambridge, Cambridge University Press, 1999.

Simone, A., *For the City Yet to Come*, Durham, NC and London, Duke University Press, 2004.

Thames Gateway Delivery Unit, *The Interim Thames Gateway Plan*, London, HMSO, 2006a: http://www.communities.gov.uk product code 06 TGDU 04176/b.

Thames Gateway Delivery Unit, *The Interim Thames Gateway Plan: Strategic Policy Framework*, London, HMSO, 2006b: http://www.communities.gov.uk product code 06 TGDU 04176/a.

Weber, M. (2007 [1922]) 'Bureaucracy', in Gerth, H.H. and Wright Mills, C. (eds), *From Max Weber: Essays in Sociology*, London, Routledge.

White, H., *Markets from Networks: Socio-economic Models of Production*, Princeton, NJ and London, Princeton University Press, 2002.

Chapter 5

Thames Gateway Oxymorons: Some Reflections on 'Sustainable Communities' and Neoliberal Governance

Massimo De Angelis

Oxymoronic Creatures and Neoliberal Governance

An oxymoron is a figure of speech in which apparently contradictory terms appear in conjunction. Starting from about the mid-1990s, a figure of speech seems to have found its host in what have been called 'oxymoronic creatures', that is 'capitalist moralists or business ethicists … lamenting the "state of the world" and drawing up new rules to generate trust in the executors of capital's will' (Caffentzis, 2006: p. 15). From about the mid-1990s, these 'oxymoronic creatures' have been increasingly influential in shaping the rhetorics and policies of national governments and supranational institutions. This happened to such an extent that even Paul Wolfowitz, once he became president of the World Bank, seemed at ease with all the inclusive talk designed to manage and articulate 'sound' business and economic priorities with social and environmental causes.[1] Talk about 'good governance', 'sustainability', 'trust', 'community', and

---

1   It is remarkable that a strong-willed neoconservative with a clear reputation for using the Prince's sovereign hammer in trying to structurally adjust recalcitrant regimes could identify with a 'social movement', although a media-friendly one. In his first speech as World Bank president, in September 2005, few months after the G8 summit at Gleneagles, Wolfowitz tells us that he 'joined 50,000 young people gathered on a soccer field in Edinburgh for the last of the Live 8 concerts. The weather was gloomy, but the rain did not dampen the enthusiasm of the crowd. All eyes were riveted on the man who appeared on the giant video screens – the father of South Africa's freedom. And the crowd roared with approval when Nelson Mandela summoned us to a new struggle – the calling of our time – to make poverty history' (Wolfowitz, 2005). Compare this enthusiasm for 'making poverty history' by means of pop concerts – a poverty that an increasing number of commentators link to the types of neoliberal policies promoted by IMF and World Bank – with the type of neoliberal policies attempted in Iraq only two years earlier by means of a sledgehammer in September 2003, by Paul Bremer, head of the Coalition Provisional Authority. This included the privatisation of public enterprises, ownership rights by foreign firms of Iraqi businesses, no limits to the repatriation of foreign profits,

even 'commons' – all terms that *prima facie* would arouse in us a sense of what is 'good,' positive and desirable, have been associated with the no-nonsense figures of speech that from the late 1970s became the landmarks of the neoliberal era: efficiency, competitiveness, the 'economy'. This oxymoronic terminology that we can call *'neoliberal governance'*, emerges as an attempt to manage clashing value practices in line with the requirements of capitalist priorities in an increasingly marketised, socially polarised and environmentally unsustainable world.

What today is called 'governance' is the name given to the neoliberal version of what Foucault called 'governamentality'.[2] Governance is a central element of the neoliberal discourse in a particular phase of it, when neoliberalism and capital in general face particularly stringent problems of accumulation, growing social conflict and a crisis of reproduction. Neoliberal governance sets itself the task of tackling these problems for capital by attempting to relay the disciplinary role of the market – evoked in endless government and supranational institution documents and reports through the rhetorical figure of 'competitiveness' and 'efficiency' and the need to 'improve' or preserve an 'advantage' in their terms – through the establishment of a 'continuity of powers' based on normalised market values as truly *common* values across the social body. Governance thus seeks to embed these values in the many ways in which the vast array of social and environmental problems are addressed. It thus promotes active participation of society in the reproduction of life and of our species *on the basis* of this market normalisation. It clearly promotes participation in political processes, but in a form that is based on the 'shared values' of the market and its 'competitiveness' requirements.

According to this logic, every problem voiced by social movements or advocacy groups can be addressed on condition that the mode of its addressing

---

opening Iraq's banks to foreign control, national treatment for foreign companies and the almost complete elimination of all trade barriers. The only things that were exempt by these neoliberal reforms were oil (perhaps to allow repayment of the costs of war) and the labour market, in which strikes were forbidden in key sectors and union rights restricted. See Harvey (2005, p. 6).

2   For a broad discussion of neoliberal governance see De Angelis (2007: pp. 87–101). Foucault understood 'governmentality' as the art of government that is not based on decree but on management. With governmentality, the question is 'not of imposing law on men but of disposing things: that is of employing tactics rather than laws, or even of using laws themselves as tactics – to arrange things in such a way that, through a certain number of means, such-and-such ends may be achieved' (Foucault, 2002: p. 211) Governmentality can thus be defined as the management of networks and flows – 'disposing things' – made of different actors (government, civil society and business institutions) –'continuity among powers' – who are encouraged to become 'partners' in a continuum called governance. In the case of 'neoliberal governance' the 'continuity among powers' referred to by Foucault allows the management of networks and correspondent practices of various actors (government, civil society and business institutions), encouraged to become 'partners'. This is established through the formation of a *common discourse*, one that is grounded on the coupling among the value practices of capital (the acceptance of disciplinary markets) and other value practices.

is through the market: for example, the environmental crisis can be dealt with by the marketing of pollution rights,[3] the human crisis of poverty in the global south can be dealt with by 'women empowering' microcredit and its articulation to export promotion policies[4] and the social, environmental and housing crisis in the urban centres of the global north such as New York and London can be dealt with by 'sustainable communities' in the context of major urban development such as the Thames Gateway project.

'Sustainable Communities'

In February 2003 the Office of the Deputy Prime Minister, John Prescott, published a Sustainable Communities Plan which laid out the government's policies with respect to major urban developments in four key growth areas already identified in regional planning guidance for London and the rest of the south-east in 2000. These are the Thames Gateway, Milton Keynes/South Midlands, Ashford and the London–Stansted–Cambridge corridor. £38 billion were committed to the development, £6 billion of which were invested in the Thames Gateway area in the first three years. The 2003 document was followed by two more specific documents in 2005, one on housing (ODPM, 2005a) – promising new developments and the dealing with the housing crisis especially for 'key workers' – and the other on local governance (ODPM, 2005b) – arguing for the importance of local participation in decision making on matters of relevance for communities. In these documents, 'sustainable communities' were marketed as

> welcoming, prosperous places to live. They have the jobs, homes, schools, healthcare, transport and other services people need. A sustainable community meets the needs of all its citizens so that the most disadvantaged aren't left behind. Our aim is to create communities that will stand the test of time; and places where people want to live. (ODPM, 2005a)

These documents' rhetoric of a 'step change' (ODPM 2003, p. 3) in the government's approach in dealing with the housing crisis is interesting in light of the approach of previous decades. In particular, what seems to be a key change is the hint that some sort of social engineering is needed as integral to policies for the built environment. The suggestion is thus made that public and private investment in fixed capital (housing) needs to be complemented with investment in social and human capital. Under the aegis of Keynesianism, the housing crisis of post-war Britain was tackled by government spending and social housing

---

3   For a critique of carbon credit in the context of a country of the Global South, see Bond and Dada (2005).

4   For a clear identification of the terms of the debate here see the video debate between Susan Davis (founder and chair of the Grameen Foundation), and Vandana Shiva in a commentary on the 2006 Nobel Peace price acceptance speech made by the founder of Grameen Bank Muhammad Yunus. See also my comment in the same blog entry at http://www.commoner.org.uk/blog/?p=106#more-106.

programmes, that is, by developing fixed capital at the social level. The poor quality of many of these council estates, the poor materials used and the designs of tower blocks that left little room for common spaces to develop community links did not help to buffer the subsequent socio-economic trends which devastated community. The waves of income and wealth polarisation, unemployment and social fragmentation brought by the systemic changes of a capitalist economy restructuring from 'Fordism' – with its emphasis on manufacturing, relatively high job security, and a wide system of social entitlements – to 'post-Fordism' – based instead on a 'service economy', job casualisation, erosion of social entitlements and disappearance of social investments in housing – combined to fragment many existing communities in East London.

There were a number of knock-on effects; for example, a real or perceived increase in crime, pervasive criminalisation of 'antisocial' behaviour (such as that of parents of truanting students from underinvested schools), the persistence of racist attacks, the increased victimisation of migrant communities and, more recently, Islamophobia. All this has contributed to turning many housing estates into modern urban battlefields and consequently mirrors of an increasingly fragmented body politic. With the mainstream media spotlight very seldom focused on the problematisation of modern conditions of work and life and often devoted to 'scandal', these trends make it appear as if this is all that goes on in housing estates.[5]

Such a situation is not only potentially destabilising for the economy but also very 'inefficient' from the perspective of mobilising the social cooperation of labour.[6] Indeed, this bears on a central contradiction. Capital requires some element of social division to be able to better mobilise social labour behind the priorities of accumulation;[7] yet these same divisions threaten the social fabric to the point of disabling the mobilisation of social labour and increasing the cost of maintaining social control to the point of non viability. It is therefore necessary for capital to recreate commons, of a type, however, that can suit accumulation.

Added to this, there is the persistent problem of affordable housing for key workers in the service sectors (teachers, nurses, fire-fighters and police among them)

---

5   It goes without saying that the centrifugal forces of fragmentation are often accompanied by centripetal forces of community recomposition, especially when communities come together to oppose some major neoliberal restructuring, such as a threatened relocation due to privatisation of the housing stock, a 'regeneration' plan of a local market threatening to replace street vendors with high street shops, or simply as in the case of the massive Poll Tax movements in the late 1980s, as part of mass civil disobedience against government policy.

6   By social cooperation of labour I understand here the articulation of both production and reproduction work, whether waged or unwaged, whether monetised or not. This is important, because the conditions of 'competitiveness' of an economy in a region, depends on how effective is this articulation between monetised and non-monetised social production.

7   This is to the extent that, to use a classic example, Margaret Thatcher anti-union laws made secondary picketing illegal, thus recognising by law that workers across sectors could find a *common* cause.

working in Inner London area, where the building of council and cooperative housing has lagged far behind the need for new accommodation, while the cost of home ownership and corresponding private rents have both skyrocketed. House prices have been pushed up year after year precisely by the 'successes' of London as a financial centre – a success that the government wants to enhance with its plan for Thames Gateway. Every round of bonuses distributed among top management in the City and every successful new deal in attracting global capital to the city adds liquidity to a housing market for which a £1 million pound house or apartment is becoming the norm in an increasing number of areas of London (with the consequent 'trickle up' effect on house prices in all other areas).[8]

It is in this context that the sustainable communities plan emerges, one that recognises the need for housing but also of social cohesion. This is because

> Communities are more than just housing. They have many requirements. Investing in housing alone, paying no attention to the other needs of communities, risks wasting money – as past experience has shown.
> A wider vision of strong and sustainable communities is needed to underpin this plan, flowing from the Government's strong commitment to sustainable development. The way our communities develop, economically, socially and environmentally, must respect the needs of future generations as well as succeeding now. This is the key to lasting, rather than temporary, solutions; to creating communities that can stand on their own feet and adapt to the changing demands of modern life. Places where people want to live and will continue to want to live. (ODPM, 2003, p. 4)

But if social cohesion is important for government planners, they have a very selective sense of what it means. The reconstruction and maintenance of social cohesion is functional to a relational mode with the rest of the world. The key is, I believe, that 'sustainable communities' are 'communities that can stand on their own feet and adapt to the changing demands of modern life', communities in other words, that do not *decline* while facing the ongoing transformations that the spinning requirements of the global economy imposes. Is this a sort of capitalist utopia in the twenty-first century – a utopia based on the full exposure of individuals and communities to the laws of the markets, while *at the same time* with the reassurance that communities can act as systemic mechanisms which are put in place to absorb shocks on the reproduction of labour power? Is the emphasis on education, training, environment, governance, participation and, last but not least, sustainability perhaps really only about this: the oxymoronic utopia that the social divisions in access to wealth and income brought by competitive markets can be buffered by social commons created again and again by communities who never tire themselves by playing competitive games with other communities somewhere

---

8   For an analysis of the link between capitalist urbanisation and the circuits of financial capital see Harvey (1985). For a report on the affordability of housing to working families in England and Wales, see Wilcox (2003). His study shows, among other things, that in London the house price to household income ratio is below four to one in only three authorities: City of London, Barking and Dagenham and Merton. This makes access to home ownership most difficult in London.

else in the world? A divisive game coupled to a '*commoning*' game the purpose of which is to keep playing the divisive game? Is this oxymoronic ontology of our condition the key to the sustainability for capital?

What Sustainability?

It seems to me that in order to address the big questions above, we need to go for a short detour on the notion of 'sustainability' as it relates to system dynamics. In other words, we need to problematise the discursive premises upon which a rhetorical figure such as 'sustainable community' is grounded. In this section we focus on trying to problematise what makes a system – like an urban 'community' – 'sustainable' and how the 'sustainability' of such a socio-economic and ecological system is reproduced in relation to the socioeconomic and ecological subsystems and supersystems to which it is articulated. Our effort here is really to come to terms with the oxymoronic character of the problematic posed by 'sustainable communities', keeping in mind that 'communities' are components of supersystems and, in turn, have components themselves.

Let us start with the unavoidable question: what is sustainability? Although the original use of the word appeared in the eighteenth century in the field of forestry, it is only recently that it gained a high political profile. In 1987, the UN sponsored Brundtland Report used it with respect to 'sustainable development', which is understood as development that 'meets the needs of the present generation without compromising the ability of future generations to meet their own needs' (WCED, 1987, p. 54). 'Sustainable development' was later adopted by the Agenda 21 programme of the United Nations, and the World Summit on Social Development in 1995 defined it as a framework of articulation among three interdependent systems, the economic, the social and the environmental. Sustainable development is thus defined as 'the framework for our efforts to achieve a higher quality of life for all people', in which 'economic development, social development and environmental protection are interdependent and mutually reinforcing components'.

In the original 1987 Report which paved the way for the term 'sustainable development' there is little or no use of the term of 'sustainability' other than with reference to the global level. It is perhaps for this reason that the 1987 definition of sustainable development reported above was echoing the philosophy of the Native American Iroquois Confederacy. Iroquois chiefs, in fact, were supposed to bear in mind the effects of their actions on their descendants for seven generations. However, they could do this only if they took their life-world within which their decisions was taken as the (supersystemic) world.

It is only subsequently that sustainability discourse was applied to *local* and *regional* areas, with UN sponsored Agenda 21 perhaps catalysing this trend, followed by the World Bank embracing the sustainability discourse (World Bank, 2003) which then become the basis of urban development in areas of the Global North as well as in London. But to convert the issue of sustainability from the global to the local is to commit the classical sin of methodological reductionism

– that the whole is the sum of its parts – and to ignore the fact that it is the interconnections and systemic *relations* among the parts (subsystems) that create the whole (system). Once we begin to approach the question of sustainability from a systemic perspective – and cast this reasoning within an understanding of what systems like global capitalism are by drawing from classic social and political economic theory – we discover that the sustainability of local systems (i.e., subsystems) is not necessarily compatible with the sustainability of the whole or that it is achieved only at the expense of other subsystems, of other localities and communities.

The communities that government planners wish to be 'sustainable' operate within a larger socio-economic as well as ecological system, which is in turn constituted by the *interactions* among other local socio-economic systems. To the extent that these *interactions* are constructed through capitalist relations of production, they are largely predicated on both functional and competitive relations among subsystems,[9] that is, two forms of integration that classical political economy from Smith to Marx have understood in terms of the problematic of 'use value' and 'exchange value'.[10]

To cut through the plethora of meanings that the term 'sustainability' generates in the literature, system thinker Alexey Voinov (1998) proposed to highlight what is common among them.[11] He argues that all of them

> talk about maintenance, sustenance, continuity of a certain resource, system, condition, relationship, in all cases there is the goal of keeping something at a certain level, of *avoiding decline*. (Voinov, 1998, p. 211, my emphasis)

However, this *decline avoidance* that the notion of sustainability seems to indicate, is at odds with both natural ecological and human-made socio-economic systems, which instead seem to follow a life cycle, rather than maintaining a certain stage. This life or renewal cycle assumes that 'a system goes through a series of stages, starting from growth, followed by conservation (inertia and homeostasis

---

9   For a discussion of how modern 'postmodern' cities such as London, New York and Tokio hold together functional integration and competition, see Sassen (2001)

10   This duality is constitutive of any process of commodity production, as functional integration of use values occurs in forms and modes that are bounded by the quantitative requirements of profitable activity upon which the production of exchange values is based. Functional integration of use values, in other words, is constituted through what we might call disciplinary integration of the parts constituting the whole. The competitive race that occurs at every level and discursive mode of aggregation of the social body (individuals on a labour market, cities, firms, countries, regions and so on) is a clear reminder that it is the *relations* among 'communities' – whether they are 'sustainable' or not – that constitute or not the sustainability of the socio-economic and ecological system as a whole. For a discussion of the market processes as processes of disciplinary integration see De Angelis (2007).

11   Voinov finds that the word sustainability refers to things such as intertemporal maintenance of resources, a dynamic relation economy-ecology, the maintenance of organisational structure in a given system through time and the non-decline of capital.

in Gumilev's terms), then release (obscurity) and finally renewal' (ibid.). The idea of sustainability therefore seems to be associated to the goal of 'breaking the cycle, of extending a certain stage in the system life pattern' (ibid.) Most likely, the stage that is to be extended is the growth or conservation stage, as from the system perspective there is little reason to extend any of the others.

Now, it must be pointed out that the goal of sustainability of a system understood in this way runs counter to the goals of renewal. The latter assumes the release phase, in which the components of the system are set free to recombine. In the release phase, the system ends and collapses, although this does not necessarily mean the extinction of the system's components. What ends or is modified is the systemic function that they perform through their interaction. These released components may again recombine in similar ways, but the system will be a different one (although it might operate through similar relational patterns). So for example, the released components of a bankrupted company are laid-off employees and sold assets. This happens when the socioeconomic system represented by the company is no longer 'sustainable', that is, in this particular case, no longer able to extend the phase of its growth and profitability. The released components, laid-off labour power and financial and physical assets, may recombine in a new socio-economic system, a new company. If this happens, this will be a phase of renewal, of creation of a new system.

The really interesting aspect of this approach is that it allows us to investigate the relations between levels of system hierarchies.[12] This is important because it is the next level up in the system-hierarchy that benefits from the renewal of components, as this helps the broader system to persist, to extend its life and to be 'sustainable'. We are reminded by system theorists that:

> For a hierarchical system to extend its existence, to be sustainable', 'its subsystems need to go through renewal cycles. In this way, death of subsystems contributes to

---

12   We must clarify here that, following system theory approaches, by levels of system hierarchies I understand here levels of hierarchy among interconnected systems and not hierarchy among people, as bearers of social roles, within a system. The difference is in the direction of the information flows that constitute organisational patterns. Thus, hierarchies within a social system are characterised by top-down control, in which the higher layers set the parameters within which the lower layers are supposed to organise their interaction. A company's organisational chart or state's bureaucracies are examples of this type of hierarchy within systems. On the other hand, the hierarchies among systems we are talking about are not constituted from the top but from the bottom. It is the interplay and thus the organisational form of the components of a system (themselves systems at lower levels) that give rise to the properties of a system that comprises them. Thus, for example, a system of social cooperation among a given number of producers gives rise to a higher productivity than the same production carried out by the same number of producers working in isolation from each other (Marx, 1976, ch. 12). This is an 'emergent' property of a system of social organisation which is not present in the individual components, themselves being a system. An organism presents features that are not discernible in the cells that comprise it, although cells are also systems.

sustainability of the supersystem, providing material and space for reorganisation and adaptation. (ibid., p. 214)

So competitive nodes *qua* components of a socioeconomic system, appear, grow, prosper and die. But it is through these life-/renewal-cycles that the overall capitalist market system *sustains* itself, persists and extends its life. The reorganisation of each particular unit-component – be this a company, a socio-economic area, a city, a region, or any other web of co-producing singularities – thus contributes to non-decay and persistence of the larger socio-economic system we call capitalism. And the same can be said by scaling down: the sustainability of a 'community' of producers – be this the expression of a social cooperation of labour at the company, city or regional level – depends on the continuous release and renewal cycles of its individual components, processes that socio-economically may take the form of 'life-long education' (renewing skills), migration (renewing skills and bodies), job casualisation and *precarious* work (renewing bodies).

Whatever level of social cooperation we are considering when we are looking at capitalism as a social system, the fact is that capitalism, as any system, is not static, but evolves as a result of the continuous renewal in its components. Its sustainability *depends* on constant change and renewal of its correspondent subsystems. The capitalist system will be more sustainable, its historical life-span extended and the 'end of history' sustained the more it continues to 'sacrifice' its components, say some individual competing 'communities'. On the other hand, an individual component of the capitalist supersystem, say a 'community', becomes 'sustainable' to the extent that it continues to 'sacrifice' its own components, individual cooperative singularities and socio-technical aspects of labour in the ongoing transformations required by keeping abreast of competitiveness.

The wisdom of the system is embedded in the neoliberal discourse that abhors all types of 'market rigidities', such as traditional welfarist forms of entitlements and rights. Thus, labour market flexibility linked to programmes of continuing education makes labour power components in principle 'trained' for dissipation and reorganisation at new and improved conditions of profitability. This stands in contrast to the classic case of post-war welfare provision and labour management that in the end turned unemployment into an opportunity of withdrawal from the capitalist system, hence reduced the potential for an evolutionary change in its organisation: 'evolution needs material for adaptation' (Voinov, 1998, p. 214), and the material for the adaptation of capital to new conditions of profitability is released through recessions, restructuring, cycles.

From a system perspective, therefore, the secret of 'sustainable communities' is, paraphrasing Giuseppe Tomasi di Lampedusa's old adage in the *Gattopardo*, everything changes (at the subsystemic level) so everything stays the same (at the supersystemic level).

The obsession with 'change for change's sake' in modern political and corporate discourse, is really an obsession for the release-renewal of individual subsystemic components triggered by pervasive competition and, therefore, for the 'sustainability' of correspondent upper-level systems, which coincides with Fukuyama's (1992) 'end of history'. This obsession – often discursively legitimised with Darwinian images of evolution and survival of the fittest and Schumpeterian characterisation of capitalist innovation as 'creative destruction' – forgets that evolution actually often implies a preference for conservation rather than change, since the 'fittest' for a particular function has already been successfully selected. It is obviously only in a world in which functions and their 'use values' are subordinated to the drive for profit and 'exchange value' that the need for change is assumed as an abstract systemic requirement rather than as contextual and contingent.

'Sustainable Communities' as Subsystems

We can now approach the problematic of 'sustainable communities' in more concrete terms and ask how a large urban community of waged and unwaged producers can be 'sustainable', keeping in mind that for the government planners such a community is subject to the constraints of having to reproduce their livelihoods in forms compatible with global *capitalist* markets. System analysis reminds us that the sustainability of a local 'community' interconnected to other communities (such as a 'community' serving a financial centre as a node in the global economy) can be ensured in most cases 'only by borrowing energy, resources (capital) and adaptive potential from outside of the system, or by decreasing the sustainability of the global system. Sustainability of a subsystem is achieved only at the expense of the supersystem or other subsystems' (Voinov, 1998, p. 220).

For our purpose here, we can refer to this 'borrowing' processes upon which the 'sustainability' of a local node in a web of highly integrated nodes of production is maintained as a *threefold accumulation* necessary for *sustainability*, that is, an accumulation of natural resources (energy, water, the mining of renewables), of financial resources (capital) and of adaptive potential ('human capital').

In the case of London, the evidence of accumulation of natural resources at the expense of other subsystems is obvious. A 'sustainable communities' plan aiming at adding a quarter of a million people to London's population, as in the case of the Thames Gateway, can only increase its energy and natural resources requirements, despite management techniques designed to increase energy, water and other natural resource efficiency. Also, a 'sustainable community' in London would have to sort out its environmentally *unsustainable* current state of sewage overflows,[13] or embark in a major renewal of its Victorian water pipes through which a third of London's clean water leaks, or cope with recurrent summer droughts by the construction of new reservoirs to compensate for the effects of

---

13   'The inadequate state of London's sewers was exposed by a storm in August 2004. Stormwater overflows prompted billions of gallons of sewage to be pumped into the river Thames, killing thousands of fish' (Weaver, 2006).

rming,[14] or plan to deal with London's increasing need for water with
zzling desalination plants.[15]

t be also pointed out that the traditional institutional response
ritiques seeks to *manage* such problems by promoting a discourse
imental protection based on *efficient* use of natural or renewable
[6] This environmental-protection approach begins with existing patterns
l and energy use, which are not problematised. What is problematised
the *efficiency ratio* at which users (individual, institutions, or firms)
eir resources. This dominant approach is highly problematic in terms
n's overall ecological sustainability because every choice of a ratio is a
choice of values that, to put it with Princen (2005, p. 89),

> just separate along the familiar divides of modern and traditional, new and
> t and slow … They separate along divides of time frame – short term and
> rcially meaningful versus long term and ecologically meaningful -- and cost
> ement – the ability to externalize the costs of production and consumption in
> d space.

fficiency claims are based on the conditions of *ceteris paribus* (all else
il). For example, a new car engine can be more fuel efficient, as it uses up
er miles, but it might use more oil per mile, or it might become obsolete
in previous generations of cars, which itself implies higher consumption
for the production of an increasing number of cars. Also, fuel efficiency
ell us anything about aggregate fuel use, which can increase with the
i car usage despite the increased efficiency of individual cars. Thus, we
in mind that the discourse of 'sustainability' of urban communities
l hide the ecologically unsustainable accumulation of natural resources
i other localities.

ns of the accumulation of financial resources, 'sustainability' is a clear
i and this is realised once we reflect on the link between sustainability
petitiveness'. The 'sustainable community' discourse is constructed
lar of competitiveness. The three-point 'challenge' set by the original
le communities plan put 'competitiveness' at the first point, before the

---

ee Toynbee, 2006.
ee Toynbee, 2006 and Vidal, 2006.
The end users and managers employing this discourse 'do not challenge the
ilitical economy'. The discourse of environmental protection 'is responsive to
pressed public desires (for public parks or for air-pollution control, for instance)
-effective industrial measures (e.g., pollution prevention or green marketing). It
is responsive to, even resistant to, attempts to change established practices such
public lands or trawling open seas or driving private automobiles. And there is
ade-off, always an exchange rate between social values (e.g. high employment)
gical values (e.g. the survival of a species). There are no absolutes, no critical
values that transcend trade-offs (e.g. irreversibilities such as loss of a species
of a heavy metal) one never has too much, just better trades at the margin'
2005, p. 29).

need to deal with housing crisis in a 'sustainable' way and with high-quality design (ODPM, 2003, p. 16). This follows a common practice in 'governance' documents in which social and ecological values are articulated to business priorities (De Angelis, 2007, pp. 94–9).

Here, it is the 'economic success' of the London region and its international competitiveness that need to be *sustained*. From a cursory look at more specific strategic documents of a variety of public institutions, we see that they all highlight 'competitiveness' as key rationale. Thus, for example, the Thames Gateway London Partnership promotes a transport strategy that is 'vital to support competitiveness of London's financial services' (TGLP, 2005). On the level of education, the Thames Gateway Technology Center at the University of East London claims to act 'as a natural channel between business and higher education … by making the facilities, resources, knowledge and expertise across the university available to local, national and international business to increase *competitiveness*' (TGTC, 2005, my emphasis).

The 'competitiveness' that is boasted of as part of what a 'sustainable community' should all be about is largely, although not uniquely, based on enhancing London's role as a financial centre and a prime location for the attraction of capital and top-end production of producer and research and development services. But what does this function mean in light of the *relation* between London and the rest of the world? In so far as the accumulation of financial resources are concerned, three things come to mind. First, the fact that London is competitive in attracting resources 'looted' (Bond, 2006) in a variety of ways through the processes of neoliberal globalisation and consequent structural adjustments, debt repayments, cuts in entitlements, privatisation of national assets and so on around the world. Secondly, the fact that London is competitive in recycling these resources into new financial instruments, converted into various forms of liquidity, new 'risk diversification' instruments, bought and sold efficiently and re-entering the spinning wheel of global finance which keeps disciplining governments to tax competition and restrained public spending (viz. social entitlements and welfare).[17] These two points are, of course, part and parcel of the growing social, wealth and income polarisation that has been registered at the global level. Thirdly, the maintenance of London as a financial centre implies a process of social polarisation also at the local level, that is, at the point of the boasted 'economic success'. One clear example is that the 'economic success' of the finance and service industry goes hand in hand with a growing army of new servant classes – underpaid, invisible, often undocumented and heavily stigmatised and open to being blackmailed (Sassen, 2001, pp. 251–325), working to clean 'competitive' transport systems, 'competitive' schools and universities, 'competitive' office blocks, or as waiters, or in fast food chains, or as onion and carrot choppers for the 'competitive' increasingly busy restaurants of the tourist and financial districts. Finally, London's competitiveness as a financial and producer service centre depends heavily on the cost externalisation of back office

---

17   For an analysis of modern form of 'looting' for the case of the African continent linked to today's general conditions of capitalist accumulation see Bond (2006).

rations to places such as Mumbai, a global functional integration that
ly on the lower costs of reproduction of skilled labour power in India.
n depends on the mass of available invisible work that is commanded
there and that can serve the reproduction needs of skilled workers.

s of the 'adaptive potential', we can recognise some complementarities
ird feature associated with accumulation of financial resources. The
London as a financial center also depends on the growth of health
tion services, which in turn, given the labour market shortages of key
se, can be filled by employing nurses, doctors and teachers from poorer
e world under heavy neoliberal structural adjustment. These, in turn,
ort of their 'adaptive potential'.

four examples, the interconnection between 'communities' is twofold:
and competitive. It is hard to imagine how the 'sustainability' of London
polis driven by the City – or, indeed, of a new community attached to the
nned by the Sustainable Communities Plan – can avoid being acquisitive
etitive, hence threatening the sustainability of *other* 'communities' ;
y are also predicated on the life-patterns of those whose poverty, hard
ttle reward, stigmatisation and criminalisation is precisely becoming,
ncreasingly *unsustainable*.

Communities

at by reflecting on 'sustainability' from a systems-analysis perspective
a critical political economy approach, we discover that the 'sustainable'
disposable' go hand-in-hand. All the moments of 'sustainable
ion' indicate that 'sustainable communities' are unavoidably linked to
e communities'. What some have called 'new enclosures' and others
tion by dispossession' are ultimately at the basis of the sustainability
itive 'communities'.[18]

is not only in light of the relation to *other* communities that the
le' is associated to the 'disposable' in current political economy. Even
ged 'sustainable communities' the sustainability of some parts is valued
ly than that of other parts, which then become disposable, and the
ocess is constructed through the discourse of 'competitiveness'. Take
le the issues linked to that moment of the Thames Gateway project
nder the name of the 2012 Olympics. Here it is becoming increasingly
at a series of smaller communities (i.e., subsystemic components of
'communities') are threatened with removal and eviction, including
ites, historical allotment gardens, common marshland, football fields

he reference here is on the literature developed in the last decade or so on the
f 'primitive accumlation' as integral part of current neoliberal policies. In a
ways, this is discussed in, among others, Bonefeld (2001), De Angelis (2004),
990), Harvey (2003), Midnight Notes Collective (1992) and Perelman (2000).

and small businesses – all because of a fetishised need for 'regeneration' in forms that are instrumental to maintain London 'competitiveness'.[19]

The Sustainable Communities Plan defines 'sustainable communities' by means of a 'shopping list'.[20] Through the lens of systems theory, we derive a less idyllic image of 'sustainable communities', and a more sober appreciation of the limitations of the combination of the values of business and the *other* values (those of systemic ecological sustainability, social justice, dignity, peace, cooperation, solidarity).

Indeed, keeping in mind the workings of the system, to couple business and ethics requires considerable skill. This is not because balancing business priorities with ethical considerations (whether on social justice or environmental issues) is difficult (companies and neoliberal governments do it all the time), but because business priorities, summarised by the famous bottom line, is itself an *ethics* – a definition of what is good and what is bad. Indeed the capitalist market is an ethical system (McMurtry, 1998), ranking producing communities according to what *it* values and not according to what *they* value. It is precisely because the market and its practice is an ethics in its own right that the problematics of articulating such different and often clashing value practices as profit, efficiency, competitiveness on one side, and social justice, environmental sustainability and a 'happy life' for all on the other, is something of an impossible challenge at the systemic level for a *sustained* period of time. To put it bluntly, what we value *qua* agents in a market (whether as workers, company directors, or middle managers) is to succeed in a competitive system, that is, by de-fetishising, to reproduce our livelihoods and our community of competing producers by threatening that of others. The system-effects of these many actions – do we need reminding? – are, if left unchecked, income and wealth polarisation, concentration and centralisation of money/power on one side and environmental degradation and catastrophe on the other. And whether it is *our* or *another* community that succeeds or loses out is, from

---

19   For a review of a variety of campaigns associated to the London Olympics, see http://www.gamesmonitor.org.

20   'Some of the key requirements of sustainable communities are: a flourishing local economy to provide jobs and wealth; strong leadership to respond positively to change; effective engagement and participation by local people, groups and businesses, especially in the planning, design and long term stewardship of their community, and an active voluntary and community sector; a safe and healthy local environment with well-designed public and green space; sufficient size, scale and density, and the right layout to support basic amenities in the neighbourhood and minimise use of resources (including land); good public transport and other transport infrastructure both within the community and linking it to urban, rural and regional centres; buildings – both individually and collectively – that can meet different needs over time, and that minimise the use of resources; a well-integrated mix of decent homes of different types and tenures to support a range of household sizes, ages and incomes; good quality local public services, including education and training opportunities, health care and community facilities, especially for leisure; a diverse, vibrant and creative local culture, encouraging pride in the community and cohesion within it; a 'sense of place' ; the right links with the wider regional, national and international community' (ODPM, 2003, p. 4).

tive of the overall ecological and socio-economic system, irrelevant.
and from this perspective, to the extent that communities at different
organise their sustainabilities and their correspondent modes of social
on the basis of a competitive practice vis-à-vis other communities
rs, there is no such a thing as a 'sustainable community'. To the extent
as agents pursuing practices that sustain capital accumulation, one
's 'sustainability' corresponds to some other community 'disposability'.
iis realisation, the fabulous oxymoronic creatures are, like the famous
vealed to be wearing no clothes at all.

06), *Looting Africa. The Economics of Exploitation*, London, Zed Books.

d Dada, R. (2005), *Trouble in the Air Global Warming and the Privatised
ere*, Durban, Centre for Civil Society.

(2001), 'The Permanence of Primitive Accumulation: Commodity Fetishism
ial Constitution', *The Commoner*, 2, September. Available at http://www.
er.org.uk/02bonefeld.pdf.

i. (2006), 'The Future of "the Commons": Neoliberalism's "Plan B" or the
Disaccumulation of Capital?', keynote presentation for 'The Commons
ce', University of Victoria, 28–30 April, Victoria, BC, Canada.

_____, M. (2004), 'Separating the Doing and the Deed: Capital and the Continuous
Character of Enclosures', *Historical Materialism*, 12 (2), pp. 57–87.

De Angelis, M. (2005), 'The Political Economy of Global Neoliberal Governance', *Review*,
28 (3), pp. 229–57.

Federici, S. (1990), 'The Debt Crisis, Africa and the New Enclosures', *Midnight Notes*, No.
10, New York, reproduced in *The Commoner*, 2, September 2001. Available at http://
www.commoner.org.uk/02federici.pdf.

Foucault, M. (2002), 'Governmentality', in Faubion, J.D. (ed.), *Power: Essential works of
Foucault 1954–1984*, London, Penguin.

Fukuyama, F. (1992), *The End of History and the Last Man*, London, Hamish
Hamilton.

Harvey, D. (1985), *The Urbanization of Capital*, Oxford: Basil Blackwell.

Harvey, D. (2003), *The New Imperialism*, Oxford, Oxford University Press.

Harvey, D. (2005), *A Brief History of Neoliberalism*, Oxford, Oxford University Press.

Marx, K. (1976), *Capital*, Vol. 1, New York, Penguin Books.

McMurtry, J. (1998), *Unequal Freedoms: The Global Market as an Ethical System*, Toronto
and Westport, CN, Garamond and Kumarian Press.

Midnight Notes Collective (1992) 'New Enclosures', in *Midnight Notes*, reproduced in *The
Commoner*, 2, September 2001. Available at http://www.commoner.org.uk/02midnight.
pdf.

Perelman, M. (2000), *The Invention of Capitalism: Classical Political Economy and the
Secret History of Primitive Accumulation*, Durham, NC and London, Duke University
Press.

Princen, T. (2005), *The Logic of Sufficiency*, Cambridge, MA, MIT Press.

Sassen, S. (2001), *The Global City. New York, London, Tokyo*, 2nd edn, Princeton, NJ and
Oxford, Princeton University Press.

ODPM (2003), *Sustainable Communities. Building for the Future*, London, Office of the Deputy Prime Minister. Available at http://www.communities.gov.uk/index. asp?id=1163452 (last accessed 15 January 2006).

ODPM (2005a), *Sustainable Communities: Homes for all*, London, Office of the Deputy Prime Minister. Available at http://www.communities.gov.uk/index.asp?id=1122851 (last accessed 15 January 2006).

ODPM (2005b), *Sustainable Communities: People, Places, Prosperity. A Five Year Plan*, London, Office of the Deputy Prime Minister. Available at http://www.communities. gov.uk/index.asp?id=1122898 (last accessed 15 January 2006).

TGLP (2005), *Thames Gateway London Partnership*. Available at http://www.thames-gateway.org.uk/(last accessed March 2005).

TGTC (2005), *Thames Gateway Technology Centre*. Available at http://www.uel.ac.uk/tgtc (last accessed March 2005).

Toynbee, P. (2006), 'Forget Drought: First We Have to End this Cowardice. Our Early Brush with Climate Change Shows What an Unequivocal Scandal the Privatisation of Water Represents', *Guardian Unlimited*, 23 May. Available at http://politics.guardian. co.uk/print/0,,329486999-107865,00.html.

Vidal, J. (2006), 'Desalination Plant Necessary to Tackle London's Water Shortage, Supplier Says', *Guardian Unlimited*, 24 May. Available at http://www.guardian.co.uk/ water/story/0,,1781658,00.html.

Voinov, A.A. (1998), 'Paradoxes of Sustainability', *Journal of General Biology*, 59, pp. 209–18.

Voinov, A.A. (1998), 'Paradoxes of Sustainabilty', *Journal of Environmental Management*. Available at http://www.uvm.edu/giee/AV/PUBS/PARADOX/Sust_Par.html.

Weaver, M. (2006), 'Sewage Overflows Threaten London Olympics', *Guardian Unlimited*, 19 January. Available at http://www.guardian.co.uk/olympics2012/story/0,,1690331, 00.html (last accessed 10 November 2006).

Wilcox, S. (2003), *Can Work – Can't Buy. Local Measures of the Ability of Working Households to Become Home Owners*, York, Joseph Rowntree Foundation.

WCED (1987), 'Our Common Future', Report of the World Commission on Environment and Development. Available at http://www.are.admin.ch/are/en/nachhaltig/ international_uno/unterseite02330/(last accessed, 15 January 2007).

Wolfowitz, P. (2005), 'Charting a Way Ahead: The Results Agenda', 2005 Annual Meeting Address, World Bank, Washington, DC, 24 September. Available at http://www. worldbank.org/(last accessed 25 February 2006).

World Bank (2003), *Sustainable Development in a Dynamic World. Transforming Institutions, Growth and Quality of Life. World Bank Report*, Washington, The World Bank.

Chapter 6

Forcing the Market, Forging Community: Culture as Social Construction in the Thames Gateway

Andrew Calcutt

> I wasn't aware until recently that I was living in a district that is set to be part of the Thames Gateway build-up. In my experience, the Thames is not so much a gateway but more of a dividing line, and I have grown up with the division that separates the two sides, North and South. (Trayler, 2006)

So wrote one of my journalism students, 20-year-old Carly Trayler from Dartford, when, as editor of *Rising East* (www.risingeast.org), I commissioned her to write a response to the Interim Plan, one of a raft of Thames Gateway documents published by the Department for Communities and Local Government at the Thames Gateway Forum on 22 November 2006.

Asked to comment on the state of the Gateway, Trayler replied to the effect that it sounded liked a good idea, but this was the first she had heard of it. She is not alone in thinking of the Gateway as something that has not happened yet. Public health minister Caroline Flint said as much in her presentation to the 2006 Thames Gateway Forum at London Excel exhibition centre:

> What's really an opportunity here is to have that chance in a regeneration project of this size, to start with pretty much a blank sheet in terms of the opportunity to design and think out of the box about how you're going to build the community; whether that's in terms of homes, business or bases. (Flint, 2006)

At 20, Carly Trayler is not much older than the designation of the Estuary and concomitant land as an area for regeneration, first badged as 'East Thames Corridor' and then as 'Thames Gateway'. She grew up alongside the growth of government policies (local, regional, national) oriented to the Corridor/Gateway and the increase of public spending in a region which thereby came into officially recognised existence. But on her mental map it does not exist; she reports only having 'grown up with the division that separates the two sides, North and South' (Trayler, 2006).

As a young woman in the street, Carly Trayler was looking up and, only when prompted to do so, recognising the prospect of the Gateway for the first time. Meanwhile, looking down on the area from the vantage point of high office,

Caroline Flint also saw it as virgin territory. This is an extraordinary oversight. Beginning with Michael Heseltine in 1979, a series of government ministers, Conservative and New Labour, have made much of redeveloping East London and its hinterlands. After more than a quarter of a century, however, a serving minister could still refer to the region as a 'blank sheet'.

That these two informants – one on the ground, the other in the upper echelons of Westminster – were seemingly oblivious to decades of Gateway policy is itself informative. Trayler is a contemporary of the plan for the Gateway, Flint is the latest in a line of ministers tasked with turning plan into reality; yet as each of them looks at the Thames Gateway from their different perspectives, too little has happened to make much of an impression on either of them. It is not that they simply forgot to mention something which is really at the core of their existence (private or public); rather, in their private and public experiences as in their references to the Gateway, there is no there, there – at least, not yet.

The aim of this chapter is to account for the not-yet character of the Gateway; and to show that the policy emphasis on culture in the Gateway is an attempt to make substantial that which has so far remained stubbornly virtual. My thesis is that culture is here called upon to do all that can be done to construct a virtual society in the absence of the scale of private sector investment and the rates of return on capital which, in these historically specific circumstances, are preconditions for realising the Gateway as a new kind of city.

Furthermore, I seek to show that where 'culture' comes to mean 'a whole way of life' (Williams, 1958a, p. 12), embedding culture into regeneration has emerged as a way of life for a whole new cohort of urban policy professionals. This life is led without the great expectations of state agency which moulded previous generations of professional planners; rather, it is conducted in the hope that private sector investment will soon flood the Gateway and float its wholesale development. In the interim, the promotion of culture is one and the same as marketing the region and attracting inward investment.

However, that the means of marketing is, of all things, culture, suggests there are forces at work other than those of the market. Of course non-market mechanisms include public subsidy via the London Development Agency and a host of other bodies. But to this degree public finance is taken for granted, like the flow of the Thames itself. Above and beyond such subsidy, however, there are particular connotations attached to culture and its recent adoption as a mechanism for regional regeneration. Throughout the modern period, culture has stood for the social organism in contradistinction to the atomising and divisive effects of economics and politics. And if culture is here a marketing mechanism aimed at organising the market in and around the Gateway, it is also an attempt to *organicise*, to create continuity and coherence throughout the region and among regeneration professionals who seek to represent its best interests. In short, culture is called upon to support the market and to demonstrate that there is more to the Gateway than the market.[1]

---

1   The point of culture (disregarding its own terms in a moment of philistinism) is its substantive opposition to both economics and politics. In his groundbreaking study *Culture*

Today, in the Gateway, the historic role of culture is to mediate between the era of state planning and the long-awaited round of large-scale, private sector capital investment which realisation of the Gateway depends on. The origins of the part written for culture can be traced back as far as George Brown's National Plan and the (then) social weight of the British labour movement. But the politics of that era are now as anachronistic as the state intervention which accompanied it. Hence the role of non-political, non-capital culture, has itself been rewritten in anticipation of decisive intervention by the market and in recognition of the exhaustion of party politics. Thus in the setting of the Gateway, culture can serve as an appeal to capital and at the same time as the elevation of ways of life over both capital and the moribund world of the political party. In that culture can look both these ways at once, orientation to culture is now *de rigueur* across the spectrum of policymakers and regeneration professionals, whether their individual origins and residual political loyalties lie on the anti-market Left or the pro-market Right.

For those of a leftist disposition, the idea of the Gateway as a profoundly cultural place is well presented in *New Things Happen*, a study by the Commission for Architecture and the Built Environment (CABE, 2006), which both codifies the social contradictions of the Gateway and expands upon its cultural significance. It is a visionary document – grounded without being pedestrian and fanciful in a positive sense – which weaves together a narrative for the Gateway encompassing its past, present and future. As an idea of the good society, it is perhaps as good as it gets; but it is unlikely to get anywhere except, and despite its own commitment to people and places, as an adjunct to the Gateway's pitch for global capital.

Those with less explicitly left-wing credentials are more likely to be relatively late converts to cultural policy as a key component in regional regeneration. But converts are often the most staunch believers. Accordingly, in her opening remarks to the seminar on 'embedding culture' at the 2006 Thames Gateway Forum, the current Secretary of State for Culture, Media and Sport, Tessa Jowell noted that the place of culture in regeneration policy requires no further justification: 'A few years ago in a discussion like this I would have started by making the case for culture. Now I can assume that the case for culture is made and accepted' (Jowell, 2006). Bringing the seminar to a close, its chairman, former Secretary of State Chris Smith, endorsed his successor's appraisal of culture's established role: 'the whether of whether culture should be an integral part, almost goes without saying: culture has to be part of any regeneration development' (Smith, 2006). Between them they personified the consensus around culture and its significance in regeneration.

---

and Society, Williams (1958b) emphasised the modern role of culture as counterpoint to the onset of market relations. More recently, Mulhern (2000) has identified 'metaculture' (the role of culture outside its own terms) as a critique of politics. Modern culture and politics, as it seems to me, have in their different ways served as the mid-point or mediation between episodes of capitalist production. In this important respect, mediation enables episodes of capitalist production to succeed one another; but it also offers a fleeting experience of the potential for capitalist relations to be succeeded by another social order.

Gateway Prospectus

Yet as culture is part of regeneration, so it cannot be the whole. Also at the 2006 Thames Gateway Forum, various high level speakers acknowledged private sector investment as a *sine qua non*. Ros Dunn, director of the Thames Gateway Strategy Division at the Department for Communities and Local Government (DCLG), observed that 'ultimately the money will probably come in large measures from the private sector' (Dunn, 2006). Her senior colleague, incoming Thames Gateway chief executive Judith Armitt proclaimed: 'I do believe that by 2016 the Gateway will be internationally attractive to global investors' (Armitt, 2006). Richard McCarthy, in charge of Programmes, Policy and Implementation at DCLG, identified the big numbers which he is hoping for: 'I want to celebrate by 2016 if not earlier that we've geared in some £38 billion of private sector investment' (McCarthy, 2006).

Thus it transpires that realisation of the Thames Gateway Interim Plan will require private sector capital to the tune of £40 billion. This puts a different gloss on the relative weight of each of the Thames Gateway documents published simultaneously by DCLG in November 2006. In media coverage, the paper most widely referred to was the Interim Plan, with its projections for 160,000 new homes and 180,000 jobs, which was also self-effacingly subtitled a 'policy framework' (DCLG, 2006a, p. 6). Such modesty was not an affectation, but fully in line with the real status of the document. For it turns out that the Plan only becomes a plan, i.e., a diagrammatic or programmatic representation of that which will be implemented, if it is framed by private sector capital of approximately £40 billion. In this context, the most significant document issued that day was not the Plan but the Development Prospectus (DCLG, 2006b), a 164-page brochure designed to market the Gateway to large-scale investors, in the hope that the market will bring capital to the Gateway and thus make it a reality.

What the state can do – 'create the conditions and drive forward to this agenda' (Dunn, 2006), in the words of Ros Dunn – is an adjunct to putting Thames Gateway on the market. But 'ultimately' government is not expected to determine what happens to the Plan, which is thus a second order document with variable outcomes dependent on the success of the primary text, the Development Prospectus, or pitch. Market forces will decide; and their decision remains uncertain.

Over decades both before and after designation as the Gateway, the market has been less than forceful in developing the region. In current jargon, the scale of investment required is way above trend.

David Marlow, chief executive of East of England Development Agency, acknowledged this when he noted that 'the greater South-East success ... is founded almost wholly on Central and West London, Thames Valley, Hertfordshire and Surrey'. By contrast: 'the East of the mega-region is actually performing relatively modestly' (Marlow, 2006).

The longstanding, local trend for modest, even meagre economic growth is exemplified by the labour market in the London Borough Newham, as identified in the Greater London Authority's recent working paper on borough employment prospects:

> Newham experienced almost continually falling employment in the 25 years to 1995. Between 1995 and 2001 employment grew before falling back slightly between 2001 and 2003 as the London economy experienced a slowdown. Overall in 2003 the level of employment in Newham was below the levels seen in the early 1980s and especially since the 1970s. (Melville and Theseira, 2006, p. 15)

Employment in Newham thus followed the recent curves of the market: down with de-industrialisation, rising with the dot.com balloon and falling again when it burst on and around 9/11. 'Trend-based projections' had suggested only 4,000 more jobs in the borough between 2003 and 2006. Thankfully the location of the 2012 Olympic Park largely in Newham is set to buck the depressed local trend, such that the Olympics effect is now predicted to raise the borough's jobs total to 125,000 by 2026.

However, whereas Newham will benefit more than most from the Olympics legacy, other Thames-side conurbations, whether London boroughs or outlying Gateway towns, have nothing comparable to count on. There is no rush to invest in the UK. Among independent forecasters, 'the consensus is for the UK economy to slow slightly' in 2007, 'along with other industrialised countries' (Lewis, 2006). Investment in research and development remains low (DTI, 2006, p. 56). Activity in the City is 'buoyant' (IFSL, 2006), but hardly recording-breaking.

The 'creative industries', hard to define but readily trailed as the sector to match growth rates previously achieved by financial services, are largely confined to the West End, Camden and the West Side of Greater London (GLA Economics, 2002). According to research compiled by GLA Economics, the data collection and analysis unit which reports to the Greater London Authority and the Mayor of London, the most significant, commercial exceptions to this Western bias are publishing, web design and fine art, which have come as far east as the City Fringe; and apart from designer-led Hoxton (Silicon Alley wired to the City's communications infrastructure), these moves are explicable as cost-cutting (publishers move from Bloomsbury to low-rent Hackney), the side-effects of deindustrialisation and the transposition of the docks downriver to Tilbury (ex-warehousing made-over as artists' studios), or as investment-avoidance (speculating on the future value of BritArt offers better returns than long-term investment).

Graham Hitchen, head of Creative London, reckons that the region 'can become a leading international creative destination', but even he concedes that 'the creative industries are not yet a major employer in East London' (Hitchen, 2005).

Rome wasn't built in a day, you might say; and if the Gateway region were already economically dynamic and socially progressive, there would be no need to regenerate it. This is a fair point. But after successive decades of supposed regeneration it is equally fair to point to the absence of leading actors in the regeneration network. The state has refused the protagonist's role; and the private sector's most celebrated names have been almost as slow in coming forward. Such is the dearth of big players that at Thames Gateway Forum 2006, Michael Heseltine joked about offering Bill Gates a peerage as long as he spends a billion pounds to build Gatestown in the Gateway (NB: this plan for realising the Plan would swamp the House of Lords since £1 billion would be required from Gates and a further 37 billionaires) (Heseltine, 2006). Heseltine later said he might settle for 'a couple of Indians and a few Chinese' to come up with the kind of large-scale, lead investment that would prompt others to follow.

Apart from the intervention of international angels, there is the widespread hope that London 2012 will put Thames Gateway on the investment map. 'Hosting the 2012 Games offers an unprecedented opportunity to build a still stronger image' (DCLG, 2006a, p. 5), boasts the Interim Plan. But 'what in the Gateway will it draw attention to', asks architect Terry Farrell, 'if there isn't a product?' (Farrell, 2006).

This is an astute question; but one aspect of the answer is that the Gateway as Planned is itself a product which is now being taken to market. Perhaps, on publication of the Development Prospectus, this is the first time that Thames Gateway has been effectively marketed; but nobody can be certain what its market value will be, and in this continuing period of uncertainty culture is called upon both to improve the offer to potential investors, and to offer some measure of improvement to the quality of life in the region. Culture in this context is as much or as little as we can be getting on with, while hoping for market intervention but without (yet) having secured a new and decisive round of private sector investment.

Culture as Leverage

The status of London as a world class city is part of the pitch for investment in East London and the concomitant region; and culture is flagged as a significant factor in the acquisition and maintenance of such status. Thus the Mayor of London's cultural strategy (2004) is subtitled 'realising the potential of a world class city', and Policy 1 reads:

> London needs to ensure its cultural institutions and events are of a high quality, world class status. (Livingstone, 2004, p. 12)

Likewise, Policy 3 states that 'London needs to develop its brand and promote itself as a world cultural city and tourism destination' (ibid., p. 14) If the richest tourists enjoy their culturally enhanced visit so much, perhaps they will buy a London company or start up a new one in the Gateway. Thus culture is itself the gateway to private sector investment.

Immediate emphasis on the cultural offer extends into the non-London sections of Gateway policy. As a 'next step' the Thames Gateway Interim Plan/Policy Framework requires that 'delivery partners will identify the cultural investments that are essential to their economic development plans; and will work with the national cultural agencies to plan investment in the Thames Gateway to create a better cultural offer' (DCLG, 2006a, p. 19). In turn, the cultural offer will play its part in 'building a global brand' in response to 'the need', recognised by 'the RDAs [regional development agencies] in common with other stakeholders', to 'create a pan-Gateway approach to marketing inward investment and development opportunities' (ibid., p. 18).

In short, culture can sell the Gateway to international investors; perhaps in the same way that cultural diversity sold East London to the International Olympics Committee.

Culture as Community

Apart from its capacity to enhance market performance by the Gateway brand, culture is also called upon to offset the atomising or marginalising effects of the market, and to act as a vehicle for the construction of community.

In his foreword to *Cultural Capital: Realising the Potential of a World Class City*, Mayor Ken Livingstone identifies culture's positive contribution in response to social and political corrosion:

> Far too many of London's citizens are socially excluded and poorly represented. Culture and creativity have a unique potential to address some of these difficult social issues. (Livingstone, 2004, p. 8)

This expectation of culture has much in common with the 'cultural agenda' pioneered in the Greater London Council, the regional democratic body led by Ken Livingstone and shut down by the national Conservative government in 1986. It is also reminiscent of the idea of cultural democracy as proposed by the community arts movement in the 1970s and 1980s:

> The ideas that constitute cultural democracy both enable and depend upon direct participation, and take as their aim the building and sustenance of a society in which people are free to come together to produce, distribute and receive the cultures they choose. (Another Standard, 1986, p. 40)

Whether at the GLC or among community artists, at that time such expectations of culture would have been aligned to 'socialism'. Now, as above, they are juxtaposed to the market. Something of a turnaround! But this is not to suggest that latterday culture champions are cynical, superficial, or any more deluded than their predecessors. Faced today with the sustained but slow growth of the UK economy, and wrong-footed by the end of the ideology of state intervention, the hope that increased participation in 'a whole way of life' (Williams, 1958b, p. 12), i.e., culture, will itself constitute a shared and hence enhanced way of life – a culture of community, a community of cultures – is as plausible as it is heartfelt.

Accordingly, the authors of the Cultural Framework and Toolkit for Thames Gateway North Kent, a collaboration between DCLG, local authorities, cultural agencies and others, define the 'value of culture' as follows:

> Culture resides within the very concept of a sustainable community as a place where people will want to live and work, that meets their diverse needs and offers a high quality of life and good services for all. Good cultural provision will attract residents and businesses which might not otherwise consider moving to TGNK; bring together new and existing communities; and help deprived communities to raise their aspirations and reach their potential. (CFTTGNK, 2006)

Similarly, www.wherewelive.org.uk is a newly-established joint venture on the part of five, national cultural agencies and the government departments which sponsor them. Headlined 'Building Communities Through Culture and Sport', the homepage announces that 'we work with a range of partners, local authorities, planners and developers, providing and supporting cultural provision that changes lives and communities for the better. Where We Live is the start of our programme of joint working that will help deliver creative, cultural and sporting activity in all communities through the sustainable communities agenda' (Where We Live, 2006a).

The site is underwritten by the Culture and Sustainable Communities Joint Agreement, signed on 13 July 2006 by Arts Council England, CABE (Commission for Architecture and the Built Environment), English Heritage, the Museums, Libraries and Archives Council, Sport England, DCMS and DCLG. Clause Three of the Joint Agreement states:

> We believe cultural assets and opportunities have a greater part to play in the business of creating new places. With greater strategic focus, collective ambition and creative leadership we can reach more people and more places, creating a step change for integration and quality of culture in achieving sustainable communities. (Where We Live, 2006b)

Beyond cultural agencies, the role of culture in building communities has been taken up by property developers such as Chris Brown of Igloo, which invests pension and charity funds in mixed use, sustainable projects. At the 2006 Thames Gateway Forum, Brown emphasised the deployment of local people in cultural schemes that are 'good for business, good for engaging – and it's fun' (Brown 2006).

Culture as a means of engaging local people and thereby constituting community is now frequently espoused by national politicians. In their preface to the Cultural Framework and Toolkit for Thames Gateway North Kent, Sports Minister Richard Caborn and Housing and Planning Minister Yvette Cooper write that: 'Culture touches and uplifts the lives of everyone in the UK. Developing access to a range of cultural activities and opportunities is an important part of the Government's vision for sustainable communities in the Thames Gateway' (CFTTGNK, 2006).

Speaking at the same seminar as Chris Brown ('Embedding Culture in the Thames Gateway'), DCMS Secretary of State Tessa Jowell declared: 'we are signed up to the vision for building new communities' by means of 'culture, sport and creative industries.' Chris Smith started the event by warning against the poverty of regeneration without culture or community:

> If you simply build buildings, if you don't think about community, you end up with sterile developments. There is no better way of thinking about community than culture in its broadest sense: arts, recreation, leisure, sport and cultural activity of all kinds. In seeking to generate those communities in the best possible way, a very large number of us think that culture has a very important part to play. (Smith, 2006)

Smith ended the session with a call for further enlargement of 'the number of us', with a special plea for other property developers to follow in Brown's footsteps: 'it's developers who now need to take this forward' (ibid.). And if they do as requested, perhaps property development will be re-categorised as part of the expanding creative industries.

Whose Community?

But what of the people who would thus be developed into communities? Opinion is divided as to whether they are communing as intended. Another *Rising East* contributor, student journalist Ian Simon, reporting on a recent community-building event hosted by a theatre company involved in regeneration, found that: 'local residents, firsthand witnesses of regeneration programmes and service closures, were in short supply. A supply of three local residents, to be precise' (Simon, 2007).

Of three recent think-tank reports on the public take-up of cultural policy, only one, published by the Institute for Public Policy Research (IPPR), accepts the positive social effects of culture at face value, while calling for a solid evidence-base from which to make the case clearer (Cowling, 2004). On the other hand, the Demos pamphlet *Cultural Value and the Crisis of Legitimacy* begins with a warning that 'cultural policy is a closed conversation among experts' (Holden 2006). In even sharper contrast, a collection of polemical essays from Policy Exchange claims that current policy does a disservice both to practising artists and the public; almost the only beneficiaries are regeneration professionals, hence the title *Culture Vultures: Is UK Arts Policy Damaging the Arts?* (Mirza, 2006).

While it remains uncertain to what extent communities are forged through current cultural policy, it is clear that much time, effort and money is taken up by regeneration professionals in the process of forming themselves into a community or series of communities.

Thus, at national level, the 'partners' to the Culture and Sustainable Communities Joint Agreement committed themselves to setting up a steering group and a task group 'empowered to set up smaller sub-groups' (Where We Live, 2006b). Membership of the task group will have been 'limited in the first instance', but 'reviewed regularly with a view to the broader cultural sector being represented in time' (ibid.). This is inclusion: the inclusion of like-minded fellow-professionals.

On a London-wide basis, the London Cultural Consortium (with Chris Smith in the chair) has been established as 'a restructured Cultural Strategy Group' to 'take forward the implementation of the Mayor's Cultural Strategy' (London Cultural Consortium, 2006). In the preamble which sets out the role of the London Cultural Consortium, the cultural strategy is characterised as the first '*coordinated* approach to arts, sports, heritage, and creative industries in the capital' (my emphasis). Under the terms of its aims and objectives the consortium is obliged to 'help the development', 'promote', 'coordinate', 'advise', 'engage' and 'maintain links' – all activities which specify bringing professional people together as a sufficient outcome.

Similarly, faced with the relative scarcity of creative industries in the Gateway region, Creative London's response is to get people together in hubs: 'a Hub isn't a building. It's a creative network within a geographical area of London' (Creative London, 2006). Apart from communication within hubs, 'they should talk to each other' (ibid.). Creative hub development consultant Debra Reay reported that various agencies were talking to each other about the 'complex task' of developing hubs as the means of taking forward the Creative London project in London Thames Gateway:

> The Creative Lewisham Agency, City Fringe Partnership, Thames Gateway London Partnership and Barking and Dagenham Council are all researching what a 'creative hub' might offer the business and cultural communities in their areas.

The professional clustering process has been replicated throughout the Thames Gateway by the regional Culture Task Group (TGCTG), as illustrated in the following extracts from the minutes of the group's meeting on 19 November 2004 hosted by Thames Gateway South Essex Partnership, Basildon.

> *ODPM* [Office of the Deputy Prime Minister, now defunct]: Sam Ashby indicated he is the new contact in the Strategy Unit at ODPM for culture in the Gateway. ODPM are making links with DCMS ... *English Heritage* [EH]: Greg Luton is keen to see how the TGCTG fits in with other networks and other pieces of work. EH has set up a Thames Gateway Group taking in East of England, the South East and London ... *Sport England East:* Sport Scoping Study ... consists of geographical mapping across the Gateway. The study is also an opportunity to engage and contribute to wider sports agenda – community, health, transport, leisure package, environment etc, and link in with other partners ... *Any Other Business*: ODPM are commissioning a photobank of images and ask members to contribute if they have any images of the Gateway ... Living East with Thames Gateway North Kent and partners had a culture stand at the recent Thames Gateway Forum. The stand attracted significant numbers of public and private sector representatives, including several VIPs. (Thames Gateway Culture Task Group, 2004)

At local level, the aforementioned Cultural Framework and Toolkit For Thames Gateway was 'created' by a

> unique collaboration between the South East Cultural Agencies; the Department for Communities and Local Government; the Department for Culture, Media and Sport; Local Authorities; Local Regeneration Partnerships; SEEDA [South East England Regional Development Agency]; the Regional Assembly; GOSE; National Lottery distributing bodies; and others. (CFTTGNK, 2006)

Visionary Thurrock, a project to envisage how the Essex town of Thurrock might benefit from cultural regeneration (it will soon be the new location of the workshops and archives of the Royal Opera House), involved Thurrock Council, Arts Council of England, the Countryside Agency, Living East, Price Waterhouse Coopers, Sport England, Thames Gateway South Essex Partnership, East of England Development Agency, Essex County Council, the Government Office for the East of England and the Heritage Lottery Fund (Visionary Thurrock, 2006).

Even when the cultural artefacts produced by collaboration are minimal, the collaborative process is multilayered. For example, launched at the 2006 Thames Gateway Forum, the Billboard Project is a multimedia container designed to enable young people to record what they think about regeneration. Organisations involved in developing the Billboard Project included Creative Partnerships, a 'creative learning programme' which 'brokers education, cultural and business sectors to effect positive change in the lives of young people' (Billboard Project, 2006); Arts Council, East and SEEDA 'via their unique shared prospectus'; Futurecity Arts, 'the UK's leading public arts consultancy'; Channel 4 Television's 4Talent which 'works with young creatives', in consultation with Basildon District Council and Southend and Thurrrock 'unitary authorities' (Billboard Project, 2006).

Far from being the work of a unified authority, the Billboard Project thus required collaboration between eight organisations to produce a big box with multimedia kit in it, otherwise described as 'a bespoke, architect-designed, shipping container which slides apart to create a multi-media filming studio and exhibition space ... brightly coloured and highly visible Tardis-like transformer' (ibid.).

This episode suggests that there are more twists and turns in the networks of regeneration professionals than in the plot of a *Dr Who* story. And if these are early days for the Billboard Project, it is not too early to suggest that the continuous process of networking among those involved in cultural regeneration has transformed them from disparate individuals on the fringes of public life to a highly influential club at the centre of twenty-first century governance. For professionals such as these the process itself provides a kind of transformation, regardless of the presence or absence of transformative capacity in the cultural projects around which their networking occurs.

Appropriately enough, the ideology of cultural regeneration now reproduces itself among regeneration professionals: it is a culture in its own right. Furthermore, this organism has acquired a high degree of authority: it has cult status. Thus cultural regeneration exists but not as advertised. Instead of groundbreaking effects on the external world, it is primarily a process internal to the middle classes which has succeeded in producing a culture to cohere the new generation of policy professionals who combined to produce total attendance of 7239 for the 2006 Thames Gateway Forum at Excel.

You do not have to be a leftover from the free market Thatcher era to feel angry at so much public money being used to establish so little. The prospect of millions spent on a prolonged process of tax-funded team building is enough to get almost anyone's back up. Yet the maintenance of social order is indeed a continuous process – more often than not, a constant battle – in which *esprit de corps* is always important; perhaps even more so when the spirit of the times undergoes substantive change and, accordingly, investment in a new *esprit* is called for.

Recent events, I suggest, have been of this magnitude: rolling back the ideology, if not the reality, of state intervention, taken together with the discrediting of the free market, the decline of the labour movement and the exhaustion of politics, have jointly posed mediation as the key question of the day: who or what will hold the ring in the absence of previous mediating mechanisms? That the current answer, cultural policy, seems as yet to be more effective within middle-class circles than across the wider population is not in itself a sufficient riposte to the advent of such policy and its role as perhaps the most important new mechanism in the mediation of social relations; rather it seems to bear out the old adage that in the kingdom of the blind, the one-eyed man is king.

In some ways, despite the waste of public money involved, it would be almost preferable if the effects of current cultural policy were restricted to those who generate it. Since culture is so multifaceted – not comprised of a single entity but an ensemble of diverse and often opposing elements – once it is adopted as a subsidised public good, it demands administration and all but invites the sovereignty of the administrator over the artist.[2] Yet opposition to administration is also inherent in culture.[3] Artists themselves are likely to resist administrative incursions into what they customarily regard as their territory, hence the fairly frequent stand-off between the demand for measurability by policy professionals and, on the other hand, autonomous artists such as the National Theatre's Nicholas Hytner, who noisily rejects the call to audit.

---

2   This tendency was famously observed and discussed by Adorno in his essay 'Culture and Administration': 'Whoever speaks of culture speaks of administration as well, whether this is his intention or not. The combination of so many things lacking a common denominator – such as philosophy and religion, science and art, forms of conduct and *mores* – and finally the inclusion of the objective spirit of the age in the single word "culture", betrays from the outset the administrative view, the task of which, looking down from on high, is to assemble, distribute, evaluate and organise' (Adorno, 1991, p. 93).

3   Adorno noted that 'culture would like to be higher and more pure, something untouchable which cannot be tailored to any tactical or technical considerations' (ibid.).

In current conditions there is even more at stake here than the artist's freedom from quantifiable outcomes. Given that culture's diversity makes it susceptible to administration, the extrapolation of culture from art into 'a whole way of life' – in other words, the adoption of the anthropological characterisation of culture as everything by cultural administrators, via Raymond Williams and Cultural Studies, has the effect of making everything in a whole way of life, i.e. culture, accessible to administration and intervention.

Bennett has explained how the radical redefinition of culture comes to be deployed and implemented as part of a revised mode of state intervention. He begins by establishing the progressive connotations of the anthropologised concept of culture:

> In advocating what at first sight seems to be a non-hierarchical and value-neutral understanding of culture, the anthropological definition appears to bring about a democratic and egalitarian plenitude in its construction of the policy field: everything is included and on equal terms. However whilst not wishing to dispute that this is so, this is not the only, or from a cultural policy perspective, necessarily the most important work that the concept performs. Its role in securing a more even spread of funding and other forms of government support across the cultural divides of class, gender and ethnicity has, to be sure, proved crucial in weakening the policy stranglehold of elitist concepts of art. (Bennett 1998: 91)

Having established this aspect, Bennett looks to the other side of the coin:

> By the same token, however, this process has brought about a parallel expansion of fields of activity which are now encompassed as fields of cultural administration. It has also done so, I suggest, in ways which are inescapably normative in the sense of effecting a governmental construction of the fields of cultural activity that are thus brought within the purview of policy to the degree that these are constructed as vehicles for in some way bringing about a reformation of habits, beliefs, values – in short, ways of life. (ibid.)

If culture requires administration and culture is comprised of nothing less than our whole way of life, then our whole way of life is now seen as needing administration and as the object of normative cultural policy. Here we are back to state intervention, but not the intervention of the state where the market once feared to tread, e.g. in the provision of health, housing, transport and communication networks. Increasingly, the market is called upon to intervene in such areas – a call which capital heeds unevenly and inconsistently. Meanwhile, with cultural policy as its inward route, the state aspires to intervene in areas of life where previously it had no recognised role.

Here the progressive ambition codified in *New Things Happen* and the self-actualising dynamic of regeneration professionals segue into something semi-authoritarian, namely, policies for improving your whole way of life which are fully in line with this very definition of culture.

The Gateway, insofar as it actually exists, is an 'ism' for the interim construction of society by cultural means. Until the market makes a decisive move to open the Gateway (when and if it ever does), in current conditions this is all that's on offer.

References

Adorno, T. (1991), 'Culture and Administration', in Adorno, Theodore, *The Culture Industry: Selected Essays on Mass Culture*, London, Routledge.

Another Standard (1986), *Culture and Democracy: The Manifesto*, London, Comedia Group and the Shelton Trust.

Armitt, J., Thames Gateway Forum, London Excel. Available at http://www.thamesgatewayforum.co.uk (last accessed 22 November 2006).

Arts Council of Great Britain (1974), *Community Arts: Report of the Community Arts Working Party*, June.

Bennett, T. (1998), *Culture: A Reformer's Science*, London, Sage.

Billboard Project (2006), 'Unique Project Gives Youth A Voice In Urban Regeneration', press release 22 November. Available at http://www.billboardproject.co.uk.

Brown, C. (2006), 'Embedding Culture into Thames Gateway', Thames Gateway Forum, London Excel, 23 November (author's notes).

CABE (Commission for Architecture and the Built Environment) (2006), *New Things Happen*, London, CABE.

Cowling, J. (ed.) (2004), *For Art's Sake*, London, IPPR.

Creative London (2006), *Get Connected*. Available at http://www.creativelondon.org.uk (last accessed 2 January 2007).

Cultural Framework and Toolkit for Thames Gateway North Kent. Available at http://www.culturesoutheast.org.uk (last accessed 2 January 2007).

DCLG (2006a), *Thames Gateway Interim Plan: Policy Framework*, London, DCLG.

DCLG (2006b), *Thames Gateway Interim Plan: Development Prospectus*, London, DCLG.

DTI Science and Innovation Investment *Business R&D and Innovation*, London, Department of Trade and Industry, 2006.

Dunn, Ros (2006), Thames Gateway Forum, London Excel, 2006. Available at http://www.thamesgatewayforum.co.uk (last accessed 22 November).

Economist, 'Survey of the World Economy', 16 September 2006.

Farrell, T. (2006), Question Time, Thames Gateway Forum, London Excel, 22 November. Available at http://www.thamesgatewayforum.co.uk.

Flint, C. (2006), Thames Gateway Forum, London Excel. Available at http://www.thamesgatewayforum.co.uk (last accessed 22 November 2006).

GLA Economics (2002), *Creativity: London's Core Business*, Section 5 'Clustering and Diversity: The Spatial Distribution of London's Creative Industries', London, GLA Economics. Available at http://www.london.gov.uk/gla/publications (last accessed 2 January 2007.

Heseltine, M. (2006), Question Time, Thames Gateway Forum. Available at http://www.thamesgatewayforum.co.uk (last accessed 23 November 2006).

Hitchen, G. (2005), 'What Will the Creative Industries Do For The Thames Gateway', in *Re:new – Regeneration News in the Thames Gateway*, 25, June, p. 3. Available at http://www.thames-gateway.org.uk (last accessed 2 January 2007).

Holden, J. (2006), *Cultural Value and the Crisis of Legitimacy: Why Culture Needs a Democratic Mandate*, London, Demos.

International Financial Services London (2006), *City Indicators Bulletin*. Available at http://www.ifsl.org.uk.

Jowell, T. (2006), 'Embedding Culture into Thames Gateway', Thames Gateway Forum (author's notes).

Lewis, C. (2006), 'Outlook for UK Public Finances Worsens Slightly in London's Economy Today', No. 52, *GLA Economics*, December.

Livingstone, K. (2004), Foreword *London's Cultural Capital: Realising the Potential of a World Class City*, Greater London Authority. Available at http://www.london.gov.uk (last accessed 3 January 2007).

London Cultural Consortium. Available at http://www.london.gov.uk (last accessed 3 January 2007).

McCarthy, R. (2006), Thames Gateway Forum, London Excel. Available at http://www. thamesgatewayforum.co.uk (last accessed 22 November 2006).

Marlow, D. (2006), Thames Gateway Forum, London Excel. Available at http://www. thamesgatewayforum.co.uk (last accessed 22 November 2006).

Melville, D. and Theseira, M. (2006), 'Borough Employment Projections to 2026: The Detailed Methodology', Working Paper 18, *GLA Economics*.

Mirza, M. (ed.) (2006), *Culture Vultures: Is UK Arts Policy Damaging the Arts?*, London, Policy Exchange.

Mulhern, F. (2000), *Culture/Metaculture*, London, Routledge.

Reay, D. (2005), 'Creative Hubs', *Re:new – Regeneration News in the Thames Gateway*, 25, June, p. 6.

Simon, I. (2007), 'The Open Question of Open Space', *Rising East*, No. 6, January 2007. Available at http://www.risingeast.org (last accessed 2 January 2007).

Smith, C. (2006), 'Embedding Culture into Thames Gateway', Thames Gateway Forum, 23 November (author's notes).

Smith, C. (2006), 'Building a Community', in *The State of the Gateway*, Thames Gateway Forum.

Thames Gateway Culture Task Group (2004), minutes, 19 November. Available at http:// www.livingeast.org.uk (last accessed 2 January 2007).

Trayler, C. (2006), 'Promising to Overcome the North/South Divide', *Rising East*, No. 6, January. Available at http://www.risingeast.org (last accessed 3 January 2007).

Visionary Thurrock (2006) *Thurrock: A Visionary Brief in the Thames Gateway*. Available at http://www.visionarythurrock.org.uk (last accessed 2 January 2007).

Where We Live (2006a), 'Building Communities Through Culture and Sport'. Available at http://www.wherewelive.org.uk (last accessed 2 January 2007).

Where We Live (2006b), 'Culture and Sustainable Communities Joint Agreement'. Available at http://www.wherewelive.org.uk (last accessed 2 January 2007).

Williams, R. (1958a) 'Working Class Culture', in McKenzie, N. (ed.), *Conviction*, London, MacGibbon and Kee, pp. 74–92.

Williams, R. (1958b), *Culture and Society*, London, Chatto and Windus.

Chapter 7

Stuff Happens: Telling the Story and Doing the Business in the Making of Thames Gateway

Philip Cohen

People live, not in places but in the description of places.

Wallace Stevens

Branding used to mean putting your name on hot metal and searing it into the flesh of animals or slaves to mark them out as your property and stop other people claiming it. It was hard, hot, and dirty work. Nowadays branding is soft, clean, cool work – it is done by advertising executives and graphic designers using computers and sitting in offices spinning stories on behalf of their business clients; this kind of branding is not only applied to the packaging or marketing of goods and services but to whole landscapes, cities, buildings, public places where people go to work or relax. Forests and rivers and parks cannot scream with pain when they are subjected to this treatment, but it can be no less a violation of their physical integrity.

Philip Kvaktum
(ex-advertising executive)

No one asked us if we wanted to be part of 'Thames Gateway'. To be honest I am not sure what it means, but if it made for better prospects for my son when he grows up, I'm all for it.

John Penn (resident of Southend)

In this chapter I want to look at the cultural turn in urban regeneration and in particular at the narrative turn in planning theory and practice which is an integral part of it. My focus will be on a wide-angled reading of long-term trends and possible future tendencies in urban planning and policymaking, but focused on the prospects – or lack of them – for that extraordinary concatenation of places which has come to be known as Thames Gateway. I am trying to find out, through a critical ethnography of its everyday business conduct and a detailed reading of its planning and promotional literatures, how the Gateway is being made up, in the double sense of being invented and implemented, as it goes along by the people who are responsible for its delivery.[1] How far are existing forms of civic

---

1   In developing this line of thought I am grateful to discussions with Syd Jeffers, Michael J. Rustin, Marta Rabikowska, Paul Watt, Tom Wengraf, Michael Keith, Michael

imagineering and urban impression management up to this task? Are we seeing a new style of governance emerge dependant not so much on media spin but upon the active conscription of potentially discordant voices and oppositional narratives on which the legitimacy of the planning process has itself come to depend?

The New Regionalism is the New Localism

The Thames Gateway project is part of a wider political and economic strategy to promote a new form of deregulated regionalism. The aim of regional policy is no longer to serve as a mechanism for the central state to tackle structural inequalities through redistributive forms of public investment, for example by channelling resources from the relatively well off south-east to the north of England; today the aim is to enhance local competitive advantage in the global economy by building upon existing or endogenous material assets by linking them to indigenous cultural or social ones.[2]

As an instance of this 'new regionality', the Thames Gateway is designed to be an elastic space of market driven economic activity whose supply chains connect downriver London to Continental Europe and the rest of the world. At the same time, in order to market Thames Gateway as the site for an inflow of major new investment and population and coordinate the area's regeneration, it has been necessary to develop a new politico-administrative apparatus of quite Byzantine complexity, one of whose key roles is to coordinate a branding strategy aimed at constructing an overall cultural identity for the region to make it seem a desirable place to live and work for its target populations.

Amongst other things this exercise involves inventing a whole new set of estuarial traditions, linked to ecological and heritage sites, in order to stitch together a Thames Gateway story to fill the vacuum created by the collapse of the old river and port economy. These traditions have partly to be woven out of the unravelled storylines associated with the maritime and industrial trades which for over three centuries materially connected communities living on the north and south banks of the Thames. These narrative threads now have to be stitched into a post-imperial and post-industrial landscape – one based not so much on the flow of capital goods but of information and cultural goods. The prime mover for the unfolding plot of regeneration is no longer the river itself – now relegated to a supporting role as a purveyor of carefully edited picturesque waterfront views – but the road, rail and air transport links which connect the region to Europe.

Wherever else this has happened the result has been what planners now call 'splintering urbanism'. This latest version of the dual city argument is associated

---

Edwards and Penny Bernstock, with the usual caveat that none of them should be held responsible for the views expressed here.

2   See the contributions to John Allen and Doreen Massey (eds), *Rethinking the Region: Spaces of Neo-Liberalism*, London, Routledge, 1998.

with the work of Stephen Graham and Simon Marvin[3] and highlights the role of specialised communications infrastructures of many kinds (superhighways, fibre optic cable networks, and high-speed transport links) joined up into one-dimensional and exclusionary nodes of activity mainly accessible to the privileged. One of the concomitants of this globalised urban landscape is a new kind of 'terminal architecture': giant shedlike structures housing logistic centres and transport hubs, sport stadia, or entertainment complexes, often existing alongside featureless dormitory-type suburbs populated by commuters still trapped in the gravitational pull of the metropolitan economy.[4] In the case of Thames Gateway, such an outcome may be one of its regeneration logics but it is also strongly contra-indicated: nothing is more calculated to put off the international companies seeking to relocate their HQs in high quality environments than proximity to such sites.

The main attempt to mitigate this effect has been to try to cultivate emotional attachment to certain imaginative descriptions – or rather re-brandings – of place. Thames Gateway is to be a 'sustainable community', to hold out the promise of new and more environmentally friendly forms of civic amenity, held together by a shared sense of belonging and 'place identity'. So just at the point when regionalism goes global in a material sense, it also goes local in purely symbolic terms.

Regenspiel

What resources are there for such a re-imagination of the Thames Gateway as offering both a prospect on the global knowledge economy and a refuge from the storms of technological hypermodernity? We might expect that Estuary English – that peculiar sociolect where the received pronunciation of the East End Cockney fuses with the standardised vowels of the suburban middle class – might provide a key to navigating the new cultural map; in so far as it communicates the flattened accentuations of a social landscape which is all blurred edges it is in fact the exact linguistic register of New Labour's social project. Yet the actual language in which the Thames Gateway story has been described as a planning project is very different. It has been captured accurately enough by the inventors of a new planning game, which has had a samizdat circulation amongst regeneration professionals over the past few years, author unknown, but rumoured to be a bored bureaucrat working for one of the Thames Gateway agencies:[5]

---

3   Stephen Graham and Simon Marvin, *Splintering Urbanism*, London, Routledge, 2001. For earlier versions of the dual version thesis and a critique of this polarisation model see P. Cohen, 'City as Image, Body, Text', in S. Watson and G. Bridges (eds), *Blackwell Companion to the City*, London, Blackwell, 2001.

4   See Martin Pawley, *Terminal Architecture*, London, Reaktion Books, 1998.

5   I am grateful to Carole Snee for bringing this little gem to my attention. It circulated in the form of an email amongst planners for several years, being added to and refined en route.

Too bored to think of a confusing, but seemingly meaningful phrase for that important report? Then try the Random Regenerator Regenerator.

Whenever you need to say something abstract to bamboozle your reader, but can't be bothered to think, just make up any three-digit number and then find the matching word from each column. For example, 424 produces 'Practical Community Involvement' – something every project needs. Or 269 produces 'Joined-up Neighbourhood Capacity' and who could manage without it?

It's the gift that keeps on giving.

Random Regeneration Regenerator					
Column 1		**Column 2**		**Column 3**	
1	Inclusive	1	Area-based	1	Renewal
2	Joined-up	2	Community	2	Regeneration
3	Consensual	3	Sustainable	3	Development
4	Practical	4	People-led	4	Involvement
5	Evaluated	5	Strategic	5	Revitalisation
6	Diverse	6	Neighbourhood	6	Synergy
7	Balanced	7	Best-value	7	Opportunities
8	Responsive	8	Sensitive	8	Initiatives
9	Supportive	9	Monitored	9	Capacity

Figure 7.1   The Random Regenerator Regenerator

What I am going to call '*regenspiel*' consists in a lexicon of portmanteau words – words that can be made to mean almost anything to anyone – which are endlessly reiterated in various permutations and sometimes collocated into catch phrases. How about Inclusive Community Opportunities being delivered through Responsive Best-value Involvement? The words are drawn from diverse vocabularies, principally those of business and management studies supplemented by social and environmental science, to constitute a distinctive syntax of governance. They permeate the diction of business meetings as much as they do the style of report writing and the audiovisual presentation of ideas.

As an example of how this language game works, consider this extract from a meeting between a local authority planner and a private developer discussing how they should respond to a new government initiative designed to strengthen the governance of Thames Gateway:

Planner:	In terms of the new strategic framework we need to ensure our responsibility matrix is tweaked to send the right signals about partnership commitment ...
Developer:	Our corporate mission statement has been updated so it is in full accord with the new guidelines ...

Planner (interrupting): That must include the community cohesion agenda
of course.

Developer: No problems there, everyone is on board for that, lets
just hope the thing gets bottomed out quickly and
DCLG get their act together on this one ...

The syntax of *regenspiel* is an extreme case of what linguists call *nominalisation*, in which actions are turned into objects and verbal processes are turned into abstract nouns.[6] At its simplest this involves the deletion of concrete human agency and attribution and their replacement by abstract entities which are invested with a performative function as the chief protagonists of the storyline. So instead of a transactive model of causality involving a) an actor, b) a process of modal action described by a verb, located in a specific time and place and c) predicated on a consequential effect, we have an account dominated by purely impersonal and often literally non-verb-alisable processes of agency and accountability.

So instead of saying 'some people a) have organised a campaign to do something b) about conditions c) in their area d)', we talk about 'consensual people-led regeneration'. Instead of telling a story about how the management of Ford Europe decided to sack 4,000 workers at its car assembly plant at Dagenham and offered to retrain them to set up their own small businesses, we talk about how Ford pioneered a new 'workforce remodelling plan'.

The preponderance of agentless passive verb forms is a notable feature of this discourse: nobody ever seemingly does anything to anyone, stuff just happens. The syntax creates a world of de-contextualised thinglike abstract entities, often reduced to acronyms which have the mysterious capacity of acting or being acted upon, but lack any attributable responsibility for the outcome. For example in a recent statement to the House of Commons, the Minister for Local Government is quoted as saying that he was going to:

> develop proposals for multi-area agreements encouraging local authorities to agree collective targets for economic development priorities and work with interested cities and sub-regions on the scope of statutory and sub-regional arrangements which could allow greater devolution of national and economic functions.[7]

which, roughly translated, means 'we are going to try to return powers of decision making over economic affairs to local level'!

Although it is sometimes possible to translate this kind of gobbledegook so that human agency can be linguistically extracted and recovered from it, in general this is an idiom of extreme de-personalisation; the fact that human actions or inactions have consequences is no longer part of the story. En route, intelligible causality and attributable meanings disappear and this process is built into the way planning is discursively organised.

---

6   See Gunther Kress and Robert Hodge, *Language as Ideology*, London, Routledge and Kegan Paul, 1979.

7   Quoted by Simon Hoggart in the *Guardian*, 13 July 2007.

Any piece of planning literature is the work of many hands, its co-construction is embedded in a complex web of interlocution, argumentation, discussion, dialogue and debate in which conflicting ideas, priorities and interests are articulated by numerous protagonists. All this normally goes on behind closed doors, governed by rules of professional secrecy and by confidentiality clauses in contracts, well beyond the reach of public scrutiny. And so in the text that finally emerges little or none of this conversational traffic – the real dynamic of authorship – is recorded. Instead we get a seamless flow of affirmative statements and propositions conveyed as an authoritative monologue through impersonally voiced prose. To mitigate this effect the document is usually prefaced by a short 'personal' endorsement by a representative of the commissioning body, often accompanied by a handwritten signature – it is this imprimatur which authorises the text, guarantees its regime of truth and, in the case of statutory instruments and policy documents, invests it with performative function in enacting what it prescribes. Yet this is an illocutionary gesture which has written the interlocutor out of the act – a form of authorisation that deletes authorial agency.

The linguistic process of nominalisation which I have described provides at once the medium and the message of this syntax of governance. So we arrive at the apparent paradox that *regenspiel* is an idiom of almost total opacity which nevertheless declares itself to be a medium of transparency. In fact we are dealing with a contradiction that has real and not merely rhetorical effects. The more human agency and accountability is repressed or deleted from planning discourses as part of the bureaucratic attempt to control all possible outcomes, the more it returns through the backdoor via popular – and sometimes populist – conspiracy theories which demonise particular developers, single out incompetent planning officials, or pillory corrupt politicians. There is a whole genre of urbanistic mythology devoted to these epic struggles of Good against Evil: visionary planners pitted against nasty NIMBYites, heroic communitarians standing firm against the bulldozers of the corporate state, the little people uniting to protect their neighbourhood and way of life from the onward march of rapacious developers and Big Capital. Even the most sober and prosaic narratives of urban renewal and decline, decked out with portmanteau buzzwords and statistical tables, often adhere to a similar Manichean plot.

However, regeneration professionals are increasingly beginning to question the bureaucratic methodology and language through which they conduct their business and to demand a more open, accessible and above all vernacular framework of public deliberation around regeneration issues. It is this communicative turn with its emphasis on critically examining the rhetorics of regeneration and with its advocacy of storytelling as part of the planner's toolkit that I now want to look at in more detail.

Two Models of Urban Modernity

In order to understand the logic of this shift and what it might or might not accomplish we have to get some of the back story.[8] In the immediate period of post-war reconstruction the planner was a public hero – it was the high moment of modernism in which urban policymakers, urban planners, designers and architects for a time combined forces to remake the devastated cities of Europe in the image of a shared rationality. This was a project organised around common norms of social regulation, spatial zoning and the scientific allocation and administration of public amenities and resource. Nevertheless, if we look a bit closer we can see that there were actually two quite different and largely incompatible models of modernity at work.

The first saw modernisation as a gradual evolutionary process of urban renovation, rehabilitation and change, building on what was viable in the existing urban fabric and infilling where possible with new structures and practices. The aim was to recreate the *polis*, build a new and more democratic urban public realm through an animation of collective memory allied to principles of common hope for the future. Organicist metaphors of growth prevail in this account; the citizen as both worker and consumer is addressed as an integrated member of the body politic, potential narrator of the city as *lieu de memoire* and as human platform for experimenting with new and embryonic forms of modernity. Urban design and architecture are given a privileged role in providing a support system for this patchworked enterprise of progressive urban reform.

We are more familiar with the second model, both because it became the dominant one, and ultimately brought the whole project of modernism into public disrepute, and also because as social scientists, or even socialists, we are more implicated in it. This is a story of modernity as a more or less violent break with the past – a process of creative destruction which produces new spaces and times and new people through the introduction of transformative technologies of production, circulation, regulation and power. The coordination of this process of abrupt modernisation is allotted to a form of social/ist-cum-scientific administration which produces blueprints for the future based on norms of efficiency and the application of rational instrumentality to every aspect of social, economic and political life. Here urban planning and policymaking (rather than architecture or design) become the key drivers of change. As a result the importance of local historical or geographical determinants in the definition and growth of cities is played down or ignored.

By the 1960s the tension between the historicist and socio-technicist dreams of modernity was coming to a head. Slum clearance, motorway building, new towns, green belts, the M25, national parks, the Right to Roam, the Coastal and Thameside Paths and the experiments in city centre renewal in Birmingham

---

8   I am indebted in what follows to the account given by Paul Rabinow 'On the Archaeology of Late Modernity' in his *French Modern Norms and Forms of the Social Environment*, Chicago, IL, University of Chicago, 1989.

and Bristol all became the site of a series of running battles between progressive conservationists and the slash and burn school of regeneration.

Let us note in passing that two very different kinds of narrative are being proposed here, each with quite distinct performative effects. In the first case, the story of regeneration is told as a series of incremental steps up a ladder of civilisational progress, the rungs being formed by inherited features of the urban landscape. The role of the plan here is to to create a secure framework – we might almost say a career structure – for its piecemeal implementation, while the role of the planner is essentially that of a social engineer. In the second case, the story is constituted in and by a moment of revolutionary rupture; it is necessary to produce a genealogy of the plan which stresses its unique *sui generis* nature and this makes the planner its sole architect or designer, building the future on the ruins of the past.

Through most of the twentieth century, Western urbanism was characterised by a running battle between these two standpoints; in different countries and at different times, first one and then the other became dominant. As with all conflicts of long duration, there have been standoffs, compromise formations and points of convergence, as well as open confrontation.

In the case of the Thames Gateway Plan it is possible detect both tendencies at work. There are those, like Tristram Hunt, who want to build on existing patterns of urban settlement and preserve their distinctive historical and geographical character whilst adapting them to the exigencies of globalisation.[9] And those stress the heroic nature of the project, in terms of its scope and scale and the massive social and economic transformation which it will bring to areas of environmental dereliction.[10]

The Plan is Not the Script

One of the fall-out effects from this lack of a unifying vision has been that architects, social scientists, designers and planners have gone their separate ways, into different silos of professional expertise from which they occasionally sally forth to accuse their erstwhile partners of betraying their preferred version of modernity.

However, both models of modernity share some common assumptions about just what has to be reformed. One concerns the failure of the ordinary citizen to 'plan ahead'. The capacity for prudential action, based on an analysis of past, present and future circumstances, is no longer considered merely an individual moral virtue; under this model it becomes a normalising administrative function to be operated on – and preferably by – the whole population. A forensic and panoptic social science develops around this concept, based on the effective deployment of statistics and forecasting models as a means to understand and

---

9   See, for example, *Heroic Change: Securing Environmental Quality in Thames Gateway*, Thames Gateway London Partnership, 2004.

10   See his article on Thames Gateway in the *Guardian* Supplement, 6 July 2007.

conform what is going on in cities in terms of certain standardised measurable indices of behaviour. This in turn enables planning to evolve into a strategy of social defence against dangerous elements inside and outside the body politic.[11]

Whether it was the failure of the attempt to planify society or its success which has brought the whole project of modernity into public disrepute and turned the planner from hero to villain of the regeneration story is difficult to say. In any case, the association of centralised top down state planning with the corrupt and dictatorial regimes of Stalinism has done much to discredit the whole enterprise. In the era of just-in-time production, state socialism with its five and ten year plans that seek to conform the vicissitudes of economic development to the iron laws of history just seems an anachronism. However, the technicist variant exerts its own tyrannies of scope and scale, with its rigid diachronic schemas for project delivery, the milestones that become millstones and the performance targets that remain asymptotically always just out of reach, all of which have created their own counter-narratives of despair.

In any case, I think we have to understand the public disenchantment with master planning and with grand projects, and how this has become focused currently on Thames Gateway, in terms of a contradictory processes between, on the one hand, the general diffusion and pervasive function of planning as a metaphor we now increasingly live by and, on the other, the incapacity of this planification to in fact deal with the instabilities, insecurities, precariousness and generally chaotic synchronicity that now characterises economic, social and cultural life in these hard global times.

In a way this is not exactly news. The map is not and never will be the territory, even in the age of GPS, as all those cautionary tales about motorists ending up in rubbish tips or nearly driving over cliffs because they are following the instructions of the talking map, not looking out of the window at the road ahead, so eloquently testify.

There is no simple correlation, or indeed any fixed principle of correspondence, between narrative and spatial form. The story of linear cities does not require to be told as the unfolding of a unidirectional plot line. Commuting is a travelling story that goes both ways. The network society may seem like an action maze, but its narratives, however fragmentary and dispersed, do not have to conform to this model. The relationship between a city centre and its periphery is not always that of a plot to a subplot and stream of consciousness is not necessarily the preferred moral compass for navigating the space of flows.

By the same token the plan is not the script, or for that matter a road map whose coordinates are already plotted and fixed in advance. In fact, scripts work only where the context or framing of the interaction is known and generally predictable because governed by stable norms. But under what Luc Boltanski

---

11   Good examples of this trend are the London Borough of Newham's Neighbourhood Information Management System (NIMS) and Knowledge East's Thames Gateway Knowledge Platform, which are producing virtual panoptica through the online collation of social statistics, often in open source formats rendering much routine social science redundant in the process.

and Eve Chiapelli have called the new spirit of capitalism, these conditions of emplotment obtain less and less.[12] Against this background the symbolic function of the plan is to conceptualise actions which cannot otherwise be configured because the action is too complicated, or there are too many partners, or the framework of participation is unstable, or the duration resists conventional periodisation. This is clearly the case with Thames Gateway. The performative role of the master plan is to attempt to regroup actions whose outcome is unpredictable by subsuming them under some higher order principle or aim. It thus offers an ordered sequence of actions governed by teleological rather than transactive causality and en route establishes a network of imaginary correspondences between map and territory. In other words, it serves as a magical defence against the destabilisation of norms, the collapse of progress and the general crisis of postmodernity.[13]

Another symptom of this crisis is the growth in popularity of life-planning classes. From lifestyle gurus to assertiveness training, from personal development counselling to career's advice, there is a whole army of professional experts to help us make our life course unfold according to a prescribed and if possible pre-scripted set of aims and objectives, to put ourselves in the driving seat of our own destinies (as one advertisement put it).

In many cases the life plan turns out to be a business plan in disguise, for nowadays everyone who is serious about making their way in the world has to have a business plan; poets, musicians, plumbers and beauticians all need a plan to minimise the costs or risks (including negative impacts) of any course of action they might undertake while maximising the benefits or positive impacts which might flow from it. Under this new regime of value every life – including the life of the most marginal and powerless – can seemingly become the centre of its own rational calculability.

In some of the more ruthless versions of life planning we can detect the trace of the original genealogy of the plan, namely as a device of military strategy or political campaigning. Military and political planning both rely on the operation of a rigid chain of command to coordinate the deployment of forces to outmanoeuvre or overwhelm the enemy's positions whilst protecting one's own. Outside the military and political establishments only the very wealthy or the very paranoid (and sometimes they are the same people) have the means at their disposal to pursue this option at all systematically.

More usually today, life planning is about how to network – how to win friends and influence people, how to insinuate yourself into important agencies of patronage and preferment, how to advance your interests or your career – for example, if you are an academic, by attending and performing at conferences and seminars.

As for urban plans, town plans, master plans and site plans, all these have at times been 'militarised' and implemented through a hermetic command structure,

---

12   See Luc Boltanski and Eve Chiapello, *The New Spirit of Capitalism*, London, Verso, 2005.

13   See Raphael Baroni, *La tension narrative*, Paris, Flammarion, 2007.

especially during the high period of modernism, primarily as a strategy of social defence against disease, deprivation and degeneration. But today urban planning is pretty much demilitarised; it has to operate within a framework of market-driven deregulation and in order to sustain any public – let alone street – credibility it has to subsume elements of both life and business planning into its vocabulary and repertoire of procedures. In other words planning has to become networky, interactive and user-friendly; it has formally to simulate a democratic process even if substantively it has little to do with it. And this is where the narrative turn in planning theory and its practice of governance comes in.

The Narrative Turn

In part, the narrative turn can be put down to impression management. Planners want to be the good guys again; they need to put a human face on what is widely seen to be a remote, bureaucratic and impermeable process of decision-making. But is there more to the current fashion for communicative planning than restoring the planner's professional *amour propre*?

One major driver is the need to reconstitute a realm of public deliberation about planning issues; this has been widely eroded by the effect of what Raymond Williams has called mobile privatism and by the associated withdrawal of large sections of the population from active engagement in civic affairs. To reverse this process the aim is to create a simulacrum of political empowerment through purely symbolic action (i.e. in a way that does not involve any actual redistribution of resource or the conflicts that this might engender); this is to be done primarily through a *re-enchantment of the public realm* as a space and time of purely cultural representation in which differences can be celebrated and consensus managed.

The need for planners to develop better communication skills for this purpose is strongly emphasised by the Egan Review.[14] The Review argues that the training of planning professionals needs to be transformed to create a new community of practice in which the arts of public advocacy and impression management take on a more central role. Planners, architects, designers, surveyors, developers and construction companies should no longer be backroom boys and girls, but should be upfront about what they do. Planning becomes a conversation not just with clients, but with all those affected by the outcome. Equally, Egan suggests that better communication needs to be established between the different planning disciplines, who must be persuaded to leave the safety of their respective professional silos if anything like the joined-up thinking required to deliver 'sustainable communities' is ever to happen.

Although it would seem that the narrative turn, as canvassed by Egan, attempts to make the planning process more transparent and accountable, it is important to point out that, within this frame, the plan is no longer a site for the exercise of the sociological imagination – how society might be differently organised in the present – but for the free play of the geographical and historical imagination.

14   See *Skills for Sustainable Communities*, London, ODPM, 2004.

How the space and time of the city be differently imagined? How can its secret or forgotten places and moments be restored to the public narrative and used for emplotting scenarios of an alternative future based upon some utopic or uchronic ideal of urban community? This kind of narrative landscaping has become an essential element in the cultural re-branding of regeneration zones as sites for prospective investment and as desirable areas to live for the high fliers of the corporate knowledge economy. They want to feel that in relocating their offices or homes, they are putting down roots into richer and more fertile soil than what appears to be just another brownfield site.

We might then ask what kind of narratives are suitable for the task.[15] Should Thames Gateway be written and read as a picaresque adventure story for boys featuring heroic bands of middle-class urban pioneers who settle in the badlands of Benfleet and Billericay and make them fit for literary and cultural habitation? Or as a *bildungsroman* in which the journey of the plan itself is traced as a series of formative stages or moments in its inner development from birth to maturity? Or perhaps as a gothic horror story about the fate of those innocents who wander into this Cockney Cyberia, get lost in its labyrinthine structures of its governance and find themselves stranded somewhere along the A13 with no destination home? Or in view of its long-running nature, episodic structure and complex set of plots and subplots, perhaps a soap opera would be the most appropriate model?

Following in the steps of Tzvetan Todorov and the French narratologists[16] we can usefully distinguish between three major types of regeneration story:

1) *Urban folk tales*, where the logic of successive actions and reactions shapes the unfolding of the plot (a.k.a. plan) and privileges the relation of historical events in terms of certain narrative roles played by their protagonists. Who does what to whom and where under which circumstances and with what outcomes is the central issue. The formal structure of the tale is organised around these moments:

   • the advent and recognition of a constitutive lack or loss of amenity or resource, which creates a disequilibrium or dislocation and also makes a starting point for the story to be told;
   • the assignation of a task or quest (with or without interdicts and sanctions) to suppress the lack or make good the loss and restore the status quo;
   • the struggle to achieve the task, through the overcoming of obstacles, the avoidance of traps, the defeat of enemies, etc.;

---

15   See Franco Moretti, *Atlas of the European Novel*, London, Verso, 2003, for a discussion of the interplay between strategies of emplotment and cartographies of the city.

16   See Tzvetan Todorv, *Genres en discours*, Paris, Editions du Seuil, 1978 and Claude Bremond, *Logique du recit*, Paris, Editions du Seuil, 1973. See also the pioneering work of Ruth Finnegan, *Tales of the City: A Study of Narrative and Urban Life*, Cambridge, Cambridge University Press, 1998.

- coda: the achievement, or lack of it, of the quest and its consequences for the narrator and the community.

Every NIMBY story I have ever heard broadly conforms to this pattern. We should note that because one action always leads to another and the relation between actions is strongly invested with causality and consequence, we get a *post hoc propter hoc* kind of explanation of the world: e.g., first there were plenty of jobs and everything was fine, then the Blacks, Poles, etc. came, then there was a lot of unemployment, therefore the Blacks, Poles etc. took our jobs. En route the narrator as chief protagonist creates a world in which there are only active heroes or passive victims, there is little scope for more subtle characterisation or the exploration of ambivalence.

2) *Grand narratives* constitute the second major genre of urban storytelling. Here, a universal rule, abstract idea or generic aim produces and guides the peripatetics of the story. This gives the story a teleological character in unfolding a particular proposition about how the world works and what drives it forward according to some ultimate law or end. Actions are related to one another through the intermediary of this formulaic proposition, often linked to the enunciation of a moral precept. For example in my study of planning business meetings I found that storytelling was often organised to illustrate such maxims as 'there is no gain without pain', 'everyone is a winner', or 'good is the enemy of great'.

    The story takes a line of argument for a walk as a series of moves along a determinate path: *disequilibrium* (the advent of the plan) – *provocation-action – sanction – re-equilibrium* (the plan modified). The plot pivots around the issue of passage to action or its blockage and, where there is such a passage, whether the original aim is achieved or not. Prolepsis – the advancement of a storyline in anticipation of objections or obstacles to its fulfilment – is the key organising principle here and one which, to jump appropriately ahead in the argument, is very germane to the Thames Gateway story. En route, human agency is either deleted altogether, or else people are portrayed as the more or less passive bearers of the structures/functions/ideas they are made to represent, at the limit becoming little more than ventriloquists' dummies for the argument, puppets of forces they neither understand or control. For obvious reasons this is still the preferred grammar for the stories which planners, politicians and others in positions of power like to tell because it authorises their actions without making them responsible for them. But the same grammar can also articulate counter-hegemonic narratives of a similarly monologic character. I have already suggested how and why nominalisation is the preferred idiom for this kind of discourse.

c) The third kind of regeneration story might be called *hermeneutic*, in that it privileges what we know and understand about a given chain of events. The quest for reflexive or critical knowledge and its obstacles (ignorance, prejudice etc) are the key dynamic here. One reflection is related to another reflection via a continual return to the events to investigate their meaning – including the nature of their narration – in search of clues for what is missing, lost, obscured. The paradigm is the detective story. The central issue is the relationship between ignorance or error and knowledge and who knows what about whom. The narrator returns to the same events again and again in order, through their retelling, to investigate and uncover their hidden meaning. This iterative search for truth brings us very close to the conjectural method of a certain kind of human science and in particular to the narrative procedures of the critical ethnographic research story. For obvious reasons this is the narrative genre best adapted to an iterative model of participative planning, and is also the approach adopted by some recent accounts of community action around planning issues.

Now clearly, these three kinds of storytelling do not exist in isolation but in a variety of weak and strong combinations. But one of the effects of the narrative turn in planning theory and practice is that, under the guise of promoting a new hermeneutics of storytelling as a means of opening up a space for a much wider range of stakeholders to have their say about the issues, there has been a covert and largely unwitting conversion of mythological stories into ideological ones, in a way that continues to legitimate the planner's tale, selectively recruiting those aspects of community narratives which endorse the authorised plan view, whilst neutralising or suppressing those 'unfortunate ' elements which do not fit – or actively disturb – the official plot. This is a form of asset stripping performed under the rhetorical guise of cultural empowerment. In the name of promoting democracy, dissenting voices are enrolled into discourses within which they are effectively neutralised.

The advocates of planning as communicative action are disarmingly frank about this. 'Stories told persuasively can be used to win people over to a planners way of thinking.'[17] Perhaps surprisingly, the community stories which carry most weight, the ones which are likely to be quoted in reports and which are used to represent the 'voice of the people' or serve as an index of effective consultation are likely to be those which echo the perspectives and priorities of the planners or their clients.

The fact that what provokes a story and makes it worth telling is something disruptive and untoward, something which defamiliarises the world or challenges the status quo (viz. a funny thing happened to me on the way to the planning enquiry – it got abolished) and that large-scale urban regeneration by definition involves a process of dislocation which is more or less traumatic in its effect on existing communities – this fact is used to suggest that the deployment of storytelling as a planning tool can have a therapeutic effect in normalising the situation and enabling people who might otherwise protest or go into a state of shock to come to terms with the situation and accept what they would otherwise oppose. To put it no stronger, this seems a rather cynical exploitation of the narrative impulse – manipulating the desire to make sense of a chaotic world by making coherent stories out of it in order to further your own ends.

---

17   From the editorial by Barbara Eckstein and James Throgmorton in *Story and Sustainability*, Cambridge, MA, MIT Press, 2003.

Yet the narrative turn in planning also holds the rather dangerous implication that the stories planners tell and the plans and reports they produce have to be understood performatively, that is, as demonstrations of professional authority and expertise or displays of communicative competence and power. Their coherence may, in other words, be purely rhetorical. The knowledge or truth claims – the claim that these statements correspond to how things really are, or how they are going to be – can just as easily become subject to challenge and counter claim.[18] Once the proverbial cat is let out of the bag and it becomes apparent that the map is *not* the territory and the plan is *not* the script, and once the discrepancy between the authorised versions of what Thames Gateway is about and what is actually happening on the ground become common knowledge, then no amount of impression management will maintain the fiction that things are otherwise. Moreover, the introduction of narrativity as a key principle for articulating urban planning issues cannot help but privilege agency over process; even if the agency in question is an abstract idea or social force, nevertheless the potential for re-inscribing individual subjectivity or collective social action is there, with all its capacity to disrupt the officially authorised storyline, to suggest alternative and perhaps happier endings than those initially envisaged, or to unsettle, even if it is rarely possible to fundamentally change, the plot.

Thames Gateway: A Case in Point

How far does the Thames Gateway plan for sustainable communities, to give it its full title, illustrate the issues I have been discussing. Certainly we find here a rich storehouse of portmanteau buzzwords which are repeated like a mantra across both the planning and promotional literatures. Thames Gateway, we learn, will be about:

i)   building economic prosperity and thriving town centres;
ii) protecting and enhancing the environment;
iii) creating decent and affordable places to live;
iv) tackling disadvantage and promoting social inclusion;
v)   establishing high quality local services and infrastructure;
vi) creating mixed and balanced communities.[19]

---

18   See James Throgmorton, *Planning as Pursuasive Storytelling*, Chicago, IL, University of Chicago Press, 1996. Throgmorton's account of his critical engagement with a popular community and environmental campaign mobilised against a hubritic form of corporate master planning in Chicago is the best example to date of the application of this approach to understanding what is at stake in the regeneration process. For a more philosophically-grounded discussion of the rhetorical turn in planning theory and practice and its function as potential space for regenerating the process of public deliberation, see John Forrester, *Planning in the Face of Power*, Berkeley, CA, University of California Press, 1989.

19   See the Egan Review, p. 46.

Note the use of agentless verbs – it is never clear who exactly is actually going to do all this, only that these will be the outcomes of the process. What is remarkable is the ease with which what are essentially moral exhortations couched in the idiom of what Marx called dumb generalities – or if you like a commonsense wish list – become performance indicators and targets indexed to highly sophisticated statistical measures, as if this would somehow enable their effortless achievement. The idea that there might be conflicting priorities and that the achievement of one of these aims (such as tackling chronic disadvantage amongst the de-industrialised working class through redistributive measures) might also put strain on another (viz. plans for maximising the economic prosperity of affluent young professionals) is never entertained. In Thames Gateway we are clearly supposed to be living in best of all possible worlds.

However, conflict there most certainly is as we can see in the competing strategies of modernisation associated with the contrasting plan views of Terry Farrell and John Prescott. In this scenario Farrell stands for urban renaissance in the inner Gateway – the contemporary version of organic historicism beefed up with the green sustainability agenda and his plan for transforming the outer Gateway into a national wetlands park. Meanwhile Prescott is made to represent technocratic crypto-Stalinist command structure planning, which will roll out cheap substandard mass housing for lower income public service workers across the whole floodplain.

Figure 7.2 *Evening Standard* **newspaper cutting – Prescottograd**

As for the narratives of decline and renewal which frame the Thames Gateway plot, there is a point of convergence around a common negative view of manufacture and its legacy. Indeed, heavy industry, rather than global capitalism has become the villain of the piece. The decline of the smokestack industries and hence of the industrial working class is heralded not as an unmitigated disaster for hundreds of thousands whose lives and livelihoods were destroyed in the process but as an unparalleled opportunity to create a new knowledge-based economy in which, however, they will play little or no active part. The treatment of brownfield sites illustrates the point clearly enough. These sites do not appear on the heritage maps – the idea that they are important *lieux de memoire* for a whole generation of workers is ignored. Instead they are marked out as sites of environmental degradation requiring special measures of remediation. But what do these sites really pollute if not the clean green image of Thames Gateway as carrying the good tidings of prosperity for all down river and up market? If brownfield sites leave such a bad smell in the nostrils of planners and property developers perhaps it is because what has to be erased is precisely the history of the urban modernities that first made them possible.

The dream might be of building the New Jerusalem (or at least a Regional Casino) in the green and pleasant marshlands of Rainham, of turning Southend into a glittering hub of the international tourist economy, or of making over Basildon and Romford into magnets for the new creative class while Chatham, now the dockyards have closed, resumes its rightful role as the guardian of our national maritime heritage. But to suggest that this kind of culture-led regeneration can be achieved through an exercise in rebranding, or to suppose that the construction of a new narrative – Thames Gateway – can do the trick in making such disparate places swing into higher economic gear, requires an effort of imagination which has nothing sociological about it. It has little to do with the actual lives of the people who live and work there but certainly requires a strenuous reinvention of history and geography.

New Things Happen

As an example of some of these tendencies I want to look at a recent report produced by CABE at the behest of Yvette Cooper, the then communities minister responsible for the Gateway, and commissioned by the Thames Gateway Strategic Partnership.[20] The project set out to map the social, cultural and environmental character of the Gateway with the aim of 'informing the strategic development of its unique identity'. The report claims that it is based on listening to what people in the Gateway have to say. A number of workshops were held, although it seems that most of the people who attended were the usual suspects – professionals of one sort or another already concerned with TG. Sir Peter Hall, the plan's original architect, and Sir Terry Farrell, both have major talk on parts. It is this rather

---

20   See *New Things Happen: A Guide to the Future Thames Gateway*, London, CABE, 2006.

narrow range of quotation and comment which is used to give the text evidential credibility. In contrast, *Gateway People*, the report by IPPR, for all that it is based on only four focus groups, gives a very different and much more negative picture of popular perceptions.[21]

The CABE report is entitled *New Things Happen*, as good an example of nominalisation as you will find, and it is divided into three main sections:

- 'Where It's At', which talks about the economic role of place making;
- 'New Things Happen', which sets out the Gateway's unique selling points (USPs);
- 'Exploring the Vision', which deals in turn with redefining work, reconnecting with nature, reasserting individualism and reinventing identity – the core values the report espouses.

The tone throughout is jaunty and upbeat and is set in the preface by John Sorrell, CABE's chair. He calls the report a 'visionary guide to TG's future' and claims that what has come through in this study is a 'pioneering culture'. He continues, 'Perhaps this comes from living at the turning of the tide. It makes the Gateway feel less like a place and more like a journey' (p. 6).

Two points are perhaps worth making here. To redescribe what purports to be a report of a piece of research in these terms effectively blurs the distinction between an evidence-based policy document and promotional literature – a typical move of the *regenspieler*. Secondly, the image of pioneers living adventurously at the edge of tidal change is a central trope of the whole document. A narrative landscape is mapped, peopled by rugged individualists whose spirit of innovation and enterprise is located both geographically as a special character of estuary dwellers (courtesy of Joseph Conrad) and historically as the special patrimony of an island race (courtesy of Winston Churchill). All kinds of stories are recruited for this purpose. The Plotlanders of Canvey Island, who built their own homes in defiance of the law and all known planning regulations, are welcomed on board, as are the decidedly dodgy dystopic denizens of Iain Sinclair's post-industrial wastelands; Bill Bragg's travelling story of the A13 and Ken Worpole's survey of Essex's radical hinterlands also make guest appearances. All these once discordant voices are made to sing in tune, their descant seamlessly blended into a harmonised discourse of neoliberal modernity. So this is how the Wild East came to be civilised – settled by a new class of ex-urban gentrifiers: by turning its erstwhile economic and social marginality into a unique selling point.

The report's green credentials are impeccable and undoubtedly the sections dealing with environmental issues are the strongest, or at least the most persuasive. Yet the report also dodges the Number 1 issue – the building of so much new housing on a floodplain at a time when some scenarios of global warming predict tidal surges well beyond the capacity of existing barrier defence systems to contain. The Canvey Island floods of 1953 are conspicuous by their absence from a document concerned to establish its roots in local history. Missing too is

---

21   See Jim Bennett and James Morris, *Gateway People*, London, IPPR, 2005.

any mention of recent experiments in designing hydraulic cities to combat flood risk. Presumably in both cases such references might have conjured up less than positive images of the areas past and future. Against this background, all the talk about promoting a new environmental aesthetic 'capable of inspiring innovation in architecture and landscape design' begins to sound like eco-elitism – greening the Gateway to enhance its desirability as a place to live and work for those whose incomes give them a wide range of choice and who can afford to pay more for a better quality environment.

The final section, on reinventing identity, draws extensively on Billy Bragg – with a sideways nod to Simon Schama's *Landscapes of Memory* – to claim that the Thames Estuary is the first port of call for every new influence and as such distils much that is common to a more general national identity. What this wider identity consists of, apparently, is the resilience required to mix local cultures with a continuous influx of new populations and ideas. This robust cosmopolitan character with its 'spirited pioneering identity' is contrasted with 'soulless suburban sprawl' – which, along with industrialism, is the real villain of the CABE regeneration story. The fact that local prides of place can sometimes

Figure 7.3 **'The truth is that identity defines us. It changes perceptions, markets, places. People are much more likely to invest in places that have a clear and valuable identity'**

Source: CABE Report.

turn nasty and be less than welcoming to newcomers, especially if their faces or cultures are visibly different, is not mentioned. Presumably it is not something about which the audience for the report – described as clients and investors in both the public and private sectors – wants to hear. Yet on the last page there is a strangely ambivalent image/text statement which manages to both indirectly recognise and disavow the issue.

On the left-hand side of the page there is an unattributed quote:

> Local people want to ensure their presence is recognised by continuity. This can come down to such simple [and inexpensive: my comment] things such as naming streets after local characters' which in its patronising crassness has surely to win some kind of prize for dropped brick of the year.

On the right-hand side of the page is a photograph of (according to the caption) lollipop-lady Mrs Sutton watching over the morning school run at Southend-on-Sea. The woman in question is shown holding a stop sign, whilst on both sides of the crossing are large billboards advertising luxury apartment interiors, presumably aimed at Southend's new creative class. So just what kind of traffic is she trying to stop? We are left to guess. Mrs Sutton's own views on Thames Gateway or the regeneration of Southend are not available. Perhaps one place to start a different kind of narrative is just there.

So just what kind of narrative turn is happening here? Clearly in terms of the Todorov schema we are dealing with a structure in which the key actants, or drivers of the story, are formulaic ideas: Sustainable Community – Pioneering Spirit, which are variously embodied and articulated by specially designated placeholders. The formal elements of the story are all present: the initial moment of *disequilbrium* represented by the TG plan itself – breaking with old ways of thinking about work, planning and the environment associated with the era of industrialism and suburbanism; the *provocation*, which the report by its very publication is supposed to elicit; the *actions* which are to flow from it – making new things happen; the *sanctions*, which are hinted at in passing if challenges are not met and opportunities missed; and finally *re-equilibrium* – the seamless blending of past, present and future in a new compact between nature and culture, symbolised by the creation of an all-embracing estuarial identity and economy. For this purpose the storyline makes continual use of flashbacks and flash forwards. It is nothing if not *proleptic*; from section to section the argument is advanced in such a fashion as to forestall all possible objections, even though exactly what these might be is never stated! Although much play is made on the notion of the open dialogical nature of the exercise, the wide consultation, and so on, this discourse is as monologic as the most prescriptive kinds of policy statement issuing from a government department.

There are, however, traces of other narrative genres. The mytho-logics of regeneration are present in the epic battle struck between the forces of enlightenment and progress, represented by the knowledge economy, green politics, the new individualism and localism versus the forces of darkness and reaction represented by industrialism, suburban sprawl and the insular solidarities

Figure 7.4   **'Local people want to ensure their presence is recognised by continuity. This can come down to very simple things such as naming streets after local characters'**

Source: CABE Report.

of Old Labour. There are also hints of a hidden hermeneutics centred on the issue of civic disengagement and the democratic deficit, because amidst all the upbeat aspirationalism there is an anxious reiteration of the need to establish a higher common principle to do with a sense of shared belonging or collective identity. There has to be more to place-building than cultivating your own selfish prospects, claiming more room and a better view, or cultivating your garden as a refuge from the storms of history

Finally, buried in all this are some rational propositions about the need to consider new ways of designing and delivering the built environment; in particular there is a useful focus on the need to encourage construction companies to experiment with new ecological building forms which challenge the cultural conservatism of home buyers.

A New Spirit of Capitalism – or Business as Usual?

The broader question raised by the emergence of narrative planning is whether this is business as usual, or whether we are seeing the emergence of a qualitatively different kind of process. Regeneration is often held to exemplify the 'destructive creativity' of modern capitalism. But the cultural turn now seems to promise to effectively mitigate, if not entirely remove, the destructive impact of large-scale urban development and to promote an entirely creative process of environmental and social renewal in which everyone is a winner.

It is perhaps worth noting that the release of this creative energy is only possible because capital has already first destroyed the material and social basis of its own earlier industrial formation and hence cleared the way for the emergence of a 'creative class', that is people who are employed in a wide range of local/global cultural services, including design, marketing and communications. As we have seen, this is the key target population for Thames Gateway and they are indeed a relatively new phenomenon, especially in their mode of attachment to place. For although they are go-getters, constantly on the move and definitely 'going places', they are as concerned with the cultural assets which make an area desirable as they are with the market value of their property; the aesthetics of a neighbourhood are as important to them as its material amenities, transport connectedness and social status. They are part of an enterprise-cum-management culture that is delivering the goods precisely by *not* talking about profit maximisation; growing the business is now about achieving harmony, balance and, of course, sustainability. Norms of efficiency and instrumental rationality are out, constructing the beautifully crafted business plan is in. Courtesy of postmodern management theory, the New Age business person and the evangelical bureaucrat reinvent themselves as artisans of the avant garde. The hip estate agent joins the poet in asserting that 'people live not in places, but in the description of places'. The *regenspieler* reborn fuses language which deletes human agency and causality with its opposite – an idiom of hyper-individualism which proclaims the expressive *jouissance* of 'living the good life'.

Obsessive self-referentiality become a necessary counterpoint to a world in which 'stuff just happens'. Luc Bolantanski and Eve Chiapello have recently discerned here a new spirit of capitalism in which art has replaced religion (more specifically Protestantism), absorbing the aesthetic critique of industrialism into its post-industrial work ethic. Here is how one of its gurus describes the phenomenon:

> The manager knows that the contemporary business world is chaotic and unpredictable, where rules of logic and rationality, let alone morality do not prevail. So he sets out to achieve some kind of aesthetic order and ethical meaning, by providing a quality product and service, and educating the client or consumer to appreciate it.[22]

---

22   John Dobson, *The Art of Management and the Aesthetic Manager*, Cass Business Studies, 2006, p. 108.

Once the irrationality of market forces is fully recognised, the way to go is to go with the global information flow and learn to ride the increasingly unpredictable waves of capitalist renewal rather than attempt to bend these forces to the corporate will. What that means in practice is protecting your own niche market through strenuous networking. So now the script itself has become the plan. Just as the launch of a new policy document becomes an end in itself, in, in terms of the publicity it creates for the 'Thames Gateway brand', so the performativity of the business plan lies in the artfulness or moral persuasiveness with which its mission is communicated to potential clients, not in any evaluation of objective measures of failure or success in its implementation.

The relationship between the cultural turn in regeneration and this aesthetic/ethical makeover of its business conduct was brought home to me in the offices of one of the UK's largest civil engineers, responsible for major development projects in Thames Gateway. The office space was open plan but subdivided by a series of floor to ceiling glass walls. Engraved on each 'wall' was a series of words derived from the company's mission statement, as shown in Figure 7.5.

Figure 7.5   Mission statements

The apparent transparency of the inscriptions – it is possible to see through each word as the eye alights on first one, then another – belies the total opacity of the concepts to which they refer. It is literally impossible to extract any connective meaning from this array of buzzwords, but the palimpsest effect impresses the viewer by its sheer scope and scale.

The narrative turn in Thames Gateway planning certainly makes for a conversational space in which civil and social engineers can once again talk to one another, if only about branding strategies; but it also offers a point of purchase for members of the professional service class who are its preferred investors, workers and residents: it is a story which they can literally buy into.

So have we really arrived at the best of all possible worlds, in which map and territory at last coincide? Unfortunately there is a catch. As Marx once put it, you cannot have a bourgeoisie without also having a proletariat. The professional service class thrown up by the new economy needs another kind of service class belonging to the old one to look after it; it needs people to wash, cook and clean for it; to mend its equipment, service its cars and yachts, mind its children and pets, minister to its recreational needs, staff its wine bars and restaurants, improve its houses, fix its drains and populate its neighbourhoods with a little local colour. This, of course, is precisely the role assigned to the post-industrial working class. The story of London used to be told as a tale of two cities. Will the story of Thames Gateway ultimately have to be told as the latest episode in this long-running saga? Or will those who have so far only been written into the script as walk-on extras somehow muster the capacity to talk back at the plan and insist that they have as large a role to play in shaping the future of Thames Gateway as they had in its past?

PART 2
Case Studies in Urban Change

Chapter 8

City to Sea: Some Socio-Demographic Impacts of Change in East London

Tim Butler, Chris Hamnett, Mark Ramsden and Sadiq Mir

Introduction[1]

The 2001 Census is the most recent comprehensive guide to how East London has been changing on the cusp of the new millennium. What was once the most solidly working-class area of London, and remained so as other areas of the city gentrified and suburbanised, can no longer be described in such simple terms. The mono ethnic white working-class backyard to London is simply no longer describable in such terms. Whilst there can be no dispute about its multi-ethnicity today, social class remains of key importance in describing its current social structure, but is also central to the contemporary dynamic of the area and the nature of the social change which it is undergoing. It is this complex interaction between ethnicity and social class that describes the social mosaic which constitutes East London today.

In this chapter we draw on work that we have been undertaking in an ongoing research project into gentrification, ethnic change and education in East London. Much of the project is devoted to survey and in-depth interview-based fieldwork about the role played by education in understanding social change amongst East London's different ethnic groupings. As part of the preparatory work for this fieldwork we undertook in-depth analysis of the main trends in the social demographics of London in general and East London in particular since 1981 drawing on data from the 1981, 1991 and 2001 censuses. The two main variables with which we were interested in mapping the changing trends were those of social class and ethnicity. This is not as straightforward as it appears: in the case of social class, the Office of National Statistics (ONS) adopted a new measure for the 2001 Census which meant that we had to convert the old measure of socio-economic group (SEG) to the new socio-economic classification (SEC); in the case of ethnicity, not only was there a rapid increase in the velocity of immigration in the 1990s but it involved a new range of ethnic groups that had not previously featured on the 'ethnic radar'. In addition, the ONS introduced new mixed race categories. We discuss the details of both these changes and their interactions

1   We acknowledge the support of the Economic and Social Research Council (RES-000-23-0793 Gentrification, ethnicity and education in East London).

in detail and suggest that they have resulted in a new and emerging matrix of social positions quite unlike anything previously experienced in Britain. In East London this new matrix of class and ethnic positions is probably in sharper focus than in any other city region in the country and the velocity at which individuals are charting their way through them is higher than elsewhere, as our fieldwork is beginning to indicate. However, the headline figures of change in London's ethnic and class structure are dramatic enough on their own to indicate the scale of what is to be investigated in East London. Between 1991 and 2001, London's minority ethnic population increased from approximately 19 per cent to 29 per cent, an increase of 53 per cent. What is critical in understanding the nature of this change is its geography: we can no longer say that the Black and Minority Ethnic (BME) population is concentrated in inner London and that the outer London boroughs are largely 'whitelands': the picture is far more complex with many of these boroughs having not only fast growing BME populations but, in several cases, this group is now, or soon will be, the majority population. In terms of social class, the same turnaround is occurring – in 1981 inner London had a lower proportion of people working in higher managerial and professional occupations (SEG 1–4) compared to outer London, the South East of England and the country as a whole whereas by 2001 the proportion in this category was higher in inner London than elsewhere (see Table 8.1).

Table 8.1   SEGs 1–4 as a proportion of SEGs 1–15 (%)

Year	E&W	SE	Greater London	IL	OL
1981	15.9	20.5	17.6	15.0	19.1
1991	20.1	24.6	24.1	24.2	24.0
2001	20.9	24.0	26.0	28.7	24.3
Ppc 81–01	5	3.5	8	13.7	5.2

In this chapter, we explore these interactions between social class and ethnic change in the context of East London. Originally the term East End – balancing the 'posh' West End of London – was shorthand for where London housed those of its poor who were working in the sweated and other trades that needed to be near to the consumer markets of the West End or alternatively where its unacceptably noxious industries or transport nodes (notably the docks) and produce markets were located. Administratively, in 1889 London was organised into 28 metropolitan boroughs constituting the London County Council (LCC) (plus the City of London giving the 29 names boroughs in the map): these included the metropolitan boroughs of Hackney, Shoreditch, Poplar, Stepney and Bow, all located to the east of the City. The River Lee marked the eastern boundary of the County of London from the County of Essex which incorporated places such as the County Boroughs of East Ham and West Ham.

However, London was always more extensive than its administrative boundaries; the de facto boundary of (East) London moved outwards with the

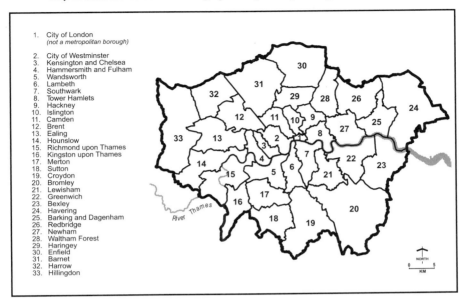

1. City of London
   (not a metropolitan borough)

2. City of Westminster
3. Kensington and Chelsea
4. Hammersmith and Fulham
5. Wandsworth
6. Lambeth
7. Southwark
8. Tower Hamlets
9. Hackney
10. Islington
11. Camden
12. Brent
13. Ealing
14. Hounslow
15. Richmond upon Thames
16. Kingston upon Thames
17. Merton
18. Sutton
19. Croydon
20. Bromley
21. Lewisham
22. Greenwich
23. Bexley
24. Havering
25. Barking and Dagenham
26. Redbridge
27. Newham
28. Waltham Forest
29. Haringey
30. Enfield
31. Barnet
32. Harrow
33. Hillingdon

Figure 8.1   The old LCC boroughs

building of the North Circular Road in the 1930s, when it was surrounded by new suburban housing in such places as Gants Hill. The construction of the largest housing estate in the world in Dagenham in the late 1920s to service the new manufacturing plants being built by companies such as Ford and (in chemicals) May and Baker marked a further expansion into Essex (Olechnowicz, 1997). The post-World War II Green Belt, which was meant to put a stop to its further outward sprawl, did little to frustrate the continued expansion. The building of the M25 orbital motorway in the 1970/80s marked another de facto boundary between London and its surrounding exurbia. In effect, however, as Buck et al. (2002) argue, London now comprises a huge travel-to-work area extending into most of the south-east quarter of England (including, for the east, out to Colchester in the north-east of Essex on the Suffolk borders).

The LCC was replaced by the Greater London Council (GLC) in 1965, bringing in parts of the surrounding counties (notably in East London the County of Essex) and incorporating into the GLC the previous county boroughs of East Ham and West Ham as the London Borough of Newham; other new London Boroughs in East London included Redbridge, Havering, Waltham Forest and Barking and Dagenham.

The GLC itself was abolished by Mrs Thatcher in 1986, following which there was no strategic government for London until New Labour set up the Greater London Assembly (comprising the 32 London Boroughs and the City of London) in 2000 with direct elections to the Assembly together with an executive Mayor, the first incumbent being Ken Livingstone, the last Leader of the Greater London

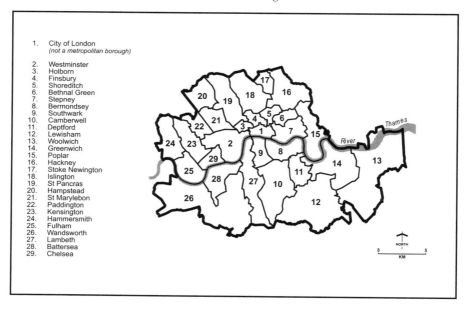

Figure 8.2   The GLC boroughs

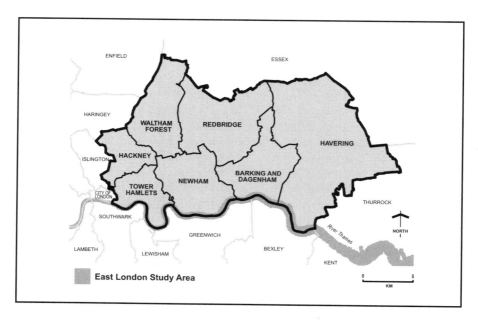

Figure 8.3   The East London study area

Council. The Mayor, who is directly elected by the people of London, reports to the GLA, which is a strategic body.

In this chapter, we treat East London as the seven London boroughs of Hackney, Tower Hamlets, Newham, Barking and Dagenham, Waltham Forest, Redbridge and Havering.

Social Class Change in East London

East London, as we have already noted, has traditionally been London's poorest 'quarter' and this has continued into the twenty-first century. The 2001 Census indicates that the only one of the seven boroughs indicated above (Redbridge) has a proportion of higher professional and managerial workers (defined as those in SEGs 1–4[2]) above the respective inner or outer London averages (Figures 8.4 and 8.5). With this single exception, all the remaining six boroughs are nearly all at the bottom of the distribution. This includes Tower Hamlets which, as we shall see, has witnessed considerable upward mobility as a consequence of the regeneration of Docklands over the previous 20 years.

Figures 8.4 and 8.5 not only show the position in 2001 but have been constructed in such a way as to indicate how these positions have changed since 1981. With the interesting exception of Tower Hamlets, which 'improved' its share of top occupational positions, particularly between 1991–2001, these positions demonstrate a remarkable lack of change. Tower Hamlets, which had the lowest share of these occupations in 1981 and was second lowest behind Newham in 1991, has had the largest increase in inner or outer London in terms of the percentage point change between 1991 and 2001 as a result of the huge regeneration programme in the Docklands areas in the south of the borough which has led

---

2   The Office of National Statistics (ONS) moved to a new form of social classification for the 2001 Census based around socio-economic classification (SEC) which replaced the previous classification by the so-called Registrar General's measurement of social class and the occupation based socio-economic group (SEG) (Rose et al., 2005).

Broadly, the new Social Class 1 of the SEC corresponds to the old SEGs 1–4 and in both cases incorporates what is termed in the narrative 'higher professional and managerial' occupations. The overlap between these two groups is high, according to Rose and Pevalin. We have converted the 2001 figures to the old SEG using a matrix supplied by Rose. For details of the transformation and a justification of its use see Butler et al. (forthcoming).

Somewhat more problematic is the conversion of what might be termed the 'middle' middle class of intermediate workers such as teachers, nurses and other routine non-manual workers which used to be found in SEG5 and particularly SEG 5.1 and is now largely, but not exclusively, classified by SEC as Social Class 2, 'lower professional and managerial occupations', although some fall into Social Class 3, 'intermediate occupations'. In London the largest social class group in the 2001 Census by a considerable margin (assuming that those who are not classified are omitted) was Social Class 2 at 22 per cent, which is approximately ten percentage points greater than either Social Class 1 (12.1 per cent) or 3 (10.2 per cent).

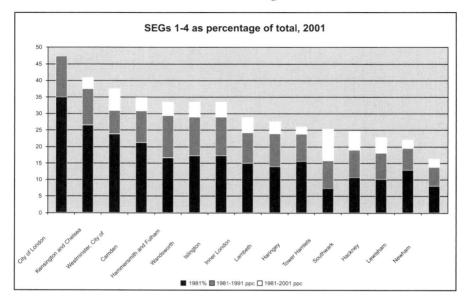

Figure 8.4   Proportion of higher managerial and professional workers in inner London boroughs 1981–2001

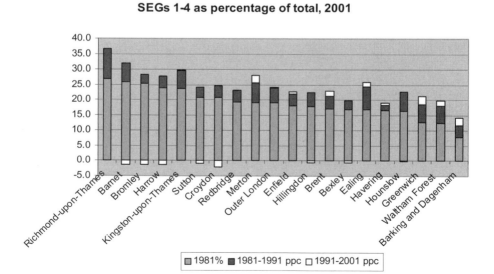

Figure 8.5   Proportion of higher managerial and professional workers in outer London boroughs 1981–2001

to widespread gentrification by – mainly childless – professional and managerial households, of which a higher than average proportion are single person households (Hall and Ogden, 1992). The percentage point change 1991–2001 in Waltham Forest and Barking and Dagenham indicates that change is beginning to take place but this is from a very low base and, unlike Tower Hamlets, the change is not noticeably higher than other boroughs; the same applies to Hackney and Newham. This, therefore, suggests that, with the exception of Tower Hamlets, there has not been a process of gentrification spreading eastwards as price rises progressively exclude even top social groups from the housing markets of inner London, particularly those boroughs to the west, south-west and north of that area. It might be expected that rising prices across London would be pushing gentrification into East London, but this does not seem to be happening in terms of social change and East London remains relatively deprived.

The interesting group to look at in this respect might be the 'middle' middle class of lower professional, managerial and administrative workers who were traditional classified by the Office of National Statistics (ONS) as SEG5 and by the more recent classification as SEC Class 2. When we do this, the position changes somewhat, as becomes clear when we compare the growth of SEGS 1–4 and 5 for the whole of outer London (Table 8.2).

Table 8.2   Growth of SEGS 1–4 and 5 for whole of outer London

SEG	Year	Mean for all outer London boroughs
1–4	1981	18.90
	1991	23.77
	2001	24.07
5	1981	11.54
	1991	14.81
	2001	25.39

There is a dramatic growth in SEG5 across outer London. The growth of the middle middle class has been the big story in London as a whole (as indeed it has for Paris (Preteceille, 2004). Studies of social change in London, particularly those that have focused on gentrification, have identified higher professionals and managers as the change agents but, arguably, what has been most dramatic in the 1990s has been the decline in the manual working-class occupations and the rise of routine lower managerial and professional occupations in the white collar sector. It has long been accepted that, with gentrification and deindustrialisation, London is becoming a more middle-class city and that there has been a process of social upgrading (Butler and Robson, 2003; Hamnett, 2003). What is now emerging are the ways in which in both inner and outer London forms of 'sorting' are taking place within the middle classes. In inner London, the growth in the middle middle classes has taken place across the city but has been particularly dramatic in eastern boroughs such as Hackney, Tower Hamlets and Newham which have not previously had a large gentrified population of higher professionals and managers. Although the middle classes are more evenly spread in outer as compared to inner London, there is an arguably even more differentiated geography emerging with particular boroughs taking on specialised occupational characteristics in relation to managerial and professional groups and also their ethnic composition. This is serving to rewrite the class geography of London in new and interesting ways – particularly in East London. The outer East London 'horseshoe' (i.e., the six boroughs excluding Redbridge – see Figure 8.3) remains largely hostile territory for the professional and managerial classes. What growth there has been has occurred in SEG5.1 but whilst this has been above the inner London average for the three inner London boroughs (Hackney, Tower Hamlets and Newham), in outer East London it has been generally lower than that for outer London as a whole with the exception of Barking and Dagenham which grew from a very small base. In this sense, outer East London appears to have 'bucked' the trend by having below average growth for both upper- and middle-'middle-class' groups and has remained much more working class in the context of an overall decline in working-class occupations (Figure 8.6).

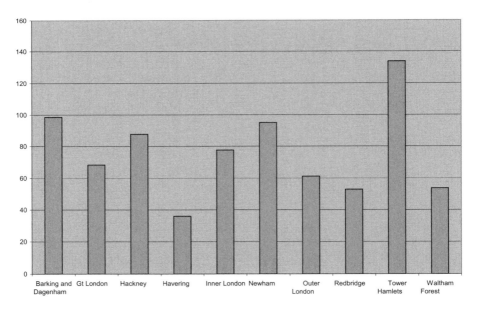

Figure 8.6   Growth in SEG5.1 1991–2001 for six boroughs

Both traditional social science measures of social stratification and more recent geo demographics (Butler et al., 2007; Hamnett et al., 2007) indicate that East London remains considerably more deprived than other sub regions in London; however, this should not be read to imply that it has avoided processes of change and restructuring that have swept the city region over the past 25 years. As we indicated at the beginning of this chapter, what was once a solidly white area which remained so longer than other areas – particularly in inner London – has witnessed significant changes in its ethnic contours. However, as we demonstrate in the next section, this is not simply a process of ethnic change it is also one of class change, as newly arrived ethnic groups begin to scramble up the social ladder both intra- and, most importantly, inter-generationally.

Ethnic Change in East London

The change in the overall structure of London's black and minority ethnic population during the 1990s, to which we referred in the introduction, was dramatic – increasing by approximately 50 pe rcent over the decade to make up nearly a third of the population of Greater London. This process has however been geographically and socially uneven; it is no longer the case that inner London is where London's BME population is concentrated nor is it that case that this population is only found on the lower slopes of the capital's social structure. Many sections of London's BME population have been upwardly mobile particularly in their second and third generations and, as this has occurred, these groups have moved upwards not only socially but also tenurially into owner occupation . This has been accompanied by mobility geographically into what used to be London's outer suburban belt around the old North and South Circular arterial roads – for example, Thornton Heath in South London and Gants Hill in East London. The continued inward migration of the expanding higher professional and managerial occupations has meant on-going gentrification, a sustained upward pressure on house prices, leaving little option to those living in inner London wanting to move into owner occupation but to move outwards to where such housing is relatively more affordable (Butler et al., forthcoming). We suggest however that housing market dynamics do not provide the whole story. For many households, particularly those in BME groups, there is (as we show in the last section of the paper) an acute awareness of the importance of education in promoting inter-generational upward mobility and they very consciously plan their moves to take most advantage of good educational facilities which tend, they argue, to be located in outer East London boroughs such as in Redbridge and Havering. These moves are motivated not just by the attraction of well-performing schools but also by the awareness that, if their children are to succeed in school, they need to be isolated from what many parents see as the negative influences of many of their peers in inner London. This is often therefore as strong an imperative to move outwards as the wish for owner occupation. We return to the question of education later.

All London boroughs, without exception, saw increases in their ethnic minority populations, ranging from just 13 per cent in Wandsworth to several boroughs with increases of over 80 per cent. It is important not to read too much into some percentage changes simply because they are on a small base. The ethnic minority population of Barking and Dagenham rose from 9,778 (7 per cent) in 1991 to 24,277 (14 per cent) in 2001: a percentage increase of 148 per cent but not a massive change in absolute terms.[3] In Harrow to the north west of London, on the other hand, the ethnic minority population rose by approximately 33,000 (63 per cent) from 52,000 (26 per cent) in 1991 to 85,846 (41 per cent) in 2001. Returning to East London, the BME population in Redbridge (largely Asians) grew by approximately 37,000 (80 per cent) from 48,421 to 87,041 and in Croydon (largely African Caribbean) by roughly 44,000 (79 per cent) from 55,114 to 98,743. Collectively, inner London lost 45,600 whites and gained 307,000 non-whites and outer London lost 185,000 whites and gained 415,000 non-whites. The proportion of the white population also decreased in London as a whole by 4 per cent but this hides large borough variations: the largest decreases in London were in Harrow (–18 per cent) and Newham (–21 per cent); the largest declines in inner London were in Lewisham (–12 per cent), Southwark (–13 per cent), and Tower Hamlets (–13 per cent), and in outer London: Croydon (–12 per cent), Redbridge (–15 per cent), Brent (–11 per cent), Greenwich (–10 per cent) and Hounslow (–11 per cent). Thus, what we are seeing in East London is a rising BME population in the context of a declining white one; there are as we have seen significant borough variations. Barking and Dagenham is interesting in this respect: whilst the overall growth is small despite the large percentage change, what this marks is a massive change for a borough that until the 1990s was an almost exclusively white place with the exception of a couple of housing estates on its western boundary with Newham. In some respects, these 'first time' increases are more significant than larger increases in actual numbers in boroughs which have lived with heterogeneity longer.[4]

In London middle-class whites are more concentrated in Inner than outer London, in the case of the non-white middle classes – with the exception of Indians, Other Asians, and 'Others' – they tend to be more concentrated in outer London. In England and Wales professionals and managers account for a larger percentage among whites than among non-whites. Chinese, Other Asians, and Others have the largest share of professionals among the non-whites groups. Employers and managers account for the smallest share among Bangladeshis. There are interesting and further distinctions to be drawn between the various constituent *situses* (i.e., divisions within social classes) within the middle class which are beyond the scope of this chapter – for the best account of social class mobility amongst ethnic groups see (Platt, 2005a, 2005b).

Table 8.3 shows that the relative growth of the middle classes as a percentage of all groups is greater in outer London for Whites, All, Caribbean, African, Chinese and Bangladeshi. It is greatest in inner London for Black Other, Indian, Asian Other and about equal for Pakistanis. This suggests that the growth of the middle and intermediate classes is taking place differentially in inner and outer London among different ethnic groups and points to more rapid suburban growth of some BME middle-class groups.

---

3   This is of course a matter of interpretation; the British National Party have used these figures to great effect to play on the perceived alteration in ethnic homogeneity to become the second largest group of councillors on the local council.

4   We are grateful to Michael Rustin for pointing out this observation.

Table 8.3   Growth in all middle classes (SEGs 1–5) as a proportion of all growth 1991–2001

	England and Wales	South-East	Greater London	Outer London	Inner London
White	73.2	74.6	120.4	131.5	108.4
Black other	−37.9	24.3	104.7	94.2	158.4
All	69	72.2	86.4	88.2	83.4
Indian	60.6	65.1	69.7	67.2	79
Asian other	49.7	52.1	56.9	46.9	109.2
Caribbean	52.8	49	62.2	63.4	62.9
Pakistani	36.4	39.6	52.7	52.6	52.8
African	47	46.6	46.9	50	44.8
Chinese	47.5	49.2	50	51.4	48.6
Other	41.2	39	39.1	41.6	35.5
Bangladeshi	25.6	25	29.2	39.7	27

However, when the analysis is broken down by SEGs 1–4 and 5 (Figure 8.7 – which is ranked by per cent growth share in inner London), it shows that the groups whose growth was most concentrated in SEGs 1–4 in inner London were Asian other (52 per cent), White (45 per cent), Indian (34 per cent), All, Other, Caribbean, Chinese, Pakistanis again with Bangladeshis at the bottom.

The group with the highest share of growth in SEG 5 as a percentage of SEG 1-15 was Whites – approximately 60 per cent in England and Wales and the South East, 63 per cent in inner London and 117 per cent in outer London. Not surprisingly this pattern is broadly replicated for All, with a much higher share of growth in SEG 5 in outer London. This indicates a growing suburban concentration of the (white) lower middle class. Most other groups, with the exception of Asian other, saw a roughly equal growth of SEG 5 between inner London and outer London.

In inner London, the distribution of non-whites across boroughs has a near normal distribution with seven boroughs having a higher than average concentration and the remaining seven having a lower than average concentration. The inner London boroughs with higher than average proportions of non-whites in 2001 are those in the east: Newham, Tower Hamlets, Southwark, Lambeth, Lewisham, Hackney and Haringey.

In outer London, eight boroughs (Brent, Harrow, Ealing, Redbridge, Hounslow, Waltham Forest, Croydon, and Barnet) have higher than average concentrations of non-whites in 2001 (compared to eleven with lower). Five of these eight boroughs are clustered in North-West and West London, four of which (Brent, Harrow, Ealing and Barnet) together with three boroughs in the East (Redbridge, Waltham Forest and Greenwich) have the largest growths in

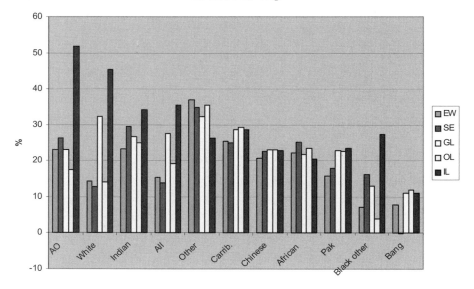

Figure 8.7   **Growth of SEGs 1–4 (higher managers and professionals) as a
proportion of all groups' growth 1991–2001**

Table 8.4   **Growth in managers and professionals (SEGs 1–4) as a proportion
of all growth, 1991–2001**

	EW	SE	GL	OL	IL
Asian other	23	26.2	23	17.4	51.9
White	14.3	12.7	32.4	14	45.4
Indian	23.3	29.5	26.7	25.1	34.3
All	15.4	13.8	27.6	19.3	35.5
Other	37	34.8	32.3	35.6	26.3
Caribbean	25.5	24.9	28.6	29.3	28.7
Chinese	20.7	22.6	23	23.1	22.8
African	22.2	25.2	21.7	23.5	20.4
Pakistani	15.8	18	22.8	22.6	23.5
Black other	7.2	16.2	13	4	27.3
Bangladeshi	7.9	-0.1	11	11.8	11

non-white populations. In other words, in outer as compared to inner London, there is a smaller proportion of non-whites overall but it is concentrated in a small number of boroughs largely in the North West and the East. Brent with 53 per cent of its working population non-white compares to the outer London average of 25 per cent and is greater than all inner London boroughs with the exception of Newham (58 per cent) and ten percentage points above Tower Hamlets.

This indicates the extent to which ethnicity is structuring the changing social structure of inner and outer East London boroughs in the context of the changes that are occurring across London as a whole. In outer, compared to inner, London there is less difference between the white and non-white proportions of the population that are middle class. In inner London, 42 per cent of non-whites are middle class compared to 60 per cent for whites. On the other hand, in outer London 47 per cent of non whites are middle class compared to 49 per cent for whites. Whites are 11 per cent more likely to be middle class in inner London than outer London, whereas non-whites are 7 per cent more likely to be middle class in outer London.

Distinguishing between Ethnicities

So far we have treated ethnicity simply as a white/BME dichotomy without making any distinction between class position or ethnic background. In this section, we attempt to draw out these distinctions with respect to our seven East London boroughs. We draw three broad distinctions here for the BME groups; firstly the Black groups in which we include Black Caribbean and Black African; secondly the Indian and Pakistani groups and thirdly the Bangladeshis. We recognise that there are many other significant groups (notably the Chinese) which have been growing rapidly in the last ten years but do not have space to consider here.

The Black groups are distinguished by the fact that they tend not to segregate themselves from the rest of the population in the same way as some of the Asian groups. Whilst they are more concentrated in inner than outer London, there is evidence that as they become middle class they tend to move away from their non middle-class co-ethnics. Hackney, for example, has a large African Caribbean population but a relatively small middle-class one – Newham is one of the only boroughs in London in which there is a roughly equal balance of middle and working class. African Caribbeans. This may be because Newham still has affordable owner occupied housing but the general pattern is one of 'class evasion' and this is repeated by the Black African group which shares the characteristic of not clustering with the African Caribbeans. Unlike the Caribbean groups, who on the whole are under-represented in East London (with the exceptions of Hackney and Newham), the Black African middle classes are over-represented in some of the East London boroughs which have a significant overall under-representation of BME populations and non middle-class Africans. Barking and Dagenham and Havering are the two exemplars of this trend. The reasons for this are not clear, although as we indicate in the last section of the chapter, this may have to do with parental educational strategies and the desire not to have their children in schools with large black enrolments.

Indians and Pakistanis both share what appears to be a 'class evasion' approach and distance themselves from their co-ethnics of a lower social class – like much of the white middle class. Middle-class Indians, as we have noted, are one of the few ethnic minority groups who have a greater tendency to live in inner as opposed to outer London – this is quite likely a class effect as this well established group is now well integrated into the higher and managerial occupations and is more likely to have acquired the material means and cultural desire to engage the relatively high status inner London gentrified housing market. Both Indians and Pakistanis have a tendency to live with other co-ethnics of the same class background but also tend to avoid sharing similar areas or indeed boroughs. Unlike the African Caribbeans who – apart from Hackney and Newham – favour South London, Indians and Asians are concentrated in the seven boroughs that make up our East London study area. Hackney and Newham (13 per cent of the population) both have above average Indian populations for inner London but in both cases below average for middle-class Indians. In Tower Hamlets there was an above average increase in the proportion of Indians but it remained below the inner London average by 2001. In outer London there were six boroughs with above average Indian populations – five of these in the west/north west of London and one (Redbridge) in the East. The trend here has been for a consolidation of growth in boroughs with an already high Indian population. When we look at middle-class Indians it appears that in Brent, Harrow and Redbridge the growth and consolidation being referred to is that of a growing middle-class population which is not the case elsewhere in north west and west London. The Indian middle classes have a tendency to consolidate in boroughs where not only are there already concentrations of Indian middle classes but where there are also high proportions of middle class of all (i.e., white) ethnicities.

Pakistanis, like Indians, have a propensity to live in owner occupied housing even if they are less middle class than Indians. Unlike Indians, who have tended to disperse amongst the population of inner London as their numbers in the middle class have increased, this is not the case with Pakistanis who have concentrated in two boroughs (Newham and Wandsworth) with a subsequent decline in their numbers in Hackney which was previously an area of high concentration in inner London. In outer London, by contrast, they have dispersed between 1991 and 2001 and much of the focus has been on East London; by 2001, Waltham Forest and Redbridge had the largest Pakistani concentrations in outer London – not far below the Newham figure. Unlike the Indian middle classes, it appears there is little difference between inner and outer London; approximately 45 per cent of Pakistanis living in inner London, in 2001, are middle class compared to 46 per cent in outer London. This contrasts with the general bias towards inner London being more middle class. As with the Indian middle classes, there is an inverse relationship between the concentration of Pakistanis and the concentration of middle-class Pakistanis. Where there are large concentrations of Pakistanis, a relatively small percentage of them are middle class. For example, while there are large concentrations of Pakistanis in Newham (8 per cent), Haringey and

Waltham Forest (6 per cent) only a small proportion of them are middle class (32 per cent, 36 per cent and 44 per cent respectively). In outer London the boroughs of Richmond, Redbridge and Havering experienced falls in the proportion of middle-class Pakistanis – this is in sharp contrast to the increase in the density of the Indian middle-class population in the same boroughs.

Bangladeshis are an exception to the general model of upward social mobility amongst immigrant groups; this is normally explained by two facts: that they arrived later than other groups and that they tended to come from poor rural as opposed to richer urban backgrounds. Most Bangladeshis in the UK originate from Sylhet (unlike the US where they tend to come from Dacca). The distribution of Bangladeshis in London is particularly concentrated in a small number of boroughs in inner London and this concentration has intensified between 1991 and 2001. Although the proportion of Bangladeshis has increased in both inner and outer London between 1991 and 2001, the greatest increase has been in inner London and is skewed toward just three boroughs: Tower Hamlets, Newham and Camden which have all increased their share. Most notably, in Tower Hamlets there has been a 20-percentage point increase in the proportion of Bangladeshis over the ten years. In outer London the Bangladeshis are spread much more sparsely than in inner London. In 2001 Redbridge contained the largest share in outer London with 1.6 per cent of the working population which is smaller than Islington (1.9 per cent) which had the eighth largest proportion of Bangladeshis in inner London in 2001. In a similar manner to Indians and Pakistanis, middle-class Bangladeshis appear to be distributed much more evenly around London than Bangladeshis as a whole. However, the middle classes are much more likely to be located in outer London. Some 42 per cent of Bangladeshis in outer London are middle class compared to only 25 per cent in inner London. This is a similar story to Pakistanis except that the difference between inner and outer is much more extreme. Furthermore, Bangladeshis in London are much less likely to be middle class than the all-ethnic population. Indeed, the Bangladeshi middle class in London is the smallest of all the Asian groups as well as being below those of Black Caribbeans and Black Africans This differential is most pronounced in inner London where in 2001 the likelihood of being middle class was 30 percentage points less than the all-ethnic average.. In no inner London borough in 2001 was the percentage of middle-class Bangladeshis greater or equal to the all-ethnic percentage. The smallest differential is found in Newham where 27 per cent of Bangladeshis are middle class compared to an average of 37 per cent for the whole population. A much larger proportion of Bangladeshis living in outer London is middle class. In a few boroughs such as Havering, Redbridge and Barking and Dagenham the Bangladeshi percentage exceeds the average. Barking and Dagenham is the only borough where the percentage of middle-class Bangladeshis (35 per cent) is smaller than the outer London average for Bangladeshis (42 per cent) but at the same time larger than the equivalent all-ethnic percentage (32 per cent). Overall in London, the growth in the relative size of the Bangladeshi middle class was less than that experienced across all ethnic groups. The Bangladeshi middle class have become more concentrated in a very small number of boroughs and it seems quite likely that the middle-class Bangladeshis will continue to concentrate in Redbridge

The Qualitative Evidence

The previous sections considered the changing nature of the East London population, in which there exists a set of identifiable inter-borough demographical shifts with respect to class and ethnicity. Particular 'ethclass' groups are clearly favouring some East London locations above others. The net result is a gradual suburbanisation of East London's BME population. This section aims to shed light on the nature of choices, and indeed constraints, informing suburban dispersal. It introduces the findings of ongoing qualitative research on the links between upward mobility, education and ethnicity in East London. Key themes to emerge here concern changing perceptions of the quality of life in East London, class evasion, housing, and, importantly, parental preferences regarding the school destinations of their children.

While some parts of East London, especially neighbourhoods nearest to the city, are becoming an increasingly attractive place to live and work for a predominantly white, elite and upper managerial and professional gentrifying class (Butler with Robson, 2003), qualitative and quantitative evidence from this study suggests that upwardly mobile members of ethnic minority groups are themselves more likely to gravitate into outer London boroughs upon signs of upward economic mobility (this is compatible with the finding in the previous section of the relatively high proportions of middle-class members of ethnic minorities in outer London boroughs with low BME populations). Semi-structured interviewing revealed a strong desire among several BME parents in Newham and Waltham Forest to move eastwards to the boroughs of Redbridge, Barking and Dagenham and Havering. Common reasons cited for (aspiring to) this relocation point towards widespread feelings amongst some BME members that their inner London neighbourhoods are increasingly undesirable locations to live and raise a family.

I:	How do you find life here?
Newham1633:	I wouldn't want to live here too long.
I:	Why not?
Newham1633:	Basically things are happening around here that shouldn't. People are getting beat up for no reason at all ... I wouldn't have a family around here.
I:	So are you thinking of moving on anywhere?
Newham1633:	Dagenham, the schools are better over there. The people are a bit better over there. It's rather quiet there; it's not as loud as down here.

The above extract from a conversation with a young mother residing in a Newham tower block illustrates common sources of unhappiness with life in inner East London: crime, youth gang activity and weak schools. Certainly, the first two of these grievances were most vociferous amongst the most economically marginal respondents who were out of work or working in insecure, low-paid employment, and who as a result were concentrated in the poorest housing. In this sense the most anxious of East London's residents are arguably those occupying the most marginal categories with respect to housing and employment prospects, traditionally the BME (and white working-class) population of East London. As we can see from this case, such anxieties may manifest themselves in a strong desire to move outwards to an alternative East London location. Such locations are perceived to offer better sanctuary from antisocial behaviour and crime, and schools that are best equipped to 'spring board' an upwardly mobile next generation towards better housing employment prospects.

It appears that anxieties are also resulting from the scale and rapid nature of social change in East London, which seems to explain the growing appeal of more residentially stable (and comparatively mono-ethnic) suburban locations. Several Inner London BME residents lamented the fact that their streets had changed from what they articulated as intimate sites of social and cultural exchange to locations of decreasing 'neighbourliness' and increasing social fragmentation. These complaints draw upon two major tropes of social change in contemporary East London: (multi)ethnicity and housing tenure.

> Leyton2631:   Once upon a time it was a really lovely place. It was quiet and it had a
>   lovely mix of people and we all sort of jogged along very well ... But
>   now, I don't get the feeling of community ... I think it it's like everybody
>   is sticking to their own communities rather than mixing in.

The above respondent has lived with her husband in a quiet residential street in Leytonstone for over twenty years and is thus well qualified to comment on the local consequences of a near continuous period of social and ethnic change across East London. A feature of her contemporary account of life in East London was notable for the frequent comparisons between the East London of today and its former, more convivial self. The retrospective view alluded to a harmonious 'melting pot' analogy of inter-ethnic interaction in East London:

> Leyton2631:   My neighbours, one was from Pakistan, one was from India...We
>   [also] had Greeks, Caribbean's [and] Chinese – anybody mixing with
>   anybody

This rather idyllic view of life in Leytonstone is in sharp contrast to her contemporary analysis in which she views such harmonious intermingling as having been stifled by the sheer diversity of migrant origins resplendent in 'new' forms of international migration to the UK, including the sizable Eastern European community now settled in Waltham Forest (and Newham). Her view is that the wide range of sending regions involved in contemporary patterns of migration is rendering such street level exchanges increasingly obsolete as they become replaced by ever-strengthening yet geographically disparate co-ethnic networks of support formed around the workplace, place of worship, café and other sites of co-ethnic interaction. Unlike the nostalgic vision of social interaction in East London propagated by this and similarly-minded respondents, 'getting to know the neighbours' is today cited as much less a social and cultural imperative owing to the proliferation of such co-ethnic cultural resources in the city, and the belief that, irrespective of one's ethnic origin, there will always be scope for co-ethnic exchange in a cosmopolitan, global city such as London.

Rather than dismiss these as defensive and deliberately confrontational sentiments, they on the contrary highlight how some East London residents, including BME members, differentiate between Commonwealth and post-Commonwealth migration on the basis of the demographic and socio-economic characteristics of the actors involved, and thus their's is a subtle, and arguably more pragmatic, interpretation of social change than one based purely on xenophobic or discriminatory prejudices. This is illustrated below with reference to the same respondent's analysis of the specific case of European migration to the UK in which she locates the source of her concern in the youthful age structure displayed by migrant groups from new EU member states (Robinson, 2002):

> Leyton2631:   With the opening of the EU a lot of Europeans are coming in. Because they are not family orientated you tend to get more rental instead of family units, so people just come and go ...

This willingness to place the immigration issue within its wider historical context demarcates a progressive, as opposed to reactionary, response in this instance. As lamentable as the neighbourhood effects of 'new' EU migration would appear, then, bitterness is tapered by a realisation that their consequences on neighbourhood cohesion are merely 'part and parcel' of life in a city that remains an important nodal point within patterns of transnational migration as it was during the period of Commonwealth migration. The indications are that these respondents are clear on the importance of international migration to the city of London and life in East London in particular, not least since many of these are themselves of migrant origin. Nevertheless, such interpretations of change flesh out trends of BME avoidance outlined previously in this chapter, in which the longest-established and upwardly mobile ethnic minority ('ethclass') groups, especially Black and Asian groups of Commonwealth origin, are striving to put physical distance between themselves and more economically marginal minority groups of which London's Eastern European migrants represent a sizeable portion.

This scenario of rapid residential change is also perceived to be contributing to a declining East London physical milieu. As neighbourhoods become more transient, with the aforementioned residential jockeying-for-positioning (in relation to 'good' housing and schools) becoming a feature of social change in East London, the ties between incoming residents/tenants and their physical surroundings are understood as having been weakened and less a source of individual and collective pride. These feelings were evident in the frustrations voiced by some interviewees who felt that streetscapes were becoming increasingly untidy. Little wonder, some said, given that to the perpetrators their neighbourhood are merely a temporary stopping-off as opposed to long-term 'home'. A number of respondents laid the blame here on the buy-to-let housing phenomenon and the spread of private rental properties, many of them multi-lets, on formerly stable, owner-occupied streets. This was seen as contributing to the increase of local residents with no (perceived) *real* connection to the area. On more than one occasion, a respondent led the interviewer to the living room window at the front of the property to point out disapprovingly the rental properties. One time this was a precursor to laying into the unconventional and/or misunderstood habits and preoccupations of the occupiers, which, in the interviewee's mind, was masquerading as anti-social, morally corrupt, criminal or suspicious behaviour (people coming and going at strange times, incomers immediately withdrawing from established trends of neighbourly interaction, lone parent mothers reliant on state handouts, etc.). Such issues led one Indian respondent to reassess her relationship to the East Ham area in Newham, somewhere she had lived for the previous 30 years:

> Redbridge7373: East Ham, I had been there for just over 30 years so ... I could see the changes – becoming more congested, more traffic – just the state of the place. I needed something different, a change. It was the crime rate. I think neighbours as well. Although we had really nice neighbours they were always changing so we didn't really get to know all the people, and just the roads and streets – they were getting really bad.

This respondent subsequently moved from East Ham to Barkingside in the outer-London borough of Redbridge. Her testimony went on to illuminate another aspect of the BME suburbanisation that is important; which is the desire of some BME members to seek physical distance between themselves and co-ethnics of lower social standing in a ritual of intra-ethnic 'avoidance'. Among the sources of her dissatisfaction with life in East Ham was the way in which she saw her own Southern Indian community developing. She felt the community had now become too materialistic with families and community members increasingly defining their status by virtue of material possessions:

> Redbridge7373: Amongst the women it was like, who has the best Sari, who had certain jewellery and who kept up with a certain fashion...people weren't allowed to think freely [and to have] a life outside that circle, so I couldn't be bothered with that.

Such competition reverberated into other elements of everyday life, including the comparative attainment of children at school:

> Redbridge7373: Everyone wanted to know your business as well. [There was] so much competition regarding children's education; whether they were playing a music instrument or whether they were [attaining] any other achievements. We didn't want to have our children sucked into that either.

Responding to the suffocating elements of her co-ethnic community in East Ham, the respondent's next residential decisions suddenly became underpinned by a desire for sanctuary and voluntary anonymity. Her new home in Barkingside was anticipated as meeting these requirements:

> Redbridge7373: That was one of the things we were looking for – we didn't want to know so many people or get into groups, we just wanted to have family life … We weren't really looking for a community base or anything like that, we had been in that, we were in that and it caused a lot of problems as well so we wanted a complete break from that – just to do our own thing; children go to school; we come home …

This indicates that social class – in turn linked to migratory history and generation – is an important source of differentiation within the East London BME population, and one that is clearly having geographical implications in the form of suburban dispersal. Suburbanisation, borrowing from Pacione (2001, p. 84), is in this case a clear 'modern message of difference' with incompatibilities in culture, class and identities underpinning motivations for dispersal. The source of this particular case of social inoculation was the respondent's attitudes towards those members of the Tamil community who arrived in London during the mid-1980s as a result of political and social turmoil in India. The respondent articulates that, while they may share ethnicity, social class and allied lifestyle preferences clearly separate them from her. Such findings demonstrate that Skegg's (2004) ideas concerning the spatial strategies by which the urban elite achieves class separation from urban 'others' are also relevant in the context of upwardly mobile BME members. These are significant ideas since they illustrate that the modern context of urban, British suburbanisation is no longer solely about a white middle class seeking to separate itself out from fellow whites of lower social status. Evidence from our work confirms that the same processes of social and residential differentiation are at work in other ethnic groups. Class is thus more of a precursor for suburbanisation than ethnicity, although it goes without saying that the particularities of the suburbanisation process, such as destination and the relative importance attached to schooling prospects, appear closely linked to ethnicity too.

The dispersal of East London's BME population is also an effect of current property dynamics linked to the gentrification of central parts of London's 'old' East End – such as our Victoria Park study area. The spiralling cost of private dwellings here, a gentrified neighbourhood bordering both Hackney in the north and Tower Hamlets in the south, has pushed the cost of terraced family accommodation beyond the financial reach of the majority of families currently residing in these boroughs. Interview findings suggest that aspirant BME homeowners and current BME homeowners intent on trading-up are increasingly refining their properties searches to the historically less fashionable yet more affordable borough of Newham, as well as various locations in Redbridge deemed within budget (which are also located in areas served by the academically worst-performing schools). Likely destinations here would include Forest Gate, East

Ham and Manor Park in Newham, and also to the southern end of Ilford, close to the Redbdrige and Barking and Dagenham borough boundaries. At the same time, these areas appear to be simultaneously undergoing a process of vacation where higher status non-whites are selling up or keeping properties for private lets, whilst moving further eastwards and northwards to more desirable parts of Redbridge – Chigwell and Woodford, for example – and Havering. Our qualitative data thus suggest that the ongoing gentrification of our most central study area is contributing towards a 'ripple in the water' effect as aspirant BME homeowners look to the core areas of BME settlement in Newham for affordable, family-size dwellings. Residents in these areas in turn seek to move further east themselves as residential social differentiation along ethnic and class lines continues, and differentiation of the East London population into various 'ethclass' constituents proceeds apace.

Access to education is an additional important motivation for dispersal from inner East London boroughs, with primary and secondary school provision in Redbridge and Havering generally considered the best in East London. They also contain academically selective state (or 'grammar') schools which are themselves a magnet for aspiring BME families who – on the whole – appear to be attaching an unprecedented amount of importance to the academic success of their children and their successful transition on to, and through, tertiary education. These schools, along with the presence of much vaunted, academically successful state non-selective schools such as Seven Kings High School, are thus important carrots within the suburbanisation process since living in close proximity to them increases the likelihood that one's children will meet the required entry criteria. The resultant neighbourhood effect is effectively a BME middle-class 'enclave' surrounding the best schools in this multicultural part of East London. This is most evident in the specific case of the Seven Kings School, where the catchment area is awash with signs of affluence including the ubiquitous front-garden-come-concrete-swathe designed to accommodate the residing family's fleet of private cars.

On the whole, it would appear that parents from all the study areas are generally happier with the provision and quality of primary schools than they are with secondary schools. This is down to the presence of more formal and critical modes of exam assessment (GCSEs and A-levels) at secondary school in which pupil performance determines access to avenues in employment and tertiary education. Primary schools are, on the contrary, seen as carrying less academic significance, although parents generally see them as having a more liberal remit of facilitating play and socialisation between pupils, as well as providing pupils with, at the very least, basic adequacy in maths, reading and writing. The importance of secondary school choice and the dilemmas it is presenting parents in East London is highlighted by the fact that many interviewees had either moved or expressed a desire to move residence as the eldest child neared 11 years old, the age of entry to secondary education. This was a view expressed across all the sample of respondents and not limited to particular ethnic groupings, although it was invariably the better off of who spoke with more conviction about moving or being able to move. It would certainly appear the case that higher social-economic groups are more empowered when it comes to making decisions with regard to residential location and schooling destination.

Conclusions

East London is experiencing a demographic transition which sets it apart from the rest of London. Whilst the horseshoe formed by six of our seven boroughs –the exception being the relatively affluent aspirational borough of Redbridge – remains probably the most deprived area in London and also retains a working-class heritage, in other respects the area has been in the vanguard of the ethnic reshaping that has been accelerating across London over the past 15 years. As we have tried to show in this chapter, the contours of this ethnic reshaping have been heavily influenced by the forces of social mobility. Whilst East London still contains a large working population who, unusually for London, still do working-class jobs, there has also been a large growth in the intermediate occupations across the sub region although this has not been as fast a growth as has occurred elsewhere in London and England and Wales more generally. Many of those in these intermediate social class groups (the new socio-economic classification (SEC) 2 or the old socio-economic group (SEG) 5) are from Black and Minority Ethnic groups. Although, unlike Platt (2005a, 2005b), we did not use longitudinal data but rather compared the cross sectional data from three censuses (1981–2001) standardising on the old SEG classifications, we are reasonably confident that what we are witnessing here are geographically specific processes of upward social mobility by different ethnic groups which is confirmed by our qualitative data. With the exception of Redbridge, in all of these areas the proportions of higher and intermediate social classes is below the London averages. Different ethnic groups however have distinctive trajectories. With the exception of Tower Hamlets and to a much lesser degree Hackney, these are not favoured destinations for white groups who are upwardly mobile into the higher professional and managerial occupations. In Hackney's case it is a favoured destination for white intermediate social groups who now appear to be driving its continued gentrification which is now no longer confined to owner occupation but embraces the private rented sector. The outer London boroughs of Redbridge, and to a lesser extent Havering and Waltham Forest, continue to be attractive to white intermediate groups who are still able to contemplate home ownership but many of these are replacing those who have left for the shire counties beyond the M25, notably Essex. Amongst the non white groups, there is a greater chance of finding higher professionals and managers in outer as opposed to inner London although two caveats need to be entered here. Firstly, as we have noted, Indians are an exception here in that they are more likely to be found in inner London as for the population as a whole. Secondly, for all Asian groups, there is a tendency to cluster in particular boroughs in outer London where there is already a high proportion of middle-class co-ethnics and, in the case of Indians, where there is also a high proportion of middle class of all ethnicities. For Black groups there is not a similar tendency to cluster and they tend to be more evenly distributed across and within boroughs but, as with all groups, they tend to avoid settling in areas with high concentrations of co-ethnics. Thus, although Hackney has a high proportion of low class African Caribbeans and Indians, it has relatively small numbers in the middle classes. Newham is an exception here for African Caribbeans but not for Indians who have left the borough as they have become upwardly mobile for the already more middle-class borough of Redbridge. Pakistanis also practise this strategy of 'class evasion' but do not tend to settle in boroughs with high proportions of Indians or indeed of other middle-class groups. Middle-class Black Africans often appear to settle in boroughs where there are low numbers of non middle-class BME groups – notably Havering and Barking and Dagenham which both have large clusters of traditional white working-class populations. We have suggested that some of this may be driven by firstly a general middle-class desire to put distance from one's working-class origins, secondly by a desire to distance one's children from groups that are perceived to be a bad influence and thirdly from the desire to move away from areas being subject to recent migration from eastern Europe and the Balkans.

East London is thus playing host to a complex pattern of social mobility. It retains probably London's largest group of working-class occupations – particularly in its outer boroughs – together with a high proportion of economically inactive ex-working-class groups. At the same time, its two inner boroughs of Tower Hamlets and Hackney, whilst (along with Newham) still high on the Index of Multiple Deprivation (IMD), are host to a process of gentrification by the new (SEC) social classes one and two. As their BME populations are upwardly mobile, they tend to move out of their (inner London) boroughs of residence both to gain access to owner occupation and to escape what they see as essentially a culture of poverty (or social exclusion) which will hold back their aspirations for their children. A process of sorting then occurs whereby Indians head for boroughs like Redbridge which already has a middle-class infrastructure and an embryonic Indian middle class, Africans and African Caribbeans head out more generally across London towards cheaper housing whilst Pakistanis also move away from their places of residence for cheaper housing in places settled by other Pakistanis and with low settlements of other middle-class Asians. The white intermediate social classes tend to head also boroughs like Redbridge, Havering and to some extent Waltham Forest where housing is seen as affordable and there is still the perception of significant numbers of people like themselves and decent schooling. We suggest that education is critical in this process of sorting and is increasingly tied to perceptions of attainment opportunities which are now firmly etched in the public consciousness through the publication of league tables and individual school assessments by the Office for Standards in Education (OFSTED).

References

Buck, N., Gordon, I., Hall, P., Harloe, M. and Kleinman, M. (2002). *Working Capital: Life and Labour in Contemporary London*, London, Routledge.

Butler, T., Hamnett, C. and Ramsden , M. (forthcoming), 'Inward and Upward? Marking Out Social Class Change in London 1981–2001'.

Butler, T., Hamnett, C., Ramsden, M. and Webber, R. (2007), 'The Best, the Worst and the Average: Secondary School Choice and Education Performance in East London', *Journal of Education Policy*, 22(1): 7–29.

Butler, T. and Robson, G. (2003). *London Calling: The Middle Classes and the Remaking of Inner London*, Oxford, Berg.

Hall, R. and Ogden, P. (1992), 'The Social Structure of New Migrants to London Docklands: Recent Evidence from Wapping', *London Journal*, 17(2): 153–69.

Hamnett, C. (2003), *Unequal City: London in the Global Arena*, London, Routledge.

Hamnett, C., Ramsden, M. and Butler, T. (2007), 'Social Background, Ethnicity, School Composition and Educational Attainment in East London', *Urban Studies*, 44(7): 1255–80.

Olechnowicz, A. (1997), *Working Class Housing in England between the Wars: The Becontree Estate*, Oxford, Clarendon Press.

Platt, L. (2005a), 'The Intergenerational Social Mobility of Minority Ethnic Groups', *Sociology*, 39(3): 445–61.

Platt, L. (2005b), *Migration and Social Mobility: Life Chances of Britain's Minority Ethnic Communities*, York, Joseph Rowntree Foundation.

Preteceille, E. (2004), *La division sociale de l'espace fancilien: typologie, socioprofessionelle 1999 et transformation de l'espace residentiel 1990–99*, Paris, Observatoire Sociologique du Changement, 145.

Rose, D., Pevalin, D.J. and O'Reilly, K. (2005), *The NS-SEC: Origins, Development and Use*, London, Palgrave Macmillan.

Chapter 9

Moving to a Better Place? Geographies of Aspiration and Anxiety in the Thames Gateway

Paul Watt

Introduction

The suburban move from inner London to outer London and beyond to the 'ROSE' (Rest of the South-East excluding London) is an important albeit under-researched part of the social geography and history of London. It is associated with a number of key social, economic and policy developments in South-East England during the post-war period. Prominent among these is the decentralisation of industry, including along the Thames Estuary the area that is currently subsumed within the Essex and Kent sections of the Thames Gateway and designated as in need of regeneration (Church and Frost, 1995). The suburbanisation of London's population has been brought about via the formation of the New Towns, the development of peripheral council housing estates, and the expansion of private housing estates in the commuter villages and small towns of the ROSE. Despite the massive scale of post-war development in South-East England and its profound demographic implications, notably the spatial dispersal of Londoners ('white Cockney on the drift' – Sinclair, 2003, p. 20), it is remarkable how few social scientific studies have been centrally concerned with this phenomenon. One has to go back to the classics from the Institute of Community Studies (Young and Willmott, 1957, 1975; Willmott and Young ,1960) for an extensive sociological analysis of London's diasporic development. In comparison, we know relatively little about contemporary suburban South-East England from the perspective of the people who live there.

This chapter begins to address this lacuna with reference to a research project undertaken in an Essex suburb given the pseudonym 'Eastside'.[1] The main aim of the project was to examine residential mobility in relation to ex-Londoners' motivational reasons for leaving London and moving to Essex. In particular, the research was concerned to understand the importance that place images play in residential mobility, not only in relation to out-migrants previous neighbourhood in London, but also with reference to their present neighbourhood in suburban

---

1   The project was funded by The British Academy, grant LRG-35374.

Essex. 'Place images' refer to the subjective meanings that people hold about areas, irrespective of whether or not such images are faithful renditions of 'real places' (Shields, 1991). Exclusionary class and racial discourses and divisions are important in relation to understanding such place images (Sibley, 1995; Watt, 2004, 2006, 2007a).

Eastside is located in the Thurrock Thames Gateway Development Corporation area in south Essex. The findings presented here address three questions that have relevance for the debate over what the Thames Gateway presently is and what it might become in the future. These questions are firstly why Londoners leave the city in order to relocate to south Essex, secondly whether the London area of origin affects their reasons for moving, and thirdly what they think of south Essex as a place to live.[2]

The Exodus from London to the ROSE

London has witnessed a remarkable demographic transformation during the last 40 years. From being primarily white and British-born in the first half of the twentieth century up until the 1960s, it is now characterised by remarkable ethnic diversity (Hamnett, 2003). This change has been partly brought about by immigration, primarily from New Commonwealth countries but also more latterly from Eastern Europe, and partly by white British migration out of London (Champion and Ford, 2000). Although post-war immigrants initially settled in inner London where cheap private rental housing was available, there has subsequently been a considerable degree of dispersal to outer London by South Asian, black Caribbean and African minorities. According to Hamnett, some of the biggest decreases in whites and increases in minority ethnic groups have occurred in outer London boroughs such as Harrow and Croydon, which has lead him to conclude that this suggests 'a process of outwards ethnic minority expansion and succession in London, with white residents moving outside London or further afield' (Hamnett, 2003, 127).

The favoured destination for white ex-Londoners leaving the capital is the ROSE, the Rest of the South-East. The ROSE has been the main recipient for post-war migration from London taking the form of middle-class movement to private suburban housing estates and commuter villages (Pahl, 1964), and working-class movement to the New Towns and suburban council and private estates (Clapson, 1998). Between 1981 and 1991, Essex gained 145,000 new residents, a 10 per cent population increase, the overwhelming majority of who were white including many from east London (Rix, 1996, p. 23). According to the 2001 Census, white ethnic identifiers made up approximately 97 per cent of the population in both Essex and Kent.

---

2   The research project was not designed to test the efficacy of housing policy in the Thames Gateway unlike Power et al. (2004) for example. This would have entailed a far larger project examining a wider range of housing tenures and types across a more extensive area.

Research on working-class suburbanisation suggests that it tended to involve movement by more affluent younger workers and their families (Deakin and Ungerson, 1977; Devine, 1992). Increased job opportunities in South-East England, notably in the New Towns, were significant in explaining migrants' decisions to move from inner London. However, according to Clapson (1998, p. 67) the major reason for migration to the New Towns and suburban estates 'was the desire for better accommodation, which usually meant a new house'. These new houses were either rented from the local authorities in the form of public housing or they were bought in the New Towns and suburbs (see Young and Willmott, 1957, 1975). Post-war suburban housing, whether rented or owned, not only came with better fixtures and fittings, but also implied a subjective sense of moving *up* coterminous with moving *out*, both for the middle class and aspirant working class (Willmott and Young, 1960). Thus, although housing played a key role in motivating migration from English inner-city areas, it was often intertwined with more intangible factors such as the desire to improve social position by escaping 'deteriorating' areas: 'they wanted to put distance between themselves and those they perceived as roughs or undesirables' (Clapson, 1998, p. 73). Clapson goes onto argue that the move out fed upon and exaggerated status differences within the working class, notably the long-standing if imprecise distinction between 'rough' and 'respectable' workers and their families. According to Clapson, this intra-class status distinction acquired racialised connotations since those perceived to be of a lower status could include 'immigrants' whose presence acted as a spur for white Britons to leave the inner city for suburban areas. Suburbanisation in relation to London and South-East England has therefore had a 'white flight' connotation (see Back, 1996; Dench et al., 2006; Watt, 2004).

Explanations for suburbanisation around London are complex and it is impossible to do justice to them in this chapter.[3] One approach emphasises material factors such as social polarisation and housing affordability. According to Hamnett (2003), there has been increasing social polarisation in London and this has taken a housing tenure form. Inner London in particular has been colonised by middle-class gentrifiers who have contributed towards exorbitant increases in house prices and private sector rents. This has in turn led to the displacement of the working class, priced out of many London areas (Atkinson, 2000). At the same time, social housing in the form of local authority rental property has shrunk radically in both absolute and relative terms, not least as a result of central government housing policies (Watt, 2001). Despite their increasingly high profile, housing associations have not made up for the overall deficit in social rental housing provision, with the consequence that there is a profound dearth of affordable rental accommodation in the capital (ORS, 2004). The contraction of social housing has contributed towards the residualisation of the sector whereby it increasingly houses the urban poor, including those in low-paid employment, the unemployed, sick and disabled, the homeless and disadvantaged minority ethnic groups (Hamnett, 2003; Watt, 2003). One impact of gentrification and residualisation is that those on middle incomes, notably skilled manual and white-

---

3   See Dench et al. (2006) for a recent controversial and flawed analysis.

collar workers as well as public sector professionals, struggle to gain access to either home ownership or social housing in London. They are therefore effectively priced or 'pushed' out beyond the boundaries of London into the ROSE suburbs where house prices are lower.

Another approach focuses on the relative 'desirability' of areas and the notion that people with similar social backgrounds (Bourdieu's habitus) attempt to live in those areas consisting of 'people like themselves' (Savage et al., 2005). This can be seen in the sifting and sorting of various fractions of the metropolitan middle classes into different London locales (Butler and Robson, 2003). In the search for sameness amidst the sea of difference that is the contemporary global city, what Bauman (2003, p. 110) refers to as 'mixophobia', one response is to simply flee the city for aspirational middle-mass suburbia (Clapson, 2003; Sibley, 1995). Rather than therefore being simply pushed out of the city, sections of the middle and working classes exercise a degree of agency as they relocate away from those areas they find 'undesirable'. This relates to the notion of 'flight from the city' as discussed by Champion (2000). Existing research on potential in-movers to the Thames Gateway from adjacent London boroughs has indicated considerable antipathy towards city life, including concerns about crime as well as the risks posed to children's safety and development (Bennett and Morris, 2006).

As suburbia itself has expanded, it has also become a far more socially complex and contested space than it once was (Silverstone, 1997). It is no longer the self-sustaining paean to middle-classdom that it once was. Instead, there is increasing evidence of 'trouble in paradise'. Gwilliam et al. (1998) have highlighted issues of sustainability in relation to a range of suburban areas, while a recent report has identified a plethora of sustainability pressures facing the London suburbs including exported inner-city problems, greater cultural diversity and transport difficulties (URBED, 2002). More worryingly, Back (1998) has highlighted the significance of racism in suburban housing estates in Birmingham. Research by Watt (1998) has indicated the contested class and racialised nature of everyday uses of public space among ethnically diverse groups of young people in the Home Counties.

The existence of the Thames Gateway regeneration scheme itself is in a way proof that all is not well in the London hinterlands. The Essex and Kent sections of the Thames Gateway have been identified as having a poor public image as well as containing areas of concentrated deprivation relative to much of the ROSE (Allen et al., 1998; Church and Frost, 1995). A small-scale study of low-income residents living in deprived areas of the Essex and Kent outer Gateway found considerable scepticism regarding the benefits of the Thames Gateway scheme plus antipathy towards prospective new residents, an antipathy that in some cases took a racist form (Bennett and Morris, 2006).

The Research in Eastside

The research was undertaken during 2004–05 in a large suburb given the pseudonym 'Eastside'. It is located in the Thurrock area of south Essex outside the M25 motorway. Eastside was chosen because it is demographically typical of this part of Essex in relation to both ethnicity and class. According to the 2001 Census, its population is predominantly white (over 95 per cent) and working class with less than one quarter of households in the professional and managerial middle classes. Eastside is an architectural hybrid encompassing a traditional rural village with church and green, a sprawling modernist post-war housing estate built by the London County Council, plus a series of newer private housing developments. Many Eastside residents commute into London for work.

The research concentrated upon recent incomers who had moved into newer private housing. Two main methods were employed. Firstly a survey based upon a structured interview schedule was undertaken with residents, either homeowners or private tenants, who had moved from an address in Greater London to Eastside during the previous 10-year period. Interviews were successfully conducted at 140 properties giving a response rate of 37 per cent.[4] The survey was followed up with qualitative data from 42 semi-structured interviews carried out with a sub-sample of survey respondents. The interviews examined people's reasons for moving along with their views on their present neighbourhood in greater depth. In this chapter, we primarily draw upon the survey findings rather than the interview data (see Watt, 2007a).

The survey respondents were in some ways stereotypically suburban. They were predominantly homeowning, white, middle-aged, married or co-habiting heterosexual couples, with both partners in paid employment. Retirees made up less than a tenth of all respondents. The vast majority (96 per cent) were homeowners, mainly mortgagees. The remainder were either in shared ownership or rented from private landlords. There was nevertheless greater social diversity than the suburban stereotype might suggest since, for example, over one quarter of respondents were single, separated or divorced. Over half (58 per cent) of respondents were women, whilst 90 per cent were white, mainly English who had been brought up in London plus a smattering of non-British whites. The non-white groups included Nigerians and Chinese among others.

In terms of housing and to some extent social class, the Eastside survey respondents can be divided into two parts. Seventy-four survey households lived in 'Woodlands', a new large private estate physically detached from the rest of Eastside. This estate is the most expensive part of Eastside, described as a 'prestigious' and 'ever popular' location by local estate agents. Most properties were detached and semi-detached houses and nearly half of the Woodlands respondents lived in detached houses. Incomes were in the high-middle zone as 62 per cent of Woodlands' households had gross incomes above £40,000 and nearly one quarter had incomes over £60,000. Just over one quarter of the Woodlands' respondents were graduates, whilst only 5 per cent had no qualifications. In relation to social class, the professional and managerial middle classes dominated accounting for over 70 per cent of all households. Occupational groups such as managers (private and public sector), teachers, financial analysts, IT consultants,

---

4   Although this is not high, the number of non-contactable households was very small since most of the non-response was made up of refusals.

civil servants and local government officers were well represented. There were also several skilled manual workers, often self-employed, such as black cab taxi drivers and electricians, but very few routine and semi-routine workers.

The second part of the sample consists of those 66 households living in several smaller private housing developments scattered around the Eastside suburb. Many of these developments are located near the 'town' section of Eastside, i.e. the small shopping area surrounded by council housing. These private housing developments have been given the collective name 'Newtown estates'. Flats and smaller terraced or semi-detached houses predominate. One third of the survey respondents lived in flats and only 3 per cent lived in detached houses. Income levels amongst the Newtown estates were lower than at Woodlands. Nearly half of Newtown households had gross incomes between £20,000–40,000, whilst only 4 per cent had incomes over £60,000. In relation to education, 6 per cent of Newtown respondents had a degree, while 19 per cent had no qualifications. The social class composition of the Newtown estates was far more working class than Woodlands. Semi-routine or routine workers made up a third of all Newtown households whereas the professional and managerial middle classes accounted for 24 per cent.

In relation to debates on social class and neighbourhoods, several features are worth noting (see Savage et al., 2005). Firstly, although neither Woodlands or Newtown were exclusively mono-class areas, the former was numerically and socially dominated by the professional and managerial middle classes, whereas the latter was more working class. Secondly, that in comparison with the urban 'new middle class' in London (Butler and Robson, 2003, pp. 116–25), the Eastside middle classes had limited cultural capital in Bourdieu's terms (1984). Less than one third of the Eastside professionals and managers were graduates compared to the majority of London gentrifiers in Butler and Robson's study. The Woodlands estate can be regarded as having a substantial 'middle' middle-class presence (Allen et al., 2007). The Newtown estates were more working-class in comparison. Thirdly, even amongst the Newtown sample there was little evidence of the poverty and deprivation which affects the council renting working class living in inner London (Watt, 2003). The routine and skilled workers in Eastside can be regarded as part of an affluent working class, one for whom 'maintaining' respectability was less problematic than for the inner London white working class (Watt, 2006).

The Geography of Moving from London

As might be expected, nearly nine out of ten Eastsiders in the survey had moved from east London, as illustrated in Table 9.1 below. Nearly half (46 per cent) came from the outer London Borough of Havering, the nearest borough to Eastside. Apart from Havering, the other main area of origin was the rest of east London, i.e. the six boroughs of Barking and Dagenham, Hackney, Newham, Redbridge, Tower Hamlets and Waltham Forest, accounting for 41 per cent. The remaining 13 per cent of the survey sample came from various parts of London.

In relation to the Thames Gateway, Table 9.1 shows that nearly 80 per cent of all the in-movers to Eastside relocated from one of the London Thames Gateway boroughs (i.e. Barking and Dagenham, Havering, Newham, Tower Hamlets, Bexley and Lewisham).

Table 9.1   London borough location of respondents' previous address

London borough	N	%
East London	*122*	*87.0*
Barking and Dagenham	13	9.3
Hackney	2	1.4
Havering	65	46.4
Newham	20	14.3
Redbridge	8	5.7
Tower Hamlets	11	7.9
Waltham Forest	3	2.1
North London	*8*	*5.6*
Barnet	1	0.7
Brent	2	1.4
Enfield	3	2.1
Islington	2	1.4
South London	*6*	*4.2*
Bexley	1	0.7
Croydon	1	0.7
Lewisham	1	0.7
Southwark	3	2.1
West London	*4*	*2.8*
Ealing	3	2.1
Hammersmith and Fulham	1	0.7

Havering is somewhat distinct from the remaining six east London boroughs. The latter are characterised by concentrations of social and economic deprivation as well as large multi-ethnic populations (Rix, 1996; Hamnett, 2003). Five of the six were among the 25 most deprived local authority districts in England in 1998, except Redbridge which was ranked 90th (Hamnett, 2003, p. 190). These six boroughs are also distinguished by large tracts of social housing, much of it in the form of estates with concentrations of deprivation and social exclusion. Furthermore, with the exception of Barking and Dagenham, the six east London boroughs are characterised by having large proportions of minority ethnic groups; at least one third of their populations were non-white in 2001, ranging from 35.5 per cent in Waltham Forest to 60.6 per cent in Newham. Redbridge has seen a dramatic transformation during the last 20 years and now has a large minority ethnic population, mainly Indian in origin (Buck et al., 2002, 75). By comparison, Havering is less deprived than the rest of east London and also remains predominantly white (95 per cent in the 2001 Census).[5] Many of the sample had previously resided in areas such as Upminster, Romford and Hornchurch which include classic inter-war suburban private developments (English Heritage, 1999, pp. 204–5). Hence a good deal of the 'suburban moves' we are considering in this chapter are actually suburb-to-suburb rather than from the inner city to suburb. If Havering is socially and materially distinctive, it also appears substantially lower down Burrow's index of neighbourhood dissatisfaction compared with the other six east London boroughs (Burrows 1999, p. 114).

Table 9.2   Previous housing tenure by area of origin in London (%)

	Havering	East London	Other London	Total
Owner occupied	45	54	28	47
Shared ownership	0	7	0	3
Rented from private landlord	6	9	50	13
Rented from social landlord	3	7	0	4
Living with parents	40	18	11	27
Other	6	5	11	6
Total (N=100%)	65	57	18	140

It is worth briefly discussing the survey respondents' housing circumstances prior to their move to Eastside. Table 9.2 indicates their previous housing tenure in relation to where they lived in London. Nearly half were already owner-occupiers before they moved to Eastside, 22 per cent of who had bought their homes from the council under the Right-to-Buy policy. The second largest category in Table 9.2 (27 per cent) consisted mainly of younger people who had been living with their parents; the latter were nearly all homeowners. This group was even larger (40 per cent) in the case of those who had moved from Havering. Private renters made up 13 per cent of the sample, whilst a paltry 4 per cent were tenants of social landlords, mainly councils, a figure that was somewhat higher for those from east London. These figures suggest that the Eastsiders are on the whole not amongst the most disadvantaged people with least choice in the London housing market. At the same time, eight per cent described themselves as having been homeless

---

5   Havering was ranked 143rd most deprived local authority in 1998 (Hamnett, 2003, p. 190).

at one time or another in London, whilst the semi-structured interviews revealed that a few had made largely failed attempts to enter social housing during their housing careers.

Reasons for Leaving London and Moving to Eastside

The survey respondents were asked several questions aimed at discerning their reasons for leaving London and moving to Essex. Given the pressures on the London housing market and the hikes in house prices well beyond what average earners can afford, it should come as no surprise that 83 per cent described moving to an area with housing that they could afford as very important and only 4 per cent considered it to be not important.

When asked an open question, more than half (58 per cent) of respondents gave more than one main reason for moving. These reflected a combination of 'push' factors, those prompting them to leave their previous London area, and 'pull' factors drawing them towards Essex. Table 9.3 below indicates what percentage of respondents mentioned each as the single most important reason for moving. Housing factors predominated with very nearly half naming such factors as the single most important reason for moving, as seen in Table 9.3. People described wanting to move in order to obtain bigger and/or better housing. Affordability was also very important, both for first-time buyers and established homeowners. When asked what had prompted the respondents to specifically relocate to Eastside, housing factors again predominated: 'more value for money, a bigger house by moving out' (S66, Havering, owner).[6] If housing encompassed the main set of reasons for moving, personal factors, such as getting married, divorced or wanting to live near relatives, were also significant (Table 9.3). Younger people wanting to set up an independent home, as well as get married, were especially important in the case of those who had moved from Havering. Moving as a result of marital or relationship breakdown was also more significant in the case of ex-Havering residents. Employment factors, such as a job change or retirement, were of minor significance being the major factor in only 4 per cent of cases.

As Table 9.3 shows, area reasons played the major role in people wanting to move in 24 per cent of cases. People either wanted to live in a 'better'/'nicer' area or they disliked their previous area. A further closed question indicated that 41 per cent of survey respondents considered moving to a better area as a very important reason for moving, whilst only 23 per cent regarded it as not important. Moving to an area with better schools was less significant since this was the main reason in only 4 per cent of cases, although 31 per cent of those with school-age children regarded moving for better schools as 'very important' when asked a direct question on education.

---

6   'S66' refers to the respondent number in the survey. The area ('Havering') refers to the respondent's previous residential borough in London and the tenure ('owner') refers to their London housing tenure.

Table 9.3   Most important reason for moving from previous address

	N	%
Housing factors:	*68*	*49*
1 Wanted affordable property	21	15
2 Wanted bigger property	16	11
3 Wanted better/newer property (incl. garden)	12	9
4 Wanted to get on property ladder	11	8
5 Wanted smaller property	4	3
6 Previous home too expensive	3	2
7 Evicted	1	1
Personal factors:	*42*	*30*
1 To get married/live with partner	14	10
2 Independence – live in own home	10	7
3 Nearer family	6	4
4 Marital/partnership breakdown	5	4
5 Health	3	2
6 Parents died/divorced	2	1
7 Other personal	2	1
Area factors:	*33*	*24*
1 Wanted better area	16	11
2 Disliked previous area	12	9
3 Wanted better schools	5	4
Employment factors	*6*	*4*
Other factors	*2*	*1*
Total	151	100

Note: Total percentage does not add to 100 for two reasons: a) 11 respondents gave two
       most important reasons: and b) rounding errors.

How do the Eastsiders' reasons for moving compare to national data on
residential mobility (Costello, 1990; DoE, 1994, pp. 166–74)? There is a good
deal of congruence in relation to the over-arching importance of housing-related
reasons. However, differences occur in relation to both employment and area
reasons. Employment-related moves are far less significant in Eastside than
nationally (Costello, 1990, 13; DoE 1994, 174), probably reflecting the fact that
Eastside is partly a commuter suburb. On the other hand, area-related moves are

more significant in relation to Eastside at 24 per cent compared to 17 per cent nationally (Costello, 1990, p. 13).

We can examine whether the reasons for moving from London to Eastside are uniform across the various parts of the capital that the respondents originated came from. Their area of origin is grouped into three: Havering, the other six east London boroughs, and the rest of London. This allows us to compare to what extent moving from the distinctive white, more affluent borough of Havering is in any sense different from the rest of London and especially from east London, an area of considerable deprivation plus with a large minority ethnic population. Table 9.4 below demonstrates a stark contrast between those who moved from Havering compared to the other six east London boroughs. Whereas moving to a better area was 'very important' for 62 per cent of the latter, this only applied to 24 per cent of the former. In fact moving to a 'better area' was not important for nearly half (43 per cent) of the ex-residents of Havering compared with a mere 4 per cent of those from east London.

Table 9.4   Importance of moving to a better area by area of origin in London (%)

	Havering	**East London**	**Other London**	**Total**
Very important	24	62	47	43
Fairly important	33	34	35	34
Not important	43	4	18	23
Total (N=100%)	63	56	17	136

Notes:: excludes 'don't knows'; p <0.01; Cramer's V = 0.333.

Other evidence from the survey points in a similar direction to Table 9.4. For example, returning to the main reason for wanting to move in Table 9.3 above, 39 per cent of those from east London gave area factors compared to 32 per cent who gave housing factors. This position is reversed for those who moved from Havering with figures of 9 and 54 per cent respectively. Respondents were also asked a hypothetical question as to whether they would have stayed in their previous area if they could have 'afforded suitable housing there'. Nearly two-thirds (64 per cent) of those from Havering would have done so, compared to only 12 per cent of those from the rest of east London.

Neighbourhood Satisfaction in London

Many survey respondents couched their place imagery in vague terms about wanting to move to a 'nicer' or 'better' area, or away from a 'rough' or 'grotty' area. In this section, we unpack further what respondents meant by a 'better area' with reference to the survey questions on their previous London area plus the interview data.

Asking about neighbourhood satisfaction is generally regarded as being a good indicator of area perceptions (Parkes et al., 2002). Respondents were asked how satisfied they were with their previous area and the responses to this question can be compared with national data from the Survey of English Housing (ibid.). The results can be seen in Figure 9.1 below for those respondents who had moved from Havering and the other six east London boroughs.[7] This shows that the levels of area satisfaction for the borough of Havering are in fact very similar to those for England as a whole with over half of ex-Havering residents very satisfied with their area, whilst only small percentages were either fairly or very dissatisfied (totalling less than 10 per cent). The contrast with the ex-residents of the rest of east London is stark. Only 14 per cent of the latter were very satisfied with their area whilst a massive one third were very dissatisfied and a further 16 per were fairly dissatisfied. The area dissatisfaction level for those people who had moved from east London was therefore both well above the national level and the level for those who had moved from Havering. Such differences in satisfaction levels are mirrored in the responses to the open survey question about what people liked about their previous area of residence. Nearly half of the ex-residents of Havering replied that there was 'nothing' that they disliked about their previous area. In stark contrast, only seven per cent of those from the six east London boroughs said the same thing about their previous areas.

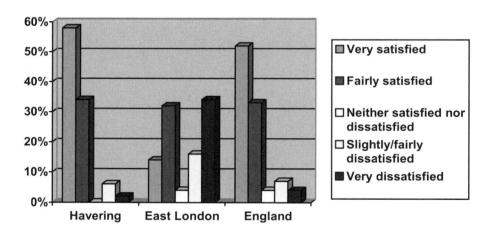

Figure 9.1   Satisfaction with area (%)

Source: Havering and East London figures from Eastside Survey, 2004; England figures
          from the Survey of English Housing, 1997/8 (cited in Parkes et al., 2002, p. 9).

In relation to questions about area dislikes and change, 'rough' people and places were routinely highlighted encapsulating perceptions of two broad but to

---

7   The rest of London respondents have been excluded from Figure 9.1 because of small numbers.

some extent overlapping issues (see Watt, 2006). The first relates to the physical environment. Comments about noise, smell, traffic congestion, lack of space and general appearance were prominent in both the survey and interviews: 'overcrowded, dirty, no greenery, the environment not good' (S133, Redbridge, owner). The respondents alluded to the notion that the city was 'dirty' in one way or another, as discussed at length elsewhere (Watt, 2007a). The second set of issues involved the characterisation of their previous area in relation to various forms of social disorder, notably crime, anti-social behaviour, drugs and the perennial complaint about 'lots of young people hanging around' (S66, Havering, owner). Examples include:

> [The area] became more rundown. ... There were more problem families moving in with six kids and four dogs and the houses were boarded up. The type of people and the class changed. (S62, Barking and Dagenham, tenant)

> The area was near to gasworks and factories, there was a stench in the air, not pleasant in the summer especially. There was high crime and vandalism, drugs on the doorstep. (S24, Newham, tenant)

As the above quotes suggest, the place images of dirt and disorder often overlapped (see Watt, 2007a). This overlapping centered upon three main urban public spaces, i.e. residential neighbourhoods, high streets and schools. In these spaces, the social bearers of dirt and disorder, those tainted with roughness, took a number of guises but included tenants or 'problem tenants', minority ethnic groups and young people (gangs, kids, etc.). The presence of these groups in residential neighbourhoods meant that many ex-Londoners articulated 'narratives of urban decline' (Watt, 2006). Working-class and to some extent middle-class communities were said to have been eroded, largely by the presence of groups associated with disorder and dirt. In Bauman's terms, those people from east London expressed a mixophobic reaction to the diversity and strangeness of cities. Disorder issues were by no means monopolised by those who had moved from the deprived east London boroughs since they also featured in the area accounts of those from suburban Havering, albeit to a much lesser extent.

The narratives of urban decline could also take a racist form as some white respondents linked the deteriorating state of their previous neighbourhood to the increased presence of loosely-classified racialised 'others' including asylum seekers, refugees, immigrants, Asians and non-whites:

> Bosnians, asylum seekers hanging around. Burglars, I didn't feel safe, mugging, gangs, high crime. The area looked tatty. (S46, Barking and Dagenham, owner)

> The area went downhill, became dirty. Immigrants did not look after their property and the area ... It was unsafe late at night with drunks, drugs and low life (S55, Newham, owner)

In Newham and Tower Hamlets, some white respondents regarded the English as being the minority in areas that had been 'taken over' by alien 'others' (see Dench et al., 2006):

> [Area got worse because] overtaken by different races, it become an area where English is in the minority. All the shops changed to cater for different cultures. (S53, Newham, owner)

'White flight' was therefore part of the rationale for some people leaving various parts of London, especially the six multi-ethnic east London boroughs. Unfortunately there is insufficient space here to discuss this important, complex and controversial issue in the detail that it deserves (see Watt, 2007a, 2007b).[8]

Neighbourhood Satisfaction in Eastside

As mentioned above, a large part of the original appeal of Eastside lay in the fact that it offered the ex-Londoners either a first step or a better step on the property ladder. Other 'pull' factors came into play, notably transport accessibility for commuting, the availability and quality of shopping and other facilities including schools. Eastside also appealed because part of its landscape resonated with what Champion (2000, p. 15) has called a 'beckoning rural idyll', for example the surrounding fields and the village church. 'It's partly a village, a complete change ... more countrified and rural, very quiet' (S7, Woodlands, owner) was a typical 'rural idyll' response.[9]

By the time they were interviewed, the new residents of Eastside had lived there for an average period of four and a half years. The survey results indicate that the majority, both in Woodlands and Newtown, were satisfied with their housing and to a lesser extent with their neighbourhoods. Area satisfaction levels were in fact very close to national levels as indicated in Figure 9.1 above. Furthermore, around 60 per cent preferred Eastside as a place to live rather than their previous neighbourhood in London compared to only one fifth who preferred the latter. However, the area the ex-Londoners came from affected these results. Amongst those from east London, except Havering, a massive 86 per cent preferred Eastside and less than 4 per cent preferred their previous area. On the other hand, 39 per cent of ex-Havering residents preferred Havering compared to 36 per cent who preferred Eastside. When asked an open question on what they liked about living in their present neighbourhood, the vast majority of survey respondents could think of something positive to say, notably that the area was quiet, peaceful, clean, convenient and close to the countryside. In fact, one quarter

---

8   'White flight' is a somewhat problematic term in the sense that some of the stigmatised groups (for example East European asylum seekers) are themselves 'white' (see Clarke and Garner, 2005).

9   In this section of the chapter, the area ('Woodlands') refers to their current location within Eastside and the tenure ('owner') refers to their present housing tenure.

could think of nothing that they disliked about the area. A benign picture can therefore be painted of suburban [self]-satisfaction based upon perceptions of order, cleanliness and tranquility as opposed to the urban disorder, dirt and angst they had left behind.

Despite this image, there was also evidence of considerable disquiet. This emerged in the survey but was even more pronounced during the semi-structured interviews. Dissatisfaction related to inadequate infrastructure, notably the paucity of non-commuter public transport as well as limitations regarding local shopping and leisure facilities. However, much of the disquiet centered upon the social texture of the Eastside area in relation to perceptions of disorder, for example crime and young people 'hanging around':

> The council estate has a high crime rate. Eastside looks a dump as you drive in. Overall it's a dump, a rundown area, a poor area financially. (S122, Newtown, shared owner)

As this quotation illustrates, the nearby council estate was routinely regarded as a blot on the suburban landscape and was associated with crime, anti-social behaviour and poverty, as well as physical decay. This estate, as well as the local state schools, shops and pubs, plus nearby Travellers' camp sites, represented stigmatised places to be avoided for several Eastsiders but especially the residents of the Woodlands estate. The latter were most likely to engage in a variety of avoidance strategies to distance themselves from 'downmarket' people and places in Eastside. One woman had moved from an affluent suburb in Havering as a result of marital breakdown. She described her own 'pure snobbery' about Eastside and not wanting to 'mix with people like that':

> The private estate [Woodlands] is like Upminster. ... Off the estate is a totally different life to what I'm used to. It's downmarket, I don't shop in the local area. (S86, Woodlands, owner)

This woman sent her children to schools in Havering. This spatial practice was by no means unusual since several of the predominantly middle-class parents from Woodlands sent their children to school outside the Eastside area, either to the affluent suburbs of London or to other parts of Essex. As well as being concerned about various blots on the suburban landscape, some Eastsiders expressed disquiet about what they saw as 'rough Londoners' moving into Eastside, a concern that also took a racialised form (see Watt, 2007a).

Towards the end of the survey, respondents were asked about their future plans. Despite the very high level of housing satisfaction and somewhat lower area satisfaction levels, 41 per cent said that they would prefer to move out of their current house or flat if given the choice. Of those who wanted to move, over three quarters wanted to move to another area. When asked why, housing factors were again important, but wanting a 'better area', including for schooling, were mentioned by nearly half of those who wanted to move. For example, one woman described wanting 'a more upmarket residential area, more rural' (S140,

Woodlands, owner). For those Woodlands' parents with children at a school outside of Eastside, moving nearer to the school was also a major incentive to relocate.

Conclusion

Most of the new Eastside residents had moved eastwards along the Thames Gateway. The search for affordable housing was a major factor in driving them away from London as well as towards suburban Essex. However, this overarching explanation conceals considerable variation dependent upon where in east London they had moved from. At the risk of over-simplification, it is possible to suggest that the suburbanisation we are discussing here encompasses two fairly distinct sets of eastward flows along the Thames. The first flow comprised those people who moved from the east London borough of Havering, whilst the second flow consisted of those who had moved from elsewhere in east London. In social class terms, there was little difference between these two flows. In the case of those from Havering, a large minority of these were younger people still living in the parental home who wanted to set up an independent home, as Table 9.2 indicates. They, alongside existing homeowners who wanted to step up to a better property or in some cases whose marriages had broken down, would probably have stayed in Havering *if* they could have afforded to buy suitable property there. Although Havering did have its share of problems, by and large these were not regarded as prohibitive. Therefore we can regard the move from Havering to Eastside as largely an overspill phenomenon as middle- and working-class people relocated from a more expensive suburb to a nearby cheaper one.[10]

The second eastward flow consisted of those who had previously lived in one of the other six east London boroughs apart from Havering. East London was routinely regarded as having gone 'downhill' as a result of increased crime and anti-social behaviour, 'kids hanging around', plus the presence of a range of racialised 'newcomers' including immigrants, asylum seekers and non-white minority ethnic groups. Those people from east London, as well as those from the rest of inner London, demonstrated a 'mixophobic' reaction to city living based upon a dislike of both social disorder and physical dirt. The city contained too many strangers, and especially those who were regarded as being responsible for the breakdown of 'community'. Leaving the city in search of a 'better area' i.e. greater social similarity and perceived safety, was an important factor in their moving to the Essex suburbs. Intertwined in this mixophobia (Bauman 2003) was a racist reaction to ethnic difference. Hence 'white flight' played some part in the move eastwards along the Thames Gateway. How many of those Eastsiders from east London would have remained there if suitable affordable housing was available is debatable. Moving away from deprived, 'rough' parts of inner and

---

10   Whether or not this should be considered a displacement effect as a result of gentrification in Havering is something that is difficult to answer with the data here (see Atkinson, 2000).

outer London to homeowning suburbia simultaneously proved and buttressed the respectability of the working- and middle-class urban escapees (cf. Watt 2006).

Having moved to Eastside, most of its new residents were generally satisfied both with their housing and with their immediate neighbourhood. Many considered it to be an improvement on their previous neighbourhood inside the Greater London boundary. At the same time, Eastside did not come upto the socially exclusive standards sought by several of its new residents and especially the middle classes living in the Woodlands estate. There were too many blots on the suburban landscape, notably the council estate, for this to be the case. As a 'spoiled suburb', Eastside was therefore only partially satisfactory for many residents since it contained too many 'rough' people and places, those same elements that they thought they had left behind in the city (see Watt, 2007a).

The research findings reported here are based upon a case study of a single suburb and as such one should be cautious about extrapolating too far in policy terms. Nevertheless the following points can be made in relation to regeneration in the Thames Gateway. Firstly, the Eastside findings emphasise what a socially complex and contested place the Thames Gateway is. Secondly, the findings here reinforce the argument from Power et al. (2004) that the provision of housing in and of itself is insufficient to regenerate the London Thames Gateway and that there needs to be major investment in infrastructure and community facilities before it will be considered as a desirable area in which to live by certain higher-income groups (see Bennett and Morris, 2006). Thirdly, it highlights what Power et al. (2004, p. 8) call 'the sensitivity of race relations in east London'. Fourthly, the Eastside findings emphasise the notion that the Essex Thames Gateway has a problem of poor image (Church and Frost, 1995), at least as far as incoming middle-class groups are concerned. This image is partly linked to earlier rounds of suburbanisation notably those that created the post-war council estates for the Fordist working class. Lastly, the Eastside findings expose what remains a fundamental contradiction in relation to contemporary suburban development generally (see Watt, 2007a). If part of the enduring appeal of suburbia lies in its socially exclusive nature comprised of aspirational, respectable 'people like us' (URBED, 2002, p. 13), then how can this appeal be reconciled with the social heterogeneity found in many suburban areas, a heterogeneity that fundamentally challenges the exclusionary class and racialised underpinnings of the aspirant suburban imagination?

References

Allen, J., Massey, D., Cochrane, A. Charlesworth, J.A., Court, G., Henry, N. and Sarre, P. (1998), *Rethinking the Region*, London, Routledge.

Allen, C., Powell, R., Casey, R. and Coward, S. (2007), '"Ordinary, the Same as Anywhere Else": Notes on the Management of Spoiled Identity in Marginal Middle-Class Neighbourhoods', *Sociology*, 41(2): 239–58.

Atkinson, R. (2000), 'Professionalization and Displacement in Greater London', *Area* 23(3): 287–96.

Back, L. (1996), *New Ethnicities and Urban Culture*, London, UCL Press.

Back, L. (1998), 'Inside Out: Racism, Class and Masculinity in the "Inner City" and the English Suburbs', *New Formations*, 33: 59–76.

Bauman, Z. (2003), *Liquid Love*, Cambridge, Polity.

Bennett, J. and Morris, J. (2006), *Gateway People: the aspirations and attitudes of prospective and existing residents of the Thames Gateway*, London, Institute for Public Policy Research.

Bourdieu, P. (1984), *Distinction*, London, Routledge.

Burrows, R. (1999), 'The Geography of Neighbourhood Dissatisfaction', *Rising East*, 2(3): 100–21.

Buck.N., Gordon, I., Hall, P., Harloe, M. and Kleinman, M. (2002), *Working Capital: Life and Labour in Contemporary London*, London, Routledge.

Butler, T. and Robson, G. (2003), *London Calling: The Middle Classes and the Re-making of Inner London*, Oxford, Berg.

Champion, T. (2000), 'Flight from the Cities?', in Bate, R., Best, R. and Holmans, A. (eds), *On the Move: The Housing Consequences of Migration*, York, Joseph Rowntree Foundation.

Champion, T. and Ford, T. (2000), *Residential Movement Into, Out of and Within London – the Part Played by Housing Associations: A Report to the Housing Corporation*, Newcastle upon Tyne, Department of Geography, University of Newcastle.

Church, A. and Frost, M. (1995), 'The Thames Gateway: An Analysis of the Emergence of a Sub-Regional Regeneration Initiative', *The Geographical Journal*, 161(2), 199–209.

Clapson, M. (1998), *Invincible Green Suburbs, Brave New Towns*, Manchester, Manchester University Press.

Clapson, M. (2003), *Suburban Century: Social Change and Urban Growth in England and the United States*, Oxford, Berg.

Clarke, S. and Garner, S. (2005), 'Psychoanalysis, Identity and Asylum', *Psychoanalysis, Culture and Society*, 10: 197–206.

Costello, J. (1990), 'How Far Do People Move House?', *Housing Finance*, 5: 13–17.

Deakin, N. and Ungerson, C. (1977), *Leaving London: Planned Mobility and the Inner City*, London, Heinemann.

Dench, G., Gavron, K. and Young, M. (2006), *The New East End: Kinship, Race and Conflict*, London, Profile Books.

Department of the Environment (DoE) (1994), *Housing Attitudes Survey*, London, HMSO.

Devine, F. (1992), *Affluent Workers Revisited*, Edinburgh, Edinburgh University Press.

English Heritage (1999), *London's Suburbs*, London, Merrell Holberton Publishers.

Gwilliam, M., Bourne, C., Swain, C. and Prat, A. (1998), *Sustainable Renewal of Suburban Areas*, York, Joseph Rowntree Foundation.

Hamnett, C. (2003), *Unequal City: London in the Global Arena*, London, Routledge.

Opinion Research Services (ORS) (2004) *Greater London Housing Requirements Study*, London, Greater London Authority.

Pahl, R.E. (1964), *Urbs in Rure*, London, Weidenfeld and Nicholson.

Parkes, A., Kearns, A. and Atkinson, R. (2002), *The Determinants of Neighbourhood Dissatisfaction*. ESRC Centre for Neighbourhood Research, CNR Paper 1: available at http://www.neighbourhood.org.uk.

Power, A., Richardson, E., Seshimo, K. and Firth, K. with Rode, P., Whitehead, C. and Traver, A. (2004), *A Framework for Housing in the London Thames Gateway: Vol. I*, London, LSE Housing, London School of Economics.

Rix, V. (1996), 'Social and Demographic Change in East London', in Rustin, M. and Butler, T. (eds), *Rising in the East*, London, Lawrence and Wishart.

Savage, M., Bagnall, G. and Longhurst, B. (2005), *Globalization and Belonging*, London, Sage Publications.

Shields, R. (1991), *Places on the Margin*, London, Routledge.

Sibley, D. (1995), *Geographies of Exclusion*, London, Routledge.

Silverstone, R. (ed.) (1997), *Visions of Suburbia*, London, Routledge.

Sinclair, I. (2003), *London Orbital*, London, Penguin.

URBED (with the TCPA) (2002), *A City of Villages: Promoting a Sustainable Future for London's Suburbs*, London, Greater London Authority.

Watt, P. (1998), 'Going Out of Town: Youth, Race and Place in the South-East of England', *Environment and Planning D: Society and Space*, 16:, 687–703.

Watt, P. (2001), *The Dynamics of Social Class and Housing: A Study of Local Authority Tenants in the London Borough of Camden*, unpublished PhD thesis, University of London.

Watt, P. (2003), 'Urban Marginality and Economic Restructuring: Local Authority Tenants and Employment in an Inner London Borough', *Urban Studies*, 40:9, 1769–89.

Watt, P. (2004), 'Narratives of Urban Decline and Ethnic Diversity: White Flight and the Racialization of Space in London and South-East England', paper presented at the Countering Urban Segregation Conference, Free University Amsterdam, 14–15 October.

Watt, P. (2006), 'Respectability, Roughness and "Race": Neighbourhood Place Images and the Making of Working-Class Social Distinctions in London', *International Journal of Urban & Regional Research*, 30:4: 776–97.

Watt, P. (2007a, forthcoming), 'From the Dirty City to the Spoiled Suburb', in Campkin, B. and Cox, R. (eds), *Dirt: New Geographies of Cleanliness and Contamination*, London, I.B. Tauris.

Watt, P. (2007b), 'Under Siege in the London Suburbs: Mixophobia, Racisms and Imagined Communities in the Thames Gateway', paper presented at the British Sociological Association Annual Conference, University of East London, 12–14 April.

Willmott, P. and Young, M. (1960), *Family and Class in a London Suburb*, London, Routledge and Kegan Paul.

Young, M. and Willmott, P. (1957), *Family and Kinship in East London*, London, Routledge and Kegan Paul.

Young, M. and Willmott, P. (1975), *The Symmetrical Family*, Harmondsworth, Penguin.

Chapter 10

Homing in on Housing

Penny Bernstock

An exploration of housing in Thames Gateway reveals the difficulty in imagining that there is a discernible housing project taking shape across this vast region that has been marked out and labelled as the Thames Gateway. What is also clear is that across this disparate space, a number of housing projects have sprung up often on watersides or brownfield sites and these schemes are contributing to meeting the now urgent government targets for more housing.

However, what these schemes also illustrate are the ongoing tensions in government policy about the need for more affordable housing, whilst creating 'balanced' communities; the need for more family housing whilst building at higher densities; the need for sustainable regeneration that incorporates employment opportunities and social infrastructure as opposed to isolated housing projects that further expand the commuter belt and the need to ensure that Thames Gateway becomes a place of choice to live as opposed to a 'buy to let' wasteland.

The government in its interim report on the Thames Gateway published in 2006 revised its housing target upwards from 120,000 to 160,000 with 35 per cent of this housing being affordable and it will undoubtedly fall to the private sector to deliver the bulk of this housing through the application of S106 agreements. Please see below for an explanation of S106 agreements (Department of Communities and Local Government, 2006). From the perspective of private developers there are considerable risks in developing housing projects in Thames Gateway, such as the high remediation costs of building on contaminated Brownfield sites; potential flood risk and the impact on profitability of the government requirements for increasing proportions of affordable housing (Gairns, 2005; Watson, 2006).

The regeneration of Thames Gateway is at a juncture. So far, the housing that has been built by the government's own omission could have been of a higher quality; included more family housing and linked more effectively to economic regeneration (Department of Communities and Local Government, 2006) The Institute of Public Policy Research have also argued that people will not want to move into such areas unless there is a mix of high quality social housing commercial developments and local facilities (Bennett and Morris, 2006).

Similarly, the findings of the study discussed below indicate that new developments are unevenly emerging across the Thames Gateway concentrating in the main around new transport links. These new developments are predominantly one- and two-bedroom flats, with a much smaller proportion of larger properties and houses being built, despite the need for such properties. In some areas maximum levels of density as indicated in urban planning documents are being exceeded. Moreover, the current model of negotiating planning gain has resulted in a scheme by scheme approach which does not lend itself well to a coherent and strategic approach, and is too dependent on the private sector. Without a more concerted effort the Thames Gateway may simply be yet another great planning disaster (Hall, 1980; Brownill, 1989)

This chapter draws on the findings of a research project undertaken between September 2005 and March 2006. The project aimed to provide a detailed picture of current practice regarding S106 planning agreements on all schemes of 100 plus units across the Thames Gateway that had either been planned or developed between January 2000 and September 2005.

Section 106 agreements were introduced as part of the Town and Country Planning Act 1990. These agreements place conditions on developers linked to the granting of planning permission and are intended to mitigate the impact of any new developments. The aim of these agreements is to ensure that developers contribute towards necessary infrastructure and the potential costs of new developments, such as the need for more school places, new roads etc. This is essentially known as 'planning gain' and may also relate to the mix of dwellings and the provision of affordable housing. Indeed, the provision of affordable housing delivered through S106 agreements is increasing to the extent that in 2006 more than half of all new affordable housing was provided in this way. (Monk et al., 2006; Rowlands et al., 2006; Watson, 2006) A range of studies have identified huge variation in the application of such agreements, and the trend is towards the implementation of a more formulaic approach based on formally agreed regional and local policies and priorities.(ODPM, 2005a).

Data related to the S106 agreements analysed was drawn from quantifiable data in the public domain. In particular S106 agreements were scrutinised along-with planning committee papers, and in some instances interviews with planning officers, developers and marketing agencies. This analysis enabled us to map the requirements of the respective local authorities in relation to each of these housing projects across the Thames Gateway, in particular exploring financial and affordable housing commitments. Data on housing type and housing density (where it was available) was recorded in order to analyse trends in these areas.

One finding of this study related to the incomplete and inconsistent way in which data was recorded both within and between authorities, with some authorities providing elaborate detail on S106 commitments and expenditure, whilst others provided minimal information. This was consistent with the findings of previous research (Monk, 2001). Moreover given that the project relied solely on descriptive data recorded in documents to make sense of S106 agreements, we have not been able to capture the complex negotiations that lead to projects either being implemented or abandoned. In total 82 schemes were identified across the Thames Gateway (see below).

We begin by considering housing targets and housing completions. We then move on to specifically consider the proportion of affordable housing being delivered through S106 agreements; the type of housing being built; the density

Table 10.1 Planning permission granted or scheme completed 2000–2005 (inclusive)

Name of Authority	Number of schemes
London Borough of Redbridge	15
London Borough of Newham	14
London Borough of Tower Hamlets	12
Havering	6
London Borough of Hackney	5
Medway	4
London Borough of Barking and Dagenham	4
London Borough of Greenwich	4
Gravesham	4
Dartford	4 (one outline for large scheme – Eastern Quarry for 7,250 homes)
Southend	3
London Borough of Lewisham	3
Thurrock	3
Rochford	1
Castle Point	0 (one large outline app)
London Borough of Waltham Forest	0
London Borough of Bexley	0 (large schemes but not subject to legal agreement – built on council sites)
Total	82

of this housing and finally we consider what other types of 'community gain' were specified in agreements.

Housing Targets and Housing Completions

A number of targets have been set for housing completions in the Thames Gateway area. Initial planning targets were for the construction of 80,000 new homes by 2016. This figure was revised upwards to 120,000, with the possibility of achieving 128,500 new homes if appropriate infrastructure was put in place; higher densities were applied; greater use was made of town centre housing; land uses were changed to residential uses and access was improved, and has since been revised upwards to 160,000. (ODPM, 2003a; GLA, 2004; DCLG, 2006)

Housing Completions Thames Gateway Authority 2000–2005

Table 10.2 shows housing completions for the period 2000 and 2005 and the initial housing targets of 120,000 set by the Office for the Deputy Prime Minister. If levels of activity continue at the same rate as between 2000 and 2005 we can predict that both London and Essex Thames gateway will reach the original target on new housing completions. However, the Kent Region of Thames Gateway is least likely to reach its target. We can also see that in order to reach the revised 160,000 target much more building will be necessary. Moreover, a study of national housing completions has suggested that output whilst increased continues to fall below what they describe as the modest targets set in the Barker Review (Palmer et al., 2006).

Table 10.2   House completions and housing targets, 2000–2005

Kent TG region 2000–05	London TG region 2000–05	Essex TG region 2000–2005
5,996 (12%)	32,126 (63%)	12,930 (25%)
Target 2001–2016	Target 2001–2016	Target 2001–2016
43,000	59,000 zones of change now by 2012 (86,000 TG authorities)	26,500

Source: ODPM, housing completion statistics, permanent dwellings completed 2000–05; ODPM, 2003a.

House Completions: London Thames Gateway

Thames Gateway Authorities within the London Region are expected to provide the bulk of housing in the Thames Gateway region and the target date for completion of 59,000 homes has been advanced from 2016 to 2012 based on London Development Agency assessments (ODPM, 2003a, GLA, 2004). The total capacity estimate for new dwellings in London is 315,237 for the period 2007/8 to 2016/17 with the East subregion comprising the largest contribution to overall capacity at 46 per cent (GLA, 2004). Indeed the revised figure of 120,000 new dwellings in the Thames Gateway region is based on significantly increasing output in the London Thames Gateway regions.

We can see from Table 10.3 that there was considerable variation in new housing completions between the London Thames Gateway Authorities. Most new housing was completed in Tower Hamlets and this has to be understood as the consolidation of the earlier London Docklands Regeneration project. Other authorities experiencing high levels of activity were Greenwich and Newham both of whom have benefited from new and planned transport infrastructure. Despite Barking and Dagenham and Havering having lots of land opportunities, activity levels were much lower indicating the uneven and slow pace of progress. We can also see that while from 2001 onwards levels of new house completions across the region as a whole increased, within some authorities this fluctuated up and down.

The proportion of housing completed by Registered Social Landlords is indicated in brackets and is 23 per cent across the region, well below the 50 per cent target indicated in the London Plan. We can see that the proportion of new housing completed by Registered Social Landlords has fluctuated across the period with no clear trend. We can also conclude that despite the need for affordable housing in London, the proportion of new housing delivered by registered social landlords ranged from 16–26 per cent. However, we need to read this data with caution as it may conceal increasing units of affordable housing being delivered through S106 agreements and possibly omitted from these figures.

Table 10.3   House completions in London Thames Gateway 2000–2005

Name of Authority	2000/1	2001/2	2002/3	2003/4	2004/5	Total
Hackney	762 (112)	612 (84)	419 (0)	283 (29)	525 (229)	2,601
Lewisham	151 (150)	289 (264)	553 (156)	632 (226)	501 (346)	2,126
Newham	484 (138)	722 (160)	426 (0)	1,092 (124)	416 (88)	3,140
Tower Hamlets	1,324 (131)	1,429 (415)	1,486 (496)	2,068 (393)	2,914 (444)	9,221
Barking and Dagenham	426 (80)	164 (57)	226 (15)	292 (101)	576 (340)	1,684
Bexley	482 (98)	223 (27)	271 (24)	784 (97)	221 (120)	1,981
Greenwich	586 (147)	1,099 (72)	1,410 (147)	1,122 (412)	1,576 (250)	5,793
Havering	274 (28)	307 (103)	263 (25)	447 (145)	457 (72)	1,748
Redbridge	159 (39)	301 (12)	510 (33)	442 (38)	650 (22)	2,062
Waltham Forest	812 (517)	129 (61)	345 (51)	191 (109)	293 (170)	1,770
Total	5,460 (1,440)	5,275 (1,255)	5,909 (947)	7,353 (1,674)	8,129 (2,081)	32,162 (7,397)
% RSLs	26	24	16	23	26	23

Kent Thames Gateway Authorities

There has been much less housing activity within the Kent Thames Gateway region. The table below details housing completions in the Thames Gateway Authorities in Kent between 2000 and 2005. We can see from this table that nearly 6,000 dwellings were completed between 2000 and 2005, and that new house completions have increased annually in this region. The target for housing completions in the Kent part of Thames Gateway is 43,000 for the period 2001 and 2016 (ODPM, 2002). If housing completions continue at this same pace then less than 18,000 properties will be completed by 2016, which is a shortfall of more than 25,000 properties. However, our own research demonstrated that lots of development activity is planned particularly in Gravesham and Dartford linked to the development of Ebbsfleet and therefore we can anticipate significant growth in this region.

The figures in brackets indicate completions by registered social landlords. We can see that 15 per cent of all new completions were completed by Registered Social Landlords and this ranged from 7 per cent–15 per cent in any one year. This is significantly below the 35 per cent figure for this region, that is now anticipated.

Table 10.4   Kent Thames Gateway: housing completions 2000–2005

Name of Authority	2000/1	2001/2	2002/3	2003/4	2004/5	Total
Dartford	229	190	433	640	380	1,872
	(16)	(5)	(55)	(82)	(52)	(210)
Gravesham	78	43	170	161	514	966
	(20)	(11)	(36)	(27)	(86)	(182)
Medway	984	562	566	516	530	3,158
	(152)	(43)	(10)	(57)	(43)	(305)
Total	1,291	795	1,169	1,307	1,424	5,996
	(188)	(59)	(101)	(166)	(181)	(697)
% RSLs	15	7	9	13	13	15

Source: ODPM, housing completion statistics, permanent dwellings completed 2000–05.

Essex Thames Gateway Authorities

The Essex Thames Gateway region has a lower overall target for new housing completions than the two other regions. We can see from the table below that Housing Activity in the Essex Thames Gateway Authorities has been uneven. Most new house building has been concentrated in three authorities, Southend, Thurrock and Basildon. Other authorities such as Rochford, Castlepoint and

Harlow have experienced much less new construction, again reinforcing the uneven nature of development across the Thames Gateway.

The figures in brackets indicate units completed by Registered Social Landlords, and we can see that these comprised 8 per cent of all completions, and ranged from 1 per cent–10 per cent of all completions across the five years. We can see that registered social landlords completed the lowest proportion of affordable housing in the Essex Thames Gateway region.

Table 10.5   Essex Thames Gateway – house completions 2000–2005

Name of Authority	2000/1	2001/2	2002/3	2003/4	2004/5	Total
Southend on Sea UA	102 (0)	82 (37)	142 (0)	134 (0)	*5128 (509)	5,588 (546)
Thurrock UA	611 (0)	983 (14)	971 (8)	819 (0)	Merged with Southend on Sea	3,384 (22)
Basildon	684 (49)	404 (12)	256 (63)	312 (18)	352 (57)	2,008 (199)
Castle Point	82 (5)	75 (0)	92 (0)	73 (0)	145 (29)	467 (34)
Harlow	237 (68)	194 (117)	145 (16)	59(0)	89 (0)	724 (201)
Rochford	180 (32)	151 (0)	144 (0)	191 (0)	93 (5)	759 (37)
Total	2,814 (154)	1,889 (180)	1,750 (87)	1,588 (18)	5,807 (607)	12,930 (1046)
% RSLs	5	10	5	1	10	8

Note: This data was compiled by the ODPM, based on local authority reported data and NHBC data. Please note local authorities may occasionally only submit partial data, sometimes omitting tenure specific data and therefore regional and county totals may not equal the sum of district figures.

Source: ODPM, housing completion statistics, permanent dwellings completed 2000–05; Southend on Sea and Thurrock UA housing completions were recorded separately until 2004/5.

We can conclude then that substantial numbers of new properties have been built across the Thames Gateway. A relatively small proportion of these have been completed by Registered Social Landlords and this has varied within the different regions. However, as noted above we need to treat these figures with caution as it may conceal an increasing proportion of housing delivered through S106 agreements, which may be included in private house completions. Let us now consider how much housing is being delivered through S106 agreements in Thames Gateway.

S106 Agreements and Affordable Housing in Thames Gateway

The development of Thames Gateway and the delivery of affordable housing have increasingly become synonymous, with targets of 50 per cent for London Thames Gateway and 35 per cent for the region as a whole (GLA, 2004; DCLG, 2006). It is anticipated that the region will play a crucial role in meeting the needs of London's expanding population and squaring the circle between low pay and housing need, whilst at the same time ensuring that communities are socio-economically balanced. The application of S106 agreements offers a tool to achieve this with private sector led development facilitating balanced communities.

However, our own research on agreements planned or delivered between 2000–2005 identified much lower proportions of affordable housing being achieved through such agreements and other research has questioned the extent to which private sector developers would be willing to provide increasing proportions of affordable housing, as this simply may not be viable (Watson, 2006). Indeed in the recent interim report on Thames Gateway it acknowledges a larger than anticipated role for Registered Social Landlords.(DCLG, 2006) Perhaps, in recognition of the problems of relying on the private sector to meet these increased targets for affordable housing.

Table 10.6 shows the average level of affordable housing specified on each of the 100 plus schemes analysed for the period 2000–2005. We can see that there is a huge range both between and within authorities in relation to the proportion of affordable housing specified. We can see that the average level of affordable housing on all schemes was 28 per cent, and this ranged from 7 per cent–100 per cent. However, we need to read this table with caution. All of the schemes providing a level of affordable housing at 35 per cent or above were developed by Registered Social Landlords. Moreover, a recent study by Monk et al. (2006) confirmed that there was variation in some instances between levels of affordable housing specified in planning agreements as compared with actual outputs.

A review of Planning Committee papers is informative in relation to understanding why some London Thames Gateway authorities gave permission for lower levels of affordable housing than indicated in the London Plan. One justification for allowing lower levels of affordable housing related to financial contributions towards affordable housing that reduced the need for Social housing grant. For example, there were schemes where levels of affordable housing were reduced from 30 per cent to 25 per cent if no social housing grant was required. Similarly the need to expand owner occupation as a policy objective in itself was also given as a rationale for lower levels of affordable housing and such negotiations were undertaken in relation to the Stratford City development. Similarly in authorities in which there were lower levels of development activity, authorities were sometimes willing to accept lower levels of affordable housing to ensure that the scheme was developed.

Table 10.6 Proportion of affordable housing stipulated in S106 agreements on 100 plus units

Name of Authority	Range	Average
Barking and Dagenham	30–71%	51%
Dartford	10–30%	22%
Gravesham	10–25%	20%
Greenwich	8–36%	27%
Hackney	31–62%	43%
Havering	15–31%	18%
Lewisham	7–35%	22%
Medway	25%	25%
Newham	15–100%	37%
Redbridge	21–35%	24%
Rochford	32%	32%
Southend	10–30%	22%
Thurrock	18–20%	19%
Tower Hamlets	17–56%	31%
All Authorities	7–100%	28%

Types of 'Affordable Housing'

The concept of 'affordable housing' is clearly contradictory; on the one hand there has been a lot of emphasis on increasing the proportions of affordable housing, and on the other there has been a failure to flesh out more clearly what constitutes 'affordable housing'. Circular 6/98 stressed the need for local flexibility in defining affordable housing, including both low cost market housing and social housing for rent. Central government is becoming more directive on this matter. Local authorities are now required to produce definitions of affordable housing in local plans. However, whilst there has been an increase in the proportion of local authorities defining 'affordable housing' there has been a tendency to simply restate national government guidelines, making these definitions meaningless (ODPM, 2003b).

We were interested to explore how the concept of 'affordable housing' was being interpreted across the Thames Gateway region. 'Affordable housing' can refer to social housing for rent provided through a Registered Social Landlord; Intermediate housing options where residents buy a proportion of their house from a developer or Registered Social Landlord; and key-worker housing aimed at specific groups either for sale or part purchase. We were interested to analyse the proportion of housing allocated to these different types of housing and the level of income that was required to determine eligibility to such options.

Disappointingly this level of detail was not available, and it was only possible to identify a breakdown of social rented and intermediate housing on some schemes.

Table 10.7 provides a breakdown of the proportion of affordable housing allocated for social rent on schemes for which the data was available. We can see that data was missing on several schemes. We can also see that where data was recorded there was a huge range in the proportion of affordable housing allocated for social rent ranging from 0 per cent–100 per cent. Furthermore we can see no particular trends within any authority on this issue. Several schemes fell short of London Plan targets that stipulate that a breakdown of 70 per cent social rent and 30 per cent intermediate options should be achieved on new developments (GLA,2004). Moreover, these findings differ from the government's own research drawn on data from 1998–2000 that argued that schemes in the South East were on average delivering more than 90 per cent social rented housing under affordable housing agreements.(ODPM, 2002) A more systematic approach to recording this important dimension would clearly be beneficial in order to more effectively plan, monitor and set targets for new provision.

Table 10.7 Proportion of affordable housing allocated for social rent

Name of Authority	% housing social rent range
Barking and Dagenham	0–58
Dartford	33–87
Gravesham	0–70
Greenwich Missing data 2 of 5 schemes	18–77
Hackney	33–100
Havering Missing data 2 of 6 schemes	0–100
Lewisham	50–73
Medway Missing data all schemes	
Newham	0–66
Redbridge Missing data all schemes	
Rochford	0
Southend	21–57
Thurrock Missing data 2 of 3 schemes	45
Tower Hamlets Missing data 5 of 13 schemes	50–73%

As this was a quantative approach it was difficult to establish the reasons why the proportion of affordable housing varied within one authority, However some reports provided more detail, and implied that the proportion of affordable housing for social rent was balanced against other objectives such as the need to ensure a 'balanced community'; and the proportion of social housing grant available. Another strategy that was applied on some schemes in Tower Hamlets was to agree financial contributions for off-site affordable housing. Clearly this mitigates against wider objectives of achieving more balanced communities in areas such as the Isle of Dogs.

Housing Density

High density development is increasingly presented as the solution to shortage of land and the key to building sustainable communities. Planning Policy Guidance No. 3 stresses the need to maximise land use and avoid developments of less than 30 units per hectare (ODPM, 2000). A range of government and quasi-government agencies have stressed the need to increase housing densities. This focus on increased density is in response to the shortage of land; the need to develop more sustainable communities and in particular a critical mass of population that will generate improved services and infrastructure and; the changing demographics of the population with the growth of smaller households. There is also an argument made for it in terms of a conception of the desirable city. The Urban Task Force's vision of renewal is characterised by high density living accompanied by high quality urban design with parks, green spaces, shops, cafes and good public transport marking out a good environment in which to live (Rogers, 2005). However, the flipside of the coin in relation to increased housing density is that we may simply have higher density housing without the anticipated benefits.

There are three related issues that need to be considered in relation to high density housing. Firstly, as developers are expected to provide increasing levels of affordable housing, they may achieve this by developing individual sites at higher densities that meet both profit and housing targets simultaneously. However, whilst these individual sites are developed at high densities they may continue to be characterised by relative isolation and separation thus achieving neither the benefits of the compact city or a coherent urban design.

Secondly, there is some evidence of a return to building upwards, so that increased densities have to be understood in part as a result of an increase in high-rise buildings. Planning applications of 16 storeys or above are not uncommon in the London part of Thames Gateway, and as each new scheme is agreed there appears to be little reflection on the perceived problems associated with this type of development, that was identified following the widescale construction of tower blocks in the 1960s, such as the unsuitability of these types of blocks for families and older people; the lack of outdoor space; poor construction and high maintenance costs (Malpass, 2005).

Thirdly and linked to housing type, there is the potential for a divide in terms of both type and density, with high density flatted accommodation accommodating mainly single people predominating in cities and lower density houses accommodating mainly families in expanding suburbs. This perspective was reinforced in a recent House of Commons Select Committee report that raised concerns about the suitability of this present trend for families (Meikle, 2006). Indeed, whilst the government's Urban Task force continues to advocate higher densities, one of its members Sir Peter Hall, contests this position and claims that the case for increasing housing densities is not proven, and may simply lead to the completion of apartment blocks, unsuitable to the needs of families (Rogers, 2006).

Housing Density in Thames Gateway

Table 10.8 shows the range and average housing densities in the different Thames Gateway Authorities. We can see from this table that there is a divide in relation to housing density within the Thames Gateway region. We can see that housing densities continue to be much lower in the outer Thames Gateway, exemplified in authorities such as Gravesham and Dartford and higher in 'inner Thames Gateway' authorities exemplified in authorities such as Newham and Redbridge.

There was also a trend within many authorities to exceed the authority's own density guidelines with a range of explanations applied for this deviation from policy:

For example:

The density of the proposed development would substantially exceed the council's normal thresholds as set out in policy H16.However, members will be aware of provisions of PPG no 3, the Urban White paper on Urban Renaissance and the 2004 London plan, which all now place an important weight on the overall indicators of the quality of new residential schemes, rather than relying on functional indicators such as simple density figures. (Re: Warton Road, London Borough of Newham)

Similar rationale can be found across the Thames Gateway region for exceeding Unitary Development Plan guidelines on housing density. Whilst building at high density does maximise land use it brings with it larger questions about design and live-ability that will need to be given much more prominence in planning debates. However, housing density has to be explored along with data on housing type.

Housing Type in Thames Gateway

The type of housing that is built in Thames Gateway is crucial for determining whose needs are likely to be met in these new housing developments and who is likely to live in Thames Gateway. One of the most worrying trends identified in this study was the mismatch between the type of housing being built and the type of housing that is needed.

Since 2000 there has been a trend nationally towards building more one- and two-bedroom flats and fewer houses. For example, in 2000/01 67 per cent of all

Table 10.8 Housing density by Thames Gateway Authority

Name of Authority	Housing density average	Range
Barking and Dagenham Data available 2 of 4 schemes	83	62–104 units per hectare
Dartford	65	50–77 units per hectare
Gravesham	43	36–47 units per hectare
Greenwich	198	81–396 units per hectare
Hackney Data available on 3 0f 5 schemes	420	151–650 units per hectare
Havering	292	102–592 units per hectare
Lewisham	420	302–802 habitable rooms per hectare
Medway Data available on all schemes	108	37–200 units per hectare
Newham Data available on 13 0f 14 schemes	827	377–1578 habitable rooms per hectare
Redbridge Data available on 10 of 14 schemes	897	157–3,104 habitable rooms per hectare
Rochford	45	One scheme 45 units per hectare
Southend Data available on one of three schemes	91	91 units per hectare
Thurrock	Data not available	
Tower Hamlets Data available on 6 of 12 schemes	212	132–372 units per hectare

Note: Some authorities record housing density based on units per hectare, other authorities use habitable room per hectare. Therefore this figure would need to be divided by three to generate an equivalent for units per hectare based on the average size properties being built.

new builds in the south-east were houses and this had fallen to 34 per cent by 2004/05 (ODPM, 2000–2005). Indeed the proportion of houses built, planned or developed in the Thames Gateway based on our analysis of schemes of 100 plus units was 26 per cent.

Table 10.9 below gives a breakdown of the proportion of houses and flats built in each Thames Gateway authority as indicated in the 100 plus schemes studied. We can see that data is missing for four authorities as these authorities either do not record this data systematically or simply record bedroom size. We can see that in eight of the 11 authorities for which data was available, flats comprised more than 70 per cent of all new developments, and in only two authorities did the proportion of houses exceed the proportion of flats.

Table 10.9 Proportion of houses and flats built in the Thames Gateway area

Thames Gateway Authority	% of flats	% of houses
Southend	11	89
Rochford	62	38
Thurrock	85	15
Havering	92	8
Dartford	73	27
Gravesham	44	56
Medway	78	22
Lewisham		
Newham		
Redbridge	75	25
Tower Hamlets		
Hackney		
Greenwich	70	30
Barking and Dagenham	77	23
Average	74	26

Source: 100+ developments across the Thames Gateway.

Meeting Need and Bedroom Type

Data on housing need indicates that there is a need for a range of housing types in relation to number of bedrooms. The pie chart below gives a breakdown of number of bedrooms for each property planned or completed during 2000–2005 for which data was available. The pie chart (Figure 10.1) gives a breakdown of number of bedrooms for each property planned or completed during 2000–2005 for which data was available. We can see from the chart that that 34 per cent of all new properties planned or developed were one bedroom; 47 per cent two bedroom and 19 per cent were three bedrooms or more. This figure is much lower than the proportion of three and four bedroom properties being completed nationally. For example according to data on housing type recorded by the ODPM in 2004/05 8 per cent of all completions in the private sector were one bedroom; 43 per cent two bedroom and 49 per cent had three bedrooms or more (ODPM, 2000–2005).

However, these figures mask considerable variation across the Thames Gateway with a larger proportion of 3 and 4 bedroom properties being completed in the Essed and Kent Thames Gateway authorities compared to the London Thames Gateway authorities.

Thames Gateway – housing type

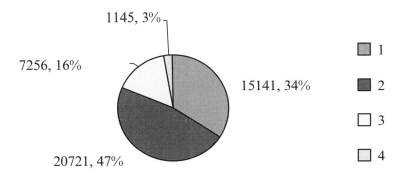

Figure 10.1 No. of bedrooms on Thames Gateway Housing Schemes

It could be argued that this simply reflects the demand for smaller properties in this area, however, an analysis of need indicators suggested that there is a mismatch between the type of housing needed and the type of housing being built, with areas of high demand such as Newham and Tower Hamlets producing smaller properties despite a demand for larger properties.

We can conclude then that despite considerable development activity across Thames Gateway there continues to be a shortfall in affordable housing both for rent and through intermediate purchasing options and there is a tendency towards building one- and two-bedroom flats at increasing densities. This suggests that without more concerted government intervention we may either see a return to overcrowding or the continued flight of families from cities. However, in addition to the provision of affordable housing, S106 agreements bring other types of benefits and it is to this that we now turn.

S106 Agreements and Community Gain

As discussed above Section 106 agreements were introduced with the intention of ensuring that developers contribute towards necessary infrastructure and the potential costs of their development, along with maximising community benefit from new developments, therefore it was interesting to explore ways in which this had been implemented on Thames Gateway developments.

Analysis of the 82 agreements identified huge variability in relation to the level of contributions and the way in which these were specified. For example, one authority might require a developer to provide a riverside walkway, whilst another might specify £1.2 million towards a Riverside walkway. There was also considerable variation in the level of contribution which may vary from £0 to £3 million plus. Sometimes a financial contribution was indicated for 'affordable housing' and sometimes it was not. This variability was indicative of the scheme by scheme negotiations and an outcome of the relative bargaining power of the different authorities. Analysis of the different authorities enabled us to identify both minimisers and maximisers of community gain. However, each scheme has its own discrete story:

> We wanted the scheme to happen, so we didn't impose too many specifications. (Planning Officer)

> The remediation costs were high so we didn't impose any financial obligations. (Planning officer)

On the other hand:

> developers who want to invest in this area, are going to have to be willing to make large financial contributions. (Local councillor)

From a developers' perspective the increasing financial costs associated with development acted as a disincentive:

> We've looked at ten sites in the Thames Gateway and only two are really feasible in terms of development, we have to pay large sums to remediate these sites and then make large contributions to affordable housing.

Community Gain in Thames Gateway

S106 agreements specified a range of benefits linked to what might be described as community gain. Practice across the different authorities varied with many of the London Thames Gateway Authority operating a more standardised approach with specific contributions for education, public art, etc. The most common contribution to be cited in agreements related to highways and public transport cited in some 63 per cent of agreements followed by education contributions cited in 39 per cent of agreements and parks and open spaces cited in 34 per cent of agreements. Less frequently mentioned were local labour clauses cited in 22 per cent of agreements and parking related issues such as car free travel agreements cited in 17 per cent of agreements. Other categories included sport and leisure facilities cited in 16 per cent of agreements; urban realm and public art cited in 13 per cent and 9.5 per cent of agreements respectively.

However, whilst developers were required to specify contributions to developments, local authorities rarely made any commitments to specific schemes, with only one authority citing a specific contribution which was in this instance for a bus stop. Moreover, there was clearly a tension on some scheme where the developers had been required by the local authority to build a school and then the local authority claimed not to have the resources to run the school and therefore the school did not open and residents had to make alternative arrangements and travel long distances elsewhere.

Overall a total cash sum of £210,745,119 was identified across the 82 schemes and it did appear that these contributions were arrived at on a scheme by scheme approach, as compared with a more strategic and coherent overview of how to use the monies to create sustainable regeneration across as opposed to simply within these schemes.

Conclusion

There are a number of conclusions then that we can draw about housing in Thames Gateway. The first is clearly that there is increasing evidence of development activity taking place across the Thames Gateway, though this is uneven both across the region and within different parts of the region. The concentration of development in particular parts of the region may lead to the kind of urban renaissance imagined with well resourced compact urban spaces emerging around more developed parts of the region with good transport connections. However, on the other hand there is also evidence that some of these schemes continue to be relatively isolated and spatially separated and therefore it may be that different housing markets are emerging in response to different markets, and those with lower incomes will be forced to move to the more isolated parts of the region.

The Thames Gateway has been marked out as a region to meet the now urgent shortages of affordable housing. We have seen that 'affordable housing' has been delivered through S106 agreements across the region, but the proportions of affordable housing being built are consistently falling below government targets and have varied considerably across the region. We have also seen that despite an emphasis on 'affordable housing' definitions of 'affordable housing' remain vague and that there has been a failure within some authorities to systematically record the different types of affordable housing provided through different schemes.

In terms of the type of housing being built we have seen that there has been a significant shift in the type of properties being built with a trend towards the production of one- and two-bedroom flats, and that this trend has been even more apparent in Thames Gateway. We have also seen that there is trend towards building at increasingly high densities and upwards with many tall residential blocks now built or in the process of construction across the Thames Gateway.

We can see that a reliance on the market to deliver housing across Thames Gateway is leading to a mismatch between the type of housing delivered both in terms of affordability and size and the type of housing that is needed. However, we must also question how this emerging housing market will interact with existing social divisions. Will lower income groups find themselves forced into purchasing overcrowded accommodation or forced to move further away to be able to purchase suitable accommodation in more isolated parts of the region, and, Who will come to reside in these new towers? Will there be polarisation here too, with the well positioned towers occupying riverside views, housing the super rich, with the poorer groups desperate to get a foot on the housing ladder crowding themselves into lower cost apartments in blocks that may quickly come to encounter the high maintenance costs that plagued the sixties tower blocks. How will the rapidly expanding buy to let market impact on this? Will migrant families be forced into multi-occupation of smaller properties simply to access housing? Will the government's now higher increased targets for affordable housing begin to generate a supply of good quality housing, or simply more high density flats of dubious quality?

The regeneration of Thames Gateway is clearly taking pace with more housing being built, and as we come closer to meeting targets on output, much greater attention needs to be placed on issues of both quality and accessibility in terms of both income and family type.

References

Bennett, J. and Morris, J. (2006), *Gateway People: The Aspirations and Attitudes of Prospective and Existing Residents of Thames Gateway*, London, IPPR.

Brownill, S. (1989), *Developing London Docklands? Another Great Planning Disaster*, London, Paul Chapman.

Department of Communities and Local Government (2006), *Thames Gateway: Interim Plan: Policy Framework*, London, Crown Copyright.

Gairns, A. (2005), *Saving Homes and Businesses, Managing Flood Risk*, London, Royal and Sun Alliance.

Greater London Authority (2004), *London Plan*, London, Greater London Authority.

Hall, P. (1980), *Great Planning Disasters*, London, Weidenfeld and Nicholson.

Howker, E. (2006), 'Illusions of Grandeur', *Guardian*, 5 April.

Malpass, P. (2005), *Housing and the Welfare State: The Development of Housing Policy in Britain*, Basingstoke, Palgrave Macmillan.

Meikle, S. (2006), 'Small Flats Pushing Families Out of Cities', *Guardian*, 20 June.

Monk, S. (2001), 'The Cutting Edge 2001: The Production of Affordable Housing through the Planning System: How Much, Is It Additional, and Who Pays?', paper to the RICS conference, Cambridge University.

Monk, S., Crook, T., Lister, D., Rowley, S., Short, C. and Whitehead, C. (2005), *Land and Finance for Affordable Housing: The Complementary Roles of Social Housing Grant and the Provision of Affordable Housing through the Planning System*, York, Joseph Rowntree Foundation.

Monk, S., Lister, D., Lovatt, R., Ni Luanaigh, A., Rowley, S. and Whitehead, C. (2006), *Delivering Affordable Housing through Section 106: Outputs and Outcomes*, York, Joseph Rowntree.

Office of the Deputy Prime Minister (ODPM) (2000–2005), 'House-building Statistical Release 2000–2005': http: www.communities.gov.uk./index.asp.?id=1156031.

ODPM (2000), *Planning Policy Guidance 3*, London, Department of Environment Transport and Regions.

ODPM (2002), *Sustainable Communities: Building for the Future*, London, Crown Copyright.

ODPM (2003a), *Making it Happen: Thames Gateway and Growth Areas*, July, London, HMSO.

ODPM (2003b), *Delivering Affordable Housing through Planning Policy*, Wetherby, Community and Local Government Publications.

ODPM (2005a), *Circular 05/05 Planning Obligations*, Norwich, TSO.

ODPM (2005b), *The Value for Money of Delivering Affordable Housing through S106*, Wetherby, Community and Local Government Publications.

Palmer, G., Kenway, P. and Wilcox, S. (2006), *Housing and Neighbourhoods Monitor*, York, Joseph Rowntree Foundation.

Power, A., Richardson, E., Seshimo, K. and Firth, K. with Rode, P., Whitehead, C. and Traver, A. (2004), 'Framework for Housing in the London Thames Gateway', CASE Brief 27, London School of Economics.

Rowlands, R., Murie, A. and Tice, A. (2006), *More than Tenure Mix: Developer and Purchaser Attitudes to New Housing Estates*, London, Chartered Institute of Housing.

Rogers, R. (2005), T*owards a Strong Urban Renaissance – Report of the Urban Task Force*, London, DETR.

Stevens, M. and Whitehead, C. (2004), 'Lessons from the Past, Challenges for the Future – Housing Policy, 1975–2000', Housing Research Summary No. 214, London, OPDM.

Watson, J. (2006), 'Understanding Planning Gain: What Works', Briefing Paper, York, Joseph Rowntree Foundation.

Chapter 11

'Alright on the Night?' Envisioning a 'Night-time Economy' in the Thames Gateway[1]

Karina Berzins and Iain MacRury

Young adults make their own nightlife, but not under conditions of their own choosing.

(Chatterton and Hollands, 2003, p. 8)

It has become increasingly recognised, London wide (GLA, 2005; New Start, 2005), nationally (ODPM, 2005) and internationally (Chatterton and Holland, 2003; Marshall, 2004; Hobbs, 2003, p. 2; Hobbs et al., 2003, pp. 25–8; Zukin, 1991; O'Connor and Wynne, 1996) that the quality of life – or 'liveability'[2] as Department of Communities has it – in a town, borough, a region, or even in a particular *street*, must include a sense of the quality of the *night* life.

The working definition of a high quality 'night' can stretch from 'getting a good night's sleep' to an all night venue crawl including drinking, dancing and a range of music, food and other entertainments – with a good deal else in between these poles. As we might imagine, 'community cultures' are (variously) affirmed, elaborated, transgressed, denied and – in a sense – *created*, in important and distinctive ways: *by night*.

In this sense evening/night-time leisure should be understood as constituted in, and through a wide array of significant as well as elusive 'places' and 'goods' which are more or less optimally provisioned. Such sites and 'goods', some

---

1   Thanks to: Phil Mullan, Julia Dane, Emma Roberts, Andrew Blake and to numerous respondents across three recent projects on NTE related development in the Thames Gateway.

2   Liveability: the liveability agenda is about creating places where people choose to live and work. This resource aims to give local authorities and their partners access to the good practice, guidance and practical tools that will help them improve the quality of people's everyday lives. See also the National Agenda for 'Sustainable Communities' – 'A sustainable community is a place where people want to live and work, now and in the future. It is safe and inclusive, well planned, well run and offers equality of opportunity to all citizens. Local authorities have a crucial role to play in creating sustainable communities and building a sense of community' (http://www.idea-knowledge.gov.uk/idk/core/page. do?pageId=80829).

basic, others complex – and various as they are – must be delivered through the development, maintenance and management of an *economy*.

The quality, range, sophistication and diversity of its night-time economy (NTE) writ large or small – village, city, or region or wide – is (we wish to argue) both index and locus, affirming (or otherwise) communities' ongoing 'livability', health and 'sustainability'.

The 'night-time economy' (NTE) describes the experiences and mechanisms attaching to the accessibility, development and provision of evening experiences; be it via a strip of bars, a new branch of Nandos, a casino, a vibrant arts centre, a famous (or trendy) bistro, an Internet café, a series of dance or comedy events, an ice skating rink, a bowling alley, a Blockbuster video store[3] or a Bollywood film festival. As a concept NTE is predicated on the recognition that citizens and consumers, and those charged with planning, governing or managing the places and spaces where they live and work, inhabit a *24-hour society*.

Times, places and spaces of pleasure, rest and play, where the public extends into domestic experience, and where the private and domestic extend into public space – are integral to how places work – so that 'night-time leisure' is no longer a 'marginal' concern (Hobbs, 2003, pp. 1–3; Chatterton and Holland, 2003; O'Connor and Wynne, 1996) and no longer apprehended (just) in peripheral vision.

NTE 'cultures' are socially based within and around sites demarcated for specialised kinds of *consumption, production* and social interaction; all together framed by systems of legal and informal governance,[4] habits, tastes and lifestyles – and by pressing commercial and economic imperatives.

It has been no surprise that when popular writers have imagined communities (sustainable or otherwise) in popular TV drama (classically in *EastEnders* or *Coronation Street*) it is to the motif of 'the local' ('The Queen Vic' or 'The Rovers') that we are so often returned. But what of the array of planners, developers and

---

3   While 'staying in is the new going out' was a fashionable phrase for a while, we focus away from domestic night-time leisure. However, the domestic sphere is a key competitor for the night-time economy – opening the likelihood of Thames Gateway nurturing a recession to the domestic amongst its numerous projected future residents. This, we think, would be a shame. Enhancements of domestic appliances home cinema etc., compulsion for families to stay home alone. This is is clearly the antithetical to community spaces and the interactional multiculturalism which in optimistic moments we may want to assign to a Thames Gateway vision. Thus Putnam's (1995) vision of bowling alone will be re-inscribed into the TG of browsing alone, notwithstanding the techo-culturalists who insist upon this being a satisfactory stand in for offline life.

4   The 2005 Licensing Act – Changes to the licensing laws (contained within the Licensing Act, 2003) are aimed at spreading the time at which customers leave venues – and the 2005 Gambling Acts (ushering in a bid process to which a number of Thames Gateway boroughs have bid (e.g. Southend, Havering, Greenwich, Newham). However there is a further and complex network of governance including doormen, proprietors, friendship networks and social habit. Since this chapter was written, the Supercasino licence was granted to Manchester – and then revoked. Casino-led development appears for the moment to be out of favour with national government.

their governmental overseers? When Thames Gateway 'sustainable communities' are envisioned, where is 'the local'? And, who and where, *are* the locals? In this chapter we argue that acknowledging NTE as a central component of 'liveability' should be made more central to thinking about how Thames Gateway is developing.

While a good degree of NTE development, anywhere, is contingent and ad hoc (alongside homes, transport and general 'infrastructure' development) the relatively rapid and large scale of Thames Gateway planning and building cannot but benefit from time to time, recalling that NTE is at the heart of development and local experience, of the life of any community and of any household – this so that NTE is planned into the region sensitively, thoughtfully and strategically.

There is considerable concern about a (generalised) 'lack of amenity' in the Thames Gateway, with headline condemnation of sprawling housing estates and 'slums of the future'.[5] It is useful to ask, (with future residents of TG in mind) alongside questions about where people will shop; where they will go to school; how they will get about; where they will get medical treatment – all core questions of practical social planning and policy – one further question: what will they (or we) do in the evenings?

While the London NTE serves a wide range of suburban communities (with the tourist markets a necessary and valuable supplementary NTE market) and with the West End NTE thriving on the transport infrastructure that services commuters by day, it is also the case that, on the outer fringes of London, and for those communities where NTE at 'commuting distance' is not an option (due to time and expense constraints) there is a strong sense of relative NTE 'deprivation' (say, in Beckon, Canning Town or Barking). Here, it is common to report a mode of 'deprivation' which is symptomatic of, and amplifying, other kinds of deprivation experienced in poorer boroughs and poorer areas – that is 'there's nothing to do round here'. This is, no doubt, a source of anxiety – linked as such sentiments often are to issues such as antisocial behaviour, drug-taking and other problems. At the same time the invigorated interest in all things property related: the 'location, location, location' phenomenon – ensures that boroughs are working, in sometimes contradictory ways – to portray the 24-hour desirability of this or that locale.

In some cases these anxieties provoke responses translated into a NTE strategy (e.g. Cheltenham, 2004; Croydon, 2003; and see GLA, 2005): local authorities have lately actively supported the inward investment and job creation attached to a thriving NTE, to promote their area in: '… proactive strategies designed to secure competitive advantage over their perceived competitors' (Hall and Hubbard, 1996). This can entail the re-packaging of urban space (Jessop, 1998),

---

5   The coverage in the popular press of a recent (2005) IPPR report into Thames Gateway residents' opinions conveys a good deal of anxiety about the level of infrastructure service provision. However, NTE did not appear high on the agenda. We argue that it should be. See *Evening Standard* (London), 20 January 2006, 'Inside Prescottgrad; Barrack-like Homes, No Local Shops, Schools, Playgrounds – Not Even a Post Box'.

often by focusing upon 'flagship' projects and the hosting of prestige events such as high profile sporting or cultural events (Hobbs, 2003, p. 3).

This chapter examines Thames Gateway NTE – with the thought that across the Gateway there may not be sufficient attention paid to this issue. The first and key point is this: Thames Gateway is not a local authority; nor does it have a Mayor's office or assembly (as London does) to devise and deliver any kind of NTE strategy (GLA, 2005). Thames Gateway could not be empowered in this way since the key NTE planning powers, through which NTE is governed and stimulated, reside in national legislation and (crucially) in local licencing. While housing and other social policy issues can be co-coordinated under the special Thames Gateway authority legislation and guided by policy statements (e.g., 'Sustainable Communities', 2003) there is a danger that NTE will 'fall through the cracks' or 'off the map', because the legislative structures are not in place to ensure any degree of coordination in the NTE sphere. NTE is bureaucratically and in terms of legislative frames 'out of sight and out of mind' in the Thames Gateway plan view.

Within the Thames Gateway there is also competition within and between city and region. As Salet et al. (2002) observe

> There tends to be a divorce between the governance of the metropolitan area and the governance of the broader region. It should be stressed again that the mayor's geographical area of responsibility only covers the area within the green belt .... Many people travel into and out of this area for employment and leisure purposes. (Salet et al., 2002, p. 55)

If we consider this in practical terms there is a nightly tension between the NTE spheres in and around the employment hubs of central London (the West End, the City and Canary Wharf), all of which have well developed NTE facilities – and the 'home' borough or suburban NTE destination. In research we conducted in Newham (MacRury et al., 2008) we came to understand that the effort to stimulate local (dispersed) NTE locations is hampered by the pull exerted by work location (central) NTE spots. As a result the centre has traditionally been advantaged (in this respect) over the periphery – with consumers and providers variously put off by the risk of a 'too quiet' or 'dead' outer London or suburban NTE opportunity.

Thus the NTE of the TG as it is currently projected in the plans for large housing developments such as East Quarry, may well, predominantly, be located on the Strand, in Covent Garden, in Brixton and around the other SE facing London train stations, because effectively the NTE economy will be an extension of the daytime work economy. This will have disastrous effects on social cohesion because unless locally based night-time amenities are nurtured and developed in interesting and sensitive ways, there will be very few incentives for workers to leave behind the bright lights of central London. When necessity demands that they return home, it will be purely for domestic leisure in the home, for child care, and for screen culture.

It is quite apparent (we think) that the NTE of the TG should include many and varied and localised instances of evening oriented third space;[6] venues to ensure that the gateway does not lapse into a hyper-trophied version of dormitory suburbia.

The Mayor's (2005) strategy (in the face of this issue) aims to stimulate dispersal *out*; igniting new centres in the Greater London areas, and taking pressure off Westminster and Camden. However, this strategic dispersal must surely also try to take account of the 'Thames Gateway effect', i.e., that 'the periphery' of London is evermore assertively *regional* rather than greater-metropolitan.

Alongside this strategy of dispersal, the main impetus to NTE development has come from local authorities' entrepreneurial competitiveness (see also Chatterton and Holland, 2003). In the Thames Gateway there is a likelihood that authorities will compete against one another – perhaps in the terms identified by Hobbs and others (2003, p. 3) above.

A related problem is that the structure of borough versus borough competitive bidding – ostensibly a mechanism to ensure that 'a locally based' case is made in structuring national regeneration – runs the risk in practice that national governmental priorities will overshadow local and regional ones,[7] rendering the 'competition' merely gestural (see Allmendinger and Thomas's (1998, p. 226) analysis of governmental control of borough's unitary development plan bids).

And, of course, this has been the case; with the casino licensing competition ushered in via the 2005 Gambling Act a perfect exemplification of the disjunction between local authority planning, regional strategic (regeneration) development and (national) governmental priorities. When, as has happened in regard to the Casino licenses we throw the Mayor's office into the mix; well, it is no surprise that the casino development has produced a somewhat intriguing series of news stories; stories alleging conflict and interference across and between the various tiers, departments and levels of government.[8]

Much of the research we have conducted and which informs this chapter indicates that the current provision of NTE in the inner Thames Gateway is not meeting the needs and aspirations of local populations. Thus, while we regularly

---

6   Oldenburg (2000) gives examples of the importance of 'third places' – between domestic and public space – as a bulwark against a diminution of a sense of community.

7   Allmendinger and Thomas illustrate this dynamic with reference to UDP in the 1990s: the boroughs were incorporated into the public-private London Pride Partnership in 1994. However, it will be seen that this new role for the London boroughs was given on the government's terms. The content of a borough's Unitary Development Plan was constrained by central government guidance – strategic guidance and the PPGs – reinforced by the appeal process which gives central government much power in the British planning system (Allmendinger and Thomas, 1998, p. 226).

8   For example: 'Today allegations appeared that Prescott's office was deeply involved in the Dome development and its casino bid, including lobbying for rival schemes to stand aside. Anna Waite, former Tory leader of Southend-on-Sea council, said: "It was made clear to me pressure was coming from on high that there should be only one bid in the Thames Gateway area and it should be the Dome. The whole thing stank from beginning to end"' (*Evening Standard* (London), 'Changing Story of the DPM', 6 July 2006).

Figure 11.1 A recent edition of *Time Out* had to work hard to highlight NTE activities 'hidden' in London's East End. It is useful to envision an East London edition of *Time Out* 2012, or for *Time Out* Thames Gateway 2015. Reproduced by permission Time Out Group Ltd

hear the rhetorical announcements – some based in sound evidence that 'London is moving East' day by day we have been made strongly aware that 'night by night' it remains overwhelmingly that NTE entertainments and activities continue to thrive and develop in the traditional locations (the West End), and in a range of NTE hot spots (Croydon, Islington (Upper Street), and Covent Garden).

However, for every Upper Street or Covent Garden there are numberless areas which have underdeveloped NTE infrastructure. And as the provisioning of such spaces falls between the public (under-)resourcing of leisure centres, art centres and community centres on the one hand, and the commercial venues owned by a number of large global providers (operating under 'super-brand' names such as Tiger Tiger, Wetherspoons, All Bar One and so forth) on the other – the concern is that these locales will become clone like night-time brandscapes, will not be sustainable, and will not meet the needs of local populations.

When NTE Goes Wrong: In Anticipation of the Thames Gateway

The night-time economy is important to sustainability for a number of reasons. First, there is a clear economic benefit – in that jobs are created. Even while these are typically low skilled and casual in may instances – perhaps especially in high volume McDonaldised non-independent venues – nevertheless the tradition of the bar job, or waiter/ressing is often valued in local employment markets, in particular in providing jobs for young adults between home and living independently.

NTE venues can bring life and light to local high streets – especially at a time when the tendency, no doubt to be amplified in the Thames Gateway – is towards mega malls and super-supermarkets.

While this is by no means a uniform quality of Night-time experience and provision, there is a case to be made that NTE venues offer an opportunity for social mixing and exchange across and between disparate groups – across dimensions of ethnicity, gender, generation and social class. Typically also however there are countervailing tendencies – such that NTE venues might be marketed towards one narrow age or income group. Nevertheless this is a plausible benefit attached to good NTE provision (see Butler and Robson, 2003, on Islington)

NTE amenity – operating evening and day – can enhance the quality of (soft-) communality, thus, as Amin and Thrift (2002) propose:

> Restaurants, football matches, musical events, golf clubs are places where ideas are developed and deals are struck, deliberately, or through casual socialization. They are places where standards are tracked, gossip is exchanged, rivals are noted and disputes are aired, rather as they are in business associations and interest groups. But these are not Marshallian spaces of interchange between members of the same community of interest (say, furniture makers in an Italian Piazza). Instead, they are more broadly constituted centres of sociability or professional gathering with a light economic touch; mixing pleasure, voice, search and business opportunity in emergent ways, (Amin and Thrift, 2002, p. 73)

They go on to add, in a point germane to considering sustainable communities, that the presence of such spaces, 'have become a significant factor in urban investment decisions' (Amin and Thrift, 2002, p. 73).

Thus, if Thames Gateway communities are really to host SMES and other businesses (providing job and local networks) in their midst, then it might be wise to plan in soft attractants such as NTE amenity can (in many instances) furnish. Without such soft infrastructure – delivered variously and to a high quality – the intention to create 'mixed' land use will be proved to have been largely rhetorical.

It is usefully to register some of the kinds of responses residents give when invited to think about the quality of a night-time economy which, largely, is understood not to be thriving. We want to suggest that the night-time economy in Newham (an inner Thames Gateway borough) can stand as a useful exemplar in thinking more broadly about the Thames Gateway NTE.

First, Newham is part of the Gateway – central to huge regeneration projects – and, especially, the Olympics. It is assertively at the cusp of old and new east London – and successes and failures in development and integration in Newham can stand usefully as in some ways more widely indicative across the projected Thames Gateway.

Second, it is anticipated that many Newham residents will be priced out of the area, such that Thames Gateway may be a medium term destination for many, in line (to an extent) with a long tradition of Eastward migration from the 'inner' East End outwards.

Detailed research into the NTE provision revealed some indication that the absence of adequate NTE provisioning can have a strong negative impact on people's sense of their quality of life – and a negative effect on sustainability (e.g., in the likelihood of choosing to stay in Newham). We report here some quantitative results as indicative of an NTE locale needing revivification:

- *General NTE offer*: how 'in general' did respondents rate Newham for going out?
- *Range of activities*: how did respondents assess the range, choice and variety of NTE offerings in the borough?
- *Restaurants*: how did respondents assess the provision of restaurants and eating-places?
- *Cinema/theatre leisure, etc*: to what extent was the provision of cinema and theatre type entertainment deemed sufficient?
- *Extent of feeling safe*: to what extent did residents and visitors feel safe and secure in Newham in the evening?
- *Transport*: how, in regarded to NTE did residents rate the provision of transport links.
- *Five year view*: this question attempted to capture the degree to which residents felt optimistic about the future development of a thriving NTE in Stratford.

So it is worth pointing out that these indicators, expressing broad dissatisfaction with an array of indices of NTE provision – including an alarming tendency to

Table 11.1   Mean and modal satisfaction indices – summary table

	General NTE offer evaluation	Range of activities	Restaurants	Cinema/ theatre leisure, etc.	Extent of feeling safe	Transport	Five year view
Mean	3.5195	3.7089	3.5181	2.8072	3.3253	2.6623	2.3158
Mode	4.00	4.00	4.00	2.00	3.00	2.00	2.00

Notes

1   Across these seven main indices of satisfaction/dissatisfaction responses have been recorded as headline data. We report both mean and modal scores to indicate both a scalar sense of satisfaction (mean) while also capturing the most frequently recorded specificassessments (modal score). This allows us to capture a sense of degree, frequency and kind of evaluations being relayed by respondents.
2   1 = very good and 5 = very poor.

feel unsafe at night – can save as a kind of warning, or premonition of a future Thames Gateway where NTE has not evolved because – in the conception NTE was 'off the map' – with regenerative effort coordinated most often towards the mega- and super-sized event and location – leaving local NTE development in abeyance.

Large regeneration projects – in housing and around the Olympics – as well as retail regeneration – should, ideally, be connected to, networked with and interspersed with the existing infrastructure (and people). There is a fear, for instance, that ExCel and Stratford circus, not to mention the Olympics – will yield event spaces but leaving new residents living *in parallel* with the present inhabitants. Thus the regenerated NTE infrastructure will serve a parallel universe of affluence – emphasising division and splitting across the locale.

In a study we conducted for Havering Council – again assessing NTE provision (in the context of their bid for a casino license) we found that over 70 per cent of respondents felt that the current leisure offer in Rainham is inadequate. The first focus group discussed the current leisure offer in some detail, and there was general agreement that it was poor. In particular, younger teenagers were pointed to as a group that had a lack of leisure provision. Alongside this, concerns were revealed in the focus groups regarding the increase in population of the local area with the proposed affordable housing agenda. There was acknowledgement that the existing leisure offer was inadequate for the present residents, and that there wasn't the infrastructure to support the increased population. Watching TV has far and away the most popular NTE activity – marking (what we see as) a regrettable recession to the domestic in that locale.

The competition from the domestic sphere is in the minds of marketers too. Thus in Mintel's (2003) assessment of the NTE markets (made before 2003 and 2005 legislation on gambling and licensing) they acknowledge the potential of a recession to the domestic, amongst some other 'threats'.

Looking ahead, it is clear that the leisure industry will have its work cut out to improve market growth rates, particularly if consumers retrench in their homes – which are increasingly geared up to provide enjoyable leisure time or opt for spending more money on eating out and holidays abroad. Town-centre locations can be problematic for many leisure venues, with their risk – or perceived risk among older consumers – of crime, violence, parking problems and general rowdiness. Addressing the needs of children, of older people, of non-smokers and non-drinkers is becoming more urgent. The industry is only partly to blame for some problems. Endless delays in pushing through modernising legislation on drinking and gambling are holding back the sector. The optimistic scenario is one in which leisure outlets continue to break down old barriers between activities and consumers. There is much more entertainment available on the high street, for example, and health clubs could have a future role as social venues. Generally, however, the spread of leisure choices is unlikely to be radically different in ten years time. (Mintel, 2003)

It is useful to consider that in addition to these pressures – there is a range of social concerns. Table 11.2 illustrates the 'aspirations anxieties' surrounding NTE planning derived from three research projects we have undertaken (2004–2006). They condense various aspirations and anxieties – threats and promises – attaching to NTE/Tourist related development.

These, we suggest, can usefully gloss future planning and debate in different areas of Thames Gateway.

Visions and Versions of the Thames Gateway

There have been a number of visions for the Thames Gateway proposed by planners, and politicians. These include Peter Hall's call for funding for infrastructure from casino regeneration:

> My personal favorite would be a gambling tax used to promote casino-led regeneration in areas like Thames Gateway: Las Vegas on the Greenwich peninsula and the Swanscombe peninsula, with the punters pouring in from the mainland on Eurostar.[9]

Perhaps most famous is the call from Sir Terry Farrell, architect and master planner for a mega nature reserve, the 'lakes district of London' where people are conspicuous by their absence. Finally, and in stark conflict with this last vision is the ambition by the ODPM for large volumes of new dwellings to be built in the TG. It is this last vision, we think, that is most likelty to conform to what finally arises.

Any one of these three visions of the TG is problematic, because overly identifying and identified with a too schematic understanding of the TG – it does however give worthwhile pause for thought.

---

9   Professor Sir Peter Hall, from his keynote lecture in December 2003. 'Talking the Talk, Walking the Walk – How to Make Paper Plans Real' (Royal Town Planning Institute's (RTPI) annual lecture).

Table 11.2   Other indicative NTE/tourism problems – aspirations and anxieties

	Anxiety	Aspiration
ExCel	That this amenity exclusively services a visitor and business tourist economy, keeping NTE spin out benefits too tightly on the 'campus'. That locals rarely utilise the surrounding development – one experienced as 'not really in Newham'	That integrated into the development of the ExCel centre are spin off benefits in terms of jobs, but also NTE leisure opportunities that can serve local communities as well as visitor and tourist users more often
Stratford City	That new NTE amenities will emerge to service incoming professional residential groups, split off, geographically and reputationally from 'old Stratford' – instituting a 'right and wrong side of the tracks' culture – such that regeneration benefits don't sufficiently extend into an existing (and unsatisfactory NTE offer – one made even less appealing as rental increased push out established local providers in favour of chain-based pubs	That the influx of residents and visitors (up to and after the Olympics) will stimulate sympathetic redevelopment of Stratford town centre linking old and new towards producing a local and specific 'buzz' in Stratford and its environs – improving ambience and reputation of the area for all.
Casino (wherever located)	That this development will service 'high-roller' international tourism and high paid city workers – with little extra spin off amenity to enhance the broader leisure offer in the locale (be it Rainham, Greenwich, or Southend)	That while the casino itself my not appeal to local residents, there is sufficient leisure amenity built in (ice rink, fitness centres, welcoming bars and pubs etc.) to ensure that there is traffic between the super-structure and the local residents, in terms of both jobs and NTE enjoyment

In each case the night vision of the TG needs to be more clearly articulated and thought through, because clearly the gateway cannot and will not be reduced to a single vision of its NTE. So we have not set out to conduct an assessment or inventory of the TG as a whole, since as we have suggested this is not possible, nor perhaps desirable, however we have come to recognise the significance of the NTE to producing a more nuanced understanding of what is at stake in the TG.

Table 11.3 **What NTE cultures are implicit in the planning? Hypothetical suggestions – but, what will happen?**

	Main 'vision'	Implicit NTE provisioning/activities
Casino regeneration	Casino Regeneration – servicing mega venues	Casino and 'trickle down' NTE leisure offer serving tourist market and affluent city and suburban dwellers
Housing driven	New town style urban sprawl	Dormitory suburbanism and domestic privacy on large estates – and high volume drinking chain pubs – 'machines for drinking in'
National park/high density	Mini-urban style clusters in parkland	Mock Elizabethan country pubs interspersed between urban villages clustering on high end chain bars (All Bar One etc.)

The NTE, Tourism and the Post-Industrial

Sir Peter Hall's picture of Casino/Eurostar-led Thames Gateway regeneration (above), while no doubt somewhat glib, indicates what we see as a mistaken view of leisure planning, especially NTE leisure planning, in the Thames Gateway. The risk, we want to suggest, is that there will be considerable incentives offered up, considerable interest in leisure related land use, particularly with the lure of international, or at least interregional tourism spend. Thus while land use maps of the projected Thames Gateway may come to record good levels of day and evening leisure provision – there is a risk that this square footage will disproportionately cater to (day and night) tourist leisure. We want to argue that while tourism and NTE provisioning are similar – it is crucial to plan in specific and locally oriented NTE provision as both complementary and supplementary NTE infrastructure – and as a predominant proportion of leisure space as the Thames Gateway as its resident populations develop.

Tourism development is prominent among the strategies available to local, national and regional governments as they attempt to address issues of economic and social development in the post industrial era. It is natural to consider the NTE and tourism at the same time. However, as we will come to see, it is important to recognise that although there are some commonalities, there are also marked differences between the two.

Tourism offers nations and regions an important supplementary industry, one to set alongside and to enhance retail, cultural and entertainment based economic activity. For example, the UK and especially London, is increasingly dependent upon tourism for economic growth and for employment. Tourism frequently emerges as a panacea in the face of anxieties connected to post-industrial decline.

The UK tourism industry's annual turnover is £76 billion, and accounts for 4 per cent of the GDP. As a growth industry, this is expected to rise to over £100 billion by 2010, however these figures were calculated without the impact of the 2012 Olympic and Paralympic Games (DCMS, 2004). Added to this, the UK tourism industry provides 2.1 million jobs, representing 7.4 per cent of all people employed in Great Britain (Great Britain Labour Statistics, 2002). In London, tourism accounts for 12 per cent of London's gross domestic product and supports 13 per cent of the workforce. It is against this financial situation that the Mayor of London, the London Development Agency and other regional stakeholders such as TourEast London have embarked upon a series of strategic plans to further enhance the tourist industries, and in particular to widen the distribution of economic gain, whilst minimising the social impact of tourism.

The Mayor of London has highlighted the fact that tourism facilities are too centralised (in the West of London), thus the LDA has committed to the devolution of budget and the delivery of strategic priorities to subregional level. One of the key vision's of the Mayor for Tourism is the principle of 'dispersal' – providing a greater provision of tourist destinations outside of West London (Great Britain Labour Statistics, 2004, p. 38). Indeed, if one examines the statistical data for London based tourist attractions, 80 per cent of both free and paid admission attractions are in West London.[10] This principle of dispersal makes it crucial that high quality, successful tourist attractions are developed in strategic area to draw tourists away from the West.

There is certainly an intention from the Mayor to draw tourists to the East, however it is quite different to consider a tourism strategy for the East of London which of course includes a good deal of the inner TG, as opposed to considering the TG as a unified whole.

Under the heading of tourism and leisure planning there is a wide range of potential activities and spaces that come to mind – from a casino at the done, to Dickens world (in Chatham), to a license for a new branch of Wetherspoons to a small local theatre space and so on. However it is important to recognise that the markets and communities which habitually might make use of such facilities and resources are widely different. Tourist based leisure is not the same thing as the leisure required and taken locally by resident communities. The risk is that planners will become complacent in too closely aligning the provision of tourism destinations; superstructures, and super-branded amenities such as bars restaurants etc., equating these with an adequate provision of nighttime economy amenity taken in general.

For the TG to develop its wider leisure economy optimally, it is important that each and all tourist groups – business tourists, international tourists, the visiting friends and family market, students[11] and local residents – are catered to in terms of their general needs and desires, for nighttime economic activities and events.

However, and at the same time, it is crucial too that, as tourism is planned in and developed, that there is a strong understanding that tourism infrastructure and

---

10   'Key Facts of Tourism for London 2002–2003', http//:www.staruk.org.uk.
11   Fn re students as tourists – fill in footfall when tourists not there.

amenity serving the various tourism markets are necessary to, but not sufficient for the proper and crucial broader provision necessary to deliver up the diverse range of amenity necessary to a sustainable NTE for residents of the Gateway. To put it bluntly, we say this: don't imagine that by building a casino or a tourist resort, an exhibition centre or super-club in the Thames Gateway, or four of five such developments, that the full repertoire of NTE needs has been addressed. Tourism NTE is not an adequate substitute for local NTE – even when synergies and cross fertilisation (as happens in London) is a very powerful stimulus to thrive.

Integrations: NTE and Tourism and the Superbrandscape

We argue that close attention needs to be paid to ensuring that NTE as part of the 'leisure economy' is planned into the Thames Gateway, that no too easy equation is made between provisioning the *tourist* economy and provisioning the domestic, local night-time economy. While necessarily tourism and local leisure consumers (day and night) cross paths, it is important to acknowledge that these are distinct constituencies, looking for different scale, scope and cost, at different times and places. The successful creation of any number of tourism venues, while increasing leisure spend and NTE classified incomes across a range of venues and outlets (restaurants, bars and miscellaneous attractions) as viewed from afar – will do little to address the project of building sustainable communities – which must be central to the proper development of Thames Gateway – in whatever forms and shapes it finally takes:

> The world of supermodernity does not exactly match the one in which we believe we live, for we live in a world that we have not yet learned to look at. We have to relearn to think about space. (Auge, 1995, pp. 35–6)

The regeneration style made apparent in suffixes such as super- and mega- (respectively attaching to 'event' like the Olympics, to 'casino' or to 'club'[12]) invite the speculation that, in the ways such developments are envisioned and enacted, there is (in terms of the area) a developmental risk; that the structures feel *superimposed* within and around the places where they spring up.

When such super-structural plans are implemented and even during the – at times – quite extended phases of anticipation and anxiety that precedes the event/ structure, the 'super-project' takes on a defining and imposing presence on future

---

12   'Superclub' definition: the term has also been used for massive, multistory, high-volume, high-profile nightclubs operating city- and region-wide. Pacha in Ibiza which opened in 1969, ia a famous superclubs; one that will be well known to large numbers of the likely future residents of Thames Gateway. It would be appropriate to categorise Bluewater and Lakeside as 'super-malls' in the same context.

horizon and then, if built,[13] on the skyline – this has subsequent impacts on the feel and reputation of an area.

It is important that there is sufficient traffic between the 'super structure' (casino, stadium, mall or theme park) and the world around it. It is important to ensure that (as far as feasible) the location does not take on too much of the character evoked by Auge in his term 'non-places'. The notion of 'non-place' is a somewhat complex and elusive one;[14] in this context it is useful to set it in contrast up against the context of 'sustainable community.'

The super-casino recently proposed for Rainham[15] provides an indicative case in point – a way of figuring the relationship between a 'notional 'non-place' (the super-casino) and a place – Rainham.

Respondents certainly understood their community to be at risk of becoming 'unsustainable'. This was recorded, typically, in the observation that in an ageing population and in a village (close to London, but with a distinctly village feel) Rainham could not properly support a living and working community in the neighbourhood. While people would continue to live in Rainham, and commute there and back to London (on the excellent transport links), a sense of community as tied to neighbourhood – one precious to a good number of our respondents, would be deemed not to have been sustained.

Sustainability depended for the respondents on young people having a viable future in the locale. Both focus groups talked in terms of the development for 'future generations' to enjoy, and wanted to see Rainham's 'untapped potential' to be realised.

The sense of community as tied to neighbourhood (Blokland, 2003) was, in the testimony of our respondents, in some imminent jeopardy. They know that in the terms of being a place where people both live and work, where industry and productive labour take place side by side with domestic life, i.e., not as a dormitory suburb, they understand that Rainham was becoming an unsustainable community.[16] It is increasingly also known as a junction, where the A13 and the

---

13   Rainham was speculatively earmarked for a development that never happened in the 1980s – with EuroDisney finally going to Paris.

14   Nevertheless Auge's gloss is relevant and illuminating: 'Clearly the word "non-place" designates two complementary but distinct realities: spaces formed in relations to certain ends (transport, transit, commerce, leisure), and the relations that individuals have with these spaces. Although the two sets of relations overlap to a large extent, and in any case officially (individuals travel, make purchases, relax), they are still not to be confused with one another; for non-places mediate a whole mass of relations, with the self and with others, which are only indirectly connected with their purposes. As anthropological places create the organically social, so-non-places create solitary contractuality' (Auge, 1995, p. 94). It might be observed (and as Benjamin (2002, pp. 512–15) has observed) that 'the gambler is involved with the world in this mode: in a solitary and contractual – non organic "contact"' – with "the cards" or a fruit machine mechanism'.

15   This was not, in the end shortlisted. See below for a discussion of the bidding process – and of the implications of this for the Thames Gateway.

16   The local industries had all but closed and Rainham continues largely to be identified as a dumping ground, with vast rubbish tips and land fill sites the 'landmark' activity.

M25 meet – it is a place becoming a non-place, and one in need of investment and development.

In their view however, and this was the prevalent one in the study – the casino was an acceptable development locally if, and only if, the attendant amenity (including an ice rink, fitness centre, restaurants and bars), was open, accessible, affordable and well managed. The casino was a necessary incidental – as none expected to gamble there. Others hoped they, or their children might find work there.

The vision Rainham citizens had of this superstructure was as a compromised hybrid space – an industry for the area, but not a leisure destination in itself. Whatever happens in Rainham, and across the Thames Gateway – when superstructural planning and development meets adjacent communities – it should be urged (through S106 and other mechanisms) that there is (at least) some degree of local input, management and planning gain' leveraged in to any regeneration deal; such that regeneration takes place in dialogue with residential groups – and not in parallel – adjacent but out of reach.

Conclusions

Mega events like the Olympics, super-casinos (wherever finally located), and the chain outlets of NTE super-brands, while obviously contributing to leisure infrastructure and to aspects of the NTE by virtue of their scale and scope, cannot satisfy what will be an emergent need for complementary, idiosyncratic, widely distributed localised facilities for night-time leisure; 'local' restaurants, independent theatres, affordable health and fitness centres, locations for night-time learning and other venues – for current, and perhaps currently unanticipated future leisure fashions, patterns and habits. This aspect of the NTE is the revenge of the multiple and specific on the general and the generalising plan view of the 'super-' this or the 'mega-' that. Currently there is no evidence that this all important dimension to the TG living spaces has been thought about, or talked about – let alone planned for. As we have argued, the rhetoric, the register and the scope of Thames Gateway – including its legislative scope – is towards delivering 'the biggest'.

This is not so much a plea for 'community' spaces; NTE venues, the Queen Vic and the Rovers notwithstanding, are no longer a 'glue' or a source of 'urban bonds' (Blokland, 2003). But it is a plea for the acknowledgement of spaces of intimacy; a plea that that plan views guiding the grand narratives of regional regeneration around London incorporate subtleties to allow for the incidental and the intimate – for these are the stuff of contemporary sustainability – and are at risk in the environments afforded by super-modern spatial plans and in the NTE arenas delivered by 'super brand' chains. So we argue for the dispersal and interspersal of spaces for intimacy – within and through the planning of tourism venues, local leisure facilities, in the planning of estates public spaces and in the mega event architecture – of the Olympics, of ExCel and the proposed Super casino. In practice this would mean a trans gateway scrutiny of emergent

NTE provision – one charged with safeguarding the intimate and diverse in the face of the 'super-'.

To build local development of NTE into regional planning is, and we are under no illusions, beyond difficult. However, and as we have argued, super projects and open market super-brand developments will not, on their own, produce the regional NTEscape required for sustainability. As Chatterton and Holland (2003, p. 66) point out regarding NTE regulation – 'there are few examples of regulators consulting consumers as to their views on solving problems, let alone defining them'. We think this is true of NTE planning as well. This was captured by one of out interviewees on the Newham NTE project. He suggested:

> Don't jump into just using ... statistics to develop the future, and how you're going to modernise the area, ask the youth and the community about what they want ... that would more likely help. (Male, 22)

Considering NTE helps us to think about an occluded aspect of the future. When Auge urges us that we need to learn to see better – in planning and living in spaces – it is particularly important that planners and those many others charged with enhancing the conditions for the building of sustainable communities to develop a capacity for a kind of 'night vision' so that the map view routinely entails serious consideration (place by place, estate by estate, venue by venue) of the question 'will it be alright on the night?'

References

Allmendinger, P. and Thomas, H. (1998), *Urban Planning and the New Right*, London, Routledge.

Amin, A. and Thrift, N. (2002), *Cities: Reimagining the Urban*, London, Polity.

Auge, M. (1995), *Non-Places: Introduction to an Anthroplogy on Supermodernity*, London and New York, Verso.

Benjamin, W. (2002), *The Arcades Project*, Cambridge, MA and London, Harvard University Press.

Blokland, T. (2003), *Urban Bonds*, Cambridge, Polity Press.

Blomley, N. (2004), *Unsettling the City: Urban Land and the Politics of Property*, New York: Routledge.

Butler, T. and Robson, G. (2003), *London Calling: The Middle Classes and the Re-Making of Inner London*, New York, Berg.

Chatterton, P. and Hollands, R. (2003), *Urban Nightscapes: Youth Cultures, Pleasure Spaces and Corporate Power*, New York, Routledge.

Clarke, D.B. (2003), *The Consumer Society and the Postmodern City*, New York, Routledge.

Cowlard, K. (1992), 'City Futures', in Budd, L. and Whimster, S. (eds), *Global Finance and Urban Living: A Study of Metropolitan Change*, New York, Routledge, pp. 224–45.

Cheltenham Council (2004), 'Cheltenham's Night-Time Economy Strategy 2004 to 2007', Cheltenham.

Croydon Night-time Scrutiny Commission (2003), 'Scrutiny Review of the Night-time Economy: Findings and Recommendations', Croydon Borough Council.

Department for Culture, Media and Sport (DCMS) (2004), 'Tomorrow's Tourism Today': http://www.culture.gov.uk/Reference_library/Publications/archive_2004/tomorrowstourismtoday.htm.

Department for Culture, Media and Sport (DCMS) (2006), 'Licensing Act One Year On – "Early Days but Encouraging Signs" –Woodward': http://www.culture.gov.uk/Reference_library/Press_notices/archive_2006/DCMS148_06.htm.

Evans, G. (2001), *Cultural Planning, an Urban Renaissance?*, London, Routledge.

GLA (2004), 'London: Cultural Capital': http://www.london.gov.uk/mayor/strategies/culture/index.jsp.

GLA (2005), *London's Night-Time Economy*, London: GLA.

Great Britain Labour Statistics (June 2002).

Hall, P. (2000), 'Urban Renaissance/New Urbanism', *Journal of the American Planning Association*, 66, p. 359.

Hall, P., 'Talking the talk and walking the walk: making paper plans real' <???>

Hall, T. and Hubbard, P. (1996), 'The Entrepreneurial City: New Urban Politics, New Urban Geographies?', *Progress in Human Geography*, 20 (2), pp. 153–74.

Harvey, D. (1994), 'From Managerialism to Entrepreneurialism: The Transformation in Urban Governance in Late Capitalism', *Geografiska Annaler*, 71 (1), pp. 3–17.

Hobbs, D. and Hall, S. (2000), 'Bouncers: The Art and Economics of Intimidation', Final Report to the Economic and Social Research Council.

Hobbs, D. (2003), *The Night-time Economy*, London, Alcohol Concern.

Hobbs, D., Hadfield, P., Lister, S. and Winlow, S. (2003), *Bouncers: Violence and Governance in the Night-time Economy, Oxford*, Oxford University Press.

Jackson, P., Lowe, M., Miller, D. and Mort, F. (eds) (2000), *Commercial Cultures: Economies, Practices, Spaces*, Oxford, Berg.

Jessop, B. (1998), 'The Narrative of Enterprise and the Enterprise of Narrative: Place Marketing and the Entrepreneurial City', in Hall, T. and Hubbard, P. (eds), *The Entrepreneurial City: Geographies of Politics, Regime and Representation*, Chichester, John Wiley and Sons Ltd.

Mayor of London, London Development Agency and TourEast London (2004), *East London Sub-Regional Tourism Development Strategy and Action Plan 2004–2006*.

Marshall, T. (ed.) (2004), *Transforming Barcelona: The Renewal of a European Metropolis*, New York, Routledge.

MacRury, I., Berzins, K., Blake, A., Dane, J. and Roberts, E. (2008 forthcoming), 'The Newham Night Time Economy: A Report to the Night Time Economy Scrutiny Commission', London, LERI Working Papers.

Mintel (2003), *The UK Leisure Business*, August, Mintel.

National Statistics (2005), *MQ6 Transport Travel and Tourism: Overseas Travel and Tourism Quarter 3*.

Nayak, A. (2003), *Race, Place and Globalization: Youth Cultures in a Changing World*, New York, Berg.

New Start Magazine (2005), 'London Communities Should Reap 'Night-Time Economy' Rewards', 25 November.

O'Connor, J. and Wynne, D. (1996), 'Introduction', in O'Connor, J. and Wynne, D. (eds), *From the Margins to the Centre*, Aldershot, Arena.

ODPM (2005), *'Cleaner Safer Greener': Managing the Night-Time Economy*, London, ODPM.

ODPM (2004), *Delivering Sustainable Communities: Joint Statement on the Need for Green Infrastructure*, London, ODPM.

ODPM (2003), *Sustainable Communities Plan*, London, ODPM.

Oldenburg, R. (2000), *Celebrating the Third Place: Inspiring Stories about the 'Great Good Places' at the Heart of Our Communities*, New York, Marlowe and Company.

Pine, J. and Gilmore, J. (1999), *The Experience Economy*, Boston, MA, Harvard Business School.

Puttnam, R.D. (1995), 'Bowling Alone: America's Declining Social Capital', *Journal of Democracy*, 6 (1), January, pp. 65-78.

Salet, W., Thornley, A. and Kreukels, A. (eds) (2002), *Metropolitan Governance and Spatial Planning. Comparative Case Studies of European City-Regions*, London and New York, Spon Press.

Sheller, M.and Urry, J. (eds) (2004), *Tourism Mobilities: Places to Play, Places in Play*, London, Routledge.

Short, J.R. (2004), *Global Metropolitan: Globalizing Cities in a Capitalist World*, New York, Routledge, accessed 20 January 2007: http://www.questia.com/ PM.qst?a=o&d=108010758).

Time Out (2006), 'East: The Real Guide to East London', Special Edition, 8 November.

Ward, S.V. (1998), *Selling Places: The Marketing and Promotion of Towns and Cities 1850–2000*, London, Spon.

Williams, G. (2003.), *The Enterprising City Centre: Manchester's Development Challenge*, New York, Routledge.

Zukin, S. (1991), *Landscapes of Power: From Detroit to Disney World*, Berkeley and Los Angeles, CA, University of California Press.

Chapter 12

From Bedsit-land to 'Cultural Hub': Regenerating Southend-on-Sea

Gareth Millington

A Town Whose Time Has Come?

Alongside other locations in South Essex such as Grays, Basildon and Canvey Island, the iconic seaside resort of Southend-on-Sea has recently been incorporated within the Thames Gateway. Building upon Southend's cultural history as the 'lungs of London' (Schama, 1996, p. 5), Thames Gateway South Essex intends to re-install Southend as a 'thriving cultural hub' and a centre of excellence for leisure and the arts. This strategy also emphasises how the 'vibrant … cosmopolitan atmosphere' of the town should 'play a key role in the regeneration and renaissance of Southend' (University of Essex, 2005). According to Renaissance Southend, the public/private partnership entrusted to promote and ultimately secure the town's regeneration, Southend 'is indeed a town whose time has come' (www.renaissancesouthend.co.uk/Southend.asp). The purpose of this chapter is to understand this optimistic rhetoric in relation to the 'unplanned cosmopolitanism'[1] (Hall, 2004) that has taken place in the centre of the town under the noses of politicians and technocrats.

The chapter proceeds in the following manner. First, a geohistory of Southend as a modern town is sketched in three phases. Second, the central zone of the town, known locally as bedsit-land (and more recently as mini-Bosnia) is elucidated by means of quantitative and qualitative data. Developments in this zone are pivotal to the argument that follows. Utilising a Lefebvrian analysis of the production of space (see Lefebvre, 1991), it is proposed that that there are three distinct 'moments' in the reproduction of bedsit-land as a racialised mini-Bosnia. This succession of moments is instructive in understanding Southend's vaunted position as a 'cultural hub' within the Thames Gateway. Finally, I comment critically on the unplanned cosmopolitanism occurring in mini-Bosnia in relation to the pragmatic rebranding of Southend-on-Sea as a centre for culture. At each

---

1   For Stuart Hall (2004, p. 2) 'unplanned cosmopolitanism' occurs because cities 'function as spatial magnets for different, converging streams of human activity'. In the case of Southend, as is argued later in the chapter, the abundance of cheap privately rented accommodation in bedsit-land continues to act as a magnet for asylum-seekers, refugees, poor ethnic minority families (often migrating from London), single people, the unemployed and homeless.

stage I utilise qualitative data collected during an urban ethnography[2] conducted in Southend-on-Sea between 2002 and 2005.

A Relic of Modernity? A Brief Geohistory of Southend-on-Sea in Three Phases

1750–1850

Up until the latter half of the eighteenth century South End was a hamlet of nineteen fisherman's houses situated at the 'south end' of the village Prittlewell. The hamlet only began to grow in response to the burgeoning trend among London's gentry for sea bathing (Pollitt, 1957, p. 2). Two hotels were built on a prime cliff-top site overlooking the Thames Estuary in order to capitalise on this fashion. To distinguish the new cliff-top resort from the old fishing village, the term 'New South End' came into being, with the original village becoming 'Old South End'. There was fierce competition for patronage of visitors between the two villages, with the inns of the lower town apparently offering 'viands and wine not at all inferior ... and on much more reasonable terms' (cited in Pollitt 1957, p. 23). Although royalty and several titled individuals visited the resort during this formative period, Southend (the boundaries between villages having blurred) was still small enough in 1848 for *Punch* to joke about the sleepiness of the resort, saying that it was 'well worth seeing – with a microscope' (cited in O'Brien, 1934, p. 42).

1850–1950

The railway reached Southend in 1856 opening up large-scale investment and settlement (Pewsey, 1993, p. 59). Trains cut journey times from London to an hour and a half and provided cheap and easy access to the coast for those who had not been able to afford a carriage or steamer ride. A select resort for the fashionable and wealthy was transformed into a Londoner's playground. Southend adjusted quickly and began to cater for the leisure tastes of working class metropolitans with an aesthetic both innocent and unselfconscious. Southend was considered a modern place and as O'Brien (1934, p. 48) wrote at the time: 'Southend is twentieth century .... It has set its face to the future.'

These developments resonate with how Lefebvre (1991, p. 58) describes the transformation of the Mediterranean coast into a leisure-oriented space for industrialised Europe. Likewise Southend was also set-aside as a 'non-work' space for working class Londoners from the City and East End – used not just for vacations, but also for convalescence and retirement. As such, Southend acquired during this period a specific role in the social division of labour in the capital: 'the Londoner who wants a day off, but also wants to be happy, and wants

    2   This ESRC-funded study (award no. R42200154335; see Millington (2006)) utilises a novel methodology comprising qualitative interviews, time-space diaries, visual ethnography and documentary analysis.

them both cheaply, has learnt to seek them in Southend' (O'Brien, 1934, p. 45). Like other British seaside resorts Southend-on-Sea was popularly constructed in the collective conscience as a 'place on the margin' (see Shields, 1991), a site for liminal cultural pursuits such as sea-bathing, singing, dancing, copious drinking and 'dirty weekends'. The town also attracted a restless ethnoscape (Appadurai, 1996) of working-class Londoners, seasonal workers, gypsies, Eastern European Jews, Italian organ-grinders and socially mobile Londoners who decided to settle by the coast (see Millington, 2005).

With ambition in keeping with the heady times, Southend required an attraction to rival the Winter Gardens in Blackpool. In 1901 the Kursaal pleasure palace opened where attractions included The Incredible Fasting Man, an assortment of caged African tribespeople, Mademoiselle Ethella the 'tattooed lady' and Al Capone's Killer Car (Pewsey, 1993, p. 37). In 1904 the imposing *Hotel Metropole* (now the *Palace Hotel*) was built and in 1908 the most elaborate Pier Head anywhere in the country was opened, a full two kilometres out to sea. Nearly half a million tourists used the pier in its first year and Pewsey (ibid., p. 53) judges that 'a visit to the Pier Head was the poor man's cruise, with deck quoits and draughts, promenades and the Pier Orchestra'. In 1938, visitors to Southend-on-Sea totalled 4,945,000 – a figure exceeded only by Blackpool (ibid., p. 53). The population of Southend also grew at an astonishing rate during this period; from 2462 in 1851 to 12,380 by 1891 (ibid., p. 59); and from 28,857 in 1901 to 120,093 in 1931 (cited in Everitt, 1980, pp. 7–9).[3] The period 1890–1914 unsurprisingly also saw the most ambitious housing developments in the town, mainly located in dense rows of townhouses to the East and West of the central cliff-top region.

1950–Present

Tourism initially boomed after World War II but numbers of visitors to Southend were in steady decline by 1950. The 'proletarian invasions' of the early twentieth century drove away the more well-to-do visitors who instead sought peace and tranquillity in places like Devon and Cornwall. Even the day-trippers, many of whom now owned cars or had even moved out to Essex (see Young and Willmott, 1957), looked further a field for outings. The town's administrators began the search for a new identity. As Harvey (1996) notes, describing the vagaries of place formation under capitalism:

> Old places ... have to be devalued, destroyed and redeveloped while new places are created. The cathedral city becomes a heritage centre, the mining community becomes a ghost town, the old industrial centre is deindustrialized, speculative boom towns or gentrified neighbourhoods arise on the frontier of capitalist development or out of the ashes of deindustrialized communities. (Harvey, 1996, p. 296)

---

3   On census day 2001 the population of Southend was 160,256.

But what future for a fading seaside resort? Consultants told Southend's councillors that the town had to 'get rid of its kiss-me-quick, whelk-eating image' if it was to attract white-collar business and reinvent itself as a centre of commerce (King and Furbank, 1992, p. 92). Despite attempts of varying success to attract investment, Southend has struggled to shake off its brash and vulgar modernity. The 1998 Index of Local Deprivation, records Southend as having the ninth greatest relative deterioration of all outer-London districts across England and Wales (fourteenth if you include London). Post-1950 hundreds of hotels, guesthouses and premises fell into disuse and were subdivided into flats and bedsits during the 1980s. During the late 1990s many of these hostels, houses in multiple occupation and down-at-heel bedsits found a purpose in providing temporary homes for asylum-seekers fleeing the crisis in Kosovo. Where Southend once represented the 'promised land' for many East Enders, nowadays large parts of the town comprise a site of peri-urban deprivation, increasingly displaying 'pathologies' of the inner city.

Little Palestine/Bedsit-land/Mini-Bosnia

The legacy of the rapid expansion of the town at the turn of the last century is a deprived central region of Southend known locally as 'bedsit-land' or 'mini-Bosnia':

> A fireman said to me the other day that he classed that part of Westcliff as mini-Kosovo, or mini-Bosnia and the Police do as well. And those are comments from people working in the forces. You think to yourself, well, if *they're* classing it like that – the Police – then that's telling you what is really going on. (Male resident aged 32)

Bedsit-land is what Löic Wacquant (1993, p. 369) refers to as a neighbourhood of exile, a place where marginalised populations such as asylum-seekers, the poor and homeless are condemned by the market. Rather than a nightmarish vision of graffitied tower blocks and deserted precincts, bedsit-land is closer in kind to a Chicago-style zone-in-transition, a hobohemia of subdivided town houses and terraces.

Officially, bedsit-land or mini-Bosnia spans the best part of one electoral ward – Milton, and creeps into two others – Victoria and Westborough. According to the Index of Multiple Deprivation (2000), which highlights the 4,000 most deprived wards in England and Wales, Milton is ranked eighty-first. Using the alternative Underprivileged Area Scale of Deprivation, Milton is identified as the poorest ward in Southend, Essex and the South East (excluding London). With an urban population of 11,000, Milton contains higher than average amounts of flats/maisonettes, single-person households, rented tenures, unfit properties, unemployment, people of non-white British origin and residents born outside the UK (2001 Census).

This space cannot be chronicled through objective measures only. Residents who live, or have lived in bedsit-land offer experiential accounts. In the following excerpt, a resident describes her friend's flat, situated in a particularly dense region of bedsit-land:

> There's these big Victorian houses that have got twelve bedsits in them. It's horrendous because some of them were beautiful family homes but they've literally had rooms sliced in half and they've put a sink in and you've got two bedsits. Half of Westcliff is like that. I've got a friend who lives that side – she's in a little basement flat tucked underneath, and she's got nothing of her own because they've crammed so many people in, put fences up to mark boundaries so no person has got a garden really, which is rotten especially if you've got kiddies, I mean where are they supposed to play? (Female resident aged 36)

What is clear from this passage is the impact upon quality of life caused by cramped and overcrowded conditions. She also reveals how there is no space for children to play – a paradox in an area where *so much* 'space' has been produced by the re-development of existing properties.

The following quote is from a young asylum-seeker who spent his first few months in Southend living in one of Milton's many hostels.

> There were different people in the hostel, from different countries. Lots of people came to visit, making lots of noise. Some were drunk. Some of them in the room were drug-users and I just wanted to move. I just didn't like it but it was out of my hands. If I could I would have moved ... but the local government supported me. I didn't choose that – they sent me. (Male asylum-seeker from Macedonia aged 17)

The excerpt conveys the insecurity that is part-and-parcel of everyday life in the hostel. Powerfully, his account demonstrates that although asylum-seekers are the *object* of fear for many, it is they who may be most vulnerable. In addition, that his future is 'out of his hands' reveals how the poorest residents of bedsit-land are effectively 'trapped in space' (Harvey, 1973).

This next excerpt, from an interview with a landlord, integrates a *subjective* understanding of space with a deeper comprehension of the *objective* market forces that combine to produce bedsit-land as a concrete entity:

> It was a road with lots of lovely houses in the '20s and '30s, but they got turned into flats and bedsits and houses in multiple occupation – which possibly started with them being guesthouses, when we hit a recession. It is the nearest road to the centre for curb crawlers, so girls started to hang out in the streets. Where guesthouses couldn't make a living because people weren't coming into the town to use them, they take the bottom end of the social class, those on the dole. You're getting fifty quid a week for each one and you've got all your rooms let out. (Landlord)

The landlord's story displays a different logic to resident's accounts. His tale is derived from an 'inside' knowledge of the *inevitability* of the housing market – devalued guesthouses are developed into flats or hostels, then over time this space is squeezed further to create bedsits and houses in multiple occupation to increase rent-value. He also adopts a disinterested perspective in relation to the social effects of market driven development.

This chapter identifies three decisive 'moments'[4] in the (re-)production of bedsit-land as a racialised mini-Bosnia. I will deal with each in turn. The laissez-faire planning regulations[5] of the 1980s provided the mainspring for the subdivision on a grand scale of the decaying Victorian and Edwardian properties in this once prosperous central region of Southend. Sensing potential, Milton ward was plundered by eager developers and landlords during the property boom of the mid to late 1980s. In fact, the ward experienced over 1000 flat conversions in a two-year spell between 1986 and 1988. This chaotic period of over-accumulation is the *first* moment in the reproduction of bedsit-land as mini-Bosnia.

> In Southend, in that central area, you've got the larger, villa-type houses. This was a prosperous time, it was the Victorian/Edwardian age – and they're huge. So, as the town expanded and you get to the 1980s, and you've got a big property boom going on, it was just ripe for subdivision. So, you even got subdivisions of the flat conversions and it went through the roof.
>
> Prices just went up and up and up and the more you could sell, the more money you made. And property was moving really quickly … so if you bought a big house for £70,000 even the house itself would have been £110,000 before you turned it round.

---

4   The concept of 'moment' is used in a Lefebvrian sense (see Lefebvre, 2003 and Elden, 2004 for a commentary). To summarise, Lefebvre views moments as attempts at total realisations of a possibility. Moments are simultaneously expressions of and the expressing of social relationships. This is why Lefebvre (2003, p. 170) argues that a moment 'defines a form and is defined by a form'. He does not believe, however, that a moment is the same as a 'situation'; rather, a moment is able to create a series of future situations. This is because an historical moment leaves traces and is able to shape the future. From a traditionally Marxist perspective, events are 'end games', the inevitable maturation of an already existing explosive (or contradictory) situation. Lefebvre on the other hand suggests that moments represent an attempt to *realise* a possibility. This explanation implies that social actors act somehow in order to 'empty' a pre-given situation of possibility.

5   Scholars widely acknowledge that the politics of successive Conservative governments led by Margaret Thatcher promoted the 'virtues of competition, freedom of choice, self-reliance and incentives, and the creation of a new type of de-industrialised society' (Edgell and Duke, 1991, p. 17). This agenda was reflected in urban planning in two key documents. Circular 22/80 (DoE, 1980) advised a 'loosening up' of the planning system entailing the release of land for development and a shift in the control of decision making (Rydin, 1986). Circular 22/80 aimed to speed up the planning system and make it more responsive to development. The circular also develops the view that planners should withdraw from aesthetic control and not attempt to influence the layout, density and size of rooms in new residential developments (Thornley, 1991, pp. 147–8). A later white paper entitled 'Lifting the Burden' (DoE, 1985) intended to de-regulate urban planning and prevent state intervention that undermined the legitimacy of market processes and individual freedoms. The traditional purpose of planning – the protection of public interest – weakened as the liberal political economy of the 1980s supplanted this with the enhancement of private interest. Ward (1994, p. 207) even suggests that under Thatcherism 'the public interest was almost redefined in terms of the functional requirements of private wealth creation'.

You turn it into two flats and you've got, like £220,000. The market drove that and there was a lot of money to be made. (Estate agent)

These subdivisions created an abundance of new accommodation that landlords (the beneficiaries of this 'new' space) appropriated in order to make a profit – initially from housing benefit claimants and later from asylum-seekers, especially from those London Boroughs declaring themselves 'full':

I've gained access to the homeless and asylum-seekers through the council, because if I'm quiet I can take half a dozen of them and that would pay my mortgage on the forty bedrooms I've got. So out of 40 bedrooms I've got six of them used by asylum-seekers; I split them all up so they're not all in the same place causing chaos, and I'm getting six grand a month for it. If I've got a quiet period I phone up an authority and say, "we've got some vacancies, do you need to put anybody up? (Landlord)

Market opportunities for landlords were also increased by the relatively low amount of social housing available in the town.[6] Some sources speculate whether in Southend there exists a pronounced entrepreneurial spirit. Two residents who moved into Southend from other areas of the country raised this point:

It's definitely more pronounced around here [the entrepreneurial spirit]. If you want to make money in Surrey where I'm originally from you commute to London. The people who stay and work in Guildford tend to be professionals like teachers, nurses. They give the impression of being more legitimate and more honourable, not quite so 'fly' as people are here in Southend. (Male resident aged 27)

It was big bucks to be had round here in the 1980s – my husband's a plasterer and I know he was working for people who were making killings ... so there is definitely an entrepreneurial spirit in this neck of the woods and I can say that because I don't come from around here. (Female resident aged 41)

I would suggest that while these comparisons clearly draw upon stereotypes of self-made Essex men whose streetwise business acumen embodies the Thatcherite ethic, the following quote (from a landlord) tends to support their observations:

As soon as you take a place that's got them sort of people you've devalued the property straight away. That's not dissimilar to what I'm saying about blacks moving into Westcliff. The same thing happens in York Road so for me as investor I can go and buy cheap flats, I was buying them for seventy, eighty grand and renting them out for £300, £350, £325 a month. I'm buying five times income and I'm making money. I don't mind what shit I put up with as long they can sign a form and I can get the cheque paid to me, I'm happy. As long as they keep the cheques coming I don't go round there, the place deteriorates, they don't give a fuck so I don't give a fuck. When

---

6   Social housing stocks depleted nation wide after the late 1980s. However, the situation in Southend was exacerbated by a historically low amount of social housing, especially in relation to neighbouring conurbations such as Basildon and Thurrock.

it becomes empty I'll do it up and I'll sell it ... I've sold my bedsits, I had them eight or nine years, I bought them for forty grand and sold them for ninety-five ... Someone else buys the bedsits and it carries on the same scale. They've bought what they think is cheap, I've had my profit and the road remains the same. (Landlord)

This passage illustrates the entrepreneurial *habitus* that residents referred to in previous quotes. The landlord describes how he buys properties in devalued areas for the purpose of letting to housing benefit claimants. There is no attempt to redevelop in a traditional sense that endeavours to improve the property and surrounding area. In fact, the place is actually allowed to deteriorate before it is sold at price that – although low – still far exceeds the initial investment. The assumption that the tenants of these properties also 'don't give a fuck' reveals how closely the landlords understanding of people, streets, buildings, rooms, rent and resale value resembles Lefebvre's (1991, p. 91) notion of 'abstract space' where the *raison d'etre* of planners, developers and landlords in advanced capitalist societies is conditioned by a logic where the ultimate arbiter is value.

If there are beneficiaries of space (and there clearly are), there must also be those who are deprived of space. The most likely scenario, described by David Harvey (1973, p. 170) is that while the 'rich can command space ... the poor are trapped in it'. With their lifeworld crushed, those individuals and families condemned by the market to live in a fragmented, restricted and devalued environment often fail to recognise themselves. The following local newspaper story hints at this sense of alienation, suggesting that life itself is opposed by the 'abstract' space of bedsit-land (where the ultimate arbiter is value).

Landlords of a house in which a refugee last week tried to commit suicide today admitted facilities were not ideal. Depressed Iranian 'KMM' doused himself in petrol and threatened to set himself alight in a house in Burdett Avenue, Westcliff, which he shares with 19 other asylum seekers ... They share washing and toilet facilities and must take it in turns to use the kitchen because it is too small. (*Southend Evening Echo*, 1 February 2000)

The built environment appears transparent and benign. Its precise configuration is often viewed as *naturally occurring* (see, for example, the work of the Chicago School on so-called 'natural areas'). Keith (2005, p. 22) similarly points to the fact that 'space becomes the medium through which particular settlements of ethics, material interest and value are made to appear normal or inevitable'. This is why Bourdieu (1999, p. 126) states that space is a particularly subtle form of symbolic violence. Symbolic violence is where restraint is exercised upon individuals by indirect cultural mechanisms rather than direct coercive social control (see Bourdieu and Passeron, 1977). From this perspective, the class struggle is inscribed, yet naturalised in space. The newspaper story, while sympathetic, carries the view that *space itself* (rather than the concealed productive forces of space) is the foundation of KMM's discontent. A further consequence of this illusory quality of space is spelled out in the *second* moment where the conditions that exist to make the presence of immigrants in Southend-on-Sea a possibility reveal a great deal about the reception they receive once they arrive.

The second decisive moment in the production of bedsit-land is the connotative switch from bedsit-land to mini-Bosnia, a clear example of how racisms become normalised in space (Goldberg, 1993, p. 185). This shift in how bedsit-land is signified is an example of what Paul Willis (1990) calls symbolic creativity, that extraordinary ability of people to humanise, decorate and invest life spaces with meaning. This kind of creativity is usually romanticised by social scientists who conveniently ignore the fact that symbolic activity often constructs what might be called an ugly resistance. This is especially the case in a spatial setting such as bedsit-land where, 'conditions of oppression do not speak for themselves but are always interpreted in ways that are subject to contestation' (Cohen, 1993, p. 2). The revised representation of bedsit-land as mini-Bosnia reflects the perception among many residents that a 'tipping point' has been reached in terms of amounts of immigrants. Unsurprisingly, this 'realisation' produces an increasingly hostile atmosphere.

> There was an elderly lady – a Romany – she's got two or three granddaughters. Anyway, they were walking together and a couple of people attacked them and were shouting 'fucking gypsies!' (Female asylum-seeker from Bulgaria aged 30)

This example demonstrates how people – like any other material object – become redolent with symbolism. The geohistorically positioned bodies of 'asylum-seekers' or 'Kosovans' in bedsit-land come to represent 'symbols of absolute cultural and moral difference' (Alexander and Knowles, 2005, p. 10).

At the heart of this connotative switch is the misrecognition by many *established* residents of bedsit-land that the deterioration of the area has been and is being caused by immigrants.

> I would have said it started getting worse over the last three or four years, I reckon – when you started to get some of these immigrants people. We seem to get a lot. Years ago you didn't have it. (Male resident aged 34)

Not uncommonly this resident believes that Milton was once a more pleasant place to live. There is little reason to doubt this view. What can be questioned however is the assumption that the deterioration of the area is caused by immigrants. This is a misrecognition because as Lefebvre (1991, p. 57) correctly points out, 'every space is already in place before the appearance in it of actors; the pre-existence of space conditions the subjects presence, action and discourse'. Simply put, the productive forces of the space that exists to make the presence of immigrants in Westcliff a possibility are concealed beyond everyday practical consciousness, within the very *naturalness* of space. This means that residents apportion blame for the deterioration of quality of life in Milton upon the most noticeable *effect* of these productive forces – immigrants.

Curiously, Milton ward has a half-remembered history of racialisation dating back to shortly after the central town was built. The reproduction of bedsit-land as mini-Bosnia contains traces of what Philip Cohen calls the 'urban uncanny' where the 'the living and the dead, the animate and inanimate become strangely confused' (Cohen, 2006). Walton (2000, p. 160) details how in the twentieth century some of strongest Jewish communities in Britain consolidated and grew in seaside settings, including Southend. He reports one resident during the 1930s bemoaning that Westcliff was a 'Little Palestine' occupied by a plethora of Jews 'driving around in their flashy cars, stuffing themselves in the best hotels' (Walton, 2000, p. 160). The relics of Little Palestine – the violently subdivided townhouses of Milton – haunt Southend today in the guise of mini-Bosnia. It is spatialised (and racialised) epithets such as Little Palestine and mini-Bosnia which give credence to Cross and Keith's (1993, p. 9) view that 'race is a privileged metaphor through which the confused text of the city is rendered comprehensible'.

The *third* moment occurs when the over-development of Milton war (*moment one*) and the misrecognition of this space as a racialised mini-Bosnia (*moment two*) fuse to produce distinctive spatial practices, thereby completing the material reproduction of bedsit-land as mini-Bosnia. Without practice (people actually *doing* things), *moments one* and *two* would remain meaningless abstractions. Structural factors such as overcrowding, poverty and lack of public space combine with the perception that these effects are caused by asylum-seekers to produce new practices, actions that practically transform bedsit-land into mini-Bosnia.

The symbolic understanding that 'asylum-seekers' are dangerous or predatory causes members of the established community to adopt routes that reduce the likelihood of coming face-to-face with an 'asylum-seeker':

> I'm not saying they're going to do us any harm, but you just don't feel safe. You won't walk past them, I'd rather come up the street and go around another road than go through the town and walk past them if there's a few together. I haven't been attacked by anybody – I know people that have been molested and their bags taken and their pension and this sort of thing – I haven't personally been attacked by anybody but I don't want to give them a chance. (Female resident aged 62)

The result is a spatiality of suspicion – a community that consciously avoids integrating with itself. Mini-Bosnia becomes a more frightening proposition when individuals choose to vent their frustrations on the perceived agents of change – asylum-seekers:

> A Kosovan refugee who was left battered and bloodied by two thugs wielding a hammer still spoke of his respect for the people of Southend. 'NK' suffered deep gashes to his face and head and bruising to his back after a frenzied attack by two men who broke into his bedsit in York Road, Southend. He said they held him down on his bed, swore at him continuously and bludgeoned him with the hammer for ten minutes. He described how he even broke free and ran for the door but was dragged back as the blows continued to rain down. (*Southend Evening Echo*, 14 April 2000)

These examples of spatial practice complete the reproduction of bedsit-land into the racialised space of mini-Bosnia. New practices are effectively the *product of* bedsit-land and the *producer of* mini-Bosnia. Such practices are *product producers:* activities that propound and presuppose space (Lefebvre, 1991, p. 36).

Yet it is a different set of spatial practices in mini-Bosnia that steer our analysis back towards understanding Southend's anticipated re-birth as a 'cultural hub' within the Thames Gateway. Recently many new independently owned restaurants, cafés and bars[7] have opened along the focal thoroughfare Hamlet Court Road.[8] This development has not been met with the approval of all members of the community:

> Hamlet Court Road was known as the Bond Street of Essex. Whether that was ever quite the case, I'm not in a position to judge, but it did have a certain elegance, a degree of charm. Now there's a shop in Hamlet Court Road advertising cheap phone calls to Zimbabwe. Now, read what you like into that. Would you expect a street like that to have a clientele that wanted to make cheap phone calls to Zimbabwe? I'm being a bit facetious now but it's a sign of the times perhaps how the populace that exists around Hamlet Court Road has significantly changed. (Male resident aged 68)

Yet despite the distaste revealed above, many residents view the revitalisation of Hamlet Court Road as an overwhelmingly positive effect of the unplanned cosmopolitanism that has occurred in the town since the mid-1990s. This scenario is reminiscent of what Les Back (1996) calls the metropolitan paradox whereby the places where racism is most rife also contain the potential to be the most progressive in terms of intercultural dialogue. More important to this analysis is how the 'exotica' on display in Hamlet Court Road offers a glimpse of an alternative and *politically expedient* reading of the unplanned cosmopolitanism that has occurred in bedsit-land.

The process through which ethnic enclaves are targeted for regeneration and/or gentrification[9] is well documented (see especially Keith, 2000, 2005). In Southend, European Union 'objective two' funding, designated for revitalising areas facing structural difficulties, has allowed the local council to formulate its own 'Hamlet Court Road Project'. The project has encouraged the burgeoning café culture by widening pavements, introducing aluminium street furniture,

---

7   In January 2007 Hamlet Court Road was home to Filipino, Italian, Thai, Japanese, Indian, Pakistani, Moroccan, Portuguese and Greek restaurants as well as three Chinese restaurants, three European style bar/bistros, two pubs, a noodle bar, Jewish bagel bar, Madeira café and a Portuguese café/delicatessen. Other signs of cosmopolitanism/ gentrification include a weave shop, an African shop, three hairdressers, two contemporary eco-furniture stores and three estate agents.

8   Hamlet Court Road is one of the oldest and most famous shopping streets in Southend and has historically been associated with independent family retailers. During the first half of the twentieth century, the road was reputedly referred to as the 'Bond Street of the east coast'.

9   Arguably due to desperation Southend Borough Council have been so eager to find a remedy for the dilapidation of its prestige shopping street that they have attempted to skip the first two 'waves' of gentrification and have moved straight onto a 'third wave' of state-assisted gentrification. It will be interesting to see whether this venture to catalyse the process of gentrification – *in reverse* – proves to be successful.

branded street banners, palm trees and CCTV in order to displace the homeless who had previously used benches in the street as meeting points.

In addition, council organised cultural festivals have stressed the use of 'diversity to enhance Hamlet Court Road for the better' (*Southend Evening Echo*, 8 December 2004). Arguably, the council's commandeering of cosmopolitan spatial practices in order to promote (and claim credit for) local economic growth confirms Lees' (2003, p. 61) suspicion that current strategies for urban regeneration amount to little more than a programme for gentrification, an attempt at 'domestication by cappuccino' (Zukin, 1995, p. xiv). It remains far from clear whether the local community that inadvertently provide the 'magic solution' for Milton's urban malaise will benefit from short-fix regeneration plans that appear more concerned to cultivate an aesthetic to satisfy middle-class 'cultural tourists'.

Moment *Four*: The 'Vision'

I propose therefore a *fourth* moment. This occurs when technocrats at both a local (Hamlet Court Road Project) and regional (Thames Gateway South Essex) level seize upon the mini-Bosnia's multi-ethnic 'buzz' and cosmopolitan spatial practices to enhance and authenticate their vision of Southend as a cultural hub. It is at this point that unplanned cosmopolitanism becomes very much *integral* to the plan. The emergent space of mini-Bosnia feeds into and feeds off the strategic repositioning of Southend. Obviously mini-Bosnia is not the *sole* driver for this re-branding exercise. Rather I propose that this dynamically evolving space functions to provide technocrats with the opportunity to represent Southend as an *authentic* (multi)cultural space. This representation of course runs congruently with catalyst developments such as the new University of Essex campus in the town centre, the end result being a neatly packaged vision for Southend within Thames Gateway:

> Southend-on-Sea has a unique cultural character and is a diverse community. The town is home to many faith communities and ethnic minorities ... Southend aims to be recognised as a regional cultural capital by 2010 and to improve the image and perception of Southend and South Essex. The University of Essex shares this aspiration .... (University of Essex, 2005, p. 11).

The mobilisation of culture as a means to transform redundant, but once prosperous areas is a well-established practice within urban policy (see Cochrane, 2003). From the securing of 'objective two' funding through to the new vision of Southend as cultural hub, it is clear that the town is learning to become successful in utilising the market advantages of cultural diversity. Through marketing ethnic diversity as a locational strength, technocrats have been able to positively spin and claim credit for the *unplanned* cosmopolitanism that has occurred. Yet, the project should not be judged too quickly a success. More perspective can be gained if the scheme is viewed in light of Sharon Zukin's (1995, pp. 273–4) warning that cultural strategies represent 'a worst case scenario' of regeneration 'when a city has few cards to play'.

Zukin (1995, p. 274) argues that culturally driven regeneration also offer *political* strategies for managing social diversity. This point is worth pursuing. Keith (2005, p. 112) ponders the 'redemptive potential' available to politicians and public institutions in the promotion of multiracial democracy. It is apparent that the adoption of a 'diversity as asset' discourse as part of the strategy of marketing Southend as a 'cultural hub' allows the local state to put a gloss on past mistakes whilst appearing to champion progressive and integrative ethnic relations. The mistake in question, from the viewpoint of this chapter, is the unchecked over-development of Milton during the property boom of the 1980s. As argued in the previous section, it was the passivity of the state in the production of this space (bedsit-land) that *made possible* the unplanned cosmopolitanism and attendant discontents of mini-Bosnia. The 'diversity as asset' discourse, whilst redemptive for the local state, is a *weak* response because it avoids the issue of moral responsibility and maintains the public and media preoccupation with 'race relations'.[10] Bourdieu's (1998, p. 38) observation that state bureaucracies and their representatives are great producers of social problems is particularly relevant here. In this instance, a 'race relations problematic' is preserved subtly; first through adoption of the 'diversity as asset' discourse and second through attempts to encourage the public (especially residents of Milton) to be more *accepting* of asylum-seekers.[11] Critically, neither strategy challenges the fundamental misrecognition (see moment *two*) that immigration is the agent of change. The maintenance of a race relations problematic merely reflects social problems and takes the effect for the cause (Lefebvre, 1991, p. 287). The redemptive potential offered by promoting diversity and the pioneering ethnic entrepreneurs on Hamlet Court Road allows local and regional technocrats to accentuate the progressive and consumption sustaining aspects of cosmopolitanism whilst obscuring responsibility for the multitude of structural disadvantages experienced by the majority in this community.

The redemptive discourse adopted by local and regional strategists in promotional material stands in stark contrast to the entrenched view among residents that Milton ward (or mini-Bosnia) is a 'dumping ground' for asylum-seekers.

> Asylum-seekers are just dumped here. The social workers have found them accommodation, they've more or less washed their hands of them. So there's no integration into the community by improving their language, their skills ... But they

---

10   In a similar vein, Imrie and Raco (2003, p. 30) suggest that New Labour's political narrative of community and individual responsibility deliberately deflects attention away from the causes of poverty.

11   This resonates with Lees' (2003, p. 65) observation that New Labour's urban policy carefully uses rhetoric that universalises responsibility for causing and alleviating urban problems.

are basically part of our community although they're not accepted by the population. (Male resident aged 60)

This penetrative view – widely held amongst those who cannot help but feel *dumped upon* – is increasingly silenced by the emerging official discourse. Yet results of the urban ethnography that this chapter is based upon (Millington, 2006) suggests this view is more deeply entrenched than technocrats care to imagine. The resentment of longer established residents of Milton's community towards immigrants (in the main) and the local council and developers (to a lesser extent) threatens to undermine the progressive practices and forms of consciousness that technocrats seek to highlight.

Future Moments

The community of bedsit-land or mini-Bosnia is beset by an array of structural disadvantages including overcrowding, unemployment, a lack of public amenities and more latterly racism. The pragmatic recasting of Southend as a 'cultural hub' in order to provoke investment and sustain consumption does not promise to alleviate these problems. Yet, this chapter does not oppose attempts to regenerate Southend as a matter of course. It is true that some developments – notably the new University of Essex campus – should bring long-term benefits to the town. Rather, this chapter aims to raise concerns regarding the continued promotion of 'signs of cultural dialogue' (Mitchell, 2003) over policies that actively remove the widespread barriers to integration and association. The path to Southend's renaissance, supposedly running in parallel to the end of a sustainable community, actually appears to have very little to do with community (aside from the state's appropriation of the commercial aspects of unplanned cosmopolitanism along Hamlet Court Road). The assurance that 'Southend's town centre strategy aims to integrate social, educational and environmental needs with local economic priorities' (ODPM, 2005, p. 21) merely adds to the suspicion that the social is continuously *reduced* to the economic by the current strategy of regeneration. This supports Imrie and Raco's (2003, p. 30) evaluation that present strategies for urban renaissance do not permit a critical questioning of the market (in particular, the persisting faith in 'trickle down' economics). Rather the actions of the business community are simply assumed to be *pivotal* to the renaissance of cities. This ignores mounting evidence that business behaviour is invariably unstable, short-term and not necessarily congruent with the politically desired creation of 'sustainable urban communities'.

The *real* community work in Milton has been left to the charitable sector.[12] In 1998 the Milton Community Partnership (MCP), comprised of a mix of professionals, representatives of the Children's Society and residents, began fulfilling its aim of providing grassroots representation for the ward whilst

---

12   This in itself is representative of New Labour's move towards communitarian strategies of self-government involving multi-agency partnerships.

encouraging local imagination and participation in the regeneration of the area. Following a quality of life report (Rayner and Fryer, 2001), the partnership sought to address the lack of public space by creating a community garden and playground. Other schemes involved unaccompanied refugee and asylum-seeker children in a project entitled *Being Here* that encouraged expressions of sense of place in Southend. MCP are also critical of the state's blinkered economic philosophy of urban regeneration. Yet by virtue of their relative autonomy from the council they have been able to practice a different understanding of urban renaissance.

> It's easy to lay everything down at the councils door but their argument is that you bring in the business, get Thames Gateway money and the quality of life will improve. I think the council are just caught up in that drip-down thing. We're very much informed by the people who actually live in the community whereas councils find it very hard to do that – it has to fit their agenda. (MCP spokesperson)

The ongoing work of MCP points towards the production a new kind of dis-alienated space, where the right to the city is extended to the many rather than the few who have the capital to appropriate it (see Lefebvre, 2002; Lees, 2004; Mitchell, 2003).

I want to conclude by advocating that it *is* possible for Southend to assume its proposed role as a cultural centre if an alternative strategy is pursued. Such a strategy would aim to establish Southend as a civic and inclusive town, with an identity that acknowledges the resorts history as a site of democratic leisure and a point of convergence for the diverse masses. A number of suggestions (aimed at a local level) are made here. The needs of the community in the central zone of the town need to be prioritised. This necessarily involves a shift away from 'trickle down' economic orthodoxy towards a programme of careful intervention that works in tandem with the grassroots approach of MCP. In addition, stricter limits should be made on the amount of subdivided dwellings permitted per street. Furthermore, the Council should consider embarking on a long-term schedule of compulsory purchase in the most overdeveloped streets. This should be aligned to a concurrent policy of re-converting unsuitable dwellings to meet lifetime homes[13] standard. This intervention would increase and improve social housing stock in the town whilst reducing exploitation of marginalized groups by landlords. Regeneration funds should be spent improving and securing the future of public facilities currently used by local inhabitants. Funds may also be used to provide new leisure, arts, work and public spaces where deemed necessary. It is also important that a politics of pluralism, based upon solidarity, trust and reciprocity, is encouraged in order to alleviate existing and forecasted social divisions.

Southend Borough Council and Thames Gateway are in a unique position to enable the flourishing of a cultural life of which the town and region can be proud. There exists the opportunity for Southend to establish a lead in the promotion of cosmopolitan citizenry on the *edges* of a global city. Yet while

---

13   Joseph Rowntree Foundation Lifetime Homes Standard.

bedsit-land or mini-Bosnia remains a racialised site of antagonism, resentment and multiple deprivations the realisation of a true urban renaissance (moment *five*) remains fanciful.

References

Alexander, C. and Knowles, C. (eds) (2005), *Making Race Matter: Bodies, Space and Identity*, Basingstoke, Palgrave Macmillan.

Appadurai, A. (1996), *Modernity at Large: Cultural Dimensions of Globalisation*, Minneapolis, University of Minnesota Press.

Back, L. (1996), *New Ethnicities and Urban Culture: Racisms and Multiculture in Young Lives*, London, UCL Press.

Bourdieu, P. (1998), *Practical Reason: On the Theory of Action*, Stanford, CA, Stanford University Press.

Bourdieu, P. (1999), 'Site Effects', in Bourdieu, P., *The Weight of the World: Social Suffering in Contemporary Society*, Cambridge, Polity.

Bourdieu, P. and Passeron, J.-C. (1977), *Reproduction in Education, Society and Culture*, London, Sage.

Cochrane, A. (2003), 'The New Urban Policy: Towards Empowerment or Incorporation? The Practice of Urban Policy', in Imrie, R. and Raco, M. (eds), *Urban Renaissance? New Labour, Community and Urban Policy*, Bristol, Policy Press.

Cohen, P. (1993), *Home Rules: Some Reflections on Racism and Nationalism in Everyday Life*, London, University of East London.

Cohen, P. (2006), *Capital Heritage: A Rough Guide to Dead Labour and the Imperial City*: http://www.uel.ac.uk/risingeast/currentissue/essays/cohen.htm.

Cross, M. and Keith, M. (eds) (1993), *Racism, the City and the State*, London, Routledge.

Department of Environment (1980), *Circular 22/80*, London, HMSO.

Department of Environment (1985), *Lifting the Burden*, White Paper, London, HMSO.

Edgell, V. and Duke, V. (1991), *A Measure of Thatcherism: A Sociology of Britain*, London, Harper Collins.

Elden, S. (2004), *Understanding Henri Lefebvre: Theory and the Possible*, London, Continuum.

Everitt, S. (1980), *Southend Seaside Holiday*, Chichester, Phillimore.

Goldberg, D.T. (1993), *Racist Culture: Philosophy and the Politics of Meaning*, Oxford, Blackwell.

Hall, S. (2004), *Divided City: The Crisis of London*: http://www.openDemocracy.net.

Harvey, D. (1973), *Social Justice and the City*, London, Edward Arnold.

Harvey, D. (1996), *Justice, Nature and the Geography of Difference*, Oxford, Blackwell.

Imrie, R. and Raco, M. (eds) (2003), *Urban Renaissance? New Labour, community and urban policy*, Bristol, Policy Press.

Keith, M. (2000), 'Identity and the Spaces of Authenticity', in Back, L. and Solomos, J. (eds) (2000), *Theories of Race and Racism*, London, Routledge.

Keith, M. (2005), *After the Cosmopolitan? Multicultural Cities and the Future of Racism*, London, Routledge.

King, T. and Furbank, K. (1992), *The Southend Story: A Town and its People*, Southend, Southend Borough Council.

Lees, L. (2003), 'Visions of "Urban Renaissance": The Urban Task Force Report and the Urban White Paper', in Imrie, R. and Raco, M. (eds), *Urban Renaissance? New Labour, Community and Urban Policy*, Bristol, Policy Press.

Lees, L (ed) (2004), *The Emancipatory City? Paradoxes and possibilities*, London, Sage.

Lefebvre, H. (1991), *The Production of Space*, Oxford, Blackwell.

Lefebvre, H. (2002), 'The Right to the City', in Bridge, G. and Watson, S. (eds), *The Blackwell City Reader*, Oxford, Blackwell.

Lefebvre, H. (2003), *Key Writings*, London, Continuum.

Millington, G. (2005), 'Meaning, Materials and Melancholia: Understanding the Palace Hotel', *Social and Cultural Geography*, 6 (4), pp. 531–50.

Millington, G. (2006), 'Racism, Community, Place: Inside the Ethnoscapes of Southend-on-Sea', unpublished PhD thesis, University of Essex.

Mitchell, D. (2003), *The Right to the City: Social Justice and the Fight for Public Space*, New York, The Guilford Press.

O'Brien, K. (1934), 'Southend', in Cloud, Y. (ed), *Beside the Seaside: Six Variations*, London, Stanley Nott.

Office of the Deputy Prime Minister (ODPM) (2005), *Creating Sustainable Communities: Delivering the Thames Gateway*, Wetherby, Crown.

Pewsey, S. (1993), *The Book of Southend-on-Sea*, London, Baron Birch.

Pollitt, W. (1957), *The Rise of Southend*, Southend-on-Sea, John H. Burrows and Sons Ltd.

Rayner, J. and Fryer, J. (2001), *Milton Ward: A Summary of Community Consultation in Milton Ward*, EEDA.

Rydin, Y. (1986), *Housing Land Policy*, Aldershot, Gower.

Schama, S. (1996), *Landscape and Memory*, London, Fontana.

Shields, R. (1991), *Places on the Margin: Alternative Geographies of Modernity*, London, Routledge.

Thames Gateway South Essex (2001), *A Vision for the Future*, Basildon, Thames Gateway South Essex Partnership.

Thornley, A. (1991), *Urban Planning Under Thatcherism: The Challenge of the Market*, London, Routledge.

University of Essex Southend (2005), *Vision 2012: Meeting Future Demand for Higher Education and the Business Community in the South Essex Thames Gateway*, Southend, University of Essex.

Wacquant, L. (1993), 'Urban Outcasts: Stigma and Division in the Black America Ghetto and the French Urban Periphery', *International Journal of Urban and Regional Research*, 17, pp. 366–83.

Walton, J.K. (2000), *The British Seaside: Holidays and Resorts in the Twentieth Century*, Manchester, Manchester University Press.

Ward, S.V. (1994), *Planning and Urban Change*, London, Paul Chapman Publishing.

Willis, P. (1990), *Common Culture: Symbolic Work at Play in the Everyday Cultures of the Young*, Milton Keynes, Open University Press.

Young, M. and Willmott, P. (1957), *Family and Kinship in East London*, London, Routledge and Kegan Paul.

Young, M. and Willmott, P. (1973), *The Symmetrical Family*, Harmondsworth, Penguin.

Zukin, S. (1995), *The Cultures of Cities*, Oxford, Blackwell.

Chapter 13

The Thames Gateway Bridge: A New 'Solution' to an Old Problem?

Andrew Blake

Based around a case study of the difficulties in planning and building a new East Thames road crossing, this chapter's focus exemplifies the problematic planning and development process in Britain. Even in the case of the Thames Gateway – a regional designation which was set up partly in order to obviate some of the problems of the planning structure – the planning process can be long drawn out and cumbersome not only because of the various local and central government organisations involved in it but also because, it is generally agreed, any planning procedure needs to address the wishes of individuals and local and national interest groups, such as, locally, the people who live near any area of proposed development, and nationally – and, increasingly, globally – the changing interests of transport and power users, and environmental groups, each of whom may bring opposing holistic philosophies to the table in any discussion of a proposed new development. The views of these interest groups are important factors in the outcome, and yet we should always remember that the planning process is overseen by central government, and here too there are significant changes to register in any story ranging, as this one does, over the best part of thirty years. In a nutshell, planning is political, and any assessment of the outcomes of the planning process has to be written within the context of shifting political power and ambition.

Planning to Cross the River, Round 1: the East London River Crossing, 1979–1993

East London and the developing Thames Gateway region have inherited a historic transport problem: it has been too difficult to cross the river Thames east of the City of London. Whether the crossing be by foot, road, tube or rail, whether over bridges or through tunnels, West and Central London have historically had many more river crossings than East London. In the late 1970s there were 19 road and rail crossings west of Tower Bridge, and only two by road and one by (tube) rail to the east; there was also a free, low-capacity, car ferry in operation at Woolwich (which also had a foot tunnel). This lack of river-crossing facilities has often been given as one of the reasons why the West and City are wealthier than the East. To an extent this problem had been mitigated by the use of the river itself; much of

East London's employment was focused on shipping, the docks, and their ancillary services. However, during the 1970s and early 1980s new container ports, served by ships too big to travel up the Thames, were built on the coast of Essex, Kent and Hampshire. As the container ports developed, and the containers themselves were trucked around the country using the relatively new motorway system, the use of the Thames upriver of the estuary faded, and the massive system of 6,000 acres of docks situated downriver from the City of London had closed altogether for business by the early 1980s. East London residents were now more likely to need to travel significant distances to work elsewhere in the capital, which made the transport problems in the east of London more urgent.

A proposed East London River Crossing road bridge (ELRC) was included in the national road-building programme in 1979, the year in which a new and aggressively pro-capitalist, pro-growth Conservative government took office. Committed to the expansion of trade and finance capital rather than traditional industry, and with a hostility to unionised labour which was embodied both in legislation to make strike action more difficult, and in the systematic use of police against strikers, the Conservative administrations of the 1980s and early 1990s were complicit with the decline of the London docks (whose labour force had been strongly unionised). The closure of the docks was part of a pattern. Other older aspects of the mass-production industrial economy, including coal mining and iron and steel production, were cut back; subsidies for car manufacture were also cut; and the utilities, telecommunications, and the national railway system were privatised.

This did not mean that all Conservative ministers were happy to abandon the areas most affected by the closure of the industrial economy. A number of schemes promoted 'regeneration': from garden festivals in Liverpool in the North of England and Stoke on Trent in the Midlands, to the planning of the Millennium Dome in South-East London, a sequence of celebratory leisure events attempted to focus attention on the new post-industrial wastelands, and tried to engender interest in, and funding for, their reconstruction.

Such efforts were complemented in the former London docks by a tailored attempt to solve the problems left by the dereliction of this huge area of the capital city. Through a 1980 enabling law, the London Docklands Development Corporation (LDDC) was set up in 1981 by Conservative minister for the environment Michael Heseltine. The LDDC had powers to cut across some of the planning powers held by local government; to buy and sell land; and to offer very significant tax breaks to developers. As a result, in a deliberate echo of the World Trade Center, New York's post-docks office complex, the grandiloquent phallic towers of the Canary Wharf 'office city' emerged to change both the London skyline and the geography of employment within the financial, information and service industries. To serve the new offices the LDDC planned and built, or persuaded government to build, a new transport infrastructure including roads and the Docklands Light Railway (the DLR – the UK's first light rail system) to take workers – and visiting City workers – to and from the new buildings, and a small airport, suitable for short take-off and landing aircraft only, to facilitate short-haul flights to and from European business centres.

Though it would have addressed the need for new river crossings east of the City (a need recognised by LDDC and local boroughs alike), in essence the ELRC road bridge proposed in 1979 did not quite fit the regeneration agenda. It was to be part of the national trunk road system. The bridge would have been part of a new multi-carriageway road which was designed to connect the A406 north circular road in North London, and the M11 motorway to Stansted Airport and Cambridge, to the A2–M2 route which goes from south London to the Kent port of Dover, as part of the planned network for longer distance traffic within and through London. Such plans included an inner ring motorway and many other schemes which would have radically altered London's geography.

The ELRC scheme went through a Public Inquiry of record length in 1985/86. A Public Inquiry allows people to object to government or private plans to build significant new infrastructure, but although such enquiries take evidence from objectors in apparent seriousness, they usually find in favour of the planner rather than the objector, and sure enough despite significant local objections the ELRC was approved by the Secretary of State for Transport in 1988. However, by this time the LDDC had given permission for the building of London City Airport on the Royal Albert dock, only a quarter mile from the proposed bridge, and the LDDC pointed out that changes to the bridge design were needed to accommodate the planes taking off and landing at this new short-haul airport. This necessitated another Public Inquiry in 1990, and the go-ahead for the full scheme with a revised bridge was finally given in 1991.

This was not the end of the story. Throughout the bridge's planning life, and throughout both Inquiries, concern was expressed not just by individual local residents but by various well-organised groups of people who were worried not about the bridge as such, but about the new roads which would be built south of the river. There were particular fears about the environmental impact of the ELRC proposals on areas of housing in Plumstead in South-East London, and – especially – on Oxleas Wood, a rare surviving patch of ancient woodland south-east of Greenwich. A Site of Special Scientific Interest (SSSI), the Oxleas woods of oak, silver birch, hornbeam and coppice hazel, crossed by a network of recreational paths, bridleways and cycleways, cover 72 hectares, and the area has been woodland for at least 8,000 years. It was and so far remains a peaceful, and much-loved, local amenity. The planned road would have destroyed a significant amount of the Wood by cutting through it, while blighting the remainder with traffic noise and chemical pollution.

Although approval for the road had finally been given, its proximity to central London was seen as an opportunity to make Oxleas Wood a national symbol for the growing environmental opposition both to the plans for road building in London, and to the national road programme as a whole – indeed, the environmental movement organised against it with military seriousness. A strategy group was set up to bring local campaigns, under the umbrella of People Against the River Crossing (PARC) together with metropolitan and national pressure groups, and environmental NGOs, making an alliance from disparate groups such as Alarm UK, Transport 2000, the World Wide Fund for Nature, the Royal Society for the Protection of Birds, Greenpeace, Friends of the Earth,

Nature and English Heritage. The planned bridge and road were fought on every level, from letter writing stalls in the high streets of Greenwich, Newham and the adjoining boroughs, to the systematic lobbying of local and national politicians. There was an 'adopt a tree' scheme (the aim of which was to get every tree in the wood adopted by an individual, family or small business); many people also made 'beat the bulldozer' pledges of disruption should building works commence; and there were regular public rallies in the Wood itself attended by thousands of local people and environmental campaigners. Once the second Public inquiry had reported there were also two further legal challenges. A High Court challenge from the London Borough of Greenwich was rejected, but a challenge from the European Commission, which claimed that the environmental assessments made by the Department of Transport at the original Public Inquiry did not comply with the requirements of the EC Directive on Environmental Assessments, proved more problematic.

The government's advisers considered that the EC challenge was likely to take a long time to settle, that its outcome was uncertain, and that construction should not begin until the case was complete. In the midst of this uncertainty, and faced by increasing and expensive road-protest militancy such as the campaign which disrupted the building of the M3 extension at Winchester, which had added several million pounds to the eventual construction bill, the Secretary of State for Transport, John McGregor MP, announced in July 1993 that the Conservative Government, whilst 'fully committed to meeting the need for a new road link across the Thames in east London as a key element in the strategy to regenerate the Thames Gateway, felt that the current scheme, designed and chosen some time ago, fails to meet the high environmental standards we now apply to new road schemes'.[1] Therefore the Department decided not to proceed with the approved scheme, but instead to examine alternative solutions which 'meet the same strategic objectives, but which will have less impact on the local environment'. They could not find such an alternative. Following a consultation by the Government Office for London, and the 1995 publication of *A Transport Strategy for London*, the revocation of the ELRC Orders was finally advertised in July 1996, and the process of removing the bridge from both national and local road building plans was completed in March 1997.

This was a very significant victory for the environmental movement. Before the Government's 1993 climb-down over Oxleas Wood, road schemes were rarely defeated, even in the face of furious national and local opposition such as that at Winchester or Newbury. But after the ELRC/Oxleas Wood decision, scheme after scheme was dropped on a piecemeal basis, and then in 1995 the national roads programme was strategically reduced from more than 500 schemes to 150, along with a government concession – acknowledging research evidence – that road building does not merely ameliorate traffic conditions for existing user

---

1   LDDC monograph *Starting from Scratch: the History of Transport in London Docklands*, LDDC 1995, available at http://www.lddc-history.org.uk/transport/tranmon2. html.

levels, but also generates further traffic growth.[2] This cultural shift encompassed changing attitudes to road use as well as to road building. In an early concession to the emerging politics of climate change (which had even impressed Prime Minister Margaret Thatcher in her final months in office) in 1993 Chancellor of the Exchequer Charles Clarke announced an 'escalator' on fuel duty – set to rise annually above the level of inflation – justifying it as a 'green tax'.

Intermission. New Labour: The Modernisers, the Lobbies and the People

Meanwhile the agenda for the regeneration of East London had moved on apace. During the 1980s Conservative politicians had identified a 'Thames Corridor' of industrial wasteland and low-lying land on both sides of the river and its estuary as suitable for redevelopment. By the time, in 1991, that Michael Heseltine officially opened the first part of the Canary Wharf complex, the name had changed, but the idea of the 'Thames Gateway' including shoreline areas of Essex and Kent as a wider area for regeneration, both for providing new jobs and for housing the semi-planned increase in the capital city's population, was firmly established.

The Thames Gateway concept was adopted wholesale by the New Labour administration which took office in 1997. Transport was among the keys to the regeneration strategy, and one principal part of the new transport structure needed by the Gateway was already in place when New Labour took office. Stratford had been identified as a major transport hub in the early 1990s, with a station for the fast rail-link to the Channel Tunnel planned to complement the tube, rail, DLR and bus interchanges which were already in place, including extension of the Jubilee Line tube to service the Millennium Dome as well as Stratford itself.

The development of such a non-car transport hub might have been the signal for significant new investment in public transport, backed by an extension of the culture shift signalled by the fuel duty escalator; and indeed some members of the new administration talked confidently of a ten-year transport plan which would shift people away from habitual car use wherever possible. Significantly for the future, however, the New Labour party's 1997 election manifesto had made comparatively little mention of transport issues. Thanks, apparently, to the views of lower middle-class 'focus groups' – among the key influences on New Labour policy – the document expressed little sentiment directly against road building or car use, instead promising a number of policy reviews. The following year the Chancellor of the Exchequer, Gordon Brown, confirmed the continuation of the fuel duty escalator, and a transport White Paper was published. John Prescott, the then deputy prime minister and transport secretary, claimed that advisers working at 10 Downing Street tried to tone down his White Paper's proposals – especially for supermarkets and other out-of-town shopping facilities to charge

---

2   A brief account of the role of road protestors in this change can be found in Alarm UK's 1995 booklet, *Roadblock,* available at http://www.roadblock.org.uk/alarmuk/roadblock.html. See also G. McKay (1996), *Senseless Acts of Beauty. Cultures of Resistance*, London, Verso.

for parking – as 'anti-car'. Nonetheless, and despite increasing rumours that the real policy-drivers on transport were not focus groups but an active and very professional 'road lobby' representing car and truck manufacturers and road hauliers, the 1999 transport Bill allowed local authorities to introduce congestion charging; there were soft targets to reduce car use; and more provision was made for rail and light rail investment.

In September 2000 the government's position began to change. A month after John Prescott had announced that 103 more of the road schemes inherited from the Conservatives had been put on hold, one of the strangest episodes of recent UK political history took place. In a reverse of the populist politics of road protest, apparently spontaneous blockades sprang up outside various oil refineries and petrol depots around the UK. An alliance of farmers and self-employed truck-drivers led the protests, which followed weeks of press-led complaint about the rising price of petrol (on the introduction of the fuel escalator, British fuel prices had been among the lowest in the European Union; at this point they were the highest). As fuel became hard to get, the government became less popular than the opposition in the opinion polls for the first time since its election. The government seemed panic-struck. In order to end the dispute, the Chancellor of the Exchequer, Gordon Brown, announced that he would review petrol duty in his November pre-Budget statement, and he did so, both cutting the current level of duty and ending the fuel escalator which the Conservatives had put in place.

Three years later (in 2003) the policy reversal was completed as Secretary of State for Transport Alistair Darling announced a £5.5bn package of transport improvements, of which over £3bn was to be spent on road-building, and very little on new tram or light rail schemes, which Gordon Brown's Treasury apparently found to be too expensive (the best known of these schemes in the UK, the DLR, the Manchester Metrolink and Croydon Tramlink, were all planned and funded under the 1979–96 Conservative administration). Having said for its first five years that it would try to cut road use, the government now began to plan for an increase. The most dramatic reverse of this new anti-green policy was the decision to widen the M25 London orbital motorway between the M3 and M4 junctions to fourteen lanes, a scheme which the Conservatives had shelved in 1995 on the grounds that its environmental cost was too high, and which the road lobby and the British Airports Authority (which wishes to carry on expanding the use of Heathrow Airport until the whole of Great Britain does indeed become Airstrip One) had been pressing for ever since.

Meanwhile in 1999 the political context for transport in London itself had been changed significantly, with the passage of the Greater London Authority Act. Transport was a key responsibility of the new elected official, the Mayor of London, and a new planning authority, Transport for London (TfL) was created. One of its key priorities was investment in London's regeneration areas, including the Thames Gateway; increasing the level of investment in this area was also among the priorities associated with the city's bid to host the Olympic and Paralympic Games in East London in 2012. The UK government and the London Assembly alike were committed to the continuing growth of London, both in terms of economy and population, and to the continuation of the Thames

Gateway development strategy in order to house the new arrivals. This meant a significant planned population increase east of the City on both sides of the river, which in turn increased the pressure for more river crossings in East London.

However, the political context had also changed with an increased awareness of global warming, which, under the more subtle designation 'climate change', had become a publicly accepted science in the final years of the second millennium. The failure of the USA to sign up for the Kyoto treaty early in September 2001 had led to a prominent political debate whose impact was tempered only by the later events of that month in the USA, and subsequently by the more immediately obvious politics of the 'war on terror'. Many government advisors, however, continued to be of the view that climate change, partly caused by the emission of carbon dioxide from cars, trucks and planes, was a far greater threat to the population of the UK (and to the rest of the world) than political terrorism.

Planning to Cross the River, Round 2: the Thames Gateway Bridge, 2003–?

In this somewhat ambivalent context, ambitious new plans for another East London road bridge emerged and were put to the test. The lessons of the previous process had been well learned by the new crossing's proponents. They started by gaining the approval of the elected Mayor of London, Ken Livingstone, whose agreement was given despite fears that the completion of the scheme would again involve pressure to build a new roadway through Oxleas Wood.[3] Having decided in the scheme's favour, Ken Livingstone then acted on its behalf, chairing the November 2002 TfL meeting which agreed to promote it.

'Promotion' is a key term here. The attempt to win public approval for a new road bridge has been carefully managed, as one might expect in the era of spin. The most important piece of planning management has been the claimed 'mission' of the new structure. It is claimed that the new bridge will *not* be built to help metropolitan or national strategic traffic flow. The Thames Gateway Bridge (TGB) is instead being promoted as a 'local crossing' to aid regeneration and employment in East and South-East London. The 'missing section' of London roadway between the A13 and the A2016 will now, it is proposed, be filled by a crossing at virtually the same place as the planned ELRC. It will cross between two rapidly developing parts of east London. North of the river is Gallions Reach, which is close to a large car-based shopping area, a new upmarket housing development, and just east of City Airport, the University of East London's

---

3   In the London Assembly on 19 June 2002 Ken Livingstone said 'I've made clear in all my meetings with ministers – there is no question of the road scheme being taken further south anywhere near Oxleas Wood. ... I will do everything possible to make it almost impossible for someone ever to actually build down to Oxleas Wood': http://www.london.gov.uk/assembly/assemmtgs/2002/assemjun19/minutes/assemjun19appC.pdf. He repeated the message in a press release, 'Thames Gateway Bridge supported by 8 in 10 East Londoners', GLA 22 November 2002: http://mayor.london.gov.uk/view_press_release.jsp?releaseid=1450.

Docklands campus and a number of development sites around the Royal Albert Dock. The Bridge would cross from Gallions Reach south to Thamesmead, which is just downriver of the equally rapidly regenerating town centre of Woolwich. On the face of it, then, this will be a significant and very useful local gateway within the Gateway.

In order to gain public consent for the crossing the proponents of the new bridge put together a systematic consultation exercise, something which had not been considered necessary for the ELRC. The local public consultation on the TGB ran from 13 May to 12 August 2003, when, in one of the largest public consultation exercises ever undertaken within London, thousands of roadshow and on-street interviews, and dozens of public meetings, were backed up by over half a million questionnaires, brochures and leaflets, in twelve languages, which were distributed across an area spanning ten London Boroughs or local authority areas. By the time the consultation period ended 85 per cent of those people who were interviewed or completed a questionnaire supported building a bridge at the proposed location. The consulters were therefore able to claim, when they reported in November 2003, that the consensus in favour of the new bridge was overwhelming.

Approval for the scheme was also gained at local government level. Planning applications were submitted to the London Boroughs of Greenwich and Newham in July 2004, and the Councils resolved to approve them on 14 December 2004 and 15 December 2004 respectively. No other local Borough raised objections to the proposal at this time; many subsequently gave evidence in its favour at the subsequent Public Inquiry (though Bexley, to the south-east of Greenwich, was and remained opposed to the scheme). So – again unlike the ELRC, which had been challenged legally by Greenwich borough council because of the planned road through Oxleas Wood – the immediately affected local government bodies were on board early in the planning process.

However, despite this apparent local consensus, there was still substantial opposition both from local residents and national environmental and public-transport campaigners. They claimed that despite the claimed local benefits, in reality the bridge would be a strategic dual carriageway link connecting the A406 North Circular, A13 and the nearby M25 and M11 in the north, to the A2, M2, M25, and M20 in the south. It would look, sound, and to all extents and purposes *be* a part of the national motorway network. The scheme was heavily backed, the protestors noted, by businesses – and not just by the local plumbers or delivery drivers who could see the advantages of being able to cross the river more quickly, but by national road hauliers wishing to use the bridge to take more road freight through London, thus bypassing a significant stretch of the M25 (and thereby saving fuel costs and drivers' tachograph time). The new bridge would, they claimed, further enable longer-distance car commuting to work by people living outside London, especially commuters from Kent who would otherwise use the Dartford crossing to get to places of work north of the river.

Furthermore, the opponents of the TGB had also learned much from the brief success of the previous decade's road protests. They were as well organised as the bridge's proponents. Groups such as Transport 2000 and Friends of the

Earth issued detailed press releases criticising both the proposed bridge and the consultation process.[4] The pressure group London Thames gateway Forum commissioned a report on the consultation process from Kerry Hamilton, Professor of Transport at the University of East London. This report (written with Calampo Focas, a research associate at UEL) concluded that TfL's consultation had been lacking in a number of respects.[5] The principal problem was that the interviewees and other respondents to the consultation were not given enough information on which to make a judgement. Only one design, a six-lane road bridge, was presented. No alternatives (such as pedestrian-only or public transport crossings) were mentioned in the documentation, and the public was not encouraged to suggest alternatives, or to engage in the planning process other than to say yes or no to the question 'would you like a new bridge in east London?', while being shown only the one design at the one spot. None of the environmental consequences of the building work, or the subsequent operation of the crossing, were mentioned – in part because the consultation had begun before the publication of the environmental assessment, which duly occurred in July 2004.[6]

Responding to the increasingly high level of opposition to the scheme, on 19 January 2005 the Secretary of State announced that a Public Inquiry would be held into the planning application and orders for the TGB. The Public Inquiry commenced on 7 June 2005 at the Valley, the home of Charlton Athletic Football Club in South-East London, and closed on 3 May 2006.

The Inquiry, chaired by Michael Ellison, heard the case proposed by TfL:

> The proposed Thames Gateway Bridge (TGB) would be a local road bridge connecting Beckton in East London to Thamesmead in South-East London. The proposed design featured separate, and segregated, dual lanes for pedestrians and cyclists, alongside a single 'public transport' lane which could be configured either for buses or for light rail. There would also be a dual carriageway for cars and trucks.

Funding would be through the Private Finance Initiative, with the approximate £380 million costs of building the new structure met with a mix of private and public funding. The private funding will be reimbursed through the bridge tolls.

The bridge would, argued TfL, improve accessibility to and within the Thames Gateway and support the regeneration of East London. Users of the bridge would see significantly reduced journey times, saving up to 40 minutes in each direction,

---

4   For example, 'Thames Gateway: Sham consultation starts on motorway-style bridge' (Friends of the Earth press release, 22 May 2003).

5   The relevant report, *A Reasoned Documented Critique of the Thames Gateway Bridge Consultation Report*, and others critiquing the TGB proposal can be found at the Thames Gateway Forum website at http://www.ltgf.co.uk/content/en/campaign_details. aspx?guid=A87CC789-B977-46B8-8794-20A1A10AAEAA.

6   The full environmental assessment can be found at http://www.tfl.gov.uk/tfl/ downloads/pdf/thames-gateway-bridge/planning-documents/Environment_Statement/ Environment_Statement.pdf.

and therefore easier access to employment and other opportunities (leisure, shopping) would be created, which would themselves generate employment.

Access to the bridge, and flow across it, would be controlled by tolls which would discriminate in favour of local users. It was proposed that users resident within the four adjoining boroughs would cross at half the cost of all other users.

The Inquiry also heard the case against. Firstly, the objectors argued that this was yet another example of the way in which London has been and is being ruined by constant development in favour of car drivers and facilitating traffic flow, and against the interests of the city's human residents, many of whom would not ordinarily use the road bridge – over 40 per cent of all households in both Newham and Greenwich do not have access to a car. The protestors agued that TfL's estimates for traffic flow and generation were far too low, and that though discrimination in favour of local users was welcome in principle, in fact the proposed level of tolling would not deter Kent and Essex commuters. When the bridge was finally built, they argued, it would immediately generate significantly higher road traffic through south London, and there would immediately be more pressure both from the road lobby and from residents disturbed by the new traffic, for the Oxleas Wood link to the A2/M2 to be built as originally planned.

Secondly, the objectors pointed out that while the design might appear, as claimed, to facilitate non-mechanical crossing, it is not in fact pedestrian or cycle friendly. At one point 8 kilometres long the bridge is simply too long, and at 50 metres too high, to be a convenient route across the river (the nearby Woolwich foot tunnel under the Thames, by contrast, is a mere 370 metres long).

The third point made by the objectors was that the crossing itself was, simply, no longer necessary, as it arguably had been in the late 1970s when the ELRC was first proposed. Since 1979, they pointed out, four new East London crossings have been built, each of which already creates the kinds of access to employment which the road scheme's proponents argue the bridge will facilitate, but without adding to the area's existing road traffic chaos; one more crossing is already under construction. The Jubilee Line Extension from Waterloo to Stratford now crosses the river three times, and this line also connects East to Central and West London, while the DLR now crosses the river from the Isle of Dogs to Greenwich and Lewisham in the south. A new DLR extension, currently under construction and due to open in 2009, will also cross under the river Thames to central Woolwich, joining the South London rail network just a mile west of the proposed new road bridge and directly connecting the area with London City Airport, Canary Wharf and the City, while another DLR extension planned to open in 2010 will facilitate travel between Woolwich and the international travel hub at Stratford. A new road crossing might be necessary for cars, but not for people.

Finally, the protestors pointed to several other schemes which are either proceeding, or which could be improved, or built more quickly, if money reserved for the bridge went instead into them, including the existing Woolwich ferry for passengers and road vehicles, and proposed light rail 'transit schemes' for the East London shoreline and the Greenwich waterfront, each of which would link into the existing public transport infrastructure while serving the emerging communities of the Thames gateway more obviously. Perhaps most significantly the proposed Crossrail would join Paddington in the West of London to the Kentish South-East of London. This new semi-fast underground rail link would cross the river just upstream from where the bridge is proposed, and would, just like the TGB, connect Beckton and the Royal Docks with Woolwich and Thamesmead. Like the TGB itself, Crossrail has the full backing both of TfL and the Mayor. The TGB's opponents claimed that the area simply does not need both Crossrail and the Thames Gateway Bridge.

In the absence of an immediate decision on the bridge, several related proposals made after the closure of the public inquiry added fuel to the protestors' ire. Firstly the London borough of Greenwich began to discuss a congestion charging scheme similar to that which has operated in Central London since 2002 (and in an expanded area of West Central London since 2006). In one of the proposals under discussion, the A102 Blackwall Tunnel approach road and the tunnel itself would be part of the charging zone – in effect this would become a toll crossing, something which the anti-bridge protestors argue would radically increase traffic demand for the bridge.[7] Secondly the Ministry of transport proposed increasing the level of toll at the Dartford Crossing, not apparently in order to raise revenue but to discourage the use of the crossing.[8] This again, the protestors argued, would seriously increase projected traffic flows across the TGB, whose proposed tolling level was set in order to discourage users of Dartford from changing to the TGB. Finally, worried by the probable increase in traffic flows of Kentish commuters coming into London, and assuming that the new bridge would generate considerable new traffic, the London Borough of Bexley declared itself an Air Quality management Zone with effect from 1 March 2007, and increased its level of opposition to the TGB.[9] Protestors demanded a re-opening of the public enquiry to take these changes into account.

There was no immediate official decision, though it was known that the Inspector had reported in November 2006. Enquiries to TfL eventually established that it had assembled a full project delivery team for the TGB, headed by Martin Stuckey, which was due to start work at the end of August 2007 on the understanding that the go-ahead was imminent. Its confidence was misplaced. The new Prime Minister, Gordon Brown, who succeeded Tony Blair on 27 June 2007, included in his new cabinet Hazel Blears as Minister for Communities and Local Government, and in that capacity she wrote on 25 July 2007 to Martin Stuckey informing him that the enquiry was to be re-opened in the light of the new evidence received from objectors.[10] Blears' letter rather underplayed the conclusions of the inspector's report, which strongly supported the case made by the objectors:

---

7   http://www.bromleytransport.org.uk/Greenwich_Road_Tolls_Article.pdf.

8   http://www.dft.gov.uk/consultations/closed/dftconsuldartford/multiconsult dartford.

9   The relevant order is at http://www.bexley.gov.uk/aqma.

10   http://www.comunities.gov.uk/pub/65/decisiononapplicationsbyTransportfor LondonforproposedThamesGatewayBridge_id1512065.pdf.

9.422

In my view the key to this is the economic regeneration benefits claimed for the scheme. If they had been robustly shown, they might have been sufficient to tip the balance. But I do not consider the evidence to be strong enough to outweigh substantially the disbenefits of the scheme in terms of increased traffic, reduced safety, increased air pollution, and a shift against walking, cycling and public transport, in favour of the private car.[11]

The bridge had been planned to open in early 2012, a magical date for London, which undoubtedly needs new cross-river transport links east of Tower Bridge for the Olympics/Paralymics to cast its regenerative spell most efficiently; the re-opening of the enquiry renders this target impossible. Whether the TGB will be built at all, and if so whether it will prove of lasting benefit to the area as it grows in population and importance, or simply allows more road traffic to flow through areas which remain stubbornly deprived, remains to be seen.

---

11   http://www.communities.gov.uk/pub/64/InspectorsReport_id1512064.pdf, p. 564.

Chapter 14

The Airport Next Door: London City Airport – Regeneration, Communities and Networks

Iain MacRury

In the context of a book about the Thames Gateway the airport at Silvertown stands as a living case study for transformative urban regeneration. The costs, consequences, benefits, opportunities and opportunisms; the intensities and disorientations of large scale regeneration projects such as the airport, are visible (especially from the air) over and across the Royal Docks sites. Some further consequences of regeneration here are manifest also in neglected interstices, forgotten corners and unvoiced anxieties. In particular the site exemplifies some the dynamic configurations of global and local referred to by Graham and Marvin (2001) as 'glocalisation'; staging conjunctions of generation and ethnicity, wealth and poverty, connectivity and disconnection, against a rapidly changing post-industrial landscape. A kaleidoscopic sense of the splintered spaces of the Royal Docks site can be captured, initially, through a number of indicative statements about the airport.

> London City Airport, at the centre of Thames Gateway London, offers direct flights to most business destinations. Executives based in the Thames Gateway can leave their offices, rapidly check-in to the uncongested London City Airport and be in the business districts of Brussels, Frankfurt and Paris within 2 hours. (Thames Gateway London Partnership)

> We had the best Docks in the world, and then ... nothing! (Long-term resident, Focus group Interview)

> There is no place here for Silvertown, yet Silvertown is the place where it happens. (Avendano et al., 1999, p. 68)

> To consider the relationship between an airport and its environs is to consider the entwining of movement, money, land, sky, matter and information. (Fuller and Harley, 2005, p. 103)

This chapter draws on research conducted in 2005 to assess the 'social impacts' of London City Airport amongst residents in the immediate surrounding areas of

Silvertown and North Woolwich, as reported by some airport employees and as understood within wider communities of interest and engagement,[1] for example local government, commercial and other stakeholders. The work was conducted at the request of London City Airport and with their cooperation, but without any direct influence or oversight from the airport management.[2] Components of the research findings contributed to parts of a larger project[3] undertaken alongside the Airport's master planning and consultation processes between 2004 and 2007.[4]

The initial phase of research focused squarely on specific indicators of satisfaction and dissatisfaction within the changing communities around the airport; finding for instance that 56 per cent of respondents saw the airport as a 'good neighbour',[5] that 20.3[6] per cent found noise to be 'a problem', and that

---

1   A note on data and methods: the study comprised a large-scale community-based questionnaire which was administered to 500 respondents across a number of areas selected on the basis of proximity to the airport and in order to sample a mixture of housing and demographic types. The research team selected the respondent addresses from the full 360° and from distances up to a mile from the airport. Approximately 300 addresses were from within half a mile of the airport and 200 from between half and one mile, using the Electoral Register, the Newham Street Index and a street atlas. The questionnaires were administered by graduate students from UEL School of Social Sciences, Media and Cultural Studies, trained in advance by LERI staff and in consultation with a member of LCY management team. The survey was undertaken in the first three weeks of April 2005. Data was coded and processed for analysis in SPSS. Qualitative work included four focus groups: long-term residents in North Woolwich and Silvertown; local youth; recent residents in newly built apartment blocks; and airport employees – baggage handlers, fire services, human resources, payroll and across a number of other air services. Interviews were conducted with other stakeholders (e.g. Transport for London, Newham Council, Thames Gateway London Partnerships, the ExCel Centre, local estate agents and hoteliers and some of the major commercial institutions in Canary Wharf). The research was carried out by a team which included Alice Sampson, Tom Wengraf Alan Walsh and Philip Cohen.

2   It was agreed from the start that the work should be conducted in a spirit of cooperative independence to assure credibility and a full range of insight and reportage. This included testimony from current employees of the airport who, like all the respondents, were guaranteed anonymity.

3   The other master plan related impact studies included close analysis of economic and environmental impacts.

4   As required by the Aviation White Paper.

5   In detail: London City Airport is reported to be a good neighbour by 56.6 per cent of respondents in the locality, and overall only 7.8 per cent suggest that the airport is a bad neighbour. It should be added that indifference is a significant and element of local response; 'indifference' is an important but hard to grasp element of the impact of the airport. So the 20 per cent of respondents who had nothing good or bad to say about the airport, while living within a mile radius are indicative of some local propensity to 'have gotten used to' the Airport as part of the background.

6   In interviews and in focus groups, noise was a recurrent talking point. This is the case even when in the survey 79 per cent of respondents to the questionnaire reported that they did not (themselves) experience noise as an immediate problem: overall however, 20.3 per cent of respondents mentioned noise as a specific, immediate and present problem for them.

only 4 per cent[7] felt that the airport brought 'new jobs' to the immediate locality. Nevertheless 60 per cent of respondents felt the airport would be 'a future asset to the area'[8] and it was clear that taken as an aggregate most respondents accept the airport as a defining feature of the locale – its soundscapes and skyline – with only 6 per cent identifying the airport as a 'bad neighbour'.

Alongside such quantitative evaluations the project also offered an opportunity to consider some of the dynamics set in train when a highly ambitious regeneration project, like London City Airport, has been located alongside and within communities which have faced and are facing the various challenges and consequences of urban de-industrialisation – to understand a little more about what regeneration projects do with, within, to and for places.

The research – especially the interview and focus group work – was able to open up some useful perspectives on the 'plan view' in this particular part of London. This invites re-engagement with analyses of certain regeneration phenomena, notably as described in Graham and Marvin (2001). The descriptions given in these accounts of *Splintering Urbanism* capture, at a conceptual level, a good portion of what is in evidence around the airport and the Royal Docks more broadly viewed – where the ExCeL Centre, The University of East London Docklands Campus, a developing business park and new retail and housing developments will soon be joined by an aquarium centre – and yet more hotels. There is an ongoing re-constitution too in terms of population composition – where multi-ethnic populations of recently arrived migrants live side by side with young professionals buying (and buying to let) commuter homes in a recently thriving property market (*Evening Standard*, 31 May 2006, p. 58; *Mail on Sunday*, 8 January 2006, p. 8). This was a topic of intense interest amongst both staff and resident respondents: 'It never used to be the best area but people here who owned houses can't believe their luck' (long-term resident). And staff in the airport noted the difficulties colleagues had in living in the vicinity of the airport:

> I don't want to go into house prices or anything, but it's getting very expensive around here. Our fellas, they move our way [Essex, Southend] or Kent. (Airport staff)

These various redevelopments produce together – on the one hand – a startling collocation productive of new network potentialities in derelict space. From another

---

7   In 2004 London City Airport required 1,101 full-time equivalent (fte) direct jobs. 66 per cent are within the local core Study Area. It is estimated that the airport supports a further 208 fte indirect jobs and 136 fte induced jobs from the region, i.e. Newham, Tower Hamlets, Hackney, Waltham Forest, Redbridge, Lewisham, Southwark, Barking and Dagenham, Greenwich. The airport is required to source 30 per cent of its staff from within Newham by S106 planning agreements. The definition of 'the area' is at issue here – so that while London and borough wide jobs are created, there is a perception that few truly local (i.e. Silvertown and North Woolwich jobs have been created.

8   60 per cent believe the airport will be seen as an asset to the area in the future, with only 6 per cent imagining it will be seen as a disadvantage to the area in the future. However it should also be noted that 36.1 per cent anticipate possible problems in the future and future expansion is cited most frequently as the likely cause of any such problems (15.6 per cent).

point of view, the regeneration has produced a random assemblage of disjointed land use affirming disconnection and to be set negatively against the (formerly and formally) coherent network spaces of river, boats, docks, homes, factories, jobs, road and rail which had previously underpinned the communities from Canning Town to Silvertown. The close urban bonds and networks are replaced by a series of premium sites networking local space into the flows of high value global commerce[9] but, arguably, and by the same process, leaving 'disfigured' (see Boyer, 1995) areas – neglected and unconnected to the renewed spatial ordering.

One resident observed 'The airport fits in well with the things around it – Olympics, ExCel, hotels'. Another agreed, 'yes, but not with the likes of us' (long-term resident).

The airport was part of very controversial series of developments, with significant and well organised opposition from within the local area (see Figures 14.1 and 14.2), and various political stand offs between Labour-controlled local authorities opposing planning initiatives aimed at fulfilling the free market political and socio-economic policies of the governing Conservative Party. Respondents in this research – some of whom have lived uninterruptedly in the vicinities of North Woolwich and Silvertown for their whole lives[10] – were conscious of this history and were able to give detailed assessments of the present conditions, now that the airport has been in place for 20 years. The strong sense of place emerging from such longstanding connections and memories is an important element in the local geography.

This opposition emerged as local communities and other interested parties became aware of a plan to regenerate previous industrial and dock land, which had lain derelict for over a decade – with an *airport*. Looking back on this period some long-term respondents recalled shocked surprise at the plan when it was announced.

> Unbelievable ... an airport on our part of the water ... unbelievable. (Long-term resident)

Unlike a number of airport protests, the issue was not so much to do with noise, or with other environmental concerns, nor was there any flavour of straightforward NIMBYism,[11] an accusation levelled at some kinds of protest. At issue was 'place' in an argument between commitments to narratives of development grounded in and oriented to spatial definitions of community redevelopment versus the dynamics of post-industrial de-territorialisation. As one long-term respondent put it: 'The Docks were a living for the people living in the area ... the airport's nothing for us.' For a

---

9   Respondents often noted that the working docks linked Silvertown to 'everywhere' so that globalisation as much a part of the local past as it is a part of present and future.

10   The 'long tern resident' respondents included individuals who had been in the area since the early decades of the twentieth century, remembering munitions being transferred under the river from Woolwich Arsenal.

11   NIMBY, i.e., Not In My BackYard.

Figure 14.1 Protest against the building of the London City Airport. Photo and banner: Docklands Community Poster Project

Figure 14.2 Anti airport poster. Loraine Leeson and Peter Dunn, Docklands Community Poster Project,1983

minority of respondents, especially amongst older residents, the airport stands as an irrelevant curiosity and even now as a target for some ongoing resentment.

The City Airport was one of a number of prominent regeneration projects developed in East London during the 1980s. The development was driven by the LDDC[12] a body created in 1981 as the government's response to 'failure – by both the market and local government to redevelop the huge area where the capital's docks had lived and died' (Travers, 1998, p. 14).

The LDDC operated by a logic of 'rigorous deregulation' (Meyer, 1999, p. 100) leading to the development of 'infrastructure without public space' (ibid., p. 101) which, over a period, has lead to 'an enormous shift in the socio-economic structure of Docklands' a place where: 'Both superior and inferior qualities are present in abundance' but however, where 'the two never meet' (ibid., p. 105) with the airport, for example, 'Seceding relationally from [the] poorer areas that geographically surround them by the use of the old docks literally as moats' (Graham and Marvin, 2001, p. 324).

While some local respondents have remained sceptical about beneficial impacts from the airport it is also the case that a dynamic regeneration process is in evidence, with the airport understood as a key element in local redevelopment. Certainly amongst the business community, a number of stakeholders supported the suggestion that had the airport not been planned and built early in the process of the regeneration of Docklands, others may not have had confidence to invest in the area, suggesting that the pace of regeneration might have been considerably slower. From its conception on, the airport at Silvertown and its environs presents a concrete, brick and glass instantiation of the major dichotomies underpinning regeneration policy and practice. This remains the case.

The airport site working pre-eminently a premium network hub surrounded by hitherto relatively 'low-value' city-space draws special attention in this context. Various accounts of airport-development understood as a particular architectural and social redevelopment 'genre' capture the ways an airport can uniquely transform space, place and experience (Auge, 1995; Fuller and Harley, 2005; Pawley, 1997) as it were excavating locality and re-mapping global and local in ways that are at once increasingly highly familiar but nevertheless always also disorienting. For instance Fuller and Harley (2005) suggest airports produce spaces 'wiped of indigenous particularities and incorporated into a totalising space of global improvement' (ibid., p. 39) Such largely abstract analyses are interesting when read through and against the testimony of local voices speaking, quite literally, at the margins and aprons of airport space. Airports, so understood, form a kind of ideal type of the enclave developments identified by Graham and Marvin (2001) as characteristic of contemporary 'splintering' urbanisms. In a useful exposition of the broad tenor of their analyses they suggest:

> It is increasingly clear that the most highly valued spaces in global city cores are being provided with their own dedicated, high-quality infrastructural connections.

---

12   In an article looking back on the LDDC Travers (1998, p. 15) described 'An unaccountable, business-dominated quango ... given millions of pounds to clear land, to build new roads and railways, and to promote the area to inward investors'.

These are configured to maximise the ease of connecting to other global city cores around the world. At the same time they are increasingly organised carefully to filter out unwanted connections with the surrounding metropolis – those that are judged to be 'threatening' or deemed to be irrelevant to the direct needs of the glocal enclave. (Graham and Marvin, 2001, p. 313)

One member of staff gave emphasis to the premium nature of the development, referring to the aspiration of the airport to be the 'Harrods' of airports. In more practical terms the airport's private jet centre offers the pinnacle of dedicated high quality private transport connectivity and is seen as an elite operation even within and amongst the airport staff – with ground crew seeing movement to the jet centre service as a promotion. Across the airport the aim is towards the speed and smoothness of transition – premium efficiency for 'businessmen who wants a 10-minute check in – or quicker now with the computer ones – they check in at home and print it out their selves' (airport staff). Noise and fumes from the jet centre specifically (as it affected a local footbridge adjacent to the airport) provoked particular concerns. The pedestrian and the jet engine uncomfortably juxtaposed as local networks abut global ones.

The airport continues to be understood by some as a pioneering project based on a novel approach to regeneration – the provision of high quality premium network facilities – such as this 'boutique' airport – small but serving key European and UK cities – centres of commerce and financial service industries – would act as an attractant and stimulus for further inward investment to the area and the relocation of businesses of the kinds that could see a benefit arising from such connectivity. Cowlard's description usefully connects the airport to other kinds of technological connectivity.

'Just 6 miles east of the City, London City Airport will give business travelers what they value most – time.' The advertising for the short-take-off-and-landing airport in the Royal Docks claims to provide rapid travel for City business people on short-haul flights to Europe. Also in keeping with the promulgated high-tech image, Docklands has two 'teleports' operated by British Telecom and Mercury to provide worldwide satellite telecommunications from the heart of the regenerating area. (Cowlard, 1992, p. 233)

Premium connectivity for the transit of 'high value' people and information is central to the operation of the contemporary economy. Regeneration architectures are predicated upon these mobilities – a conception of space out of kilter with more territorial notions where space and place more readily serve a *grounding* function for communal identifications and relations.

London City Airport is consistently described as a valuable local asset, although it is generally not distinguished as *the* key regeneration driver (either by businesses or by local residents), but rather as an integral part of a wider picture of regeneration initiatives and certainly as an important element of the local transport infrastructure. More broadly, Thames Gateway, as a regeneration zone on a grand scale, can usefully be thought about in this context.

Thames Gateway is a conception of 'place' predicated on a variety of regeneration locations and modalities, up and down river; rural, urban, brownfield and lately mega-event and theme park centred renewals. The regeneration of Docklands – begun in the 1980s and ongoing – provides a useful focus to consider the dynamics, anxieties and experiences attaching to the making and remaking of places in and around London – where complex populations, embedded histories and shifting geographies abut global flows of information and capital – co-evolutions of place and 'non-place' as Auge (1995) phrases it (see also Avendano et al., 1999, p. 69).

London City Airport, its environs and networks, are key constitutive parts of the Thames Gateway development (Al-Naib, 1990, 2003; Foster, 1999; Mayor of London, 2004). At the same time, and notwithstanding important specificities, the airport stands as an early instance of Thames Gateway development – one permitting useful retrospection.

Zurich ZRH	LX451	8:25		3	Final Boarding
Manchester MAN	VG426	8:30		8	Final Call
Rotterdam RTM	VG274	8:30		6	Final Boarding
Amsterdam AMS	KL1556	8:45		7	Final Call
Luxembourg LUX	VG302	9:00		4	Boarding
Frankfurt FRA	LH4801	9:10			Checkin
Glasgow GLA	BA8722	9:15			Checkin
Edinburgh EDI	BA8704	9:25			Checkin
Dundee DND	CB919	9:45			Checkin
Amsterdam AMS	VG218	9:45			Checkin
Milan Linate LIN	AP4217	10:05			Checkin
Isle of Man IOM	3W802	10:05			Checkin
Edinburgh EDI	BA8706	10:10			Checkin
Rome FCO	AP4221	10:10	10:30		Checkin
Dublin DUB	AF5115	10:30			Checkin
Geneva GVA	LX445	11:20			Checkin
Antwerp ANR	VG104	11:30			Checkin
Dublin DUB	AF5125	12:00			Checkin
Luxembourg LUX	LG4593	12:10			Checkin
Zurich ZRH	LX457	12:15			Checkin

Figure 14.3 Indicative list of some destinations[13] from 'live' online departure board, June 2007

---

13   London City LCY on the global database system of airport destination alludes to a network of location codes DUB, LU, IOM and so on which links passenger tickets, baggage tags, flight numbers and departure boards at a level of abstraction where 'place' is effectively forgotten. It is interesting to contrast the local names of Dockland sites (such as

In particular (and since its conception) the airport has been understood as a concretisation, more effectively realised as a growing array of new routes have developed (see Figure 11.1) of the idea of the Thames Gateway as primarily a 'Gateway to Europe'. Thus just after the airport opened *The Economist* reported:

> London will be in the absolute forefront of Europe. International companies will want facilities they cannot find in the City, and that is another reason why the success of Canary Wharf is an inevitability. A model working environment for the next century, unparalleled in Europe. (*The Economist*, 9 August 1989)

This is Europe understood as a primary economic centre and is consistent with a conception of European-ness, and lately globalisation, which is primarily about financial connectivity. The political importance of Europe in the 1980s, and the intimate link between European unification, Docklands and the famously pro-European figure of Michael Heseltine (Al-Naib, 2003; Travers, 1998), coincided with some background legislative changes highly relevant to the developmental context of City Airport – important European regulation changes described by Cowlard (1992) at the time as follows:

> The year of the Single Market of the European Community, 1992, will give further impetus to the internationalisation of financial markets, and London will be a part of that process. The Second Banking Directive will, for example, enable any bank authorised in one member state to operate anywhere in the Community as a step towards a single market in financial services (Cowlard, 1992, p. 240)

This, as much as local regeneration imperatives, accounts for the initial and particular relevance of an airport as a defining iconic development alongside the Canary Wharf office space developed – with financial services companies (understood in part in terms of their mobility needs) as the major likely future tenants. This 'regeneration' strategy has proved effective (in its own terms) and is at the heart of a good deal of the promotion of London Thames Gateway. Gateway to London, who are responsible for marketing business space in London to corporate employers suggested that 'we would have had 80 per cent less success in attracting new office developments if London City Airport did not exist'.[14]

The Royal Docks regeneration is understood primarily in terms of attracting corporate investors as tenants for developments such as the Royals Business Park, a joint development between Standard Life Investments, Development Securities PLC and the London Development Agency. Building 1000, a prominent glass and mirror office building, is the first completed phase of the development and comprises 252,273 ft^2 (23,436 m^2) of office space. This building faces the airport on the opposite

---

'Cyprus' – a DLR station – on the Dock facing the airport – or Canada Water – a Jubilee Line tube station – or Canary Wharf itself). These allude of course to the distributed place names of Empire trade and to wharves and quays (the lifeworld of the Docks).

14   Stakeholder interview: with thanks to Richard Karberry and Louise Congdon of York Aviation.

side of the Royal Albert Dock. The business park will ultimately comprise some 1.6 million ft^2 in a highly landscaped 50 acre premium environment. The airport is cited as a major attractant for corporate office tenants, standing as a potent emblem of, and as a practical contribution to, the kind of 'premium connectivity' and manicured spaces deemed essential for contemporary service industries.[15]

Local authorities stand firmly behind the ongoing strategy even while enforcing planning regulations ensuring a good degree of restriction on flight times and frequencies.[16] The Newham Council UDP states that the airport forms:

> a major strategic asset to the Borough and to London as a World City, linking business centres in the West End, City, Docklands, East London and elsewhere in the Thames Gateway with a wide range of European business destinations. It is an incentive to further development in the Royal Docks and is an important direct and indirect generator of employment. The Council's policy towards London City Airport is one of support and encouragement in recognition of its strategic and economic importance to the Borough and sub region. (LB Newham UDP)

The borough has direct responsibility for planning decisions affecting the airport. Some Silvertown respondents were critical of the way that the borough had represented their particular local interests. Again, and with political representation the underlying issue, the debate requires attentiveness to the definition of 'space', and to interpreting the balance of interests of one area against the aims and strategic ambitions of the borough. This is played out in the main in the scrutiny of, and on the airport's part, adherence to, the strict limitations on aircraft movements at the beginning and end of each day, and at weekends.

Respondents agreed that this was a contributory factor in the assessment of the airport as a 'good neighbour' with the borough successfully mediating between the needs of the airport and the community. Nevertheless, in terms of more general anxieties respondents were unsure about the extent to which local-political governance was a reliable safeguard for them.

> Newham gives the planning permission for them to do all this. We have no say...we're in the outback here ... Newham don't know we exist. (Long-term resident)

At the metropolitan level the London Plan (Mayor of London, 2004) also cites the airport as a key nodal point linking London to continental Europe as part of a 'Gateway'.

---

15   Thames Gateway London Partnership reported that existence of the Airport is vital to efforts to attract new investment to the area, particularly in the office market: 'We would have had 80 per cent less success in attracting new office developments if London City Airport did not exist.' Stakeholder interview with thanks to Richard Kaberry and Louise Congdon of York Aviation.

16   Local respondents agreed that the airport was good at adhering to such restrictions.

East London should become London's gateway to mainland Europe, building particularly on the Stratford International Railway Station, but also on access to the City and Stansted airports, the Channel Tunnel and the Port of London. Economic development should be geared for the long-term opportunities these present. (Mayor of London, 2004, p. 244)

London-wide, the airport offers a degree of iconic place-making, signalling an intention towards service driven regeneration, the provision of premium transport links and a practical contribution to the economic life of the city. It is, in this sense, a part of the 'figured city' (Boyer, 1995) – a construction of space that can however leave elements of degeneration untouched and unthought. It is important to note that Silvertown residents continue to register a sense of disconnection from London. The airport seems not to 'map' their space as the working Thames had done, and, as they anticipate, the DLR will now do (see Figure 11.4 below). Such a sense of spatial refiguring amplifies the impacts of redundancies and withdrawals associated with the decline in value of manufacturing labour and the communities supporting 'heavy' industry. Such a dynamic is likely to be resonant in some cases, considering the prospects for the re- and dis- and yet-to-be-located sites and people up and down Thames Gateway as it develops. This in turn highlights the centrality of issues about transport and ICT connectivity, necessary for fulfilling a movement-centred (re-)conception of communal geographies – perhaps with the sense of connectedness increasingly important (economically and for individuals and groups) as the sense of 'place' becomes attenuated.

Regeneration projects such as London City Airport, as in the 1980s, are predicated on the future and elsewhere – the focus on intention and becoming. As Fuller and Harley (2005) argue, it is the logic of airports that they grow – with expansion the default mode of each individual airport installation as well as for the global network – an airports-city they name 'Aviopolis'. The risk is that in such a mode of thinking (as routinised in the professional imagination of regeneration planning) *past*, *present* and *here* can seem to be 'bracketed' or even entirely occluded from the visions, processes and products of 'growth' and 'regeneration' – with quantitative expansions and efficiencies standing in for palpable improvements in quality of life, i.e. connectivity, relationship, 'sustainability' or 'liveability'.

The permanent anxieties about connection and disconnection to Europe and debates about various kinds of union mean that planning, managing and delivering transport connectivity (the Chunnel, Cross Rail, City Airport) have often been overlain, spurred but also inhibited (in debate and execution) by anxieties and fantasies about London's and Britain's changing place and status and relationships the world.[17] Today the important European dimension must be

17   One might speculate that City Airport symbolised a 'light touch' engagement with Europe privileging financial connectivity, as opposed to the Channel Tunnel, a more concrete connection, and associated with freight and heavy lorries and with anxieties about immigration and the body of the nation – even despite the pseudo airline marketing of the Eurostar brand.

understood alongside three further and more recently emphasised practical and political 'geographies'; those of 'community', regionalism and globalisation. These are not issues to be ducked – and the Gateway is usefully conceived as a spatial project articulating elements of engagement with globalisation – and with the airport key to this vision. But the airport, like the Gateway is also and assertively also *here* and *now*; it is Essex, Kent, Newham, Silvertown – places existing in past and present as well as in regeneration 'future-speak'.

As has been well documented, the docks and adjacent manufacturing industries closed down in this part of East London in the 1960s and 1970s (Carr, 1986; Meyer, 1999).[18] The airport complex stands adjacent to a runway built on a strip of land surrounded by large dock basins – flanked on two sides by water – once part of a 'world famous Docks ... we were the centre of the world' (respondent, long-term resident).

The Royal Docks terrain – 'the product of a past geared to the carriage of goods rather than people' (Cowland, 1992, p. 240) – was a surprising location for an airport. The London City Airport is in fact a STOLPORT (short take off and landing airport), this for environmental reasons (restrictions on size and type of aircraft) and because the runway is necessarily limited in length. The sense of continuity in 'transport' function – for instance with air cargo – and associated work is minimal. The airport is primarily a 'light' service industry and not a substitute for the heavy industry that had once occupied the Docks.[19] As an example the work of maintaining the aircraft is largely handled away from London City, so that the particular skilled jobs that might otherwise have come into the area are distributed more widely; as exemplified in the instance of Belgian airline, VLM. Their crew and maintenance bases are located in Antwerp, i.e. elsewhere – even while London City Airport acts as the main hub on its network, but without the presence of ground-based crews. Nevertheless there are fire service and other skilled jobs at London City – but perhaps not as many, even proportionally, as there might be in a larger international airport.

This is consistent with the initial aim of the airport. In essence, the concept was to replace the global colonial-commercial and industrial gateway role of the original docks with a new modern technological air service gateway to European financial networks and flows, and so, it was hoped, to catalyse the redevelopment

---

18   As Travers (1999) describes it: 'London docks handled their maximum tonnage in the early 1960s, yet by 1981 virtually all docking activity had gone from the upstream part of the Thames. Between them, antiquated labour practices and containerisation caused fatal damage to the old Port of London. Such docking activity as survived had migrated to Tilbury.'

19   However, ground staff respondents described the jobs they did in baggage handling – commenting on cargo '90 tonnes a month and on the increase' (respondent baggage handler), primarily the airport is designed for the quick, smooth and efficient passage of business people to European and UK destinations – usually linked to financial services and other commerce. However, baggage handlers' observations of increasing amounts of large luggage, suitcases and backpacks indicates an increase in non-business travel and increase in tourist travel corroborating a sense amongst staff of a more heterogeneous customer base in recent years.

of the area. There was a political-economic choice implicit in the decision in that the materiality of the service industry is light not heavy; it is people and information, not things. The City Airport (qua icon) emerged from a particular interpretation of the degree and kind of Europeanisation the UK was prepared and preparing for in the 1980s. This has had consequences locally.

Young people in the area reported that they were largely unaware of the types and kinds of jobs the airport could offer, and sought work in the remaining factories, such as Tate and Lyle – maintaining continuities with a local history and habitus disposed to manual labour. However such continuities are not readily served in the prevailing regeneration ethos – where the transformative educational projects needed to link past and future habitus have been under developed or misaligned.

The airport, now 20 years old – so that some respondents 'had grown up with it' as a permanent presence in the area – remains nevertheless as a kind of symbol of novelty, standing as a sign of regeneration and change, of course in particular to those members of an older and long established community who were 'born to' the sounds, sights and smells of the working Royal Docks. As Avendano et al. (1999, p. 68) observe:

> The residents of Silvertown sit sandwiched between two landmarks of London's global economic history. On the one side is the Tate and Lyle sugar refinery, one of the last vestiges of the industrial past, and on the other is London City Airport, landmark of the post-industrial present ... physically and socially the divisions between the two worlds are constantly reinforced.

This sense of novelty the airport carries may, for some, lie in the paradoxically remote but proximal character of the airport; a resolutely strange local element – even while lending its now highly familiar and visually 'spectacular' backdrop to the area – alien in terms of habitus and use value. In terms of daily functional engagement the airport remains 'distant' from the lives of a large proportion of the people who live next door to it. Even in terms of 'news and gossip', there was, for the older residents, used in the past to knowing about all sorts of local coming and goings, a real sense of deficit: 'they never tell us what's going to happen ... how do we know?' (long-term resident). The sense of local pride and ownership is not well served if people feel ill informed. Such anxieties about information flow to do with airport developments was counterproductive for the airport too – feeding local anxieties and suspicions.

The survey element of the research confirmed the anecdotes about low usage – where respondents talked about going occasionally for coffee and meals, but where flying was a rare and expensive thing to do. The airport is not heavily used by residents from within the immediate locality with any great frequency. Seventy-five per cent of survey the respondents had 'never flown from or to London City Airport' and 41 per cent had never been to the airport 'for any reason'.[20] This

---

20   This low usage is primarily a function of the specialist nature of the airport, selectively serving a relatively small number of European and UK destinations. It is also a

paradoxical relationship between local people and the airport echoes a number of theorisations of contemporary urban change (Graham and Marvin, 2001).

The 1980s wave of Docklands regeneration seemed in many ways to bypass and further undermine communities ravaged by unemployment and various other forms of deprivation– as opposed to regenerating them (Carr, 1986; Foster, 1999; Meyer, 1999; Butler and Rix, 2000; Jerram, 2000). The airport, planned as an iconic regeneration project to the East of Docklands – extending the regeneration further out of the centre (around Canary Wharf) was the first of a number of regeneration project in the Royal Docks.

The specific geography of Silvertown, North Woolwich and the airport produces something of a 'peninsular' feel, It may be that this geographical isolation exacerbates the sense of being cut off, from the main swathes of the City, from Newham borough and from the more positive energies and experiences emerging around Docklands. It may be that the 'village' will remain something of an outcrop as there is not much buildable or urbanisable land around the airport. The huge dock basins on one side and the river on the other, isolate the installation. Land is so expensive (the north side of the Royal Victoria Dock is reserved for new business parks) that there is little scope to build more inclusive or mixed settlements. And the river on the other side is another obstacle. This geographical fact of life is one of the reasons why some Silvertown people may feel like an enclave of earlier times.[21] As one respondent suggested, this has been a long standing feaure of the area:

> You never got no bother cos the only way out of here was East Ham and the only other way was Canning Town, so nobody ever got any bother cos they could get you at both ends … you were in trouble, the police were there, you couldn't get out. (Female 70s)

And an airport staff member recalls:

> When I joined there was only one road into the airport – think if there was a burst pipe or something … we'd be in trouble. (Staff member)

---

function of the size and capacity of the airport and in part reflects the business level pricing. Fifty-nine per cent of passengers using London City Airport are travelling on business, which is a far higher proportion than for any other UK airport, including Heathrow. Sixty-three per cent of all passengers using the airport come from socio-economic groups A and B; again much higher than for any other UK airport. Airport staff expected an increase in volume and diversity of passengers as the DLR link ties the airport more closely into non-business networks and puts the airport 'on the map' (staff respondents) and less remote. Of the 22.5 million air passenger trips originating in or destined for the London boroughs making up London City Airport's main catchment area within east and central Greater London, only 4 per cent were via the London City Airport. It remains a niche airport. Any democratising impact of budget airlines has not directly influenced the LCY service, though increasing tourist travel is a future aim.

21   With thanks to Michael Rustin for this observation.

suggesting that as there was only one way in and one way out, a certain order was maintained in a relatively closed community space. This 'geography' and its psychosocial correlates (in the facts and senses of local intimacies, identifications and rights) is no longer affirmed in the regenerated settlement – where the airport signals wide dispersal and unintelligible comings and goings.

Politically also – in terms of any broadly 'local' sense of control and ownership – there have been shifts, as development companies, local authorities and planning and regeneration bodies have at various times held sway in decisions about present and future change. The lack of reliable information for local people was identified as a problem.[22]

Concluding Points

When Monopoly launched its new seventieth anniversary limited edition, designed to reflect the changing face of London, it was something of a coup for London City Airport to appear as a square on the revised game board. This recognition in the new version of the highly popular game 'map' of London is poignant. Alongside a variety of more substantive developments; regeneration projects such as Stratford City, the continuing expansion around Canary Wharf, the Olympics[23] and the Thames Gateway itself, the airport stands alongside a great number of other incidental indications of a reconfiguration of city space to the East of London – iconic affirmation of a reconnection between the East of London and the familiar names, places and spaces of the City and the West End.[24]

City Airport then, even 20 years on from its controversial opening in 1987, is iconic of novelty – of a new turn on the London map. In keeping with this recent appearance on the Monopoly board, the City Airport stands as a token, associated as much with the flow, direction and movement of capital as with planes, people and places. This square on the monopoly board, replacing Kings Cross Station, also asserts the necessarily global and international character of (East) London and Docklands – the extension and tightening of aviation based 'connexity' (Mulgan, 1998); to Europe, to global business, and, as Fuller and Ross (2005) have it, to the flows and transits of the global network they term 'Aviopolis'. The question is: does London city Airport stand as a place (to live and work) or as a token – a square on a board – a card in the regeneration game? A place or a non-place?

---

22   Shortly after the consultation the airport took positive steps to enhance this aspect of community engagement strategy.

23   The 2012 bid document was taken from London City Airport to the IOC offices in Lausanne, Switzerland, by 14-year-old East London basketball prospect Amber Charles' (*Daily Mail*, 7 July 2005, p. 92).

24   In practical terms this is registered in the figures recording borough of departure for passengers flying from London City Airport. The two leading boroughs are Westminster and x..

Figure 14.4 London City Airport square on the 70th anniversary edition of the Monopoly board game

Certainly the employees, many of whom have now worked theire since before it opened feel like a community. 'We are a close knit group' in a place with 'a special atmosphere' (employees' focus group).

A point made quite powerfully by longstanding residents, who remember the arguments set out (promises made) at the time the Airport was first developed, is that the existence of Newham-wide employment targets is beside the point; it is those parts of Newham which are directly adjacent to the airport and which bear proportionately the most costs in terms of disruption and necessary accommodation, that should be positively transformed by benefits such as employment opportunities. Respondents did not feel that such benefits were consistently apparent to the locality (as tightly defined in Silvertown and North Woolwhich) though they were able to point to friends and relatives who worked in the airport an saw that the jobs created were valuable – even if not routinely taken up by local people.

However, some informants from the stakeholder interviews were of the view that there were some strong and clear secondary benefits from the LCY which improved (or will come to improve) local employment. All the community interviewees thought that the airport had attracted or helped to attract other businesses into the area; most notably the hotel industry, which provides local employment opportunities. The bars in the hotels also provide a place for local people to meet and are popular places for socialising. However, one interviewee thought that the new leisure businesses were City businesses and not ones that benefited Silvertown people. The community interviewees also felt that the presence of the airport had resulted in the extension of the DLR, which they felt would not have happened without the Airport and its willingness to lobby for the extension. The DLR staion opened during the period of the research and was a long awaited and highly valued consequence of the airport – by staff and residents alike.

The DLR and the Airport

Perhaps the most significant event from a local point of view in the development of the airport has been the opening of the DLR link connecting the airport, Silvertown and King George V to Canning Town (and the Jubilee underground line) and on to Tower Hill, Bank and Canary Wharf and to Stratford – and the Olympic site (see Figure 11.5).

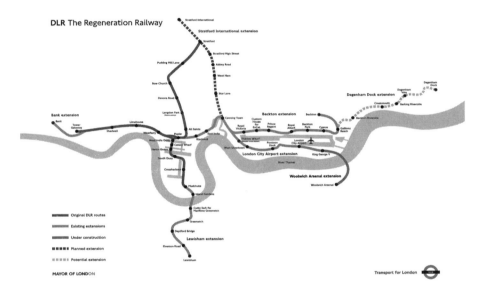

Figure 14.5 The DLR extension was finally opened in 2006

I don't think we would have got the DLR extension if it hadn't been for the airport and that's something I'm looking forward to. (Long-term Resident)

It's an easy way of getting out of the area and I just wish it had been there when I was working. (Long-term resident)

Airport staff say that DLR means that:

at last people know we exist ... they don't think it's Heathrow when we say London City Airport!

Bruce Jerram's (1999) tour of Dockland noted ruefully that the airport is not linked to DLR:

> The Docklands light railway, itself a local paradigm for the priority of movement over permanence, passes tantalisingly within sight of the airport, but in the non-plan regime of Docklands development it runs past the far side of the runway with no station connecting to the planes (Jerram, 1999, p. 40)

Belatedly, then, this omission has been addressed with the positive development for Silvertown. The link to the DLR is important practically and figuratively in that the benefits of connexity enacted for the City by the airport are now (only now) affirmed also for the local community (see Figure 11.4). Importantly the DLR is not a premium network connection – though it provides high quality local and commuter service across the Royal Docks and a connectivity that was impossible in the 1980s – and not even envisaged as recently as 1999 (see Jerram (1999) and Avendano et al. (1999) whose scenario views of Silvertown point out the lack of a smooth network link to the airport).

In thinking about 'splintering urbanisms' I would argue that the DLR can be contrasted positively, from the point of view of building local amenity and connectivity for Silvertown, against the Heathrow Express which Graham and Marvin (2001), contrariwise, cite as 'excellent example of glocal bypass', premium connectivity outstripping the poorer transport system – at a premium price. They go on to discuss an example of the politics of transport connectivity in an era where the regeneration tendency is towards the profitability, security and efficiency of premium networks and less supportive of public infrastructure development serving more elaborate, localised life-worlds. They cite the example of a change in public transport policy following the Labor (sic) victory in the Federal State of Victoria, Australia, in 1999.

> In most cases, scope continues to exist at the level of local and national state and governance regimes to reassert and even strengthen leverage over the production and regulation of premium networked spaces. Local municipalities and planning agencies can renege on licence agreements and bring networks back into direct connection with public network operations. (Graham and Marvin, 2001, p. 397)

They give the example of an Australian development which:

> paved the way for the possible linkage of Melbourne's international airport to the city's public transit system, even though the developers of the CityLink e-highway had negotiated a contract with the previous Conservative government that promised them exclusive connectivity to that most lucrative of sites. With the right political backing, traditional policy intervention through the construction of public duct space, public investment, leeway rights and planning instruments can do much to (re)socialise benefits from premium networked infrastructure investments. (Ibid., p. 398)

The DLR is of course a much smaller and different type of facility, and the City Airport a far smaller airport. However the porosity and accessibility of some elements of premium network space means that the positive regeneration benefits of some development can be felt in more inclusive ways. In this connection the Cross rail development is highly relevant – for the airport, for Thames Gateway and for local and regional regeneration. Linking the East of London to Heathrow and eventually Paris cross-rail could prove to

In the meantime and in general terms there is an ongoing aspiration around the London City Airport towards community links and engagements which are more than cosmetic. The community, young and old have come to accept the airport as a defining feature of the area, and while anxieties remain in general about regeneration, housing and change, the airport is no longer sense as the unwelcome intrusion it once was. Indeed it is seen by some as an ally against further regeneration, as the flight path of the planes precludes high rise building in quite a wide area of Doclands and beyond[25] opening the skyline and providing a sense of space relatively rare in London.

The process of embedding a premium regeneration enclave is a slow one – and one that is never complete. As Avendano et al. (1999) suggest concisely:

> The aim is to create the overlapping conditions between place and Auge's non-place by disassembling the existing physical borders so that one can start to include local cultures and societies.

This is a laudable aim, and in a design project about the airport they proposed a largely architectural solution aimed at making the airport more of a destination (by giving it accessible amenities and inducing a night time economy via a night club for the late hours when the airport qua airport is not in operation). It is a compelling vision, if somewhat fanciful. However, the overlapping of place and non-place which Avendano et al. (1999) suggest – and as a broad aspiration for Silvertown and thinking about Thames Gateway – must be resolved not just on the plane of architecture, but through practical arrangements across the region. The routing of the DLR into Silvertown in 2006 is exemplary here.

Further developments need to emerge providing a genuine connectivity continuous and contiguous with the airport transits and flows, in terms of enhanced exchange and flow of information and people between the airport complex and the community – via communications but also through jobs and other deep-seated forms of participative engagement and dialogue. Place and non-place converge only in such concrete and continuous processes.

Fuller and Harley (2005, p. 48) suggestively propose a connection between Foucault's observation that:

> We are in an epoch of simultaneity; we are in an epoch of juxtaposition, the epoch of the near and the far, of the side by side, of the dispersed. We are at the moment I believe, when our experience of the world is less that of a long life developing through

---

25   This factor has caused some conflict between the airport and various regeneration plans.

time than that of a network that connects points and intersects with its own skein ...
(Foucault, 1986, p. 22)

and the network cultures epitomised and enacted in airports and their spatially
transformed milieus. The generations of residents and employees who live
and work at the airport now accept, express and embody much that Foucault
articulates. However, and at the same time, the airport and planners, and policy
makers, implementers and politicians must be alert to the power and necessity
(however complex) of continuities in place and narrative.

Important too is the overlapping of connectivity (premium and local, as per
the DLR), producing sustainable narratives of place and space and inclusive inter-
and intra-site communications and exchange In the face of an urbanism prone to
the enclave and the enclosure it is important to 'plan in' and develop 'points of
interconnection, not hermetically sealed objects' (Thrift, 1997, p. 143)

> You'd never believe that the area could change so much, in what? ... 20 years; you'd
> never believe how this could go from a little village, because that's all it was (Long-
> term resident, Silvertown)

The identification of a 'village' points to the close knit community that
developed around the Docks and factories. Of course it was anything but a 'village'
as now understood in the national imaginary, though it had a far higher level of
amenity as it has had in recent years.

> Like everyone knew everyone and we had lots of shops, the park and the swimming
> pool, cinema, a little cinema, it was lovely ... the council ruined it when they broke
> the community up and let all the places out, you know all through different ideas they
> had..the council broke the community up. (Long-term resident, Silvertown)

But Silvertown, North Woolwich, Canning Town and many other 'villages'
continue to serve the memory and desire for place and for narrative. For the
Gateway to become something more than something to pass *through* on the
way to somewhere else, for it to become a place of connection and development
attentiveness to the micro-politics of place must remain a priority. Boddington
(1999) argues 'places such as airports reconstitute synthetic gateways and
borderland territories' (Boddington, 1999, p. 5). It is important in Silvertown
and across the Gateway that that synthetic comes to mean integrative rather than
'unreal' and that the Airport can become more of a bridge between the local
community and the processes of regeneration rather than being (as some longer
standing residents see it) an outward sign of a regenerative processes to which
they cannot contribute and from which they can see few clear benefits so that:

> forces of disintegration can be...used as the medium for new forms of integration and
> affirmation. That is how and why people survive in cities and rebuild their lives out
> of so much rubble, injustice and disappointment'. (1996, 67) (Graham and Marvin
> 2001:393 check)

The Thames Gateway Regeneration Agenda needs to be alert to the provision of physical but also social linkages, new and emergent networks of association grounded in systems of movement and re-connection. The development (and preservation) of such systems offers practical redress – in policy agendas – to some of the excesses of glossy but dystopian developments of inequitable 'glocal' network regeneration.

While a romanticisms about locality can be readily dismissed regeneration professionals need to acknowledge that the uncompromised and uncompromising primacy of premium network regeneration in the production, renewal and reproduction of space – up and down the Gateway cannot, on its own, deliver the sustainable and liveable futures anticipated.

References

Al-Naib, S. (1990), *London Docklands: Past, Present and Future*, London, Thames and Hudson.

Al-Naib, S. (2003), *London, Canary Wharf and Docklands: Social, Economic and Environmental*, Romford, Research Books.

Amin, A. and Thrift, N. (2002), *Cities: Reimagining the Urban*, London, Polity.

Auge, M. (1995), *Non-places: Introduction to an Anthroppology of Supermodernity*, London, Verso.

Avendano, S., Murphy, D. and Old, A. (1999), 'Bewteen London City Airport and Silvertown'. in Cruz, T. and Boddington, A. (eds), *Architecture of the Borderlands*, London, John Wiley.

Butler, T. (2000), 'Eastern Promise: Education and Social Renewal in London's Docklands', London, Lawrence and Wishart.

Carr, R. (1986), 'Dockland: An Illustrated Historical Survey of Life and Work in East London', London, NELP/GLC.

Cowlard, K. (1992), 'City Futures', in Budd, L. and Whimster, S. (eds), *Global Finance and Urban Living: A Study of Metropolitan Change*, New York, Routledge.

Daily Mail (London) (2005), '2012 by Numbers', 7 July, p. 92.

Daily Post (Liverpool) (2004), 'Air Links Claimed as Region's Right; Tony McDonough Looks at How Global flights Would Benefit Merseyside', 17 November, p. 8.

The Economist (2005), 'A Tall Storey', 17 November.

Evening Standard (London) (2006), 'Next Stop Europe Via the DLR; A Small Step in Improving Transport Links has Resulted in Impressive New Leaps for Business Mankind', 10 January, p. 54.

Evening Standard (London) (2006), 'Canning Town Goes for Gold Goes for Gold: Canning Town Has Gone from No-Go Area to Hot Tip in Just a Few Months, Says David Spittles Homes & Property', 8 February, p. 4.

Evening Standard (London) (2006), 'Back in the Docks: The First Docklands Property Boom has Peaked, but New Developments Are Opening Up Fresh Frontiers', 31 May, p. 58.

Foster, J. (1999), *Docklands: Cultures in Conflict*, Worlds in Collision, London, UCL Press.

Foucault, M. (1986), 'Of Other Spaces', *Diacritics*, 16 (1).

Fuller, G. and Harley, R. (2005), *Aviopolis: A Book About Airports*, London, Black Dog.

Gordon, A. (2004), *Naked Airport: A Cultural History of the World's Most Revolutionary Structure*, New York, Metropolitan Books.

Graham, S. and Marvin, S. (2001), *Splintering Urbanism: Networked Infrastructures, Technological Mobilities and the Urban Condition*, London, Routledge.

Landry, C. (2000), *The Creative City: A Toolkit for Urban Innovators*, London, Comedia.

*Mail on Sunday*2006),'So You Want to Live In. Silvertown', 8 January, p. 10.

Mayor of London (2004), *The London Plan: Spatial Development Strategy for Greater London*, London, GLA.

Mayor of London (n.d.), 'Sustaining Success', Economic Development Strategy for London: http://www.lda.gov.uk/upload/pdf/EDS_Strategy.pdf.

Meyer, H. (1999), *City and Port: Transformation of Port Cities London, Barcelona, New York, Rotterdam*, Utrecht, International Books.

Sunday Mirror (London) (2006), 'Where to Invest in Property', 13 August, p. 7.

Thrift, N. (1997), 'Cities Without Modernity, Cities with Magic', *Scottish Geographical Magazine*, 113 (3), 138–49.

Travers, A. (1998), 'Thatcher's Gift to the East-Enders', New Statesman, 127 (4378).

Chapter 15

Involving Local Communities in the Thames Gateway Developments

Alice Sampson

Introduction

This chapter considers current policy approaches to community participation and their relevance to the development of the Thames Gateway 'project'.[1] The intention of central government is that community participation will improve strategic planning, service delivery, and social cohesion, and that the benefits gained from these improvements will be sustainable. It is envisaged that participation by communities will enable disadvantaged localities within the Thames Gateway area to be revitalised, and for the planned new communities to be integrated into the area to create a socially vibrant and economically thriving region.

The problem is that community participation has always been difficult to achieve and successive policies have been unable to involve the local communities, particularly in disadvantaged areas, in any meaningful sense and with tangible benefits.[2] The heart of the problem has been defined by central government as institutional failure; it is recognised that statutory agencies are reluctant to include 'the community' in decision-making, to put in place mechanisms to increase the involvement of more local people, and to encourage problem-solving by, and for, local people. For these reasons central government neighbourhood policies have recently included the creation of new institutions and extensive target setting with the purpose of supporting the implementation of a community participation policy with community empowerment as the mechanism to bring about changes

---

1   The discussion in this chapter draws on government policy documents and academic studies on the performance of government initiatives on urban renewal, and findings from our own research on urban regeneration issues at the Centre for Institutional Studies, University of East London. I would particularly like to thank Michael J. Rustin for his useful comments that contributed to improving this essay. I would also like to thank colleagues at the Centre for Institutional Studies for their very helpful comments on an early draft: Jessica Datta, Jon Griffith, Gladius Kulothungan and Mike Locke. The usual disclaimer applies.

2   Local and national evaluations of urban policies have all reported on the struggle to involve community representatives and the community sector. See, for example, Robson et al., 1994; Fearnley, 2000.

in decision-making and practice. These changes in practice aim to ensure that statutory agencies are more responsive to the problems of local communities, and provide an opportunity to rejuvenate local services.

Whilst community participation discussed in this chapter is considered as a method of bringing about improvements to services, community life and how it is organised, community participation can also be understood as a political tool in negotiations between central and local government for the re-distribution of power and influence. In the ongoing struggle to establish central control and to bypass local authority influence, centrally-funded initiatives are one type of strategy and the role of community participation within these initiatives is to enable central government to make such initiatives attractive to local people. Community participation is used as a way of appealing directly to local people. From this perspective it may be argued that there is no real commitment to community involvement.

Although the 'politicisation' of community involvement is outside the scope of this chapter, the ongoing negotiations for relative power and influence between central and local government informs how organisations respond to the drive to place community participation at the heart of the Thames Gateway developments. The research findings discussed in this chapter illustrate how responses to community participation vary even within small geographical areas, different social 'experiments' are taking place underpinned by different understandings of the benefits of community participation.[3] Where issues about the relationship between active involvement by citizens and democratic participation arise and influence practices, they are included in the discussion. But the complexities of the problem of community involvement are probably far more complicated than suggested by the brief descriptions given in this chapter. It is likely that the developments described reflect many agendas which surround, and inform, debates about community participation; policies and practices arise out of compromises, struggles for influence and power, and a genuine commitment to the moral right of people to be part of decision-making processes where they are affected by the consequence of the decisions.

Thus the Thames Gateway 'project' provides a unique opportunity to develop more systematic policies and practices to promote community participation. The region has pockets of poverty side-by-side with affluence and areas of entrenched disadvantage along the northern and southern banks of the River Thames.[4] The planned influx of thousands of new residents into areas of existing settlements and the creation of new areas for development provides a unique opportunity for

---

3   Many of the examples used in this chapter draw on our recent research (see, for example, Locke, 2000; Ahmad et al., 2006; Knight, 2006; Sampson and Selman, 2007; Sampson, 2006). Our knowledge of all the developments which are taking place is limited but the importance of the examples used in this chapter is to give a flavour of some of the different types of practices which could be more systematically explored in the Thames Gateway area. Most of our research has taken place within the Thames Gateway area.

4   See the report by Oxford Brookes University (2006) which summarises social and economic information about Thames Gateway.

encouraging community participation in a 'growth area'.[5] A particular challenge for community participation in the Thames Gateway region is highlighted by a study in Tower Hamlets which concluded that: 'The people who are most put out by Bangladeshi settlement are precisely those with the longest involvement in the community and greatest stake in the area.'[6] Furthermore, a study which interviewed existing and prospective Thames Gateway residents found potential tensions between existing residents and incoming minority ethnic communities. Existing residents perceived incoming groups from different ethnic groups as a threat to the 'Englishness of the local community',[7] suggesting that inclusive participation will be difficult to achieve.

It is argued in this chapter, however, that the new institutional arrangements set up to facilitate community participation may increase community involvement but they do not provide the mechanisms necessary for transferring decision-making to the local community in ways that will secure systematic and routine improvements in services. Three reasons for this are discussed in this chapter. Firstly, that these institutional arrangements will impede the development of the Thames Gateway project due to the attempts by central government to control the process and outcomes of community participation through Local Strategic Partnerships and Local Area Agreements. Secondly, by over-centralising administrative controls creativity and flexible local responses to local problems are stifled. Thirdly, it is argued that centrally set targets can undermine sustained participation as they encourage activities which seek to meet targets rather than understand local social problems and how best to respond to them. The final section brings together some of the promising approaches which are discussed in the previous sections to consider a way forward and the government's approach to urban renewal and sustainable communities, which places community participation at its centre, is discussed.

The Centrality of Community Participation

To develop a model of neighbourhood participation the government drew on the lessons learnt from urban regeneration initiatives such as City Challenge and the Single Regeneration Budget Fund, commissioned reviews of studies to find out more about 'what works' and funded research to assess the initiatives which they introduced to find out about the effect of community participation in

---

5   Four areas in the south-east of England have been designated as growth areas for housing. Thames Gateway is one. Again, see the report by Oxford Brookes University (2006) for details about anticipated migration.

6   This quotation summarises findings from a study which explored how East Enders live now and the effect of immigration, contemporary politics and social policies on their lives (Dench et al., 2006, p. 184).

7   This study was designed to find out more about the housing aspirations of groups of people planning to move into Thames Gateway and the needs and concerns of existing residents (Bennett and Morris, 2006).

practice.[8] The studies found encouraging indications that promoting community participation has promising effects. Community participation in strategy and planning led to a broadening of agendas to include additional social goals, increased communication fostered trust between public, private and voluntary sectors, and in some places working practices changed in response to community members requests for improved services, and community involvement generated a sense of inclusion and self-respect. Increased participation also improved residents' identity with an area.[9]

A raft of government initiatives describes the importance of engaging with the community from children's programmes, Sure Start and the Children's Fund, to urban renewal, Neighbourhood Renewal Funds, and Crime and Disorder Reduction Partnerships. The theme for the Thames Gateway region is the same: at the heart of the Thames Gateway project is a notion that communities should be sustainable, and to achieve this they should, amongst other things, be 'well run – with effective and inclusive participation, representation and leadership' and that people should be put in control and given the 'tools to shape their future'.[10]

To achieve this, the government has introduced initiatives which put these intentions into practice. The Safer and Stronger Communities Fund (SSCF) guidance written by the Neighbourhood Renewal Unit (NRU) makes clear its expectations: 'The NRU expects local residents to play a key role in the development of new structures and the delivery strategy from the outset, including representation in a decision-making role' (OPDM, 2005a, p. 9) and that the neighbourhood is 'the place for increasing community engagement and improving the effectiveness and responsiveness of services' (ibid., p. 5).

Funds from a Community Empowerment Networks scheme were also made available to provide community representation on Local Strategic Partnerships (LSPs) with the opportunity to work with other community representatives to become an effective 'voice' at strategic meetings and have a central role in supporting the delivery of services. It is argued that these arrangements provide '*a platform for building strong and cohesive communities in which everyone regardless of race, faith, gender, age, sexual orientation, and disability has a real stake and where services are tailored to meet local needs*' (Neighbourhood Renewal Unit, 2005, p. 10; italics original).

In outlining how neighbourhoods should be renewed community empowerment is described as a key component:

---

8   These studies include a review of the literature for the Home Office on what works in community involvement in local areas (Burton et al., 1994), a study funded by the Office of the Deputy Prime Minister and the Economic and Social Research Council describes the dimensions and challenges of sustainable communities (Kearns and Turok, 2004), and a review of lessons learnt from past regeneration schemes that are applicable to the Thames Gateway (Oxford Brookes University, 2006).

9   These findings draw on research findings described in reports by McArthur (1995), Burton et al. (2004) and University of West of England et al. (2005).

10   These texts draw on two documents on sustainable communities in Thames Gateway produced by the Office of the Deputy Prime Minister (2005a and 2005b).

Evidence from the implementation of neighbourhood renewal clearly shows that community empowerment is a vital tool in the delivery of sustainable change. Community empowerment generates commitment from local people, improves the quality of local initiatives by sharing local knowledge and skills and improves sustainability by nurturing a sense of ownership. This is particularly true at the neighbourhood; this is the level at which most people identify with their community. (Ibid., p. 24; italics original)

It is recognised that previous initiatives have failed where solutions were imposed from above and were *'designed and delivered by people who had no real knowledge of the problems and potential in an area'* (ibid., p. 21; italics original). And that effective community action

often requires innovation in decision-making and governance structures that allows representatives, VCS (Voluntary and Community Sector) and citizens from all backgrounds to be able to influence and shape public service delivery and that to achieve this there is a need to increase the capacity of local communities so that local people are empowered to participate in local decision-making and are able to influence service delivery … the engagement of local communities is crucial. (Ibid., p. 22; italics original)

The above extracts from government policy documents outline a clear approach to community involvement in neighbourhoods. It specifies that local people should have control, and be given the skills and knowledge to make strategic decisions, and decisions which influence the delivery of services to meet local needs. This 'empowerment' approach is expected to result in strong and cohesive communities that are inclusive of all its members, and to foster a sense of ownership of the local area. Implicit in this model is an assumption of institutional failure; that statutory agencies are too insensitive and rigid to respond to the problems of local communities, and an assumption that community participation is the key mechanism that promotes the responsiveness of these institutions to provide better and more appropriate services.

Promoting Participation: Central Institutional Arrangements and Local Accountability

To put in place its proposed model of community participation the government has introduced Local Strategic Partnerships (LSPs) as intermediary institutions. These partnerships are responsible for neighbourhood renewal and for delivering Local Area Agreements (LAAs). Integral to their activities are incorporating representatives of voluntary and community organisations into the partnership arrangements and actively encouraging and supporting community participation. Financial support from central government for these activities was forthcoming through the Community Empowerment Network Fund (CEN). This Fund was designed to increase the capacity of the community and voluntary sector to be effectively represented at LSP meetings by giving financial support to increase the skills and knowledge of community groups. This Fund is now integrated into the Safer and Stronger Communities Fund.

In creating LSPs it was recognised that community representatives and representatives of community organisations are more 'in tune' with the problems experienced by residents than service deliverers from statutory agencies, and have a better understanding of solutions which will make a difference. Thus one of the purposes of these new institutional arrangements is to influence decisions made by statutory agencies about the planning and delivery of services within local areas. However research studies about how the LSPs and their associated initiatives operate have found little evidence that the ability of the community sector to influence decision-making has grown as a result of the activities of LSPs.[11]

Rather findings from research studies show that the new institutional arrangements tend to reinforce existing practices. Where the community sector was vibrant and active before the introduction of initiatives to support them, the CEN funds have not added any value, and in areas where the influence of the community sector was weak and ineffective at influencing decision-making, it has remained so.[12] The difficulty is that statutory partners – local authority, health and the police – remain unwilling to cede power, resources and decision-making to community and voluntary organisations. Findings from a NCF study about the efficiency and effectiveness of LSPs illustrate how statutory agencies can easily maintain their dominance: 'Where a statutory body – or even an individual officer – chooses to ignore community voices, it is extremely difficult for communities to have any influence' (see NCF, 2006, p. 22). This dependence on the willingness of statutory agencies to achieve positive outcomes arising from community participation is particularly challenging for policymakers who wish to change the balance of power. For community participation to occur, and for the engagement to continue, it is necessary that community representatives feel their views are welcomed, that statutory agencies have something to offer and that community representatives and community groups can see tangible benefits from their participation.[13] The difficulty is that an ongoing problem of management failure, and residents feeling 'disempowered in decision-making processes', has been identified.[14] As a result in some places participants have experienced frustration and alienation as a consequence of participation and certain groups are typically not included; those with disabilities and black and

---

11   Work by researchers at the University of West of England and other colleagues (UWE et al., 2005), the National Audit Office (NAO 2004), and the National Community Forum (NCF 2006) all make these arguments although a strong theme runs through the UWE and NCF studies that it is too soon to expect LSPs to have identifiable impacts. It is the argument in this chapter that whilst there may be some changes in the amount of community participation, these changes do not necessarily translate into increased decision-making and influence by communities.

12   See the following studies referred to above: UWE et al. (2005), National Audit Office (2004) and NCF (2006).

13   These findings can be found in the review by Burton et al. (2004).

14   This is one of the conclusions from a study that explores 12 of the most disadvantaged neighbourhoods in England and Wales and assesses the effect of government policies on the areas since 1997 (Lupton, 2003, p. 212). This problem which has been found by other studies (see Foley and Martin (2000) for example).

minority ethnic communities, for example, and particular issues are not typically addressed including those related to gender, to refugees and asylum seekers, and travellers.[15] The marginalisation of issues related to gender and minority ethnic communities at a neighbourhood level is of concern since women often play a key role in community development and emerge as leaders in their communities, for example.[16]

Other difficulties have been identified in the way in which LSPs can work in practice. At meetings where community representatives have conflicting ideas about decisions made by other LSP partners conflictual relations can become embedded and disempowering.[17] Where statutory agencies do involve 'the community', their practices tend to reinforce existing divisions within an ethnic group. The South Asian community in Bradford is one such example where minority groups within the South Asian community such as lesbians, gays and those with mental health problems were not consulted and this lack of consultation reinforces their marginalisation and exclusion.[18]

Another problem is that where participation has increased the increasing participation has been with those who are already active. The active have simply become more involved, rather than new participants becoming active thereby broadening the participation base of the local community.[19] Other studies have also found that the 'usual suspects' are approached by representatives from statutory organisations to participate in neighbourhood renewal initiatives and that these people become 'overloaded', a position which is not sustainable. Community leaders in East London talked about their satisfaction with their achievements and improvements in their area but also about the high costs to

---

15   See studies conducted by UWE et al. (2005, p. 28) and EIUA et al. (2006). Similarly local evaluations of Sure Start programmes have found that parents/carers have become frustrated when they have participated despite their willingness to become engaged and many have many skills and experiences to contribute (Sampson, 2005; Knight, 2006).

16   A recent study funded by the Joseph Rowntree Foundation on neighbourhood security and urban change notes the importance of the role of women in local governance (Innes and Jones, 2006). See also Lupton, 2003.

17   See UWE et al. (2005).

18   See the findings from a study where academics worked alongside community researchers who were participant observers in their own communities (Blakely et al., 2006).

19   This is a finding from a study conducted by Demos designed to find out if policies that promote community participation in governance build social capital (Skidmore, 2006). Another study conducted by researchers in South African found that community empowerment was sustained when large numbers of local people were 'empowered' through increased information, and training (Lyons et al., 2001). Thus the findings from the Demos study suggest that the governance in neighbourhoods in England are not sustainable as they are drawn from a narrow base of participants.

their personal and family life, and how they had been 'railroaded' into taking up positions on partnership boards.[20]

As the above discussion shows, despite creating a new intermediary institution and to facilitate the promotion of community participation the new institutional arrangements are unable to check the power of statutory agencies if they choose not to listen or to be influenced in their decision-making by preferences expressed by the community sector. And LSPs can work in ways which are detrimental to establishing a broader base for community participation; they are not necessarily inclusive of all community members, nor to they tend to incorporate new citizens. So where do the problems lie? And how can they be addressed? Three inter-related problems are identified and discussed below.

Firstly bringing about changes through community 'empowerment' requires new practices. However, the two mandatory targets for community empowerment in LAAs require changes in perceptions. The indicators are: the percentage of residents who feel they can influence decisions affecting their local area, and the percentage of residents who feel that people from different backgrounds can get on well together. But 'empowerment' occurs through persuasion and by getting decisions made which are compatible with the wishes of community members, rather than just 'feeling' that there is a difference and the motivation to be involved depends on the likelihood of producing tangible results, that is by experiencing improvements through the decisions made.[21] For these reasons the targets set out in the LAAs are inadequate particularly where practitioners are reluctant to involve community members in decision-making.[22]

Secondly a set of problems is centred on the reluctance by statutory agencies to genuinely involve local people and community groups in decision-making. For this to happen statutory agencies will need to relinquish some of their control and to understand that the outcomes of participation with the community will have some unpredictable outcomes; that there will be more uncertainty. To respond to these deep-seated reluctances it is suggested that underpinning community participation with the values enshrined in the rights agenda will create a more 'level playing field'.

Many elements of a rights agenda are, in fact, already in place but not systematically utilised. One of the main aims of the Human Rights Act, introduced in 1998, is to ensure the delivery of quality services which meet the needs of service users and that the rights enshrined within the Act will be incorporated

---

20   The findings from this study on community leaders in East London are described in a publication by Locke and colleagues (Locke et al., 2000).

21   Several studies record these findings including Lyons et al. (2001), Beresford and Hoban (2005) and Dalziel et al. (2007).

22   A small study in Thames Gateway found that interviewees from local authorities, development companies and community group representatives thought that the community sector were not fully participating in the Thames Gateway developments, but rather they were consulted on some issues and their views not necessarily taken into account (Sampson, 2006).

into all policymaking.[23] People can expect the application of human rights principles for example to be treated with dignity and respect which will improve the experiences of service users and lead to better quality services for local people.[24] Connections have also been made between human rights, equalities, and service improvement and the Greater London Authority has demonstrated this by incorporating a 'rights-based' approach into their equal opportunities agenda. A rights approach gives community participation additional legitimacy. It changes how statutory agencies perceive the process of engaging with 'the community' because participation becomes an obligation or duty, and gives individuals within a community and community groups a better opportunity to be persuasive and to negotiate changes that solve their problems and meet their needs. In this way a 'rights agenda' changes how statutory agencies engage with communities. A rights agenda also changes the expectations of local people. People can expect to be involved in the developments in their community and the entitlement to participate is likely to increase motivations to participate.

An example of how a rights-based approach to participation is being championed can be found in Haringey.[25] The Children's Fund programme led by the local authority, funded a project to engage young people in the development and delivery of the Children's Fund programme. The work is informed by the values enshrined in the United Nations Convention on the Rights of the Child article 12 which states that a child has the right to express their views on anything that affects them and for their views to be taken into account; and, by a belief that participation by young people should be inclusive, that is where systems should change to accommodate the values and participation of children rather than integration where children participate in predefined ways in predefined structures.[26] A group of six young people, the 'Participation Crew', were educated about their rights and visited Children's Fund projects to gather the views of other children about services and to inform them, and project staff, about children's rights and about how to involve young people in decision-making. Training sessions run by the young people and adults enabled projects to practice

---

23   The Department of Constitutional Affairs has produced guides to the Human Rights Act (DCA (2006), for example). The Audit Commission report on the Human Rights Act demonstrates that there is little systematic inclusion of the Act in policymaking and rather, statutory agencies make changes only in response to case law (Audit Commission, 2003).

24   See the Audit Commission report on the Human Rights Act and policymaking (2003).

25   We have been involved in the evaluation of the Haringey Children's Fund for the last five years and the following account draws on our research for this programme.

26   For children's rights see the UN Convention on the Rights of the Child. Rights are also mentioned in Every Child Matters and The Children's Act 2004. An assessment of the Haringey Children's Fund participation project has been conducted (Sampson and Selman, 2007) and there are some informative academic texts on participation of children and young people in policymaking and the delivery of services (for example, Bessant (2003), Cutler and Taylor (2004), Hill et al. (2004), Percy-Smith and Malone (2001) and Sinclair (2004)).

participation and through the experience of engaging children in decision-making in the running of projects, managers and staff were able to experience first-hand the positive advantages of this approach. The rights-based approach articulated by young people themselves made it difficult for staff to avoid engaging with children in the planning, delivery and assessment of Children's Fund services.[27]

Structural changes are also underway in Haringey to enable children and young people to have an influence in strategic decision-making within the local authority. A Youth Council is being set up and will consist of young people who are elected to represent children in the borough and who will aim to make a difference at a policymaking level. The Participation Crew will join the Youth Council and act as participation trainers and advocates for young people. In this way participation by young people will become integral to policy and practice development.

The purpose of the above account about how participation by children and young people has increased using a rights-based approach is to demonstrate the potential of this approach. How it would work in other settings such as in neighbourhood forums or within Local Strategic Partnerships has not, to our knowledge, been explored. A more systematic use of the Human Rights Act is another possible course of action. The Act provides recourse through the courts for local groups who feel discriminated against on grounds of racism or disability, for example. In this way the effect of underpinning community participation with a rights agenda should, in principle, facilitate inclusionary practices. The Act is also being used where victims' families feel that the police fail to protect the victims' right to life in cases of domestic violence which end in murder.[28] Where the police fail in their duty to take action to protect the victim cases are being bought under the Act to bring the police to account.

A third set of problems is related to accountability. However there are various types of accountability which can act either to facilitate, or mitigate against, a shift in power to increase the influence of community representatives and organisations. A thoughtful empirical study by Day and Klein (1987) examines accountability in public service organisations and gives an insight into how accountability works in practice and how practices arise from the context within which organisations work.[29] The authors describe the clarity of accountability structures in a water company. The objectives of the company's work are clearly defined, and there is a direct relationship between inputs and outputs; that is, effective and efficient performance of services can be defined in terms of the outputs. And the process

---

27   See a report by Sampson and Selman (2007) and an earlier assessment of the Haringey Children's Fund programme (Amad et al., 2005) for a fuller description of the activities of the participation project. Local authority policymakers were still found to be reluctant to commit to the participation agenda, and preferred to consult with children if, and when, they thought it necessary, what is known as 'tick-box' participation to meet the requirements of central government and other funders.

28   See a special report on domestic violence entitled 'My sister was killed while the police did nothing', in the *Observer*, 11 March 2007.

29   The organisations included in this research were the National Health Service, police, social services, education and the water authority.

of supplying water and mending leaking water pipes is not difficult for managers to control because its activities are visible.

The clear lines of accountability were due to objectives which are easy to understand and operationalise, performance defined in terms of outputs, and visible activities that are not difficult to control. These factors quickly dissipate in settings where a collection of agencies are delivering services and there is ambiguity about the contribution of a specific service to achieving a common goal. Much more uncertainty surrounds the process of service delivery – the lack of visibility, and the outputs and outcomes are the performance of numerous agencies making it unclear who is responsible for the final outcome. These complexities are illustrated in the example given below which describe how the London Borough of Lewisham has developed a neighbourhood policy within the guidelines set by central government.

The London Borough of Lewisham has pooled funds from numerous funding streams, the Children's Fund, Teenage Pregnancy etc, and has streamlined its commissioning and its strategic plans so that all services delivered by the statutory and voluntary sector meet LAA targets. Voluntary sector organisations are involved in the LAA strategic planning and in sub-groups including finance and performance. There is also a review process by the local authority which regularly assesses the extent to which the LAA targets are being met. These structural changes made by Lewisham local authority provide a good example of what central government is trying to achieve at a neighbourhood level: joined up working at a strategic and practice level through joint commissioning, pooled budgets, and shared service level agreements, and all working together providing a 'seamless service' to meet targets set by central government.[30]

But in this situation what about accountability: who is accountable to whom and for what? Much of what is described above is illustrative of a complex shared system of outputs and outcomes which makes it impossible to assess performance of an individual organisation leading to what Day and Klein describe as 'dead-end' accountability. As the framework practiced in Lewisham shows, managerial accountability is dominant and local voluntary sector organisations and community groups are part of the administrative structures which are intended to ensure that the framework for delivering the LAAs is making a difference. Furthermore, given that the 'accountable body' is the local authority then this model reinforces the dominance of the statutory agencies. Accountability to central government is also prevalent simply because the purpose of the activities is to meet their targets. The effect of these institutional arrangements is however to give ambiguity to democratic accountability. A lack of clarity about the accountability of LSPs has been identified as problematic by the national evaluators of LSPs.[31] In

---

30   To give one example of how central government is influencing the local agenda, a directive was sent to all Children's Fund managers in January 2007 from the Government Office for London to remind them to pool the Children's Fund funding into their Local Area Agreement.

31   An action research study was undertaken between 2002 and 2005 to assess the initial processes of implementing Local Strategic Partnerships (EIUA et al., 2006).

the example of the actions taken by Lewisham Local Authority local democratic accountability appears to be weakened.[32] Any developments in the Thames Gateway would benefit from finding out how to strengthen these links and to reduce uncertainties about who is accountable to whom for what.

Central Administrative Control and Local Creativity

The discussion above considered the strategic framework within which neighbourhood policies are shaped. In this section the focus of the discussion is on practice; on the delivery of services and on those who receive services, the service user. How practices are influenced by the targets within the strategic framework are considered.

Target setting has been shown to be an effective way of influencing the development of strategies, what interventions are put in place and how they are managed. At a strategic level the main activities of the Local Strategic partnerships reflect their performance indicators; crime, education and training, health and inequalities.[33] By establishing targets, outputs and outcomes and regular reviews of performance through monitoring progress central government administrators are able to maintain control of 'what happens'.

A resumé of the target setting that is required for neighbourhood funding illustrates its extensiveness of the controls. A Local Area Agreement (LAA) which is a three year agreement between central government, local authorities and key partners through Local Strategic Partnerships (LSP) sets out priorities for a local area. The outcome framework for a local area agreement states that 'The elements of the framework reflect what central Government believe to be key priorities of the communities we serve'.[34] For LAAs there are national outcomes, national mandatory performance indicators, PSAs and floor targets. Each LAA has a primary objective and four secondary objectives, and six mandatory outcomes, four of which pertain to crime and crime-related activities and anti-social behaviour, and one on health improvements and the other on empowering local people. The full outcome framework for LAAs runs to 11 pages of mandatory and optional outcomes under four sections: children and young people; safer and stronger communities; healthier communities; and economic development.

---

32   Researchers have emphasised that direct public participation is at odds with traditional understandings of representative local democracy (Foley and Martin, 2000). This has been found to be causing tensions in Thames Gateway (Sampson, 2006). It also raises issues about the different understandings of accountability and its relationship to representativeness which adds further uncertainties to the complex relationships within the community sector (Gaventa, 2004) and may serve to undermine the ability of the community sector to work together and with statutory agencies.

33   See the executive summary of the national evaluation of the LSPs (EIUA et al., 2006, p. 7, Fig. 1).

34   See the implementation guidance for the Safer and Stronger Communities Fund: The Neighbourhood Element and the Local Area Agreement Guidance for Round 3 and Refresh of Rounds 1 and 2: March 2006 (Neighbourhood Renewal Unit, 2005).

Where an area receives funding from several funding streams information on a total of 18 mandatory outcomes with 24 mandatory indicators are required. The other outcomes and targets listed in the 11 pages are optional, but encouraged. Six monthly meetings occur to review progress.

By having such an extensive system of controls the effect is to take away opportunities from local decision-makers. The priority given to meeting the requirements of the funding institutions is in effect, about self-preservation by administrators rather than responding to the needs of local communities.[35] This approach therefore stultifies opportunities for problem solving and creatively seeking solutions, the process through which empowerment can occur. As Landry and Bianchini note in an essay on fostering creativity in the city: 'Everybody is potentially creative, but organisational structures, habits of mind and working practices can squeeze creativity out' (Landry and Bianchini, 2995, p. 10).

Indeed, omitted from the current model is the 'empowerment' of front-line practitioners. Where research has explored how empowerment works, practices have included ongoing training to give all staff the confidence and skills to problem-solve with service users and to feel able to work creatively and flexibly to find solutions.[36] A review of empowerment practices within local Sure Start programmes found that parents/carers in some areas moved from feelings of vulnerability to having an increased sense of control over their lives.[37] With their new-found confidence some Sure Start parents/carers partook in activities for the benefit of their community. Creating a working environment where open discussions between staff and management take place to understand problems and concerns are also part of the 'empowerment' of staff. And working with a non-judgemental and respectful style as well as being willing to learn from parents enables responsive and supportive services to be developed. The Sure Start national evaluation found that where staff had the confidence to respond creatively to the problems parents were experiencing, they moved beyond the remit of the Sure Start targets.

Achieving genuine participation also requires a 'shift' in organisational culture for service providers from one in which they protect themselves by asserting their professional status to one which involves sharing knowledge and skills with service users. Findings from a study on the participation of social care users using voluntary organisations, including homeless people with addiction problems, those with communication impairments, and with dementia, illustrates where participation is integrated into everyday activities, it is a positive experience for service users and service providers.[38] In this study participation arose out of a

---

35   See Marris and Rein's account of the poverty reforms in America between 1960 and 1964 (1967).

36   See for example; Lyons et al., 2001: Gaventa 2004; Williams and Churchill 2005; Knight 2006.

37   See the review on empowerment in Sure Starts as part of the national evaluation (Williams and Churchill, 2005).

38   For a report and model of good practice on engaging seldom heard from groups, see Robson et al. (2007). Some of the voluntary organisations which participated in the study were located in Thames Gateway.

respect for, and in recognition of, the skills and knowledge of service users. Staff valued the contribution of service users to improve the responsiveness of their services to their needs, and developed strategies to improve the confidence of users to participate through establishing a rapport and the reciprocal relationship in which advice and support were exchanged. The effect of this approach was to make the service user feel valued, to feel able to support other service users, and in doing so to 'give something back', and importantly, to have the confidence to raise problems with a range of services they used.

Overcoming the reluctance of service users to voice their critical opinions of services is a significant step in the process of bringing about change; it makes problems visible and enables actions to be taken to solve the problems. For service users to continue articulating problems with services they receive, staff responded by accepting criticisms, working with service users to solve the problems and crucially included taking action to remedy the difficulties. Indeed research studies have found that service providers who have an advocacy role can effectively meet the needs of service users, particularly where users have complex problems, new migrant groups, survivors of domestic violence and racist violence, for example.[39]

Central Target Setting and Sustained Participation

A third issue relevant to considering community involvement in the Thames Gateway 'project' also reflects tensions between central planning and local conditions and problems. In particular, it considers how centrally determined targets have implications for sustained community participation in local neighbourhoods. In essence difficulties arise where targets and their measures, do not address issues as defined and understood locally, because as described in earlier sections of the chapter, even though participation may increase initially, the social problems are likely to persist.[40] These issues are discussed in more detail using crime and disorder as illustrative examples.

Reducing fear of crime is one of the LAA targets but as a social problem it is complex, and may not be sensitive to crime reduction initiatives.[41] The meanings given to the 'fear of crime' and how it can be explained by respondents participating in surveys can be different from how politicians and policymakers conceptualise the problem. In fact there was 'no 'fear' of crime in Britain until it

---

39   See research studies conducted by researches at the Centre for Institutional Studies: Knight (2006) and Parmar and Sampson (2007), for example.

40   This argument is discussed in more detail in a paper on conducting robust evaluations (Sampson, 2007).

41   A large Home Office evaluation of the Safer Cities interventions found that whilst the areas which invested most in crime prevention activities reduced burglary at the greatest rate, but in these areas worry about burglary increased (Ekblom et al., 1996). And more recently the British Crime Surveys have found that crime has declined but concern about victimisation has not fallen to reflect these changes (Walker et al., 2006).

was discovered in 1982' by politicians and policymakers who feel that it is more amenable to being reduced than crime itself.[42] Over the years research studies have refined our understandings about the 'fear of crime' and it is far more complex than a simple expectation of becoming a victim.[43] 'Signs of crime' increase worry; including graffiti, litter and strangers 'hanging around' and those living in run-down areas tend to amongst the high levels of anxieties about victimisation. Those who are most afraid of crime have other anxieties that are not related to crime; anxieties due to feeling physically vulnerable, and worries about job insecurity, and family illness, which increase their 'fear of crime'. Another aspect of the 'fear of crime' problem is the dark: women feel more unsafe in the dark than men. Collectively the findings from these studies demonstrate that the 'fear of crime' has diverse roots which are not necessarily related only to crime. Having an impact on the fear of crime target through crime and crime-related reduction programmes alone may not impact upon the problem and the absence of tangible results will undermine people's willingness to participate.

Responses to crime also vary in different localities and this provides an example of how different solutions to the 'same' problem may be required in different neighbourhoods within Thames Gateway. Ethnographic studies in areas where there are regeneration initiatives have found that reactions to crime are complex, even contradictory. In some areas crime is 'talked up' whilst in others it is concealed.[44] This may be understood by learning more about the 'logic' of neighbourhoods, that is residents follow and re-produce behaviour according to a set of social 'rules' which are applied locally and this 'logic' explains different responses to crime.[45] In some neighbourhoods residents withdraw and a spiral of decline occurs and residents are unable to stop crime and disorder becoming a cause as well as a consequence of the decline.[46] In other neighbourhoods criminality and crime-related behaviours are protected and drug dealing and taking can be concealed due to the benefits of such activities for residents including financial rewards and a reduction in other types of crime such as burglary and car crime.[47] Thus effective interventions in one place will be ineffective or irrelevant in another.

---

42   Extensive research has been undertaken on the fear of crime and its measurement by a group of criminologists funded by the Economic and Social Research Council. A summary of some findings relevant to the LAAs can be found in Criminal Justice Matters (Ditton et al., 1998).

43   There are many relevant research studies and they include Hale (1996), Donnision (1998), Farrall et al. (2000), Killias and Clerici (2000), Pantazis (2000) and Moore and Shepherd (2007).

44   The two ethnographic studies are Foster (1995) and Hancock (2001).

45   See Heley (2006) for a detailed explanation of neighbourhood logic and Sampson forthcoming for a discussion on how the concept can be used to understand responses to crime on housing estates.

46   See study on decline and disorder in American by Skogan (1990).

47   See a study on drug dealing and taking on housing estates in England by May et al. (2005).

It is argued that a preferable starting point is to understand how social problems are formulated locally and how best to respond rather than adopting the current approach which is more about setting up services to meet targets. What is happening at the moment is that representatives of statutory agencies engage with 'the community' because they need to 'prove' that they have completed the activities necessary to meet government targets; they need to 'tick the right boxes'. But pre-set targets might not influence actions that provide solutions to local problems and similarly indicators used to measure performance may not assist to resolve local social problems. This issue is encapsulated by an old saying by the police 'what gets measured, gets done'. Thus problems like the fear of crime have demonstrated their resilience to interventions exactly because they have been poorly understood, and its component parts not responded to because the targets are not suitable measures for resolving the problem. Where local problems are not addressed in a meaningful way at a neighbourhood level tangible results are unlikely to occur and community participation is therefore unlikely to be sustained.

Another aspect of thinking more about the effect of targets on promoting particular behaviours can be illustrated using the crime and crime-related targets as an example and asking: is engaging local people in crime-related issues the best way to build sustained participation?

Of the six mandatory outcomes for LAAs, four are about crime and anti-social behaviour and the targets are about reducing 'bad' behaviour. This approach for neighbourhood actions puts most energy and effort into overcoming unlawful and disruptive behaviour in order to create 'strong' communities. By for example, tackling anti-social behaviour, drug-taking, reduce re-offending, and the fear of crime.

The presumption is that residents will be motivated to participate in the knowledge that they will make judgements and decisions about negative and anti social behaviour of their neighbours and in the belief that the outcome of being an active citizen will be to reduce crime.

Using crime and the threat of crime to increase participation is likely to be divisive where convicted criminals live in the area, as they are neighbours and members of the same community. As the effects of the current policy on issuing Anti-Social Behaviour Orders show, local people who have not committed a crime but have been anti-social, receive a criminal conviction if they breach their Order.[48] Again the actions of one set of local people against another can have divisive, rather than inclusive, consequences.

In comparison, research has found that encouraging the involvement of as many local residents as possible in decision-making occurs through positive and enjoyable activities and it is suggested that this approach is more likely to be self-sustaining and to have long term benefits. Community participation is after all a voluntary activity and coming together to enjoy oneself and have fun, is a more attractive proposition. Indeed where Sure Start teams 'held regular and

---

48   See research report by the Youth Justice Board on Anti-Social Behaviour Orders (Youth Justice Board, 2006).

well attended events celebrating parents' achievements or the diversity of the community, they had a better chance of involving parents'.[49]

Feelings of safety affect how people think, feel and act in their neighbourhood and safety is related to knowing others living in the same neighbourhood and where people feel safe it changes the atmosphere and encourages social interaction between residents. Projects which are about positive experiences, for example designing public neighbourhood play spaces and services, have reported tangible results both for individual participants in terms of increased social and personal skills, and by providing a valuable community meeting place.[50]

Moving On: Policy Developments for Thames Gateway

The account presented in this chapter is a description of a well-intentioned central government policy designed to create thriving neighbourhoods based on a credible theoretical model of sustained development with community participation at its heart. A number of tensions, even contradictions, have been identified and in particular the difficulty of reconciling the aim of central government to lead on improving public services and to increase the influence of local communities by 'empowerment' and increased participation. In practice, despite the creation of new intermediary institutions and extensive administrative controls, there is little evidence of the transfer of power, influence, and decision-making to local communities.

It has been argued that the Thames Gateway project offers a unique opportunity to address these difficulties. The implications of the arguments presented in the chapter for moving on are that: firstly that there need to be are a very few highly selected targets and performance indicators which will encourage flexible and creative practices which are problem-solving and responsive to local problems and that promote positive behaviours and having a good time. Central government leadership and direction to motivate change and improvements can occur through the central funding of voluntary and community organisations[51] and can be designed to include funding for minority interests and to fund those who advocate on behalf of service-users. The intention would be to promote community participation practices and to empower community groups to influence the policies and practices of statutory agencies to have a checks-and-balances system in place. The funding by central government enables voluntary and community groups to gain independence from the dominance of statutory agencies.

Secondly the 'right-to-participate' raises expectations and encourages participation. The integration of the human rights principles provides stronger

---

49   See the empowerment study of the national Sure Start evaluation (Williams and Churchill, 2005, p. 65).

50   See, for example, Innes and Jones (2006) and Kapasi (2006).

51   This action is recommended in the report by the National Community Forum (2006).

values to inform policymaking, and a route to a complaints process through the courts of law if necessary. Within this framework community participation would be an obligation and duty rather than an activity that is required to be completed in order to 'tick the box' to secure further funding.

Thirdly intertwined with the reduction in targets and performance indictors and a 'right-to-participation' is the difficult but important issue of strengthening community participation and local democratic accountability. This will ensure, amongst other things, that policymakers and politicians will be assessed on tangible results, on actual practices.

Finally Thames Gateway provides a unique opportunity to put in place some policy and practice experiments to find out more about how to strengthen the sustained involvement of local people and organisations. The new developments provide the context for a new creativity and imaginative ways of engaging with the Thames Gateway communities.

References

Ahmad, E., Rice, R. and Sampson, A. (2006), 'Making a Difference: the Progress of Haringey Children's Fund Programme 2003–2005', Centre for Institutional Studies, University of East London: http://www.haringey.gov.uk/the_progress_of_haringey_childrens_fund_programme_2003_-_2005.pdf.

Audit Commission (2003), *Human Rights. Improving Public Service Delivery*, London, Audit Commission.

Bennett, J. and Morris, J. (2006), *Gateway People. The Aspirations and Attitudes of Prospective and Existing Residents of the Thames Gateway*, London, Institute for Public Policy Research.

Beresford, P. and Hoban, M. (2005), *Effective Participation in Anti-Poverty and Regeneration Work and Research*, Findings: August, York, Joseph Rowntree Foundation.

Bessant, J. (2003), 'Youth Participation: A New Mode of Government', *Policy Studies*, 24 (2/3), pp. 87–100.

Blakey, H., Pearce, J and Chesters, G. (2006), *Minorities within Minorities: Beneath the Surface of Community Participation*, Findings: December, York, Joseph Rowntree Foundation.

Burton, P., Goodlad, R., Croft, J., Abbot, J., Hastings, A., Macdonald, G. and Slater, T. (2004), 'What Works in Community Involvement in Area-Based Initiatives? A Systematic Review of the Literature', Home Office Online Report 53/04: http://www.homeoffice.gov.uk/publications, accessed 16 January 2006.

Cutler, D. and Taylor, A. (2004), *Expanding and Sustaining Involvement: A Snapshot of Participation Infrastructure for Young People Living in England. A Report of the Carnegie Young People Initiative*, London, Department for Education and Skills.

Dalziel, D., Hewitt, E. and Evans, L. (2007), *Motivations and Barriers to Citizen Governance*, London, Department for Communities and Local Government.

Day, P. and Klein, P. (1987), *Accountabilities. Five Public Services*, London, Tavistock Publications.

Dench, G., Gavron, K. and Young, M. (2006), *The New East End. Kingship, Race and Conflict*, London, Profile Books Ltd.

Department for Constitutional Affairs (2006), 'A Guide to the Human Rights Act 1998', Third Edition: http://www.dca.gov.uk/peoples-rights/human-rights/index.htm, accessed 26 March 2007.

Ditton, J., Farrall, S., Bannister, J. and Gilchrist, E. (1998), 'Measuring Fear of Crime', *Criminal Justice Matters*, 31, Spring, pp. 10–12.

Donnison, D. (1998), 'Creating a Safer Society', in Jones Finer, C. and Nellis, M. (eds), *Crime and Social Exclusion*, Oxford, Blackwell Publishers.

Ekblom, P., Law, H. and Sutton, M. (1996), 'Safer Cities and Domestic Burglary', Home Office Research Study No. 164, London, Home Office Research Statistics Directorate.

European Institute for Urban Affairs, Office for Public Management, University of Warwick and Department for Transport (2006), 'National Evaluation of Local Strategic Partnerships: Formative Evaluation and Action Research Programme 2002–2005', Executive Summary to Final Report, London, Office of the Deputy Prime Minister.

Farrall, S., Bannister, J., Ditton, J. and Gilchrist, E. (2000), 'Social Psychology and the Fear of Crime: Re-Examining a Speculative Model', *British Journal of Criminology*, 40 (3), pp. 399–413.

Fearnley, R. (2000), 'Regenerating the Inner City: Lessons from the UK's City Challenge Experience', *Social Policy and Administration*, 34 (5), pp. 567–83.

Foley, P. and Martin, S. (2000) 'A New Deal for the Community? Public Participation in Regeneration and Local Service Delivery', *Policy and Politics*, 28 (4), pp. 479–91.

Foster, J. (1995) 'Informal Social Control and Community Crime Prevention', *British Journal of Criminology*, 35 (4), pp. 563–83.

Gaventa, J. (2004), 'Representation, Community Leadership and Participation: Citizen Involvement in Neighbourhood Renewal and Local Governance', prepared for the Neighbourhood Renewal Unit, Office of Deputy Prime Minister, London, Office of Deputy Prime Minister.

Hale, C. (1996), 'Fear of Crime: a Review of the Literature', *International Review of Victimology*, 4, pp. 79–150.

Hancock, L. (2001), *Safety and Regeneration in Urban Neighbourhoods*, Basingstoke, Palgrave.

Heley, L. (2006) 'The Institutional Logic of Neighbourhoods', *Learning for Democracy* 1 (3), pp. 41–55.

Hill, M., Davis, J., Prout, A. and Tisdall, K. (2004), 'Moving the Participation Agenda Forward', *Children and Society*, 18, pp. 77–96.

Innes, M. and Jones, V. (2006) *Neighbourhood Security and Urban Change*, Findings: November, York, Joseph Rowntree Foundation.

Jones Finer, C. and Nellis, M. (1998), *Crime and Social Exclusion*, Oxford, Blackwell Publishers.

Kallias, M. and Clerici, C. (2000), 'Different Measures of Vulnerability in their Relation to Different Dimensions of Fear of Crime', *British Journal of Criminology*, 40 (3), pp. 437–50.

Kapasi, H. (2006), *Neighbourhood Play and Community Action*, Findings: November, York, Joseph Rowntree Foundation.

Kearns, A. and Turok, I. (2004), 'Sustainable Communities: Dimensions and Challenges', ESRC/ODPM Postgraduate Research Programme, Working Paper 1.

Knight, R. (2006), 'Abbey Children's Centre Evaluation: "We Should Be Sewn Together, Not Tightly, Just Gently"', unpublished report to Barking and Dagenham Education Department, Centre for Institutional Studies, University of East London.

Landry, C. and Bianchini, F. (1995), *The Creative City*, London, Demos.

Locke, M., Sampson, A. and Shepherd, J. (2000), "'A Lot of Friends. A Lot of Appreciation and a Phone that Never Stops Ringing": Voluntary Action and Social Exclusion in East London – A Pilot Study', CIS Commentary No. 96, Centre for Institutional Studies, University of East London.

Lupton, R. (2003), *Poverty Street. The Dynamics of Neighbourhood Decline and Renewal*, Bristol, The Policy Press.

Lyons, M., Smuts, C. and Stephens, A. (2001), 'Participation, Empowerment and Sustainability: (How) Do the Links Work?', *Urban Studies*, 38 (8), pp. 1233–51.

McArthur, A. (1995), 'The Active Involvement of Local Residents in Strategic Community Partnerships', *Policy and Politics*, 23 (1), pp. 61–71.

Marris, P. and Rein, M. (1967), *Dilemmas of Social Reform. Poverty and Community Action in the United States*, London, Routledge and Kegan Paul Ltd.

May, T., Duffy, M., Few, B. and Hough, M. (2005), *Understanding Drug Selling in Communities*, York, Joseph Rowntree Foundation.

Moore, S. and Shepherd, J. (2007), 'The Elements and Prevalence of Fear', *British Journal of Criminology*, 47 (1), pp. 154–62.

National Audit Office (2004), *Getting Citizens Involved: Community Participation in Neighbourhood Renewal*, London, The Stationery Office.

National Community Forum (2006), 'Removing the Barriers to Community Participation', Report Commissioned by Neighbourhood Renewal Unit, Communities and Local Government: http://www.neigbourhood.gov.uk/publications, accessed 22 January 2007.

Neighbourhood Renewal Unit (2005), *The Safer and Stronger Communities Fund: The Neighbourhood Element. Implementation Guidance*, London, Office of the Deputy Prime Minister.

Nelson, V., Quan, J. and Forrester, P. with Pound, B. (2005), *Community Development Work in North Kent: An Evaluation*, London, University of Greenwich.

Office of the Deputy Prime Minister (2005a), *Creating Sustainable Communities. Delivering the Thames Gateway*, London, Office of the Deputy Prime Minister.

Office of the Deputy Prime Minister (2005b), *Sustainable Communities: People, Places and Prosperity*, London, Office of the Deputy Prime Minister.

Oxford Brookes University (2006), 'Thames Gateway Evidence Review', London, Department for Communities and Local Government.

Pantazis, C. (2000), ''Fear of Crime, Vulnerability and Poverty: Evidence from the British Crime Survey', *British Journal Criminology*, 40 (3), pp. 414–36.

Parmar, A. and Sampson, A. (2007, forthcoming), 'Evaluating Domestic Violence Initiatives: Transferring Practice Principles not Projects', *British Journal of Criminology*.

Percy-Smith, B. and Malone, K. (2001), 'Making Children's Participation in Neighbourhood Settings Relevant to the Everyday Lives of Young People', *PLA Notes IIED*, 42, pp. 18–22.

Robson, B., Bradford, M., Deas, I.,Ham, E. and Harrison, E. (1994), *Assessing the Impact of Urban Policy*, London, HMSO.

Robson, P., Sampson, A., Dime, N., Hernandez, L. and Litherland, R. (2007), 'From "Add-on" to "Everyday Participation": Practice Guidance on Participation of Seldom Heard Users of Social Care Services', Report to Social Care Institute for Excellence, Centre for Institutional Studies, University of East London.

Sampson, A. (2005), 'Sure Start Thames View: Taking Stock', unpublished report to Barking and Dagenham Education Department, Centre for Institutional Studies, University of East London.

Sampson, A. (2006), 'The Involvement of Local Communities in the Thames Gateway Developments', unpublish ᵓ report to Denton, Wilde, Sapte, Centre for Institutional Studies, University of East London.

Sampson, A. (2007), 'Developing Robust Approaches to Evaluating Social Programmes', *International Journal of Evaluation Theory, and Policy*, 13 (3), pp. 477–93.

Sampson, A. and Selman, J. (2007), 'An Assessment of the Progress of Haringey Children's Fund Participation Project', unpublished report to Haringey Local Authority, Centre for Institutional Studies, University of East London.

Skidmore, P., Bound, K. and Lownsbrough, H. (2006), 'Do Policies to Promote Community Participation in Governance Build Social Capital?', Findings: November, York, Joseph Rowntree Foundation.

Skogan, W. (1990), *Disorder and Decline*, New York, Free Press.

Sinclair, R. (2004), 'Participation in Practice: Making it Meaningful, Effective and Sustainable', *Children and Society*, 18, pp. 106–18.

University of the West of England, COGS, European Institute for Urban Affairs (2005), 'Making Connections: An Evaluation of the Community Participation Programmes', Executive Summary, Research Report 15, Neighbourhood Renewal Unit: http://www.neighbourhood.gov.uk, accessed 22 January 2007.

Walker, A., Kershaw, K. and Nicholas, S. (2006), 'Crime in England and Wales 2005/06', Home Office Statistical Bulletin: http://www.homeoffice.gov.uk/rds/pdfs06/hosb1206.pdf, accessed 12 March 2007.

Williams, F. and Churchill, H. (2005), 'Empowering Parents in Sure Start Local Programmes', prepared for the National Evaluation of Sure Start, CAVA Research Group, University of Leeds.

Youth Justice Board (2006), 'A Summary of Research into Anti-Social Behaviour Orders Given to Young People between January 2004 and January 2005': http:/www.yjb.gov.uk/publications, accessed 12 March 2007.

Chapter 16

Blue Sky over Bluewater?

Michael Edwards

Introduction

The Thames Gateway project poses daunting choices for those with the power to decide on the future development of South East England. Government and the Mayor of London both agree that most of the region's growth should be concentrated in the Thames estuary. They share the assumption that London has to expand East, not West, and that the supposed rationality of capitalist growth is the only telos in (or out of) town.

But is this even a good project on its own profit-driven terms? A toxic mix of de-regulation, state subservience to corporate interests, political cowardice and collective amnesia about how to do urbanisation, all the signs are that Thames Gateway will be UK regeneration plc's biggest debacle so far.

It doesn't have to be this way. The new city could be a laboratory for innovation in ways of living, ways of building and ecological relationships. The reality may be somewhere in between. In this article I will sketch my worst and best case scenarios. First, a bit of background.

Capital Problems

London is a problem region and its eastern part has special problems. London sucks in wealth created around the world, staffs its hospitals and services with people trained in poorer countries and drains the skilled people from much of the UK (Amin et al., 2003; Massey, 2006). Meanwhile its internal unemployed 'surplus population' (of many ethnic groups including poor whites) remain largely overlooked within the city, squeezed between low wages or benefits and high living costs.

One result of this sucking in of resources and of highly educated people is economic growth, hailed as 'wealth creation'. The growth package comes with expanding employment and population and even faster price increases, especially for housing. The government and the Mayor of London just welcome all this expansion and insist that London somehow has to go on growing. We are told that any restriction of this growth could kill the goose that lays the golden egg: investors would go elsewhere.

Expansion along the radial corridors to north, south and west could be a good solution but there is a taboo on that because of the strength of resistance from the property-owning classes who defend themselves so vigorously in the green belt round London. The county of Buckinghamshire fought off the threat of urbanisation in the 1960s by telling the government that, in return for preserving the leafy Chiltern Hills, they could have a free hand around the stinking brick kilns (and Labour voters) of Bletchley. That's how we got Milton Keynes. Now we get the Thames Gateway for much the same reasons: the people east of London could do with more jobs and the NIMBY forces simply are less powerful out that way.

London has a long history of problems to the east. This is where the most polluting industries went, outside the environmental and safety controls of the old London County Council – east of the River Lea on the north bank and east of Greenwich on the south bank. It was the backyard of London with power generation, garbage disposal as landfill in the Mucking marshes, car-breaking and the rest. It also had the Ford plant at Dagenham, oil refineries, cement, armaments, paper and cardboard manufacture among its main industries. With the destruction of manufacturing in the UK since the Thatcher period this part of England suffered catastrophic job losses which produced an abandoned working class and a fertile ground for racism.

Figure 16.1 Slogan on a site in Hackney: a workshop demolished to make way for luxury housing. Photo: Michael Edwards, 2005

A little away from the rivers, the east has long been a dormitory area to which east Londoners have moved when they could afford to do so, and these movements have been disproportionately of white people. London itself may (and should – see *Mute*, 2006) celebrate its diversity but at the edges of Greater London and especially in the counties beyond its boundaries the social landscape is very white.

Employment growth has been strongest in central and western London. That trend follows the market, reinforced by decisions to expand Heathrow and by Ken Livingstone's determination to foster finance and business services in the centre. London cannot house its growing labour force so it has to suck more commuters in from outside – especially from the dormitory areas of the east which are the least self-contained parts of southern England. From the point of view of employers in the City, West End and Docklands, their future growth depends on even more commuting from Kent and Essex. But the trains which bring them in are jam packed and central London employers (and property owners) are pushing for investment to increase their commuter capacity. Services from Kent will start running on the Channel Tunnel Rail Link tracks in 2007 and there is strong pressure for that to be followed by 'Crossrail', although the wider economic and social justifications for it are weak.

Ken Livingstone now has some influence over the privatised suburban railway system of the region, but Transport for London (TfL) is struggling to find ways to enlarge the system's capacity to get the new workers in to the centre, even with massive state investment and maintaining a 2006 level of overcrowding on the trains. And it is very wasteful: every packed train coming in to the centre runs back nearly empty for the next load of Kent and Essex commuters. This is less of a problem going out of London in other directions to places such as Milton Keynes, Watford, Reading and Gatwick. There are more jobs out there and thus more reverse commuting. Major population growth in the east thus has disadvantages from an energy point of view.

Another problematic feature of this eastern region is ecological. The modern parish of Mucking, for example, has been described as one of the most derelict on the north shore of the Thames (Astor, 1979): the higher land worked for sand and gravel, and the marshes along the river covered by London rubbish (Middleton, 1994). The Thames Gateway needs a major investment to clean-up polluted land; the huge landfilled marshes at Mucking may be damaged beyond repair and many of the areas proposed for urban development are vulnerable to flooding – either now or as a quite likely result of global warming in the future.

Worst Case Scenario ...

If the Thames Gateway project goes ahead with some of these major challenges unresolved, pessimistic foresight suggests the following outcomes.

The cost of making it happen at all – building transport and social infrastructure as well as subsidies for clean-up of land – is an endless drain on state investment. The 2012 Olympic and Paralympic Games helps a bit in this respect because the sheer imperative of being ready on time for the Games permits normal decision-making and consultation to be compressed and ensures that budgets will be found to do roadworks and other bits of infrastructure in the national interest. Even that is not enough, however, and much of the infrastructure lags years behind the need.

The growth of the region's population and income in turn boosts growth of property values in the south of England, leaving the west and north of Britain to struggle. Government statements about regional policy – already very feeble – become even less convincing as state expenditure on the Olympics, and then on urban infrastructure and housing, further overheats the South East. As house prices (and rents) are driven up in this way, low- and middle-income people suffer worsening housing conditions, more overcrowding and dependence on housing benefits.

Mass private house-building firms are cajoled into building thousands of houses a year but each development serves just a single market segment and income group. The higher ground and fine landscapes get the 'executive' homes; the marshes and degraded areas get denser blocks of apartments, euphemistically called 'starter homes', and 'affordable' housing. The house-building industry remains profitable, though this is largely because selling prices are growing year after year: housing in Britain remains poor value for money in European terms and more than half of what you pay for a dwelling is payment for the scarcity of land, not for the dwelling. A steady influx of workers from eastern Europe cushions the construction sector from the need to modernise itself.

Apart from jobs in construction, the economy of the Thames Gateway grows only slowly, so its population remains dependent on long-distance commuting, mainly to Central London. There are more trains running, but they still have cattle truck conditions. Stratford, Ebbsfleet (aka Bluewater) and Ashford have high speed, and expensive, services to St Pancras but many areas are only served, at best, by ludicrous extensions of the Docklands Light Railway – in truth just a tram – with dozens of stops between home and work. Anyone who has sat for an hour on the Athens tramway to the southern suburbs (built for the Olympics) will know what I mean.

Some prestige architecture will decorate this messy picture, with flagship projects here and there. There are wonderful designs by Zaha Hadid, AHMM, Bernard Tschumi and Colin Fournier. But these are fragments lost in a sea of mediocrity, dominated by routine architectural firms commissioned by big development companies and the 'Registered Social Landlords' who have already shown that they often do no better.

A lot of money is made even in a low-grade development of Thames Gateway. Pressure of demand for space in London is so strong that everything sells sooner or later and property values grow through the agglomeration of activity and the new infrastructure. But the profits from this are all private because successive governments have not had the nerve to hold any long-term land ownerships or equity shares. Governments insist on getting 'planning gain' contributions out of private developers for social housing, infrastructure and so on. But they do it in year 1, just when the developers can least afford to pay and long before the trees have grown and the serious land values built up. In this worst case scenario it is always the state and public bodies that come to the rescue, firefighting on service provision, patching infrastructure. There may be some exemplary water-management and local-energy schemes – these are being promoted hard just now by the Deputy Mayor and likely to figure strongly in the next London Plan. But these schemes need continuing management to work and if all the profits have been given away – either to initial developers or to individual owner-occupiers – these costs will be hard to cover.

The British appear to have forgotten the positive aspects of the twentieth century new towns programme. One of the great strengths of that programme was that it was financially sustainable in the medium and long term. Large scale urban development involves heavy initial costs while the benefits are reflected only very slowly in rents and property values as each city matures. In the new towns of Britain the government agencies which built them retained ownership of a lot of the land and buildings and could thus recoup the investment and pay off the loans. This is just what we are failing to do in the Thames Gateway: as with Mrs Thatcher's Docklands project in the 1980s, all the valuable assets end up in private hands and there is no flow of public or collective funds to pay for maintenance or services or repay the debts incurred in the initial infrastructure.

And the Best Case …

Instead of wallowing in amnesia, our professions and politicians could do a little remembering what their predecessors were good at, a little learning from foreigners and a lot of innovation. This is a more optimistic view from about 2025.

Thames Gateway develops, but more slowly than in government plans of 2006. This is partly because major elements of government and cultural institutions have been spread to other regions, partly because other development corridors are evolving: through Watford, Berkhamsted and Tring to Milton Keynes and Luton; through Surrey and Sussex to Gatwick and through east Hertfordshire to Stansted and Cambridge. London's old 'green belt' plan is being replaced with something more like the 'finger' plans of Copenhagen and Stockholm. Almost all those living in the new areas can leave home and walk one way to a good shopping centre and railway station, the other way to green space and allotments, stables or golf course. The choice between urban and rural situations is over: most people can have both, not just those in Hampstead, Richmond or Stanmore.

Within these new 'fingers' all the land has been taken in to the ownership of Land Development Trusts. They are very diverse but what they have in common is that they retain all the freeholds and grant building leases subject to ground rents which are annually revised in line with market conditions. This means that these collectivities gather about half of the growth in property values while the owner-occupiers or other users of land get the other half. It's a fair exchange because this revenue covers all the costs of infrastructure and services, maintenance of ecological systems and community services. It is a good long-term investment and is financed with bonds which have proved very successful in an increasingly volatile world financial system. These have been investments in real things (infrastructure and service spaces) which actual people use and pay for so they are more robust than the highly speculative investments which the geographer David Harvey (1982) called 'fictitious capital' – investments made in the hope of capturing some imagined future profit.

From about the year 2000, many countries – led by the USA – created a new kind of tax-exempt investment company for holding real estate – 'Real Estate Investment Trusts' (REITs) there and with other names elsewhere. These brought a lot of new money into property investment, mainly in shopping centres, offices and so on. But from about 2005, these funds began moving into the large-scale ownership of housing on the assumption that money could be made by speculative selling or by jacking up the rents being paid by tenants. In Germany many hard-pressed municipalities and social housing organisations sold thousands of (occupied, tenanted) dwellings to these investors, causing severe alarm. Following the rent strike against Real Estate Investment Trusts across the whole of Germany in 2008, international investors have switched from asset-stripping social housing to safer investments like Land Development Trusts.

The bond-financed equity-sharing system used in the London region from 2007 is a modified version of the site leasehold system which gave us Bloomsbury in the eighteenth and nineteenth centuries and many other high-quality urban areas in Britain. In those early cases it was a private owner who held the freehold and thus got the long-term benefits – indeed it was mostly aristocrats. But the system works as well or better when the long-term owner of the collective rights is a public or collective body with no outside shareholders. It is similar to the Hong Kong system which produced half the income needed by the colonial administration, enabling tax to be kept so low. And it draws on the lessons from Britain's post-war new towns which Margaret Thatcher privatised just when the profits were really rolling in.

Another great innovation in the Thames Gateway has been in the configuration of street systems and shopping/service centres (see Edwards, 2001 and Marshall, 2004). No longer do we have hierarchies of main and 'distributor' roads, with shops and services in isolated islands away from passing trade. Instead the frontages to main urban roads are all lined with shops, schools, offices and other services, with parallel service roads for cycles, buses, trams and cars. Passers-by can (and do) stop for services and everyone has shops within 10 minutes walk and a B+Q within 10 minutes drive. There is so much of this commercial space that rents for it are rather low and the new development areas have become a breeding ground for new business: only here can shopkeepers combine local customers, online customers and the regional customers who come and hunt them out. There are no double red lines here.

The London Plan has put a lid on further office development in and around the centre of London, just as Paris did to ensure that its suburban employment centres took off at La Défense and at Marne-la-Valée. These two huge centres were not much use, however, to the impoverished residents of the working-class suburbs of Paris who have been widely excluded from the general economy – but they did show what could be done to make a region more polycentric.

The British real estate fraternity was furious initially but now finds there are plenty of good investments in these prospering London suburban nodes, and they are much less volatile than central London, which was all they knew about until about 2010. Communities living round King's Cross, the Elephant and Castle and London Bridge breathed a sigh of relief and got on with life, the threat of displacement much reduced.

Because employment growth in Central London has slowed, more jobs are being created out in the suburban nodes. There is quite a bit of reverse (outwards) commuting so the trains are used in both directions. The massive investment in Crossrail was not needed and has been re-directed into a better network mesh of routes linking suburbs, using a mix of trains, trams and buses.

But probably the biggest transformation has been in housing. Barratt, Persimmon and their like, whose main skill was managing their land banks and timing their developments, have re-directed most of their work to Dubai and Shanghai. In their place we have a whole new industry based on cheap and plentiful land supply. Users of land pay over the long run through their ground rents (see above) instead of up-front. A consortium of Stuart Lipton, Ikea and John Lewis dominates the production of modular building components so that building enterprises get economies of mass production whether they are big or small. It is the modernist dream come true but with a thoroughly post-modern outcome: every dwelling can be different. Whereas new housing used mainly to be aimed at first-time buyers and new households, current output targets a huge range of market segments – often in the same development. So thousands of elderly Londoners have moved out of their big houses and flats where they could afford neither the maintenance nor the Council Tax and now live in the Thames Gateway. This was displacement dressed up as 'consumer choice'. It begged the question of why these people could not have cheaper maintenance and council tax so that they could continue living in the city amongst family and friends. Indeed the key attraction of inner city living for many of them was dwellings with few but spacious rooms, bookable guest rooms for visiting friends and families nearby, plenty of children and younger people around (but out of earshot) and an easy transition to more supported form of living as they get more decrepit. The housing associations, co-ops and developers who understood this, and the architects who helped them, have become immensely successful.

Part of the buzz in the Thames Gateway comes from this shift away from totally individualised housing, highly popular with people in all age groups including young workers. The growth of co-housing and of various forms of cooperatives has produced both a revived sociability and a major reduction in the environmental impact of falling household size (see Williams, 2006).

Another distinctive feature of development in the Gateway is the wide range of densities of building, ranging from 20 to over 1,000 habitable rooms per hectare. All the developments have to meet a zero carbon emissions standard and all the low density developments have to make big net energy contributions to the local or national grid to compensate for the fact that their residents are bound to drive a lot more. A good example of the results is at Mucking in Essex where the high river terraces (with long views across and down the estuary) were intensely settled by Romans and Anglo Saxons in the first millennium. They were then removed by gravel quarrying in the 1970s and are now re-settled as a busy town, mostly below ground, but with balconies, terraces and gardens on all the space not covered with photo-voltaic panels.

Thames Gateway is neither bound to succeed nor bound to fail. But it will be hard to make into a great success. It is not the kind of development which the property market, left to itself, would undertake. But government is determined to impose it on a reluctant market, aided by its success in securing the Olympics for 2012: the Games helps to keep the speculative housing bubble inflated and provides patriotic legitimation for state expenditure.

There are some major changes we could make in the organisation of urban development so it is driven less by speculation, more by needs, productivity and creativity. We could do it if we had a mind to – but who is the 'we'? Contemporary Britain does not have the sort of collective decision-making system (i.e., kind of government) which makes such changes possible.

Postscript

As this work goes to press the government has published its White Paper *Planning for a Sustainable Future* (DCLG, 2007) and consultation about its proposals are now under way. The main proposals in the White Paper which could have an impact on Thames Gateway appear to be three: taking major infrastructure decisions out of the hands of local authorities and resolving them through an Infrastructure Planning Commission, commercial criteria for deciding whether new developments should be within, alongside or apart from established centres and some weakening of public consultation requirements in various planning processes.

The proposals for the Infrastructure Planning Commission are highly controversial in so far as local objectors and local authorities would have much reduced power to prevent affected developments where these formed the local implementation of policies agreed at national and regional levels. The change is presented by government as a way of ensuring that facilities which are needed nationally (and which would benefit large numbers) cannot be vetoed or delayed by vociferous locals (typically few in number but resisting negative local effects like aircraft noise). The primary aim is to prevent events like the Heathrow Terminal 5 decision which took seven years, including an inquiry so expensive that Hillingdon council had to pull out on cost grounds. The proposals also include a plan to unify the very different approval regimes for different sorts of infrastructure (energy, railways, ports, airports and so on) and that will probably we widely welcomed, not least in the Thames Gateway. However, the reduction of local powers to resist unpopular installations or to propose root-and-branch critiques and alternatives is meeting with strong opposition from local authorities, NGOs and environmental campaigns and there is great scepticism about how public debate can be more than tokenism at a national or regional scale. The present chapter has not been concerned with the complex challenges of decision-making and 'governance' of the Gateway but this author's provisional view is that the White Paper's Commission proposal could simply add yet another non-democratic element to the existing maze and thus make it even more difficult for plans and policies to gain effective scrutiny and support in this sprawling region.

Proposals to reconsider the criteria governing the location of services (especially retailing) are a rather fluid part of the White Paper and likely to be much debated in the coming months. Essentially the dilemma is whether to follow the neo-liberal line (coming from Kate Barker's review (2006) of the planning system) that the market broadly responds to consumers – and consumers know their neeeds best – or to retain some variant of current practice in which planning authorities can shape the retail system in other ways in pursuit of environmental objectives or to protect services to immobile groups, support SMEs and so on. These issues are going to be very complex indeed in the Gateway, given the mix of established and (presumably) new retail and service centres and the extreme disparities of income and of needs to be served. We have Bluewater creaming off the luxury trade across a wide region at a high environmental cost in car travel; at the other extreme we have small town centres like Grays, no longer hosting many multiple shops because of the success of Bluewater and Lakeside but able instead to make a low price retail offer to a relatively poor clientele. Making wise decisions about centres and services in this context will be very difficult, as argued earlier in this chapter, and it is hard to see how generic national policy rules will affect the problem.

The White Paper's proposed changes to the public participation regime are tricky to evaluate since they are expressed in 'apple pie and motherhood' language which is hard to penetrate. The proposal to replace the very specific new – and still untested – requirement for Statements of Community Involvement in town and country planning with a more generic obligation on public authorities to consult across all policy areas could be a fine reform if applied in a democratic way but sceptics will fear that it is just another weakening of public participation. The other main proposal is to place the primary responsibility for public consultation about developments on the developer. This we know to be open to manipulation and bias and likely to undermine local authorities' fundamental need to be in close communication with their citizens, businesses and organisations. And, with so much of the territory subject to development proposals, the Gateway could be badly hit if this provision is enacted.

The final comment to be made on the White Paper is that it does not contain any innovations on the financing and land policy issues which have been the main focus of this chapter. The main thrust of policy is a further fine tuning of the neoliberal development agenda which this chapter has criticised. We are heading towards my pessimistic vision.

References

Amin, A., Massey, D. and Thrift, N. (2003), *Decentering the Nation: A Radical Approach to Regional Inequality*, London, Catalyst.

Astor, M.D. (1979), 'The Hedges and Woods of Mucking, Essex', *J. Panorama*, Thurrock Local History Society, 22, pp. 59–66.

Butler, T. and Rustin, M. (eds) (1996), *Rising in the East: The Regeneration of East London*, London, Lawrence and Wishart.

Department for Communities and Local Government (2007), *Planning for a Sustainable Future*, London, HMSO.

Edwards, M. (2001), 'City Design: What Went Wrong at Milton Keynes?', *Journal of Urban Design*, 6 (1): 73-82, 2001 http://taylorandfrancis.metapress.com/(gv5r3k55 uskqviihnchfv3f2)/app/home/contribution.asp?referrer=parent&backto=issue, 5,6;journal,17,20;linkingpublicationresults,1:104633,1.

Gordon, M. (1994), 'Thames Gateway: Sustainable Development or More of the Same?', *Town and Country Planning*, 63 (12), pp. 332–3.

Harvey, D. (1982), *The Limits to Capital*, Oxford, Blackwell.

Marshall, S. (2004), *Streets and Patterns*, London, Spon, Space Syntax: http://www.bartlett. ucl.ac.uk/research/space/overview.htm.

Massey, D. (2006), 'London Inside-out', *Soundings: A Journal of Politics and Culture*, 32, pp. 62–71.

Mayor of London (2004), *The London Plan: The Spatial Development Strategy*, London, GLA.

Middleton, C. (1994), 'The Road to Mucking: How Does a Banana Skin in a Bin End Up in Essex?', *Evening Standard* 25 November, pp. 10–12.

Mute (2006), 'Dis-integrating Multiculturalism', 2 (2): http://www.metamute.org/en/Dis-integrating-Multiculturalism.

Williams, J. (2006), 'Innovative Solutions for Averting a Potential Resource Crisis – the Case of One-Person Households in England and Wales', *Environment, Development and Sustainability*, 8 (3), pp. 1–30.

Chapter 17

After London's Turning: Prospects and Legacies for Thames Gateway

Philip Cohen and Michael J. Rustin

The contributions to this book have highlighted a number of strategic issues which pivot on the political, economic, social and cultural implications of London's eastwards turn. The purpose of this concluding chapter is to engage with these arguments, not in order to draw the threads together into a single narrative – for the reasons already discussed in our introduction, we think this is both an impossible task, and in so far as it imposes an editorial foreclosure on the debate we hope this book will help stimulate – a counter-productive one.

However it may be as well, before proceeding one step further, to focus on some aspects of these contributions which we think are especially salient for the line of argument we want to pursue here.

New Economies for Old?

The first theme we want to explore concerns the nature and consequences of de-industrialisation and its role in reproducing a dual urban economy in a post industrial setting. As John Marriott shows in Chapter 3, although London was hardly best known for its manufacturing industries, by comparison with the Midlands and North, there was in fact a very substantial industrial complex, and hence a large industrial working class. Initially this was made possible by the import of coal by sea and river, and then by the national electricity grid, as well as by the needs of the large population of the capital city. The decline of this manufacturing base, epitomised by the downsizing of Ford Motors in Dagenham has been mainly an effect of the broader competitive failure of British manufacturing in the post-war period, exacerbated by policies of deflation and high exchange rates in the Thatcher years which led many industrial sectors to go to the wall. An additional factor in East London was the closure of the London Docks in the 1960s, which had brought many linked industrial activities connected with sea-faring, and the processing of raw materials (Tate and Lyle's sugar plant in Silvertown is a rare survivor of these.) Symbolically, what had been the centre of the dock industry in the Isle of Dogs has now become a prime centre of what is now the leading edge of the financial and business services sector, concentrated in its new eastern node around Canary Wharf. Nevertheless, industrial activity on a small and medium-size scale does remain significant in the region, and remains vital for the employment opportunities of its residents.

As the British economy shifted in its emphasis from its previous focus on manufacturing, to the greater prominence of the service-industries, more attention became focused on cities themselves and especially capital cities with their political and cultural centrality, as generators of wealth. As Bob Jessop has stressed in a series of articles, the international competition between cities to host global spectacles, such as the four-yearly Olympic Games is a central aspect of the creation of the entrepreneurial city. Many cities found that major quarters of industrial and port activity had fallen out of use, and the trend began to recycle such spaces for such post-industrial economic purposes as financial and business services, tourism and entertainment, and modern retail facilities. In the ports, what had been the essential functional resource of sheltered deep water now became a primarily aesthetic amenity, as in the redevelopments of port zones in Boston, Baltimore, Sydney, and Barcelona, as well as in London. Hans Meyer in Chapter 1 outlines two historical conceptions of port-cities, those in which the port was fully integrated into the fabric of a city (of which Amsterdam and Venice are prime instances), and those where the port was a specialised function separated from it either by location, or by physical barrier, as in the case of the Dock Wall which surrounded the London Docks in its prime.

William Mann in Chapter 6 picks up the threads of this argument in terms of East London's urban fabric, pointing out that the commercial redevelopment of the Isle of Dogs has in fact reproduced the spatial segregation of the former enclosed docks in a new form. Whereas the Docks were surrounded by a peripheral Dock Wall, built for security, the complex of corporate buildings around Canary Wharf is also effectively cut off from working-class Poplar to the north by a six lane highway, which, (like its Battery Park City equivalent in New York) offers only a single footbridge as its mode of pedestrian access.

The considerable success achieved in the commercial redevelopment of the London Docks into a major hub of activity for the variously called knowledge, cultural and information economy is one of the factors which led attention to be given to the wider East London area, as a greatly under-utilised asset from the point of London's competitiveness as a city region. Could what had been achieved for Docklands – or at least the western end of it – be achieved downriver and on a broader regional scale? De-industrialisation had led to the under-utilisation of potential economic 'assets', in particular that of human resources or labour power. There was relatively high unemployment or 'economic inactivity' – withdrawal from the labour force – in the east of the city, especially in those areas poorly served by the rail and road systems, yet there was a scarcity of labour in more central metropolitan areas. The dispersal of manufacturing across the eastern side of London in earlier years had created local labour markets – for example in the area surrounding the Woolwich Arsenal – but when manufacturing declined, the populations who had serviced employers in these areas found themselves cut off from available work. So the thinking was that if transport could be improved, London as a whole would have the benefit of a larger and better-integrated labour market.

An example which influenced thinking on London's development in this respect, in particular through the advocacy of Peter Hall, was Paris, whose Regional Express Railway network (the RER) had sought to improve the economic integration of the greater Paris region. The Paris Metro (like the London Tube) was most efficient in providing local transport, because of its many stops. The main line commuter services had the disadvantage, as they have they have in London, of arriving at terminus stations on the edge of the city's central zone, which required changes of transport mode if one wished to cross the city. The RER by contrast provided a high speed link between destinations located in all quadrants of the city, passing through its centre, and producing a lattice-like network to complement the familiar hub-spoke pattern of the earlier rail system. In London, Crossrail (whose funding is not yet agreed), Thameslink 2000 (which is agreed but is many years behind its construction schedule), and a slowly developing orbital railway system which is supported by the Mayor's office, are the equivalent initiatives for this urban region. Andrew Blake in Chapter 13 discusses the long drawn out process of gaining agreement for another river crossing, to repair another deficit in connectivity within the Thames Gateway region.

Another scarcity which development in the east is intended to alleviate is that of housing, especially for middle-and lower-income people whom it is feared are being excluded from the London housing market by high and continuous increases in house prices. There are in particular anxieties about the availability of housing for the modestly-paid professionals required to staff schools, health, caring and police services, and there are schemes to make housing specifically available and affordable for these populations. There is also, in a modern city, as Saskia Sassen (1993) has pointed out in relation to New York, a growing labour market for the low-paid, doing 'McJobs' in the tourist and retail sectors, and providing cleaning and domestic services for affluent sections of the population who choose to pay for such services in order to devote time to high-earning employment. Thus a new kind of dual economy is appearing. Where are these populations, the considerable numbers of legal and illegal migrants who fill the needed spaces in the London labour market, actually to live?

The provision of housing on a large scale in the Thames Gateway region is seen as a solution to this problem, and indeed the commitment to build 200,000 housing units over the next 20 years in this area is the most solid and definite element, so far, in the planning of developments for the east side of London, but its mode of delivery has been intermittent and the outcome far from certain. Penny Bernstock in Chapter 10 noted both that development is taking place more slowly than was intended and an unexpected decline in the average size of dwellings, no doubt a 'downsizing' response to problems of affordability for many actual or would-be residents.

Thus both in regard to the labour and housing markets, it can be seen that the primary objective of the development of the eastern quadrant of the city is to enhance the wealth and competitiveness of London as a whole, by bringing an under-utilised, and 'underperforming' zone into fuller activity. This seems to be a situation in which there need be few losers, since as they become able to make a larger contribution to the metropolitan economy, the inhabitants of London

East will surely gain benefits from their own better access to work, housing and other amenities. But here the argument becomes more complicated.

This is because the justification of major development in the Thames Gateway has been implicitly set out in terms of two objectives, not one. The aim has been put forward not only of making a contribution to London's and Britain's economic competitiveness, but also of redressing the historical inequity and injustice of the relative positions of the east and west of London. Plainly it is easier to mobilise commitment and idealism around a project to make East London into the near-equal of the west, as an environment and locus of opportunities, than for a development which will merely reproduce its relative disadvantages, even if some absolute gain is achieved. The goals of enhanced competitiveness and of achieving greater equity are in fact rather confused in the advocacy and planning of the Thames Gateway developments, no more so that in its master concept of 'sustainable community', and this in a way rather characteristic of the larger politics of the New Labour era.

This blurring of the goals of efficiency, or enhanced competitiveness, and those of greater justice and equity, has also been in evidence in London's 2012 Olympics Bid, itself a major component of the plans for the broader Thames Gateway. The bid made much of the aspect of urban regeneration of disadvantaged East London, and of London and especially East London's multi-ethnic and multicultural population. Yet the Olympics is in reality a global festival on its never-ending tour, rather than by any means a local or even national event set on an international stage. Most of the large resource streams which flow in and out of it are corporate ones, including the quasi-corporate brand of the International Olympics Committee itself. Given the huge investment costs of staging the Games, it is not obvious that the winning city and its national economy will even necessarily gain economically from doing so. In Britain there are certainly many disadvantages in concentrating further investment in London, at the expense of other regions.

Even so, the distribution of benefits (and costs, as Massimo de Angelis points out in Chapter 5 where he discusses the contradictions within the concept of sustainability) from the location of the 2012 Olympics in Stratford is not easy to predict. There will be major investments in environmental improvement, new buildings and facilities, and in housing. But these are likely to be accompanied by rises in land-values which will lead to population movements, both of lower-income groups and small businesses out of the Stratford area, and of higher income groups into it, albeit with some cashing-in of their up valued assets by existing property-owners. Stratford will achieve a more favoured position in London's various competitive markets, in part through its unrivalled position as a transport node, and this will make a contribution to the wider eastern economy. But how much of this benefit will accrue to existing populations, and how far they will rather be excluded and displaced by it, remains to be seen.

The broader question here then is how far the development of the Thames Gateway is likely to break with, or merely continue, the existing patterns of relative disadvantage between the subregions of London. It certainly seems unlikely that the provision of housing in itself is going to be sufficient to end the relative deprivation of the region.

In Chapter 8 Tim Butler and his colleague's analysis of the findings of the 2001 Census, describe very complex patterns of relocation, noting the different routes of geographical mobility which are being followed by groups defined by class, educational and ethnic identity. This chapter charts a demographic complexity which has so far found little articulate expression in cultural or political terms, in contrast to the strongly marked traditions and political identity of the old East End. Paul Watt in Chapter 9 notes the poor image of the Gateway from the point of view of middle class groups with suburban aspirations, and the continuing preoccupation with class and ethnic differences among socially mobile residents seeking improvement for their families. Where so many people are seeking to escape at the same time from what they experience as relative deprivation, places of escape can prove elusive. Both chapters, in their different ways, show how earlier predominance in inner East London of white working-class people is shifting, as a consequence of gentrification, outward suburban migration, and the inward movement of black and minority ethnic populations. However, inner East London remains relatively deprived.

The Cultural in London's Eastwards Turn: Towards a New Orientalism?

In 2004 the Greater London Authority announced a commission to establish the boundaries of the capital city, and to recommend whether they should be extended. At the time many commentators saw this as a cynical exercise by the Mayor of London to enlarge his domain of governance. But it addressed a real enough question. Just where does London, considered as an imagined community of self-styled 'Londoners', now begin and end? Is the metropolis defined by the range of its transport system? Or by what is left of its green belt? Or by the widened scope of its function as a global city? Or by some conventional mental image as of the city's limits? Or is there a separate cultural dynamic which generates its own relatively autonomous mappings of space, place, identity and belonging?

The question of city limits is not exactly a new one. From the mid-Victorian period onwards the informal economy radiating out from the Docks operated through social networks and supply chains which stretched from the heart of the West End to Mile End, from Bond Street to Beckton. Drugs, the 'black market', organised crime, the sex trade and all manner of other dodgy business created an economic hinterland that was certainly not registered on official maps and confounded the largely precinct-based structure of the metropolitan police. Only the under-manned river police were sufficiently mobile and savvy to intercept some of this traffic. Otherwise the 'just in time' provision of illicit goods and services through constantly shifting centres of supply linked through a myriad of conduits operating on an irregular basis, defeated both the logistical and imaginative capacities of the state even as it prefigured the kind of economic activity space that would one day be produced by post-Fordism.

It is also worth remembering that East London's cultural economy has a provenance that long predates the advent of so-called 'creative industry'. For example the 1960's explosion of youth fashions (Mods, Rockers, Skinheads, Crombies et al.) confirmed the area's already well established position as a laboratory of sub-cultural innovation; the presence of the rag trade, on the cusp of passing from Jewish into Asian hands ensured that what began as a very localised way of white working-class youth negotiating their changing class and race habitus turned into internationally marketable teenage fashion in double quick time. Do-it-yourself creative industry started here.

From the early 1980s the inner East End saw a major influx of young professionals attracted by the area's growing reputation as a style centre associated now with the Young British Artists scene and general multicultural 'funkiness', not to mention its lower rents and proximity to the city. This coincided with an exodus of 'old' East Enders as a result of the closure of the docks. As several of our contributors have noted, the figures of Essex Man, not to mention Essex girls, came to symbolise in the public imagination what had happened to the newly affluent working class in Britain – it had apparently deserted the labour movement, voted for Thatcherism, and become completely absorbed in a culture of consumerism and possessive individualism.

Yet in and sometimes against these 'new times' the legacy of Empire was being re-valorised. Not just in the 'little Englandism' that sometimes powered local-style resistance to regeneration, as in the campaign by 'Islanders' on the Isle of Dogs against the plans of the LDDC, but in the re-invention of the East End as an internal Orient (Cohen, 2005). In the 1880s Jewish immigrants from eastern Europe found themselves assimilated to the positions of Lascars and Chinese, misrecognised as Sephardim rather than Ashkenazi, on account of their 'oriental' features. This characterisation included a marked duplicity – the respectable hard-working nature of these communities was read as a mere façade behind which lurked perverse and dangerous impulses. A century later Islamophobia updated the scenarios of the barbaresque, and it was the turn of the Bangladeshi community to be lumped together with Vietnamese/Chinese refugees as the new 'enemy within' the citadels of Western civilisation, as represented by Canary Wharf. And now of course the wheel has come full circles with the influx of young economic migrants from Eastern Europe ....

In the same idiom a picture of 'white flight' was drawn in which Cockneys fled en masse from the racially tense inner city neighbourhoods where they had grown up to places associated with 'England's green and pleasant land', or at least to the mud flats and sandbanks of the Thames estuary which they had previously only visited for a day out. Whereas the move from inner to outer East End in the 1930s and again in the 1950s was widely hailed as a step in the direction of modernisation, linked to the advent of Fordism, the more recent migration further downriver from Barking Reach to Brightlingsea is seen to represent not just the end of the industrial economy but the end of the line for the English working class as a whole. For this diaspora coincides with and is seen to represent the weakening and even collapse of forms of white working-class culture that hitherto supported a narrative of collective aspiration communicated from generation to generation amongst manual workers and their families; the individualisation/fragmentation of this narrative is widely held to have opened the fissures through which an always latent racism could 'leak' and become more manifest. The closure of the 'fictive kinships' of class, hitherto anchored to workplace solidarities, around a more mobile, even virtual, but still decidedly matrifocal sense of imagined community was an alternative response, albeit one which has been less recognized and commented upon.

With the advent of New Labourism, the position of those left behind by the knowledge economy and who found themselves trapped in welfare poverty or 'backyards industry' was often assimilated to that of an underclass, a new kind of 'residuum', occupying what planners refer to as holes or tears in the urban fabric; it was but a step to characterise them as the denizens of some 'Cockney Cyberia' and associate their presence downriver with Thames Gateway. Not surprisingly then these groups came to be demonised as suffering from 'poor whites syndrome'. Cockneys, having been comprehensively rehabilitated by their contribution to the myth of the Blitz, courtesy of their legendary cheerfulness, resilience and sense of humour under fire, now found themselves no longer the backbone of the post-nation but resuming their traditional pariah status as a race apart. The work of Iain Sinclair, however great its literary merits has performed a valuable rebranding service for the Thames Gateway project by landscaping the area and its inhabitants with all the narrative devices of the gothic imagination, rendering the 'wild east' into a new urban frontier to be explored and settled by middle class 'pioneers'.

Elsewhere it has been the potential affinities rather enmities between poor Whites and Asians that are stressed. Both groups could be sentimentalised as the standard-bearers of close knit extended family and community life that was elsewhere being lost; Brick Lane for example was glamorised, as poverty went multicultural and dressed up in ethnic drag, providing local colour useful for marketing the inner East End as a venue for cultural tourists. The 1990s saw the birth of Schlockney, erstwhile pearly queens camping it up for the passing trade in radical chic, whilst young Asian comedians stepped into the shoes of Charlie Chester and stood up in 'Cockney' pubs to tell anti-racist jokes that would have made the cheeky chappy turn in his grave.

Those with their ears to the ground detected many new sounds of the multicultural times emanating from the East End. In the 1980s Madness and Ian Dury's Blockheads blended ska and pub anthems with rock 'n' roll to give a distinctive two tone flavour to white men talking the blues. More recently Nitin Sawhney and Dizzy Rascals gave a musically sophisticated but still raw edge to the diasporic groove. Nowadays Chas and Dave sound like the end of pier concert party they always were. Meanwhile on the streets, and largely through the medium of playground banter the Cockney vernacular was being taken up and transformed by young British Asians and Blacks and made over into a rap attack on adult authority with which many white Easter Enders could and did identify. Meanwhile on the other side of the tracks there was the birth of a new cool: Estuary English – the cockney guttural softened to an Essex burr – came to epitomise the new cultural melting pot that social mobility and the 'end of class' was meant to be creating.

Whatever the real, as opposed to imagined changes taking place, it is certainly the case that as a result of these shifting identifications the sense of being an East Ender has become increasingly de-territorialised: it no longer corresponds if it ever did, to living in a physically demarcated area of East London, let alone within the sound of the proverbial Bow Bells (Cohen, 1999). Just who is, or who is not, an East Ender is much less a contested topic these days amongst White, Black and Asian young people; fings, or at least cockney credentials, are no longer quite the cultural resource they used to be. The decline in popularity of *EastEnders* from the nation's favourite soap to casualty in the rating wars has added its own twist to the tale. In the wake of 7/7, its original winning formula of popular multiculturalism – the whole world rubbing along together in a street market with just enough friction to keep the audience wanting to find out what happens in the next episode – no longer carries quite the same street cred.

In fact, on the ground the cultural traffic between city and sea continues to generate actor-networks which have as little to do with the intense face-to-face localisms of Albert Square as they do with planners' maps of commuter flows. Any summer evening on Southend's hot mile sees boy racers from all over East London and Essex converge to track their own very different lines of desire. In Chapter 12 Gareth Millington shows clearly how the attempt to develop this resort into a hub of creative industry and cultural tourism has to connect with these forms of mobility, yet remains hamstrung by its own pretensions to civic respectability as well as by problems of poverty and multiple deprivation which it shares with other formerly prosperous seaside towns. In similar vein Chapter 11, Karina Berzins and Iain MacRury's study of the night time economy in Stratford suggests that there is more to creating a 'cultural quarter' than a cluster of performing arts venues.

All these recent developments have been the subject of intense journalistic speculation and public comment. East London has always been a favoured site for the projection of public anxieties about the state of the nation. Will the spur of the Olympics turn Stratford into the centre of a new wave of creative industry that spreads across Outer East London, uniting the rappers of Romford with the cultural hipsters of Shenfield? Will the Lower Lea Valley become Britain's silicon valley, silently humming with eco-technology, while herons and up-market house hunters nest happily along the riverbanks? Or is this just a planners and estate agents wet dream? Will ethnic gentrification spread its net ever wider, and Essex Girls take to wearing the hajib? Will white flight go entrepreneurial and make Jaywick Sands London's new Edge City? Will we see the development of global villages characterised by a very English form of rural cosmopolitanism, or will popular NIMBY-ism join forces with what is left of the Tory squirearchy in closing ranks against the new multicultural middle class?

These questions are rhetorical – that is they are posed in such a way as to be unanswerable in any strictly empirical or evidential sense, but rather to dramatise a pervasive sense of cultural dislocation and social unease which cuts across – but also links – numerous sites of representation about how London, and the country as a whole is changing. This emerging 'complexity without voice' makes it difficult to find or assign coherent meaning to the regeneration of the Gateway, but it also fuels various conspiracy theories about the political process of which it is a part.

The most recent, and hotly debated thesis, advanced by the authors of *The New East End* (Dench et al., 2006) and endorsed by a whole genre of popular and academic commentary on what life is like on the wrong side of the tracks, is that the white working class has been sold down river by an unholy alliance of politically correct ultra-leftists and Black or Muslim extremists who have seized control of local labour councils and driven through policies maximally calculated to alienate Labour's traditional (sic) support.[1] There is a certain irony in this, since once upon a time, within living memory, it used to be the Trotskyites who accused the old reformist Labour Party of betraying the workers; now the big boot in the sky is on the other foot, and it is Respect who is accused by erstwhile Labourites of *trahison des proles*!

There are four separate charges, which are linked together into a single indictment:

1) by abandoning historical entitlements to scarce amenity and resource (most notably housing) derived from the post-war settlement, the sacrifices and struggles of the working class in uniform have been repudiated or ignored;
2) by applying universalistic criteria of social need in a way that rebounds to advantage of arrivant communities, the long-established communities have been put at a systematic disadvantage;
3) by endorsing moral symbolic and doctrinaire forms of anti-racism, white people find themselves continually placed under suspicion and surveillance for latent or unconscious racism;
4) by promoting a form of multiculturalism in which the values and ways of life of white working-class people are either marginalised or ignored, at best tolerated, at worst ridiculed, the conditions for a white backlash were created.

Whether these arguments can be separately justified by the evidence produced in the book, or indeed elsewhere, is a moot point.[2] But certainly these are popular perceptions and it would be wrong to dismiss them as groundless. Some of these outcomes may be unintended effects of well-intentioned policies, others may be more engineered, and still others the result of processes that could not in any case

---

1   This argument is advanced with widely varying degrees of subtlety, often drawing selectively on ethnographic research or using ethnography to underwrite. See, for example, Michael Collins' (2004) recent 'biography of the white working class' on South East London and Gillian Evans' (2005) study of educational failure amongst white working-class children in Bermondsey. A much more nuanced account is to be found in the work of Roger Hewitt (2005) also on South East London and in the forthcoming comparative study of young people in Deptford and the Isle of Dogs (Rathzel et al., 2007).

2   Mumford and Power (2003) give a less divisive description of East End community politics.

has been avoided or contained. But it is the way the arguments are joined up that gives us cause for concern. For the result is not only to simplify the complex and shifting community politics of East London but risks creating a new victimology which can easily be, and in fact has been, successfully exploited by the British National Party, as their recent electoral gains in Barking and Dagenham and in areas of Essex indicate.

An alternative line of argument about the political concomitants of structural change in East London replaces conspiracy theory with a version of modernisation theory which rests on technological determinism. This view portrays globalisation as an irresistible, technologically-driven force, against which the local is merely a sometimes immovable and usually reactionary object. Here the white working class are seen as simply an obstacle in the path of progress; they are pathologised for failing to adapt to changing circumstances, by clinging to a culture of manual labourism and masculinity which is out of step with new economic times and for failing to grasp the opportunities that have landed on their doorstep. If only they could somehow be wired up and plugged into the new circuits of the network society!

In our view what these different theories of change attempt, but fail to adequately address is the political consequences of the weak correspondence between London's socio-economic structure and its cultural and political geography. This is not to do with any failure of social engineering, still less a lag between the dynamism of material infrastructure and the conservatism of mental maps; rather it articulates an absence within the political realm itself, a gap between the existing forms of urban representation and what needs to be represented about the urban realm; it is this hiatus which is one of the outcomes of 'splintering urbanism' (Graham and Marvin, 2001) which a number of our contributors are concerned to address and to which we now turn.

Making Things Public

There is first of all the obvious fact that the Thames Gateway does not fall within any political boundary and strides across many; it includes numerous governmental jurisdictions including those of parts of Essex, Kent, the Greater London Authority and various boroughs and district councils exercising authority within these. This has meant that it has been necessary to create a plethora of administrative authorities charged with a range of sometimes overlapping tasks, generating a bewildering array of acronyms and initiatives. For example the annual Thames Gateway parliamentary junket is sponsored by Thames Gateway South Essex, Thames Gateway Kent Partnership, the Thames Gateway London Partnership, the London Thames Gateway Development Corporation, Renaissance Southend and Thurrock Thames Gateway, and will be attended by representatives from dozens of local authorities, regeneration agencies, and other bodies, the 57 varieties of governance only be spoiled by the fact that the congregation will be overwhelmingly made up of white middle-aged men wearing dark suits!

At the same time Thames Gateway is a name which many inhabitants of its territory do not identify as the place where they live, or to which they belong. In this respect it is quite unlike many of its component locations, such as East London, or the Isle of Dogs, or Dagenham or even Docklands, which have long had a strong sense of place.

The gap opened up by these dislocations, is filled by visionary cartographies advanced by architects and planners offering competing ideal typical accounts of what should be happening[3]. As a result the Thames Gateway comes to denote a planners' aspiration, a signifier of governmental intentions more than it refers to an authentic or recognisable place. In their chapters, Philip Cohen and Andrew Calcutt draw attention to some of the consequences of this situation. In Chapter 2 Cohen suggests that the Thames Gateway is being invented through a new style of governance centred not just on existing methods of civic imagineering or urban impression management but on a whole new syntax of governance in which human agency is dissolved into agentless and/or non-human causality in a way that floats free of any attributable sense of consequence. This void is filled by the narrative turn in planning which enables some 'peoples stories' to be highlighted for their appositeness in confirming the rhetorics of the master-plan, appearing to give it an authentic plebiscitary voice, whilst effectively confiscating their power to unsettle the pre-established consensus. In Chapter 7 Calcutt argues that in the Gateway 'culture' is increasing deployed by government to 'make substantial that which has so far remained stubbornly virtual.' One might say that what can't be readily be debated or decided by rational means, instead becomes shaped by less rational kinds of representation and persuasion.

So the problem remains of how to give real meaning and shared identity to the Thames Gateway in a way which is anchored in some form of popular participation in its planning and delivery. In default of some such countervailing force it seems likely that developers will continue to cherry-pick their preferred sites for higher-value projects, while building on less desirable areas at much lower specifications, and even then only where government provides financial inducements for them to do so. Michael Keith in Chapter 4 and Michael Edwards in Chapter 16 see large opportunities and risks in the current pattern of development, and set out the alternative futures for the Gateway with starkness and urgency. Keith warns against a 'default model of low-quality, economically suboptimal suburbanisation', arguing that this would be a waste of the opportunity of a generation. Edwards sets out best and worst case scenarios for the Gateway, contrasting the exemplary development that *could* take place, especially if the question of land values were tackled by government for the public

---

3   Although their design aesthetics are radically different Terry Farrell's postmodern vision of urban renaissance (1994) and Richard Rodgers' argument for a fit for purpose modernism have many points in common; through their work at the Architecture and Urbanism Unit at the greater London Authority they have helped break with the idea that large scale urban development has to be driven by mass produced standardized building units to achieve economies of scale.

good, with an alternative poor-quality outcome from which property developers would be the main beneficiaries.

New thinking about governance being developed by Bruno Latour, in part in response to environmental issues, may be helpful in devising solutions to these problems. Latour, in his book *Politics of Nature* (2004) and in a recent symposium and exhibition (Latour 2005b), argues that before decisions can be made, all the 'objects' relevant to these decisions have to be assembled and given a voice. These objects include human subjects for example workers, people at different stages of their life-cycle, even people as-yet unborn – and many non-human subjects on which human existence in various ways depends. In the Thames Gateway, the human subjects include all the different categories of people who live and work or come to visit in the region, or who may do so in the future, between whom there are many differences of experience, origin, interests and value. The non-human protagonists include, for example, the River Thames, the atmosphere, the brownfield and greenfield sites, the wetlands and the bird-life, the mud flats, archaeological and heritage sites, modernist and industrial ruins, the existence or non-existence of fish, to name only a few. There are innumerable hybrids, Latour (1993) has pointed out – those entities that are 'invented' and become effective only through interactions between man and nature (such as microbes, pulleys, genes and electrons), since it is on the interactions between human and non-human agency that all meaningful life depends.

Latour argues for a new kind of 'bicameralism', or 'separation of powers'. In one 'house', human and non-human subjects need to be assembled, their relations clarified, their various claims, real and virtual, made articulate and some kind of aesthetic or narrative coherence given to their existence. From such carefully curated assemblages options and choices can be formulated. In the other 'house', these same evidences are reconvened within the framework of political democracy, constituted on a franchise which gives equal voice to all citizens; it is here that decisions can be made, but now with a fuller recognition and articulation of all the elements that need to enter into them if they are to be adequate to the complexity of the situations that need to be addressed. Latour's argument is that political institutions as they are present constituted cannot assemble all that needs to be represented, or map the complexity of their environments. Because it becomes widely recognised that they cannot do this (politicians plainly cannot carry in their heads all the many kinds of understanding and knowledge that are relevant to each situation) they lose the trust of the public, and default, in defence of their own positions, to habitual evasiveness and to the manipulation of opinion through techniques of public relations management and phoney consultation exercises.

Latour's argument points to a problem which is, of course, widely recognised by political scientists, by politicians and by large sections of the electorate who vote with their feet every five years: namely the 'democratic deficit'. Alice Sampson in Chapter 15 discusses the deficits often found in the attempts to involve local communities in decision-making, but the problem has wider ramifications. New Labour's so-called double-devolution agenda – the return of initiative from central to local government and from local government down to the neighbourhood, is a top-down attempt to create bottom-up solutions. So too is the current fashion for exercises in public place-making. Despite its more rootsy vernacular, the attempt to create a virtual public realm according to e-democracy principles (open source software, open access websites and light touch moderation) has failed to turn the chat room into an agora. The use of citizens' juries to provide local forms of adjudication on issues of public amenity that fall through the normal mesh of planning law and public enquiry is a more interesting example and one which could be pushed further. The recent announcement that a pilot scheme of 'participatory budgeting' is to be introduced in some areas, enabling citizen panels to decide on certain allocations of public money to improve neighbourhood facilities is a step in the right direction although the matters allowed for jurisdiction are predictably small in scope and scale.

The difficulty with all these initiatives is that despite – or perhaps because of – their rhetorics of community empowerment, they singularly fail to engage with the real levers of power; these remain massively concentrated in the higher reaches of government and in public and private corporations. Nor do such measures counteract the erosion of intermediate civil institutions between state and market; instead they fill the void created by the corrosive effects of targetology and deregulation with simulations of the democratic process. Inevitably the initial enthusiasm for more inclusive forms of planning quickly dissipates when it becomes apparent that nothing much is going to change on the ground as a result of all the effort. The result is likely to be withdrawal from further civic engagement and even greater disillusionment with the political and planning process.

The recent government White Paper on planning reform makes interesting reading in this context. It wants to streamline the planning process, by abolishing the regime of multiple consent whereby planning proposals may have to meet the requirements of many different kinds of planning regulation before they can be validated. The paper argues that the planning process as presently constituted is too lengthy, too costly, too legalistic and too bureaucratic and discourages all but the most determined and articulate of objectors from taking part and having their say. All of which is true. The White Paper has some interesting things to say about 'changing the culture' of planning to ensure that ordinary citizens can take part on an equal footing with professional advocates, but like all such 'culture change' statements, the actual prescriptions of how to do it are infuriatingly vague.

One of the main problems the White Paper has set itself to tackle is the fact that public enquiries are adversarial. They are modelled on judicial proceedings and consist of objections to a proposed plan being answered by its defendants – usually the property developers or planning authorities who have put it forward, or lawyers acting on their behalf. In that sense the planning enquiry reverses the situation in a court of criminal law, where it is the state which prosecutes and the defendants are usually ordinary members of the community. The fact that the head of a planning enquiry is both judge and jury in the case is of course a flaw, albeit one that could indeed be easily rectified by empanelling a citizens' jury. But the aim of the White Paper is not to improve the adversarial system by giving it a more democratic frame, but to abolish it, and replace it with a system of managed consensus which will in effect narrow rather than widen the scope of public deliberation. This is to be done in two ways. The creation of an independent

Planning Commission will make all the major strategic planning decisions about national infrastructure – the road and rail network, airports – projects of importance to national security. This has, on any reckoning, to involve a further centralisation of power and a reduction in democratic accountability. But this is balanced by proposals to enhance public participation at a local level, partly as a means of heading off objections and hence reducing the need for public enquiries and partly to free up the operation of market forces and make the system more quickly responsive to client/consumer demand.

Adversarial procedures are seen to be a stumbling block to realising both these aims. The notion that a properly-supported widely-accessible space of public deliberation in which different views could be put forward and cases argued might actually be a means of tackling the democratic deficit does not seem to have entered the official mind. But perhaps after all there is another way to do it.

Towards a New Practice of Regional Assembly: A Modest Proposal for the Political Regeneration of Thames Gateway

The government now proposes to abolish regional assemblies, because they have come to be widely seen as a useless carapace of the existing already lugubrious system of decision making. We think that this actually offers an opportunity to rethink the relationship between regionality and planning regulation. For this purpose we need to bring together and articulate the widest possible range of choices and stakeholders within a framework which encourages multivocal accounts and exercises the dialogical imagination. We do not need to institutionalise yet another dialogue of the deaf in which everyone believes their own propaganda and no-one else's!

So let us take Latour's model of political representation and operationalise it by drawing on some of the work which John Forester and his colleagues have done in constructing a critical theory of public deliberation linked to a practice of participatory planning (Forester and Fishcher, 1987, 1993; Forester, 1999). What would such a framework look like and how it might be built in Thames Gateway. What should be its organising principles?

One place to start might be to consider the multiple meanings of 'region'. It means, literally, an area over which rule (from the Latin *regere*) is exercised. But rule is here interpreted in a dual sense; firstly it is a means of deciding the scope, scale and spatial distribution of certain phenomena (such as a plant or animal species, or a set of linguistic or cultural characteristics of a human population settled in a particular area). This involves taking the measure of the phenomena and assigning them a value or a place in the wider scheme of things. Such calculations may indeed be purely approximate – a region is a range of variation around which a figure (say the cost of a house) might fall.

The second sense of the word relates more to its function in political discourse. As an image of the body politic, it is defined by its special and usually unequal relationship to an organ of proximal governance – we talk about 'regional' seats of power, for example. Region also connotes a defined administrative space, over which a particular kind of jurisdiction is exercised. In many contexts it has become a synonym for a province; a periphery defined by a centre which it itself lacks but which either remote controls it or acts at a distance as a pole of attraction or influence.

So region in its dual usage refers us to Latour's two houses and equally the Thames Gateway is a region in both these senses; it is an assemblage of disparate and indeed discontinuous entities whose relations are approximate. And it is an administrative space whose periphery is everywhere and centres nowhere, or perhaps more accurately it is organised poly-centrically around a series of discrete hubs of governance.

The next step is to consider what kind of assembly might be appropriate to such a form of regionality? Our first suggestion is that the assembly should be peripatetic; rather like the Assizes, it should move through all the zones of change in turn following a regular itinerary and its work should be undertaken in each place over a limited period of time, say a fortnight. What are assembled during this time would be two things. Firstly the collection of documentary evidence generated by locally situated knowledge concerning topical planning issues and secondly its preparation in the form of propositions for subsequent public debate and evaluation.

The first part of the process resembles the way an exhibition is curated – and indeed such an exhibition may be produced as a backdrop to the deliberative proceedings. We propose to call the people who do this work curators for another reason. There is an interesting evolution of the term from someone who had the care of troubled souls, and who was the guardian of their interests, to someone whose task is to assemble artefacts or artworks for the purposes of public exhibition. We see our curators as performing both functions – that is having a special duty of care to all those who are troubled by a particular plan, a duty which is discharged by helping them firstly to assemble all the evidence (objects, artefacts, oral testimony, visual documentation) they need and then helping them articulate this material into a publicly performed (and possibly multimedia) statement about their distress or grievance in way that gives it narrative coherence and aesthetic form. The process of giving symbolic value and dialogic form to deeply felt beliefs tends to reduce their toxicity and aid reflexivity. It is a process which militates against political, religious or ideological extremism, without for all that stage-managing consensus. Although the arguments of such groups as the British National Party (BNP) or radical Islamists might well be put forward within such a process, it seems unlikely that they would flourish in a context which encouraged reflective deliberation. In any case curators are not political lobbyists or professional advocates of any hue – their task is primarily to assemble as representative a range of voices as possible and facilitate conversation between them.

The team of curators would travel from zone to zone through the region working with schools, youth centres, community organisations, senior citizens clubs and a range of other voluntary organisations, as well as collecting evidence from a wide range of representative bodies. We propose that this 'progress' should be accomplished in the form of a Mobile Observatory, combining the function of Mass Observation and a Mobile Information Unit.

Mass Observation (MO) in its original conception was an attempt to construct a 'social poetics' of everyday life, based upon diaries and reports produced by a network of correspondents who each month responded to a different directive; the chosen topic might relate either to a current political event, or to a more personal and intimate issue (viz. sex lives, friendships, health). In the case of the more public topics correspondents were supposed to note down conversations they heard or took part in, and to summarise their gist. These reports were then collated so as to distil from them the pattern of popular sentiment and belief on a particular issue, to help inform and influence policy making as well as being of general public interest. Our proposal adapts this principle to the age of the Internet. It involves recruiting a team of correspondents in each zone of change, each of whom produce their own blogs, focusing on an agreed topic each month, giving their personal views, but also sounding out opinion amongst, family, friends and workmates, to provide a monthly digest of information. The blogs could then be linked to a virtual Thames Gateway Assembly site on Second Life.

Mobile Information Units (MIU) have a long history and have been put to many uses: from the agitprop trains and 'revolutionary excursionism' organised by the early Soviet urbanists, to Ken Kesey's Merry Pranksters; from the political campaign trail bus to the traveling road show. In the UK they have largely been used as means of targeting public services at hard-to-reach communities (in both a geographical and social sense). Lending libraries and mobile radiography units are just two of the better known examples. Most of these initiatives aim to break down social isolation amongst groups perceived to be in some way 'left behind' by economic developments.

The experience of MIU, like that of recent experiments in e-democracy, indicates that whether the vehicle of information is a bus or a laptop computer, it only works in so far as it is part of a wider, socially embedded, process of capacity-building *and is not a substitute for it*. In this case the Mobile Observatory is embedded in the political process of assembly; as it travels around from place to place it not only accumulates evidence, and relays information from and about one community to another, but in its very trajectory helps bring into being a Gateway wide network of informed deliberation which reflects, challenges and reconstructs what is meant by sustainability as it goes.

The second 'moment' of Assembly – which we propose to call a convention – stabilises the region as a singular site of coordinated deliberation and decision-making at set times and places In this 'other house' made up of representatives from all the zones of change, presentations are made based on the local work done by the curators relating to topical planning issues. These presentations would be made directly by the parties concerned with technical assistance from the curators where necessary. They would adjudicated by a citizens' jury made up of one elected representative from each zone of change, supported by a professional panel of convenors.

The convenors' panel would comprise a mixture of academics, planners, architects and others with relevant professional expertise drawn from both public and private sectors; it would advise the citizens' jury on points of planning procedure and law and on other technical matters. They could question the presenters as could members of the jury. Following the presentations – which we might add could take many discursive forms – including film, video and performance arts – there would a period of open debate with speakers from the floor. This would be followed by a further session held *in camera* at which the presenters would meet together and with the convenors to see if agreement in principle could be reached and a joint statement of planning intent submitted. If this was not possible the assembly would reconvene to hear a summing up from the professional panel and adjudication by the citizen's jury. This in turn would be translated into an indicative planning statement setting out the key policy options and the proposed terms and conditions for realising a particular piece of urban development. The statement would then be submitted to the National Planning Commission for approval within three months; if such approval were refused then the mechanism of a Public Enquiry would finally come into play.

There are two further points. The first concerns the process of deliberation itself.

We think that all planning propositions must clearly identify self-interest – what the proposers or opposers of a given plan hope to gain if their case is upheld and what they think they would lose if the argument went against them This must be stated at the outset; then and in a separate statement the proposition must be justified in terms some higher common principle which in this case would be the concept of sustainable community as adumbrated in the Thames Gateway Plan. This proviso achieves two things. Firstly the level of mystification is reduced; it will be much more difficult to pass off self interested actions as a disinterested pursuit of the common good. Secondly, the requirement to produce a metanarrative foregrounds the issue of values. What regimes of value (moral, economic, aesthetic etc.) are being used to justify the claims about a particular project realising its definition of sustainable community? We have already suggested that the Thames Gateway Plan is characterised by conflicting values – for example winning competitive advantage versus achieving redistributive justice. We want to make the Thames Gateway Assembly into a 'values tournament' around the notion of sustainable community, and to test the robustness of the concept in terms of what it means in practice across a range of contexts. In this way the public evaluation of a proposal comes to depend not just on its technical merits or the rhetorical power of its argumentation(although these tests must also be passed), nor on the range and depth of locally situated knowledge which is deployed in its favour or against (though this too is important) but on the *quality of articulation* between the substantive case (linked to declarations of interest) and normative frame (highlighted in the statement of values); the extent to which this allows for more than a formal audit of outcomes and actively encourages continuous public evaluation of the unfolding process would be a crucial test. The grounds of judgement are thereby shifted away from an apparently 'value free' assessment of means, or an ideological rationale of ends to a consideration of what constitutes a realistic programmatic effort to define and construct sustainable community.

The second point concerns the way this process is to be institutionalised. It should be clear that our proposal for a Thames Gateway Assembly has nothing to do with adding yet another layer of governance to the already Byzantine complexity of the existing apparatus. The aim rather is to give some real identity through participation to a geographical space that currently has little or none, creating a form of 'imagined community' (to use Benedict Anderson's terms) which is appropriate to a diversified and complex region. This process is iterative, in that it involves working through the issues year on year, at different stages of the realisation of the plan. Although some elements of the Thames Gateway plan are already approved and in place (for example, the plans for Ebbsfleet and Shell Haven) so that in these cases there may be only limited scope for local negotiation around modes of delivery, in other cases there is an opportunity to develop a whole new culture and apparatus of participative planning which has a long term strategic bearing on outcomes. Equally, given the very long time span involved between design and delivery, existing plans, however well formulated or advanced, are inevitably going to be subject to 'events, dear boy, events'. The volatility of the global economy, interacting with local fluctuations in the housing and labour markets may substantially change some of the key parameters, and it is important to have a strongly embedded framework of public deliberation which can respond flexibly and just in time to such eventualities.

A Case in Point

Let us finally take a concrete example of the kind of issue that might be deliberated by the process we have outlined. There is currently an influential group of architects and urban planners centred on the City East initiative, launched by the Greater London Authority (GLA), whose aim is to implement the strategic objectives of the London Plan to the east of City Hall and to map out a vision for the area over the next 25 years. They have been encouraged to engage in blue sky thinking and they have come up with the idea that the skies around the Royal Docks would be bluer and better off without airplanes, but with skyscrapers. The proposition is that London City Airport should move downriver to the mouth of the Estuary and the docks be built over to provide a mix of residential and commercial development à la Canary Wharf.

Now it might be thought that the existing residents of the Royal Docks (including UEL) would support this initiative, as it would remove a major source of multiple pollution (noise, fuel, smell), and contribute to a local reduction in carbon emissions. But as Iain MacRury shows in the study reported in Chapter 14 the local response might be more ambivalent. Not only is there a (fragile and unevenly distributed) sense of local ownership ('our airport') but one of the great indirect benefits of the airport's presence is to prevent the construction of high rise office blocks – owing to flight safety regulations. With these removed the way would be open to build another cluster of iconic skyscrapers similar to those at Canary Wharf. However not only would such intense commercial development accelerate the gentrification of the area, driving up house prices, it would be unlikely to generate many new jobs except for low wage, low skill -office cleaners to replace the higher-paid skilled jobs lost as a result of the airport closing. In terms of the Big Players, the City East solution might be good news for the new Biota Centre – and let's face it for the University of East London's staff and students who would have a more pleasant environment in which to work and study – but less so for ExCel Centre who rely a good deal on business visitors via the airport and the connectivity to Europe.

At present there is no way in which the City East proposal can be publicly deliberated. It is not yet official GLA policy, hence it is not subject to any official consultation process; the draft area Master Plan for the Royal Docks makes no reference to the proposal. Moreover, apart from informal discussions with key institutional stakeholders (including the university) there has been no engagement with local community forums. Indeed the whole proposal is under wraps because of a legal injunction awarded to London City Airport to prevent publication of the plan because it represents a threat to their business interests as a result of planning blight. But the issues are not going to go away and nor are they just local to the Royal Docks. The proposal bears directly on the national policy for civil aviation, and the international strategy for tackling global warming. Any decision to relocate London City Airport would of course affect the reception area – and might trigger all kinds of NIMBY-style protests elsewhere in the region. The international travel and visitor economy of East London would also be directly affected. More locally, if the docks are paved over there will be no more water sports, and plans to open up the docks through the use of water buses would be dead in the water. Environmentalists, speaking on behalf of the wild life, the water, the foreshore – everything that makes up the natural ecology of the Royal Docks would also have a strong case to make and might opt for an altogether different vision – remove the airport, but keep the waterscape and build a small scale version of Venice using the latest hydraulic engineering to put low density housing on floating platforms across the dock.

So here is a whole array of potential issues, protagonists and visions, varying greatly in the scale and scope of their concerns and in their political clout and articulacy. Here, in microcosm are all the conflicting priorities and perspectives animated by the Thames Gateway plan. Our proposal for a bicameral regional assembly organised according to Latourean principles is simply a way of providing a level field in which all these different matters of concern could for once be put on an equal footing.

We have worked this proposal through in some detail because we think it incumbent on anyone with an idea like this to demonstrate that it is feasible. There are altogether too many glib exhortations to 'build to a human scale' or 'create a sense of place identity' issued by politicians or policymakers (and sometimes by academics) who appear exhausted by their utterance, and who collapse into silence or vacuity before the redoubtable task of thinking through how any of these laudable principles are to be put into practice! We think the multimodal procedure we propose is realistic, in so far as it based on precedents that have worked in similar contexts, and robust, in that it is capable of being tried and tested. Our proposal whilst retaining the adversarial principle, would also encourage compromises and trade-offs of one interest or voice against another. It would be a step forward if such compromises were openly debated and negotiated, in a search for positive-sum outcomes where possible, rather than being determined by stealth or default, as the strongest force imposes its will.

In putting forward a new kind of deliberative agency for Thames Gateway we are attempting to accommodate the new level of complexity in urban planning which is entailed by the goal – appropriate in itself – of achieving development on this large geographical scale. Neither 'government as usual', nor letting the market decide, nor the ad hoc creation of quangos with little money and less authority will meet the planning needs of this situation, nor, come to that, those of many other city regions in Britain.

References

Cohen, P. (1999), 'All White on the Night?', in Butler, T. and Rustin, M. (eds), *Rising in the East*, London, Lawrence and Wishart.
Cohen, P. (2005), 'A New Orientalism? The Anglo-Gothic Imagination of East London', *Rising East On Line*, 2: http://www.risingeast.org.
Collins, M. (2004), *The Likes of Us – A Biography of the White Working Class*, London, Granta.
Dench, G., Gavron, K. and Young M. (2006), *The New East End: Kinship Race and Conflict*, London, Profile Books.
Department of Community and Local Government (2007), *Planning for a Sustainable Future*, London, HMSO.
Evans, G. (2005), *Educational Failure and White Working Class Children in Britain*, London, Palgrave.
Farrell, T. (1994), *Selected and Current Work*, London, Images Press.
Forester, J. and Fischer, F. (eds) (1993), *The Argumentative Turn in Policy Analysis and Planning*, Durham, NC, Duke University Press.
Forester, J. and Fischer, F. (eds) (1987), *Confronting Values in Policy Analysis: The Politics of Criteria*, London, Sage.
Forester, J. (1999), *The Deliberative Practitioner: Encouraging the Participative Planning Process*, Cambridge, MA, MIT Press.
Graham, S. and Marvin, S. (2001), *Spintering Urbanism*, London, Routledge.
Hewitt, R. (2005), *White Backlash and the Politics of Multiculturalism*, Cambridge, Cambridge University Press.
Latour, B. (1993), *We Have Never Been Modern*, London, Harvester Wheatsheaf.
Latour, B. (2004), *Politics of Nature: How to Bring the Sciences into Democracy*, Cambridge, MA, Harvard University Press.
Latour, B. (2005a), *Reassembling the Social: An Introduction to Actor-Network Theory*, Oxford, Oxford University Press.
Latour, B. (2005b) 'From Realpolitik to Dingpolitk: How to Make Things Public', in Latour, B. and Weibel, P. (eds), *Atmospheres of Democracy: Making Things Public*, Cambridge, MA, MIT Press.
Mumford, K. and Power, A. (2003), *East Enders: Family and Community in London*, Bristol, Policy Press.

Rathzel, N., Hieronymous, A., Cohen, P., Back, L. and Keith, M. (2007), *Finding the Way Home: Young People, Place Identity and Belonging in Hamburg and London*, Berlin, Das Argument.

Rodgers, R. and Power, P. (2000), *Cities for a Small Country*, London, Faber.

Sassen, S. (1993), *The Global City: New York, London, Tokyo*, Princeton, NJ, Princeton University Press.

Index